LUXORIUS

A LATIN POET AMONG THE VANDALS

NUMBER LXII

RECORDS OF CIVILIZATION

SOURCES AND STUDIES

LUXORIUS

A LATIN POET AMONG THE VANDALS

BY MORRIS ROSENBLUM

TOGETHER WITH A TEXT OF THE POEMS
AND AN ENGLISH TRANSLATION

IN LITTERIS
LIBERTAS
1754·1893

COLUMBIA UNIVERSITY PRESS

NEW YORK AND LONDON 1961

The Stanwood Cockey Lodge Foundation
has generously provided funds toward
the cost of publication of this work

PRINTED IN THE NETHERLANDS

LIBRARY OF CONGRESS CATALOG CARD NUMBER: 60-6547

Uxori meae

D. J. R.

PREFACE

This book is a study of the work, life, and times of Luxorius, a writer of epigrams who lived in or near Carthage during the last years of the Vandal occupation of North Africa in the sixth century.

Its chief purpose is to interpret Luxorius' poems through an English translation and a detailed commentary. This is the first translation in any language of all of his extant poems. It has been made without embellishments; the language and the order of ideas are as close to Luxorius' own as possible so that the reader may get an understanding of the poet's style and manner of expression. The commentary is equipped with historical, cultural, linguistic, grammatical, and literary notes: this edition of Luxorius is the first modern one of its kind and the only one in English. A fascinating aspect of Luxorius' poems is that they lead the student into many varied bypaths of research, including art, athletics, sports, horticulture, ornithology, medicine, and folklore. Modern as well as ancient parallels are given in this book whenever appropriate.

Another aim is to present Luxorius as a writer who wrote in the classical tradition but also bridged the period between the end of the classical period and the beginning of medieval Latin. Therefore, due attention is paid to the grammatical, linguistic, and metrical tendencies of medieval Latin as they apply to the poems of Luxorius.

A third aim is to bring the history of Luxorian scholarship up to date. Comparatively little has been done on Luxorius in the twentieth century; most of the studies of his poetry were written in the last century. These consist mainly of articles in periodicals, many of them almost a hundred years old. There is need of reappraisal and reinterpretation, especially because certain scholars have attempted to rewrite Luxorius according to their ideas of what they would have written if they had developed the themes of Luxorius' poems. With rare courage these scholars then aver that, *ohne Zweifel* or *senza dubbio* or *sine dubio* or *sans doute,* Luxorius did write what they say he wrote. Conjectures are always in order and probabilities may be explored, but they should be labeled as conjectures and probabilities. Exception must be taken to conclusions which are first offered as a mere possibility and then accepted by the proposer as an indubitable fact. In turn, these conjectures are transmitted by later commentators as established facts. I have examined as many of these as possible and have weighed their merits.

To understand Luxorius, it is necessary also to know something of the following:

1. The history and culture of North Africa, especially Carthage.

2. The Vandals. The Romans living in North Africa despised their new lords as barbarians. Nevertheless, under these barbarians, poetry was written, mainly of a noncontroversial nature as fitted the times: trifles, light verse, descriptive pieces, and epigrams.

3. The *Latin Anthology.* The poems of Luxorius are found in the *Latin Anthology,* a collection presumed to have been compiled in Carthage in the sixth century. The relationship of Luxorius to other poets of the *Anthology* will be studied. Finally, the manuscript tradition of the *Anthology* will be treated; a few necessary corrections in the reports of my predecessors will be made and some new information supplied.

Except for a small number of changes (listed below, Appendix II), the text of my edition is substantially that of Alexander Riese, *Anthologia Latina,* 2nd ed. (Leipzig, 1894). All translations of authors cited are my own.

This book was undertaken at the suggestion of Dr. Gilbert Highet, Anthon Professor of the Latin Language and Literature, Columbia University. I should like to express my appreciation of his aid and encouragement, for he gave freely of his time and vast fund of knowledge. Every effort has been made to meet the high standards of accuracy and clarity which characterize his own teaching and writing. As it is customary to declare, any deviations from those standards are my own responsibility.

Special thanks are also due to Dr. Moses Hadas, Jay Professor of Greek, Columbia University, for his tireless efforts to help this book achieve publication, thereby exemplifying the highest ideals of teaching.

The book is being published with the aid of a grant from the Stanwood Cockey Lodge Fund, to which I express my sincerest appreciation.

I acknowledge with thanks the valuable information and suggestions given to me by many scholars, either in person or through correspondence: Mlle Marie-Thérèse d'Alverny, Assistant Conservator of Manuscripts, Bibliothèque Nationale, Paris; Dr. C. H. Benedict, Columbia College; Dr. John Day, Barnard College; A. F. Dekker, Manuscript Division, Royal Library, The Hague; L. M. J. Delaissé, Assistant Keeper of the Department of Manuscripts, Royal Library of Belgium, Brussels; H. G. Fletcher, Public Library, Art Gallery and Museum, Cheltenham, England; Dr. E. Gose, Rheinisches Landesmuseum, Trier, Germany; Dr. W. T. H. Jackson, Columbia University; Dr. E. Jammers, Head of the Manuscript Division of the Library of Heidelberg University; Dr. Erhart Kästner, Duke August Library, Wolfenbüttel, Germany; Dr. K. A. Meyïer, Department of Western Manuscripts, Library of the University of Leiden; A. N. L. Munby, King's College Library, Cambridge, England; Dr. Martin Ostwald, Swarthmore College, Pa.; Mlle Colette Picard, author of *Carthage*; Dr. H. N. Porter, Columbia University; Dr. J. F. C. Richards, Columbia University; Dr. A. Lytton Sells, Indiana University, Bloomington; Mlle Jeanne Vielliard, Director of the Institut de Recherche et d'Histoire des Textes, Paris.

Indebtedness is acknowledged to the staff and facilities of Avery Library, Columbia University, especially to Mrs. Rosaline Halperin and Adolf K. Placzek; Butler Library, Columbia University; the Library of the Brooklyn Botanic Garden; Brooklyn Public Library; the Library of the Metropolitan Museum of Art, New York; Bibliothèque Nationale, Paris; Alaoui (Bardo) Museum, Tunis; and the Lavigerie Museum, Carthage.

I also wish to give special thanks and to express my deep gratitude to my friends for reading this manuscript and for offering me many helpful constructive suggestions: Leo Dressler, Franklin K. Lane High School, Brooklyn, New York; Dr. Morris Leider, New York University Post-Graduate Medical School; Maxwell Nurnberg, Abraham Lincoln High School, Brooklyn, New York; and to the staff of the Columbia University Press for their sympathetic assistance, above all to Miss Elisabeth L. Shoemaker, Editor.

Let me here indicate my appreciation to my wife and traveling companion, Dora J. Rosenblum, who trudged with me through many museums and clambered over the ruins of Carthage in search of first-hand material.

Finally, I wish to acknowledge my debt to all the scholars before me who toiled in the same Luxorian vineyard and who are named in this book upon the appropriate occasion. *Ferveat opus et procedat!*

New York, N. Y.   MORRIS ROSENBLUM

CONTENTS

PLATES

following page 108

ABBREVIATIONS

R after a number denotes the number of a poem in Riese's edition of the *Anthologia Latina*.

L. after a number denotes the number of a poem of Luxorius in the text of this book. It is used when there is a need of avoiding confusion with the poems of other authors.

AJP	American Journal of Philology
ALL	Archiv für lateinische Lexikographie und Grammatik
BSCP	Berliner Studien für classische Philologie und Archäologie
CAH	Cambridge Ancient History
CIL	Corpus Inscriptionum Latinarum
CJ	Classical Journal
CMH	Cambridge Medieval History
CML	Corpus Medicorum Latinorum
CP	Classical Philology
CQ	Classical Quarterly
CR	Classical Review
CRAI	Comptes rendus de l'Académie des inscriptions et belles-lettres
CSEL	Corpus Scriptorum Ecclesiasticorum Latinorum
CW	Classical Weekly
DarSag	Daremberg and Saglio, Dictionnaire des antiquités grecques et romaines
EB	Encyclopaedia Britannica
GL	Keil, Grammatici Latini
IG	Inscriptiones Graecae
JP	Journal of Philology
MCAAT	Musées et collections archéologiques de l'Algérie et de la Tunisie
MGH	Monumenta Germaniae Historica: Auctores Antiquissimi
MPAI	Mémoires présentés par divers savants à l'Académie des inscriptions et belles-lettres de l'Institut de France
NE	Notices et extraits des manuscrits de la Bibliothèque Nationale et autres Bibliothèques (Bibliothèque Impériale before 1871)
NJbb	[Neue] Jahrbücher für Philologie und Pädagogik; Neue Jahrbücher für das klassische Altertum; Neue Jahrbücher für Wissenschaft und Jugendbildung (the three forming a continuous series)

OCD	Oxford Classical Dictionary
OED	Oxford English Dictionary
Phil	Philologus
PL	Migne, Patrologia Latina
PLG	Bergk, Poetae Lyrici Graeci
PLM	E. Baehrens, Poetae Latini Minores
RE	Pauly-Wissowa, Real-Encyclopädie der klassischen Altertums-wissenschaft
RhM	Rheinisches Museum für Philologie
SchH	Schanz-Hosius, Geschichte der römischen Litteratur
TAPA	Transactions of the American Philological Association
TLL	Thesaurus Linguae Latinae
ZöstG	Zeitschrift fur die oesterreichischen Gymnasien

PART ONE: THE POET

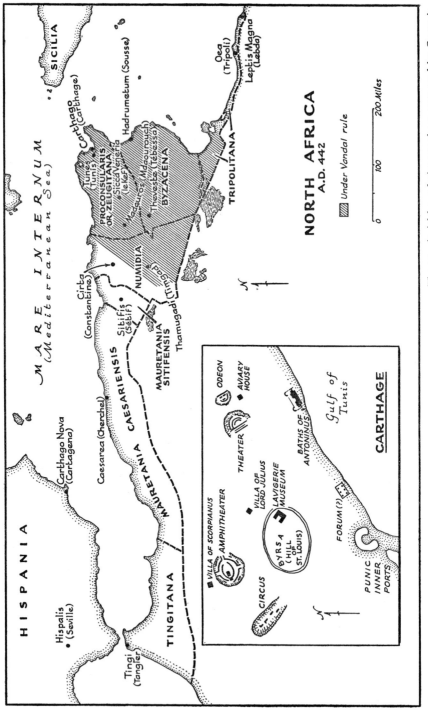

NORTH AFRICA
A.D. 442

///// Under Vandal rule

0   100   200 Miles

The provincial boundaries are those proposed by Courtois.

CARTHAGE

- VILLA OF SCORPIANUS
- AMPHITHEATER
- CIRCUS
- BYRSA (HILL OF ST. LOUIS)
- VILLA OF LORD JULIUS
- LAVIGERIE MUSEUM
- THEATER
- ODEON
- AVIARY HOUSE
- BATHS OF ANTONINUS
- FORUM (?)
- PUNIC INNER PORTS
- Gulf of Tunis

HISPANIA

Hispalis (Seville)
Carthago Nova (Cartagena)

MARE INTERNUM (Mediterranean Sea)

SICILIA

Carthago (Carthage)
Tunes (Tunis)
Hadrumetum (Sousse)
Oea (Tripoli)
Leptis Magna (Labda)

PROCONSULARIS OR ZEUGITANA
Sicca Veneria (le Kef)
Mactaris (Maktar)
Thysdrus
Thaenae
BYZACENA
Theveste (Tebessa)

NUMIDIA
Cirta (Constantine)
Sitifis (Sétif)
Thamugadi (Timgad)

MAURETANIA SITIFENSIS

MAURETANIA CAESARIENSIS
Caesarea (Cherchel)

TINGITANA

Tingi (Tangier)

TRIPOLITANA

I. THE VANDALS AND CARTHAGE

A. The Vandal Conquest of North Africa

1. Destroyed in 146 B.C., Carthage was situated in a location too attractive and advantageous to remain long unoccupied. Disregarding the curse laid upon any future settlers, Gaius Gracchus attempted (but failed) to establish the colony of Junonia near Carthage in 122 B.C.[1] After his victory at Thapsus and the capture of Utica in 46 B.C., Julius Caesar planned to found the colony of Julia Concordia Karthago, a plan cut short by his death.[2] However, the site must have been inhabited, for references are found to the damage done to Carthage by Lepidus, to whom Africa and Numidia had been given by Octavian after the battle of Philippi in 42 B.C.[3] In accordance with a memorandum left by Julius Caesar, Octavian sent colonists in 29 B.C. to resettle Carthage close to the site of the destroyed city, so as to avoid the ancient curse.[4] Later, he felt strong enough to disregard and even defy this curse, so that the work of erecting a new city within the limits of Punic Carthage began; the publication of the *Aeneid*, with its description of the building of the first Carthage by Dido, is believed to have aroused enthusiasm for the building of a Roman Carthage.[5]

2. During the reign of Claudius and before A.D. 44 North Africa was divided into four provinces: Africa or Africa Proconsularis (called

[1] Appian, *Punica* 20.135-36, *Bella Civilia* 1.3.24; Plutarch, *Gaius Gracchus* 11; Aymard and Auboyer, *Rome et son empire*, pp. 50, 165; *CAH*, IX, 73-74, 80-81, 100.

[2] Appian, *Punica* 20.136; Dio Cassius, *Roman History* 43.50-51; Julien, *Histoire de l'Afrique du Nord*, pp. 122-23; Lapeyre and Pellegrin, *Carthage latine et chrétienne*, pp. 67-69.

[3] Dio Cassius, 52.43.1: Octavian settled Carthage anew because Lepidus had laid waste part of the city; Tertullian, *De Pallio* (*PL*, II, 1085), "post Gracchi obscena omnia, et Lepidi violenta ludibria, post trinas Pompei aras, et longas Caesaris moras, ubi Statilius Taurus imposuit, solemnia Sentius Saturninus enarravit." See also *CAH*, X, 30, 120, 206.

[4] Appian, *Punica* 20.136. See also Strabo, *Geography* 17.3.15.

[5] Julien, *Histoire*, p. 124; Lapeyre and Pellegrin, *Carthage*, p. 69.

Proconsularis for short and sometimes known also as Zeugitana), with its capital at Carthage; to the west of that province, Numidia, with Cirta (modern Constantine) as its capital; still farther west, Mauretania Caesariensis, with Caesarea (modern Cherchel) as its capital; and to the extreme west, below the Strait of Gibraltar, Mauretania Tingitana, with its capital at Tingi (modern Tangier). Later, especially in the reign of Diocletian (284-305), the African provinces were divided into smaller units. From the eastern part of Mauretania Caesariensis was carved a new province, Mauretania Sitifensis, whose capital was Sitifis (modern Sétif); likewise, Africa Proconsularis gave up part of its eastern territory to form the province of Byzacena, with Hadrumetum (modern Sousse) as its capital. In return, Proconsularis received the large city of Theveste (modern Tébessa) from Numidia. Tripolitana, formerly under military rule, became a separate province, with Leptis Magna (modern Lebda) as its capital.[6]

3. Proconsularis was the most important of these provinces. Carthage itself grew in population and influence until it became one of the most flourishing of all Roman cities, second in many respects only to Rome.[7] Destroyed by fire in the second century but rebuilt under the Antonines and the Severi, through its splendor Carthage well merited the official epithet of *Felix*.[8] Salvian of Marseille (*fl.* A.D. 430-50) describes Carthage in these terms:[9]

I am content to speak of only one city in Africa as an example, the leader, and so to speak, the mother of all the cities in Africa. I mean the city which was always a rival of Roman might, once the competitor of Rome in war and

[6] Albertini, *L'Afrique romaine*, pp. 31-37; Bouchier, *Life and Letters in Roman Africa*, p. 1; Courtois, *Les Vandales*, pp. 70-79, and map, p. 66; Julien, *Histoire*, pp. 143-46, and map, pp. 136-37; Schmidt, *Geschichte der Wandalen*, pp. 41-44, and maps, pp. 203ff.; Warmington, *The North African Provinces*, pp. 1-2.

[7] Augustine, *Epistulae* 118.2.9 (*PL*, XXXIII, 436), "Duae tantae urbes, Latinarum litterarum artifices, Roma atque Carthago"; *De Baptismo contra Donatistas* 2.11 (*PL*, XLIII, 137), "in Africae capite et notissima civitate Carthagine"; Aurelius Victor, *De Caesaribus* 40.19, "Carthaginem terrarum decus"; Martianus Capella, *Liber de Nuptiis Mercurii et Philologiae*, ed. by A. Dick (Leipzig, 1935), p. 333, 6.216G.669, "Carthago inclita pridem armis nunc felicitate reverenda"; Herodian, *Ab Excessu Divi Marci* 7.6.1, says of third-century Carthage that it was surpassed only by Rome in wealth, number of inhabitants, and greatness.

[8] Cagnat, *Carthage, Timgad, Tébessa*, pp. 10-11; Julien, *Histoire*, pp. 78-79; Colette Picard, *Carthage*, p. 13, "Colonie romaine, la seconde Carthage est officiellement une portion de Rome sur le sol africain."

[9] Salvian, *De Gubernatione Dei*, in *CSEL*, VIII, ed. by M. Petschenig (Vienna, 1883), 7.16.67-68, or in *PL*, LIII, 143 A-C. There is no evidence that Salvian ever visited Carthage; he appears to be talking about Carthage before the Vandals conquered it. See O'Sullivan, *The Writings of Salvian*, p. 7.

courage, later in splendor and prestige. I speak of Carthage, both as the most formidable enemy of Rome, and now a second Rome, as it were, on African soil. She alone will do as my example and witness because she contained within herself the necessary means by which the power of a state is managed and governed anywhere in the wide world.

In that city were found all the paraphernalia of public offices, in that city existed all the schools of liberal arts, in that city were the workshops of the philosophers, and finally, in that city were all the academies for instruction in languages and morals; in that city were stationed also troops and officers to command them; there was the proconsular position, there in that city was a permanent judge and governor holding indeed the name of proconsul but acting with the power of a consul; finally, in that city were all types of functionaries, differing from one another not only in rank but also in title, the supervisors, so to put it, of all the streets and crossroads, governing almost all the places of the city and all the individuals living in it.

4. Many diverse ethnic groups inhabited North Africa in the fifth and sixth centuries.[10] Most numerous were the Berbers, whose ancestors had lived there before the arrival of the Phoenicians.[11] Other inhabitants were the Libyans, a tall, blue-eyed people of Indo-European origin,[12] some descendants of the early Punic settlers; Moors; Roman soldiers, colonists, merchants, and officials; Greeks; Jews; and various representatives of other parts of the Roman world.

5. A multiplicity of creeds flourished in North Africa at this time. The orthodox Catholic religion, Athanasianism, was in conflict with rival and dissident sects: Arianism, Manichaeism, and Donatism.[13]

[10] Boissier, *L'Afrique romaine,* pp. 5-9, 351-60; Bouchier, *Life and Letters,* pp. 4-12; Courtois, *Les Vandales,* pp. 104-12; Julien, *Histoire,* pp. 48-51, 214-16, 232-34; Lapeyre and Pellegrin, *Carthage,* pp. 118-25, 214-31; Mommsen, *The Provinces,* II, 304-6; Schmidt, *Geschichte,* pp. 1-23; Haywood, *Roman Africa,* pp. 102-9.

[11] *EB* (11th ed.), XVIII, 812, "Tribes known to the Romans as Moors were undoubtedly Berbers." The Romans called the latter *Numidae, Gaetuli,* or *Mauri* (*EB* [14th ed.], III, 428). See Martroye, *Genséric,* pp. 74-75; also Snowden, "The Negro in Classical Italy," *AJP,* LXVIII (1947), 268, on the Romans' use of *Maurus* to designate a Negro. Modern Moors are hybrids of Arab and Berber; the Berbers, although dark-haired and black-eyed, are whites. They have persisted in spite of foreign conquests of Africa; many of them live in primitive villages today.

[12] Bouchier, *Life and Letters,* p. 9; *EB* (14th ed.), III, 427, says that the Berbers were indigenous Libyans; Sallust, *Jugurtha* 18; Livy, 35.40.5, calls Muttines, one of Hannibal's generals, a Libyphoenician (cf. 21.22.3); Pliny, *Natural History* 5.3.24, Libyphoenices vocantur, qui Byzacium incolunt; see also Martianus Capella (cited above, n. 7), p. 333, 6.216G.670.

[13] Bouchier, *Life and Letters,* pp. 72-83; Lapeyre and Pellegrin, *Carthage,* pp. 114-17; Leclercq, *L'Afrique chrétienne,* I, 312-80. Monceaux devotes Vols. V-VII of his *Histoire littéraire de l'Afrique* to Donatism. See also Augustine, *Confessions* 3.7.12-14 (*PL,* XXXII, 688-90), 5.3.3-6 (*PL,* XXXII, 707-8), and 7.2.3 (*PL,* XXXII, 734).

Judaism was strong and influential.[14] Faith in the old Punic gods had not died out entirely; many North Africans still adhered to pagan cults. In addition, belief in astrology, magic, and superstition was popular, especially in Carthage, where the *magus* was a familiar figure.[15]

6. The economy of North Africa was based mainly on agriculture. In spite of dry winds, treeless wastes, salt lakes, proximity to deserts, and the absence of extensive fertile plains, North Africa, through a system of irrigation and careful farming, was on the whole a productive region.[16] Wheat was the chief product; Cicero had grouped Africa with Sicily and Sardinia as a granary of Rome.[17] Olives, grapes, pomegranates, dates, and vegetables were other important staples. The North Africans also engaged in commerce and industry; marble was quarried on a large scale and the manufacture of dyes and woolens ranked high. The wealthy Romans in Africa acquired huge holdings of land and, notwithstanding stern measures taken against them, rich proprietors continued to consolidate large estates until the Vandal conquest.[18]

7. In 429 the Vandals crossed from Spain into this rich and inviting land under their able leader Genseric (also known as Gaiseric, Geiseric, Gizeric, or Gyzeric). The Vandals were a Germanic people originally living near the Vistula, who had crossed the Rhine in 406, marched into Belgium and Gaul, and penetrated into Spain, most of which they wrested from the Roman Empire in 412. The Vandals consisted of

---

[14] Bouchier, *Life and Letters,* p. 92, mentions synagogues at Cirta, Sitifis, and Carthage, and a Jewish cemetery north of Carthage. M. Loewenthal, *A World Passed By* (New York, 1933), pp. 408-10, describes the synagogue and necropolis at Carthage, also the collection of Hebrew inscriptions and artifacts in the Bardo and Lavigerie Museums; see *MCAAT,* VIII, 13-69 and *CIL,* VIII.5.2, p. 241, *s.v. Judaica.* On the Jews in Carthage, see also S.W. Baron, *A Social and Religious History of the Jews* (New York, 1952-58), I, 176 and 374, n. 13, where Baron summarizes the theories that the Phoenicians were absorbed by the Jews in North Africa; II, 164-66, where he is of the opinion that Christianity spread more rapidly in southern Gaul, Spain, and North Africa because there were large settlements of Jewish origin; and III, 7-8, on the Jews in North Africa under Justinian, who considered the Arianism of the Vandals a Jewish movement. (See Pl. III, C.)

[15] Augustine, *Confessions* 4.3.4 (*PL,* XXXII, 694-95); *De Civitate Dei* 8.19 (*PL,* XLI, 243-44); Bouchier, *Life and Letters,* pp. 54-56; Keenan, *Life and Times of St. Augustine,* pp. 111-16; Lapeyre and Pellegrin, *Carthage,* pp. 54-56; see also Poem 13 by Luxorius.

[16] Bouchier, *Life and Letters,* pp. 2-4; Mommsen, *The Provinces,* II, 336-37.

[17] Cicero, *De Imperio Pompei* 12.34, "haec tria frumentaria subsidia rei publicae."

[18] Schmidt, *Geschichte,* p. 49; Warmington, *The North African Provinces,* p. 64. See also Pliny, *Natural History* 18.7.35, "verum confitentibus latifundia perdidere Italiam; iam vero et provincias—sex domini semissem Africae possidebant, cum interfecit eos Nero princeps."

two large tribes, the Hasdings and the Silings; they were joined by the Alani, who had originally inhabited the land between the Danube and the Tisza (Theiss). In addition, a large number of Suevi and Goths accompanied the Vandals.[19]

8. In 416 the Visigoths descended into Spain, wiped out the Silings, and destroyed the power of the Alani, who then allied themselves much more closely with the Hasdings.[20] The remnants of the Vandals and their associates fled to the extreme south, took Cartagena and Seville from the Romans in 425, and were preparing to invade Africa when Guntheric, their king, died. After his death, Genseric, his brother, became the king of the Vandals.

9. In the meantime, Honorius, the emperor of the West ruling from Ravenna, had died in 423, leaving no heir. His nephew, the future Valentinian III, son of Constantius and Galla Placidia, the sister of Honorius, was only four years old at the time. Two able generals, Aetius and Boniface (Bonifatius) commanded the Roman armies, the former in Gaul and the latter in Africa. Either of these two men, according to Procopius, merited the title "Last of the Romans."[21] Galla Placidia counted on the support of Boniface to install her son as Augustus; Aetius favored a usurper.

10. Either because of the pressure of the Visigoths, or because of his own decision to settle his people in the fertile lands of Africa, or because, as some authorities imply, of an invitation extended by Boniface,[22] Genseric crossed into Africa in 429 and seized all of Mauretania,

---

[19] CMH, I, 407-14; Courtois, Les Vandales, pp. 11-14, 21-37, 40-41, 51-58, 217; Leclercq, L'Afrique chrétienne, II, 143-213. Pliny, Natural History 4.14.99, first mentions the Vandals, calling them Vandili. The Vandals and Goths were often considered the same; see Procopius, Bellum Vandalicum 1.2, and Martroye, Genséric, pp. 307-10. According to M. Rostovtzeff in CAH, XI, 94-97, the Alani were a nomadic tribe of Asiatic origin coming from the vicinity of the Aral Sea. They migrated to South Russia and, merging with the Germans, formed part of the Gothic-Alanic kingdom there.

[20] Later, the king of the Vandals was addressed by the title "King of the Vandals and of the Alani." See CMH, I, 305, 317; Courtois, Les Vandales, pp. 218, 237; Julien, Histoire, pp. 233-34; Schmidt, Geschichte, p. 161; and Procopius, Bellum Vandalicum 1.24.3. Books 3 and 4 of Procopius' History of the Wars are Books 1 and 2 of the Vandalic Wars.

[21] Procopius, Bellum Vandalicum 1.3.14-15.

[22] CMH, I, 409; Julien, Histoire, p. 235; Martroye, Genséric, pp. 85-87; Schmidt, Geschichte, p. 27; Procopius, Bellum Vandalicum 1.3.17-32; Jordanes, De Getarum sive Gothorum Origine et Rebus Gestis, ed. by C. A. Close (Stuttgart, 1861), or, under title De Origine Actibusque Getarum, by A. Holder (Freiburg and Tübingen, 1895), p. 33, "Sed Gizericus, rex Vandalorum, iam a Bonifacio in Africam invitatus, qui Valentiniano principi veniens in offensam, non aliter se quam malo reipublicae potuit vindicare." Boniface had been engaged in machinations against Aetius and presumably turned to the Vandals.

Numidia, and Proconsularis except the fortified cities of Cirta and Carthage. Although the entire Vandal host consisted of 80,000 persons, of whom only 15,000 were soldiers, yet the conquest of such a large area was surprisingly easy.[23] The Vandals were aided by rebellious native tribes, by groups of itinerant workers known as *circumcelliones,* and by peasants rising up against their Roman overlords.[24] In addition, the Donatists and Arians looked upon the Vandals, who were Arians, as liberators.

11. Genseric then defeated Boniface, who had been restored to favor by Galla Placidia and put in command of an entire army including Visigoth mercenaries. Thereupon the court at Constantinople sent an army under Aspar to aid Boniface, but Genseric defeated their combined forces in 431. The Vandals and Romans finally signed a treaty in 435 whereby the Vandals received both Mauretanias and a large part of Numidia. In turn, they were enrolled in the service of Valentinian as *foederati* and were called upon to pay a slight tribute.[25]

12. Having established himself in Africa, Genseric strengthened his army and navy, consolidated his power, and, without warning, marched upon Carthage, which he took with ease in 439. The Romans were subsequently powerless to prevent either his incursions into other parts of Africa or his naval raids on Sicily and other islands.[26] Finally, in 442 another treaty ceded to the Vandals the richest parts of North Africa: all of Proconsularis and Byzacena, and sections of Numidia and Tripolitana. The Empire retained the two Mauretanias and a portion of Numidia.[27]

13. In this way conditions were stabilized in North Africa and the Vandals held power without interference by the Romans for almost a century. Carthage was kept as the seat of their government. Be-

---

[23] Schmidt, *Geschichte,* pp. 31-32; Procopius, *Bellum Vandalicum* 1.5.18; Victor of Vita (Victor Vitensis), *Historia Persecutionis Africanae Provinciae,* Vol. VII, *CSEL,* ed. by M. Petschenig (Vienna, 1881), 1.2 (*PL,* LVIII, 182C).

[24] Courtois, *Les Vandales,* pp. 140-48. According to Courtois (p. 147), the *circumcelliones* were Donatists merely by a fluke ("*de raccroc*"). See his n. 8, p. 140, for references in St. Augustine on the *circumcelliones* as Donatists; see also *RE,* III.2, 2570.

[25] Procopius, *Bellum Vandalicum* 1.4.13-15; Courtois, *Les Vandales,* pp. 169-70; Julien, *Histoire,* p. 237; Schmidt, *Geschichte,* p. 64.

[26] The Vandals became a naval power; they sacked Rome in 455, and in 468 they won a tremendous victory over the combined fleets of Leo and Marjorian, emperors of the East and West, respectively. See Procopius, *Bellum Vandalicum* 1.6.17-24, and Courtois, *Les Vandales,* pp. 205-9.

[27] *CMH,* I, 307; Courtois, *Les Vandales,* pp. 173-75; Julien, *Histoire,* p. 238; Schmidt, *Geschichte,* p. 71. See also Courtois, p. 182, and maps, pp. 172-73.

ginning with the date of their conquest of that city, six kings[28] ruled over them: Genseric, 439-77; Huneric, son of Genseric, 477-84; Gunthamund, nephew of Huneric, 484-96; Thrasamund, another nephew of Huneric, 496-523; Hilderic, son of Huneric, 523-30; Gelimer, great-grandson of Genseric, 530-34.

14. The reputation (or rather, notoriety) of the Vandals is such that their name has given to English, French, and other languages words synonymous with destroyers and destruction.[29] However, when viewed dispassionately and disinterestedly, the history of the Vandals does not indicate that they were more destructive of life and property than any other "barbarian" tribes. Certainly, once they were established in Africa, they were gentler than had been the Goths under Alaric or the Huns under Attila. In fact, even when depicted by their most hostile, bitter, and impassioned critics, the Vandals appear to have been milder than were the Romans on many occasions. The latter slaughtered multitudes of Gauls on orders of the merciful Caesar and wiped out garrisons of rebellious Jews in Palestine. When they felt that policy made such a course necessary, the Romans, so much more cultured and civilized than the Vandals, razed Carthage and decreed that Corinth, "the light of all Greece," should be extinguished for no more weighty reason than that Roman envoys had been addressed somewhat too haughtily.[30]

15. The Vandals were eventually obliterated as a people after their defeat by the forces of Justinian in 534; there were apparently no writers among them, and even if there were, we do not have their writings; the records that we do possess of that period are those of the survivors, the Romans of North Africa and elsewhere. Their tablets are, so to speak, etched in venom.[31]

[28] See Courtois, *Les Vandales,* "La Galérie des Rois," pp. 260-71, and p. 409, table and chronology; also Schmidt, *Geschichte,* genealogical table after p. 203.

[29] The use of the words *vandal* and *vandalism* as terms of opprobrium in English date to the late seventeenth or early eighteenth century (*OED,* XII, 34-35). Voltaire may have been the first French writer to use *vandale* in this sense (in 1732); Henri Grégoire, Bishop of Blois, coined the term *vandalisme* in 1793 or 1794; see Courtois, *Les Vandales,* p. 59.

[30] Cicero, *De Imperio Pompei* 5.11; see also *De Officiis* 1.11.35, and 3.11.46, where Cicero admits it was a cruel act.

[31] Martroye, *Genséric,* p. 381, "Seuls les Romains et les Catholiques savaient écrire; ils nous ont transmis l'expression de leurs justes ressentiments, et la postérité, jugeant par leurs écrits, n'a vu en Genséric qu'une sorte de pirate. Suivant un mot attribué à Louis XVI, les Vandales ne furent pas aussi vandales qu'on l'a dit, mais ils n'en demeurèrent moins des barbares." This is echoed by Cagnat, *Carthage,* p. 128, "Il ne faudrait pas, toutefois, prendre à la lettre toutes les accusations qui ont été dirigées contre les Vandales. Seuls,

16. It is easy to understand the bias and bitterness with which some contemporaries wrote about the Vandals, who were Arians, consequently heretics and far more detestable than mere barbarians. Strong religious differences and the loss of their positions may have affected the accounts of Possidius, bishop of Calama (*fl. ca.* 435), and of Victor of Vita (*fl. ca.* 484-86). Animosity engendered by religious conflicts also enters into the work of Prosper of Aquitaine (*fl.* 429-55) and of Victor Tunnunensis (*fl. ca.* 564), who continued the *Chronicon* of Prosper.[32]

17. It cannot be determined to what extent the atrocities enumerated by Possidius and Victor of Vita should be attributed to the religious enemies of the African Catholics, to exiles who returned from the desert, and to the agricultural gangs, the *circumcelliones,* who had suffered so long on the Roman latifundia and who now settled scores with their Roman oppressors.[33] Beyond the demands of military necessity few of the Roman edifices were torn down by the Vandals, who in fact preserved Roman culture, such as it was, in a period of decadence. The Roman cities in Africa were destroyed not by the

à cette époque, les Romains et les catholiques savaient écrire; nous avons conservé l'expression de leurs doléances, de leurs ressentiments, de leur indignation, sans contre-partie d'aucune sorte." Leclercq, *L'Afrique chrétienne,* II, 169, writes, "Il semble que malgré des brutalités et des violences impardonnables, les Vandales valurent mieux que leur reputation proverbiale." There does not seem to be in the story of the capture of Rome by the Vandals any justification for the charge of willful and objectless destruction. See *EB* (14th ed.), XXII, 971; Courtois, *Les Vandales,* pp. 59-64; and Julien, *Histoire,* p. 223. However, the tradition continues to this day; see *Carthage autrefois,* pp. 12-13, "Deux haines les [the Vandals] animent; celle du barbare contre la civilisation, celle de l'hérétique contre le catholicisme.... Six rois obéissent à leur sauvagerie native et à leur insatiable cupidité.... Carthage, évoquant le souvenir de la gloire passée, appelle à son secours les Empereurs d'Orient."

[32] The tone of their writings is illustrated by Possidius, *Vita Sancti Augustini Episcopi* (*PL,* XXXII, 57-58), "nulli sexui, nulli parcens aetati, nec ipsis Dei sacerdotibus vel ministris, nec ipsis ecclesiarum ornamentis nec instrumentis nec aedificiis." Victor of Vita, *Historia Persecutionis* (cited above, n. 23), continues his complaints against the Vandals from 1.1 to the very end of his book. Prosper, *Chronicum Integrum* (*PL,* LI, 598), shows clearly why he and other churchmen wrote so vehemently against the Vandals. He says of Genseric, "praecipue nobilitati et religioni infensus, ut non discerneretur hominibus magis, an Deo bellum intulisset." Julien, *Histoire,* p. 233, so characterizes Procopius and Victor of Vita, "Nos deux principales sources littéraires sont suspectes. Procope, si précieux pour la conquête byzantine, dont il a été témoin, doit n'inspirer qu'une confiance mitigée pour les périodes antérieures. Quant au livre Victor ... écrivit ... ce n'est pas à coup sûr un livre d'histoire."

[33] The local orthodox Christians were naturally inflamed against the Vandals as heretics, but what must have aroused their anger even more was the fact that pagans, Donatists, and heretics of every kind were free to satisfy their resentment against the Catholics when the Vandals arrived. See Martroye, *Genséric,* p. 443, "Pour tous les proscrits, si nombreux en Afrique, l'arrivée des Vandales marquait l'heure de la vengeance."

Vandals but by the Byzantine conquerors and African tribes during the expulsion of the Vandals in 534 and by the Arabs in later centuries.[34]

18. A laudatory account of the Vandals is given by Salvian—a Christian writer.[35] He pictures them as virtuous and chaste, instruments chosen by God to punish the sinful Africans. Of course this too can be recognized as special pleading, purposeful and tendentious. The truth lies in between: the Vandals were not angels but neither were they demons and ogres. "The Vandals were not little saints, it is true, and there is no doubt that their invasion was cruel. But it is false to say that it ruined the country."[36]

19. The government of the Vandals was an absolute monarchy, with the king in control of both the army and the church. The richest fields in Proconsularis were assigned to the soldiers; the crown kept the peripheral regions of Byzacena and Numidia. The Roman landowners either fled from Africa or were allowed to remain as virtual serfs or *coloni*. Many features of Roman administration were retained. The organization into cities and municipalities was left undisturbed; even the office of "proconsul" was attached to the court in Carthage. For practical reasons Latin remained the official language. With no culture of their own, the Vandals soon learned to adopt Roman ways. However, there was no fusion of Vandals and Romans.[37]

20. Under Genseric and Huneric there was a systematic and severe persecution of the Catholics which was, however, alleviated under Gunthamund and Thrasamund.[38] The latter was the most intellectual of the Vandal kings, surrounding himself with theologians, rhetoricians, and writers. During his reign both Vandals and Romans met to listen to Felicianus, teacher of the poet Dracontius.[39] Although the polemist Fulgentius was a Catholic, Thrasamund invited him to his

[34] See n. 65, this chapter, on the use of Roman structures as marble quarries. See also Cagnat, *Carthage,* pp. 11-12; Courtois, *Les Vandales,* p. 315.
[35] Salvian, *De Gubernatione Dei* 7.11-23, 45-108 (*PL,* LIII, 138B-152C).
[36] Courtois, *Les Vandales,* p. 168.
[37] Bouchier, *Life and Letters,* p. 106; *CMH,* I, 307, 316-21; Courtois, *Les Vandales,* pp. 218, 252, 258-59, 312; Julien, *Histoire,* pp. 239-47; Lapeyre and Pellegrin, *Carthage,* pp. 125-26; Martroye, *Genséric,* pp. 263-81; Schmidt, *Geschichte,* pp. 148-49. See also Procopius, *Bellum Vandalicum* 1.5.11-17, for Genseric's treatment of the Libyans.
[38] *CMH,* I, 312-13; Courcelle, *Histoire littéraire,* pp. 152-65; Schmidt, *Geschichte,* pp. 93-96, 103-14, 186-88. Huneric was at first somewhat milder than Genseric, but Victor of Vita, 2.1 (*PL,* LVIII, 201B) was suspicious: "Qui in primordio regni, ut habet subtilitas barbarorum, coepit mitius et moderatius agere." Victor of Tunnuna, *Chronicon* (*PL,* LXVIII, 944), says that Huneric was worse than his father but that Gunthamund (*PL,* LXVIII, 946) "nostros protinus de exilio revocavit."
[39] See Dracontius, *Romulea, Praefatio* 1.12-15,

court.[40] This learned king not only encouraged literature but also engaged in the building of parks, country seats, public works, churches, and palatial structures.[41]

21. Upon the death of Thrasamund in 523, Hilderic, a feeble old man who had been passed over for thirty-nine years in the succession to the throne, became king. He adopted a lenient policy toward the Catholics and authorized the recall of banished priests. However, in 530 he was deposed by Gelimer, a most repressive ruler. Justinian, emperor of the East, who had befriended Hilderic, now intervened, and after the breakdown of diplomatic relations with Gelimer, sent Belisarius with an army into Africa. The Vandals were crushed.

22. Then the victorious Justinian acted in a manner more befitting the mores of "barbarians" like the Vandals, to whom so many atrocities were attributed, than those of an enlightened and civilized monarch. He deprived the Vandals of their property, turned the Arian churches over to the Catholics, killed or enslaved the soldiers of Gelimer, and handed over their wives to his own soldiers. Gelimer himself had previously reduced the ranks of the Vandal nobility by massacring Hilderic and his nephews, Hoamer and Oageis, and their followers. Two of Gelimer's brothers were killed in battle. Gelimer and some of his retinue were captured, exhibited in the triumph at Constantinople, and then exiled. The few Vandal nobles remaining in North Africa lost their property and submerged their identity in the masses.[42] Practically all traces of Vandal occupation were wiped out; the Vandals ceased to exist as a people after 534.

B. Carthage, a Roman Metropolis

1. When the Vandals entered Carthage in 439, they came into a

---

Sancte pater, o magister, taliter canendus es,
Qui fugatas Africanae reddis urbi litteras,
Barbaris qui Romulidas iungis auditorio,
Cuius ordines profecto semper obstupescimus.

Hallowed father, O teacher, so must you be extolled in song, who are bringing back to the African city the learning that had been driven away, who unite Romans with barbarians in a lecture hall, at whose rows of seats we are truly amazed at all times.

[40] Schmidt, *Geschichte*, p. 189.
[41] See Poems 210R-214R, and 376R.
[42] Courtois, *Les Vandales*, pp. 353-57; Martroye, *L'Occident*, pp. 258-59, notes that the Moors joined in the massacre of the Vandals.

rich and magnificent city, a true Roman metropolis filled with great public buildings, a *praetorium*, temples, churches, baths, a circus, theaters, and an amphitheater. The Baths of Antoninus Pius, for example, were among the most beautiful in the Empire.[43] Carthage also had a forum of which the inhabitants were very proud. Although the ruins today are rather extensive, little is left of all that splendor:

> Giace l'alta Cartago; appena i segni
> Dell'alte sue ruine il lido serba!
> Muoiono le città, muoiono i regni,
> Copre i fasti e le pompe arena ed erba.[44]

> Here lies great Carthage; scarcely does the sea bank protect the traces of its lofty ruins! Cities pass away, kingdoms pass away; sand and grass cover their history and glory. (See Pl. III, B.)

2. Public buildings were made of marble, of almost every kind of marble then known: costly Numidian marble—white, pink, and green —cipolin, green porphyry, and pink onyx. The columns in the Baths of Antoninus were made of Egyptian granite and Carrara marble.[45] Limestone reinforced by volcanic rock imported from Sicily and Sardinia was also widely used; the homes of the poor were made of tufa coated with pitch.[46] The inner walls of the houses of the rich consisted of plaster over which frescoes were painted or in which small pieces of marble were inserted; capitals and columns in these homes were also constructed of marble.

3. Remains of rich homes and suburban villas have been discovered in North Africa.[47] Among these are the Aviary House, so named because of the designs in the mosaics, and the Villa of Scorpianus, a

---

[43] Lapeyre and Pellegrin, *Carthage,* p. 34; C. Picard, *Carthage,* pp. 51-52.

[44] Tasso, *Gerusalemme Liberata,* 15.20.1-4.

[45] Albertini, *L'Afrique romaine,* p. 57; Bouchier, *Life and Letters,* p. 4; Cagnat, *Carthage,* p. 24; C. Picard, *Carthage,* pp. 13, 54. Audollent, *Carthage romaine,* p. 629, says that Parian marble or marble like it was used. See Poem 6.5.

[46] Pliny, *Natural History* 36.22.48, asserts that tufa (*tophus*) was not suitable for building but was used in Carthage because the Carthaginians had no other material. He facetiously remarks that they used pitch for houses and lime for wine. See also Bouchier, *Life and Letters,* p. 52, and Lapeyre and Pellegrin, *Carthage,* p. 26.

[47] C. Picard, *Carthage,* pp. 37, 44-45, 50, 68, describes the villas excavated in Carthage. See also Lavedan and Besques, *Histoire de l'art,* I, 261-64. For descriptions of works of art, statuary, gardens, etc., see Poems 18, 26, 27, 34, 46, 60-62, 70, 83, 85, and 88.

charioteer.[48] These villas are characterized by porticoes, marble colonnades, large rooms, and abundant mosaics. Examples of such mosaics are now to be seen mainly in the Lavigerie Museum, Carthage, or in the Alaoui (Bardo) Museum, Tunis; some, however, have found their way into the British Museum.[49] (See Pls. II, A, and IV, A.)

4. The Aviary House had an octagonal *viridarium* or garden in the center of the court.[50] An atrium opened up on a second garden, in which there was a fountain decorated with statues of Venus, Cupid, and Bacchus. This was fed by a stream descending over mosaic slabs arranged in steps.[51] Here, as in other villas of North Africa, the subjects of the mosaics are flowers, hunting, fishing, and farming. In another villa, which is called the Villa of Lord Julius, dating from the fourth century, there are mosaics of the four seasons.[52]

5. As an example of the extensive estates in the North African countryside, Boissier describes in detail the remains of a villa unearthed between Constantine and Sétif. The atrium was thirty feet long; the thermae attached to this villa were large enough to serve a town. The swimming pool was surrounded by a semicircular gallery containing twenty-one rooms, each paved with mosaics, from which the life of the owner can be reconstructed. It was like that of rich Romans in other parts of North Africa, as indicated by similar mosaics found elsewhere. From some of the poems of Luxorius, it is evident that the manner of living did not change for the opulent landowner when the Vandals dispossessed the Romans.[53]

6. The mosaics of this villa bear the name of the owner; a certain Pompeianus, and legends describing each scene.[54] The owner's private

---

[48] See n. 74, below.

[49] See *A Guide to the Department of Greek and Roman Antiquities in the British Museum* (London, 1928), pp. 54-55.

[50] See Poem 18. The outline of this *viridarium* is still visible; see C. Picard, *Carthage*, p. 44.

[51] See Poems 34, 61, 62, 69, 70; also C. Picard, *Carthage*, p. 45.

[52] See Bouchier, *Life and Letters*, pp. 44-46; Julien, *Histoire*, pp. 164-65; Lapeyre and Pellegrin, *Carthage*, pp. 24-26; Merlin, *CRAI* (1920), pp. 337-38; C. Picard, *Carthage*, Pls. 12 and 13; also note on Poem 18.13, below.

[53] See above, n. 8; Poems 18, 19, 46, 83; also Boissier, *L'Afrique romaine*, pp. 153-74; Julien, *Histoire*, pp. 164-67; Mommsen; *The Provinces*, II, 333-34; Schmidt, *Geschichte*, pp. 49-51.

[54] For mosaics of such estates, see n. 68, below; *Inventaire*, II (1914), 362, 940; *MCAAT*, VII, 23-24, Nos. 103-5, Pl. 6. See also notes on Poems 18 and 67. Pantings were rare; mosaics, the rule; in Pompeii, the reverse was true. On African mosaics, see Albertini, *L'Afrique romaine*, p. 92; Audollent, *Carthage*, pp. 638, 659-66; Bouchier, *Life and Letters*, p. 52; Cagnat, *Carthage*, pp. 116-17; Lavedan and Besques, *Histoire de l'art*, I, 269; Leclercq, *L'Afrique*, II, 34-35.

stable is depicted, as are his horses, whose names are given—Delicatus, Pullentianus, Titas, Scholasticus, Altus, and Polidoxus. Scenes of the hunt are the subject of two mosaics; even the names of the dogs are affixed—Fidelis and Castus. There are pictures of rustic life: the management of the farms and the gathering of the flocks, the forest keeper's home, an orchard, a young man leading a little dog and protecting a lady's face from the sun with a parasol. The caption for this last vignette is *filosofi locus*. Boissier, who writes with a vivid imagination, romanticizes that in such a setting as this, little poems were being read, poems of the type in vogue in Africa, some of which have been preserved, *selon lui*, in the *Anthologia Latina*!

7. The public buildings were also sumptuous. The small theater or Odeon, built in the third century, and the large theater built in the second century, were both destroyed by the Vandals, according to Victor of Vita.[55] It has been explained by some writers that these were demolished because the Vandals did not want to leave any structures that could later be used as fortresses against them.[56] Some idea of the former magnificence of the Odeon and the Theater can be gained from the statues found there, most of which are now in the Bardo. From the Theater came a colossal statue of Apollo and statues of Hermes carrying Dionysus, of Venus and Cupid, Ceres, and some emperors; from the Odeon, a huge Jupiter, a statue of Venus and a dolphin, and a beautiful statue of Hadrian.[57]

8. Apuleius, who once spoke in the Theater, gives an embroidered rhetorical description of it:[58]

We must consider in an auditorium of this kind not the marble of the pavement, nor the boards of the stage floor, nor the columns of the stage, nor the lofty height of its roof and the splendor of the fretted ceiling, nor the extensive rows of seats, nor the fact that here can be heard the deception of the mime, the

[55] Tertullian, *De Resurrectione Carnis* 42 (*PL*, II, 901), "Sed et proxime in ista civitate cum Odei fundamenta . . . collocarentur." Tertullian wrote early in the third century. See also Lapeyre and Pellegrin, *Carthage*, p. 33; C. Picard, *Carthage*, p. 43. Victor of Vita, 1.3.8 (*PL*, LVIII, 184B), "Nam et hodie si qua supersunt, subinde desolantur, sicut ibi Carthagine odium [Odeum], theatrum, aedem Memoriae, et viam, quam Caelestis vocabant." However, Courtois, *Les Vandales*, p. 79, notes that Victor later (4.4.17; *PL*, LVIII, 239C) talks about a meeting in the "destroyed" Aedes Memoriae. See also Courtois, p. 41, where he lists contradictions in Victor, and pp. 64-87, where he expresses doubt concerning Victor's reliability.

[56] Procopius, *Bellum Vandalicum* 1.5.8-9; Cagnat, *Carthage*, pp. 25-26.

[57] For photographs, see Cagnat, *Carthage*, pp. 25-27; C. Picard, *Carthage*, pp. 43-44.

[58] Apuleius, *Florida* 18.

dialogue of the comedian, the ranting of the tragedian, that here can be seen the perilous turns of the ropewalker, the juggler's sleight of hand, the gestures and movements of every type of performer. . . .

9. The Theater has been partly reconstructed; in it plays are occasionally presented and large gatherings are convened. The Odeon and the Theater are situated in an elevated part of Carthage, opposite the Byrsa, the old acropolis of the city, now called the Hill of St. Louis. The setting lends itself to oratory, and it was to this setting that Winston Churchill referred when he addressed the Eighth Army there, early in June, 1943.[59]

10. The stately Forum and its public library are mentioned by Luxorius in Poem 3.2:

Pomposique fori scrinia publica.

Apuleius refers to this library in the same passage in which he describes the Theater. No remains of the library have been unearthed; in fact, the ruins of only a single ancient library have been found in North Africa—the one at Timgad.[60] St. Augustine alludes to the Forum of Carthage in his narration of the adventure that befell Alypius, his pupil and townsman.[61] He mentions the *Vicus Argentarius* as one of the settings of the episode; we possess the names of some other streets and sections of Carthage,[62] but the location of the Forum has not been established, although some authorities think it was near the harbor.[63]

---

[59] According to Colette Picard, *Carthage*, p. 16, "La guerre mondiale de 1939-1945 a même rendu à Carthage une place dans l'histoire du monde: c'est dans son théâtre, là même où Apulée avait jadis lu les Florides que M. Churchill prononça son discours à la VIIIe Armée. . . ." Churchill's account of the occasion follows, from *The Hinge of Fate* (Boston, 1950), p. 828, "I addressed many thousand soldiers at Carthage in the ruins of an ancient amphitheatre. Certainly the hour and setting lent itself to oratory. I have no idea of what I said, but the whole audience clapped and cheered as doubtless their predecessors of 2,000 years ago had done as they watched gladiatorial combat." Churchill says he spoke in the Amphitheater, but Mlle Picard, who was once the conservator of the ruins of Carthage, says he spoke in the Theater and confirmed this in a letter dated December 20, 1956. A personal investigation of the sites in May, 1957, and the questioning of eyewitnesses at the Theater itself convinced me that Churchill must have spoken in the Theater.

[60] Cagnat, *Carthage*, pp. 103-6; Julien, *Histoire*, p. 178.

[61] Augustine, *Confessions* 6.9.14-15 (*PL*, XXXII, 726-27).

[62] Audollent, *Carthage*, p. 310; Bouchier, *Life and Letters*, pp. 18-19. See also n. 55, above; *Acta Proconsularia Sancti Cypriani* 2 (*PL*, III, 1561A), "In vico qui dicitur Saturni, inter Veneream et Salutariam mansit"; *Expositio Totius Mundi*, ed. by J. Gronovius (Leyden, 1700), pp. 268-69, "Et iterum praecipuum invenies opus publicum in eam, vicum argentariorum."

[63] Audollent, *Carthage*, pp. 230-33; Lapeyre and Pellegrin, *Carthage*, pp. 30-31; C. Picard, *Carthage*, p. 30.

11. The Amphitheater, situated west of the Byrsa and close to the ramparts of the city, equaled the Roman Colosseum in size and splendor.[64] All that is left of it today is the arena floor, on which a camel occasionally grazes, some substructures and stalls, and a few ramps of the *vomitoria*. However, it was still standing in the twelfth century and excited the admiration of the travelers and geographers El Behri and Edrisi (or Idrisi).[65] (See Pl. II, B.)

12. The great Circus, frequently mentioned by Tertullian, was near the Amphitheater.[66] Its dimensions, 675 by 100 meters, rivaled those of the Circus Maximus in Rome; it could seat 200,000. El Behri says that the columns were so large that twelve men could sit on top of one of them with their legs crossed and eat and drink at a table. The area is now used as farm land and has been cut by a road; a few sections of the spina, which was more than 300 meters long, are barely visible.[67]

13. The Africans, especially the Carthaginians, were fond not only of hunting, but also of racing.[68] Africa was the home of skilled horsemen and spirited horses. Livy describes the maneuvers of the famed Numidian cavalry;[69] the names of Gaetulian, Garamantian, and Numidian horses appear in lists of Circus Maximus winners.[70] African riders won triumphs in other parts of the Empire—among them a certain Scorpianus, winner of 700 races, whose name appears on an

[64] Cagnat, *Carthage*, pp. 29-32; Julien, *Histoire*, p. 33; C. Picard, *Carthage*, p. 68.

[65] El Behri (also known as Al Behri, El Bekri, and Al Bakri), is the author of *Al Masâlik W'al Mamâlik* (The roads and the provinces), from which a part was excerpted and translated by MacGuckin de Slade, as *Description de l'Afrique septentrionale* (Algiers, 1913). El Behri calls the Theater (Amphitheater) a most remarkable monument and is enthusiastic about the aqueducts, reservoirs, and marble statues. El Behri (1090-94) refers (p. 93) to the abundance of marble in Carthage in his day. Al (or El) Edrisi or Idrisi (1100-64) wrote *Kitâb Rudyār* (Book of Roger), which was translated by R. Dozy and M. J. de Goeje as *Description de l'Afrique et de l'Espagne* (Leiden, 1866). Edrisi also notes the aqueducts and the carting away of marble; he is most enthusiastic about the Amphitheater (pp. 132-33), "Le théâtre, qui n'a pas son pareil en magnificence dans l'univers." For more on Carthage by these two writers, see Cagnat, *Carthage*, pp. 29-30; Lapeyre and Pellegrin, *Carthage*, p. 33; Sladen, *Carthage and Tunis*, I, 52-53.

[66] E.g., in *De Spectaculis* 5.7-9 (*PL*, I, 711-15).

[67] Lapeyre and Pellegrin, *Carthage*, pp. 33-34; personal visit to the site, May, 1957.

[68] Boissier, *L'Afrique romaine*, pp. 241-48; Getty, *Life of the North Africans*, pp. 37-56; see also Augustine, *Confessions* 6.7.11-13 and 6.8.13 (*PL*, XXXII, 724-26). For mosaics of racing, see below, Ch. III, n. 7; *Inventaire*, I (1922), Pls. 712, 785, 1236, 1611; II (1914), Pl. 18, 124, 126, 321, 375, 540; *MCAAT*, VII, 12, No. 19; XV, 19-20, No. 262, Pl. 8, showing a victorious charioteer, the names of two horses, Amandus and Frunitus, the stables of the Circus, and the legend, *Eros, omnia per te*; and XX, 4, No. 351, Pl. 1, and 14, No. 386. See also Reinach, *Répertoire de peintures*, pp. 290-93. Poems 7, 20, 26, 27, 34, 38, 41, 42, and 50 by Luxorius contain references to the Circus, racing, and charioteers.

[69] Livy, 35.11.4-10.

[70] *CIL*, VI.2, 10047, 10058, 10082.

inscription found in Germany,[71] and Porphyrius, in whose honor epigrams were composed and statues erected in Constantinople.[72]

14. As is well known, there were four racing factions: the Blues (*Veneti*), Whites (*Albi*), Greens (*Prasini*), and Reds (*Russei*).[73] These existed in Rome under the emperors and were eventually transported to other parts of the Roman world.[74] The factions had serious political and social implications: the Greens and Reds represented the lower classes, the Blues and Whites, the aristocracy.[75] When political parties disappeared under dictatorial emperors, these factions took their place. Gibbon describes most vividly and graphically the bitterness and power of the factions in Constantinople.[76] From the evidence of Poems 38 and 42 by Luxorius, it is apparent that factions continued to exist in Carthage even under the Vandals, but we have no information concerning any political import they might have had at that time.[77]

15. As has been seen above (A5), the Carthaginians were devoted to the cult of magic. Their addiction to the use of charms and to methods of warding off the evil eye was directly bound up with the "sportsmanship" of Circus habitués. A great number of charms written on lead tablets (*tabulae plumbeae* or *tabulae execrationum*) have been brought to light; many of them are in the Lavigerie and Bardo

[71] *CIL,* III.3, 12013.9. He is called here [*agita*]*tor factionis, natione Afer;* he may be the Scorpianus of the Villa; see above, B 3, and *Inventaire,* II (1910), 273, No. 816.

[72] *Anthologia Palatina* 16.344. Bailly, *Byzance,* p. 56, says that charioteers were idolized more than movie stars today; they were exempt from taxes, and practically above the laws. Their statues were placed alongside those of emperors.

[73] For the origin and use of these colors, see Tertullian, *De Spectaculis* 9 (*PL,* I, 715); Cassiodorus, *Variae* 3.51 (*PL,* LXIX, 606). According to Bailly, *Byzance,* p. 54, the Blues and Whites merged, as did the Reds and Greens. For mosaics of the four factions, see *Inventaire,* I (1909), 6; I (1922), Pl. 712; II (1914), No. 18; *MCAAT,* VII, 12, No. 19; H. W. Johnston, *The Private Life of the Romans,* rev. by Mary Johnston (Chicago, 1932), frontispiece, a color plate of a mosaic found in a villa near Rome, showing charioteers wearing the colors of the four factions.

[74] In Germany, see above, n. 71; in Spain, see Burmann, *Anthologia,* II, 249, Book IV, Epigram 340.1, *Factionis Venetae Fusco;* in Constantinople, *Anthologia Palatina* 15.46, 49; 16.47; 338-40, 343, 344, 348, 349, 354, 363, 368, 376, 380-87; in Carthage, Luxorius, Poems 38, 42; and Tertullian (cited in n. 73, above).

[75] Goossens, *Byzantion,* XIV (1939), 205-9; Friedlaender, *NJbb,* LXXIII (1856), 745-50; Pollack, *RE,* VI.2, 1954-58; see also Mayor, *Juvenal,* II, 218-19, note on Juvenal, 11.198, for citations of Latin authors on factions. See also Suetonius, *Caligula* 55.2, *Vitellius* 14.3-4, *Domitian* 7.1.

[76] *The Decline and Fall of the Roman Empire,* Ch. 40, Part 2. See also Bailly, *Byzance,* pp. 51-60; Procopius, *Bellum Persicum* 1.24.1-10, 17-58, on the Blue and Green factions and their rioting in Constantinople.

[77] See Poem 191R.5 about Bumbulus, who did not belong to the same faction as his father: "Dilexit genitor prasinum, te russeus intrat." Boissier, *L'Afrique romaine,* p. 243, gives a charming but not penetrating explanation of one's allegiance to a faction.

Museums; their text can be read in the *CIL*.[78] A racing fanatic who wished to cast a spell upon a horse or a charioteer would have a magician write out his wish, which he then placed in the tomb of a newly buried person. These imprecations are written in Latin and Greek or in Latin words with Greek letters. They contain the names of both horses and charioteers and call upon a spirit or deity to render them ineffective, cripple them, and topple them over. Part of a Latin inscription runs as follows:[79]

> Excito te, demon, qui hic conversans; trado
> tibi hos equos, et deteneas illos et inplicentur
> nec se movere possint.

> I call upon you, O spirit who dwells here. I am delivering these horses to you. Hold them back; let them become entangled and unable to move!

16. A Greek inscription against the Greens ends with this urgent plea:[80]

> Ἤδη ἤδη ἤδη, τάχυ τάχυ ταχέως.
> Κατάδησον κατάδησον κατάδησον αὐτούς.

> At once, at once, at once, quickly, quickly, more quickly, cast a spell, cast a spell upon them!

17. A few poems in the *Anthologia Latina* mention other forms of entertainment enjoyed in Carthage under the Vandals. No. 111R beautifully depicts the art of the pantomimist, who interprets by gestures the songs of a chorus; No. 112R deals with the skill of a rope-walker; Nos. 113R-115R are about singers and dancers. Luxorius refers to a pantomimist in 24L and to a female musician and dancer in 75L. Mimes and pantomimes had replaced comedy and tragedy in the late Empire; because of language difficulties pantomimes would

---

[78] *CIL*, VIII, Supp. 1, pp. 1288 ff., describes some tablets found in or near tombs, attached to the walls of a *cippus* with the help of a copper nail that perforated the leaves of the tablets. The execrations are not confined to racing; some are also of a more personal nature. See *MCAAT*, VIII, 87-91; XV, 118, No. 60, 137, No. 50, 138-39, Nos. 61-65; XX, Nos. 164-66; *CIL*, VIII, Supp. 1, 12504, 12506, 12508-11; for translations or summaries, see Cagnat, *Carthage*, pp. 27-29; Lapeyre and Pellegrin, *Carthage*, pp. 119-20; Sladen, *Carthage and Tunis*, I, 97-99.

[79] *CIL*, VIII, Supp. 1, 12504.

[80] *CIL*, VIII, Supp. 1, 12509.

certainly be pleasing to those Africans who knew no Greek and whose Latin was poor.[81]

18. So devoted were the Carthaginians to the pleasures of the theater, circus, and amphitheater that, just as in Belgium's capital on the eve of Waterloo, there was a sound of revelry in Carthage while an invading army was at its gates and upon its very walls. In the words of Salvian:[82]

The arms of barbarian people were resounding against the walls of Cirta and of Carthage; and yet the Christian population was going wild in the circuses and enjoying itself in the theaters. Some were having their throats cut outside the walls; others were fornicating inside the walls. Some of the people were captives of the enemy outside the walls; others were captives of their own vices inside the walls. . . . As I have said, there was a sound of battle outside the walls and of games within the walls; the cries of the dying were intermingled with the shouting of the revelers; the cries of the people falling in the fighting could scarcely be distinguished from the uproar of the people shouting in the Circus.

C. Carthage, a Center of Learning

1. On the other hand, the Carthaginians, as well as the other Romans in Africa, were devoted to learning and literature.[83] Ever since the second century A.D., Africa had been a center of education, especially in rhetoric and law, so much so that Juvenal applied to Africa the oft-quoted epithet *nutricula causidicorum* (7.148).

2. Schools flourished even in the smallest towns.[84] The system of education was the same as that which prevailed in the rest of the Empire; pupils learned to read, write, and count under a teacher known as a *litterator* or *primus magister* or *magister ludi.* Then they were

[81] Boissier, *L'Afrique romaine,* pp. 253-65; Getty, *Life of the North Africans,* pp. 37-56. See also Poem 386R and Apuleius, *Florida* 5, 18.

[82] Salvian, *De Gubernatione Dei* 6.12. 69-71 (*PL,* LIII, 122 B-C, 123 A-B). See *ibid.* 6.2.10 (*PL,* LIII, 110A-111B) on the evils of games. On Salvian, see above, n. 9.

[83] Mommsen, *The Provinces,* II, 341, "More value was set upon the Latin, and along with it on the Greek instruction, and on its aim of general culture, in Africa than anywhere else in the world, and the school system was highly developed." See also Monceaux, *Les Africains,* pp. 459-91, on Carthage as an intellectual center and on the literary life there.

[84] On education in the Roman Empire, see Boissier, *La fin du paganisme,* I, 145-218, and *L'Afrique romaine,* pp. 267-71; Bouchier, *Life and Letters,* pp. 32-35; Dill, *Roman Society,* pp. 385-451; Graham, *Roman Africa,* pp. 128-30; Julien, *Histoire,* pp. 180-81; Leclercq, *L'Afrique,* II, 6-20; Marrou, *Histoire de l'éducation,* pp. 359-83; Monceaux, *Les Africains,* pp. 48, 58-77; Warmington, *The North African Provinces,* pp. 103-4; also Augustine, *Confessions* 1.13.20 (*PL,* XXXII, 670); *S. Fulgentii Episcopi Ruspensis Vita, Prolegomena* 1.5 (*PL* LXV, 119C).

taught literature, grammar, and composition by a *grammaticus*.[85] Among the poets of the *Anthologia Latina,* Calbulus, Coronatus, and Luxorius were *grammatici.* Faustus, the friend of Luxorius, was also a *grammaticus.* Greek was not taught to any great extent in the Western Empire in its late days but there were Greek *grammatici* in North Africa, plays were given in Greek, and, according to St. Augustine, Greek was taught even in small towns.[86]

3. When they reached the age of fifteen to seventeen, students who wished to continue their studies went from their native small towns to larger cities where renowned teachers (*rhetores*) taught. Cirta, Theveste, Madauros (modern Mdaourouch), Hadrumetum, Oea (modern Tripoli), and Leptis Magna were noted educational centers. St. Augustine, for example, went from his native Thagaste to Madauros and then to Carthage, the intellectual center of the province and the equal, if not the superior, of Rome as a seat of culture and learning.[87]

4. The intellectual fervor of Carthage is well expressed by Apuleius in the speech he made in the Theater:[88]

Every one of you throughout the city is most educated; you possess every form of knowledge, which small children learn, young men display, and old men

[85] The Latin of the educated Africans has been held to be superior to that spoken in Italy. African Latin was characterized by a wealth of archaisms and by the literary use of vulgar forms. See Audollent, *Carthage,* pp. 701-8; Boissier, *L'Afrique romaine,* pp. 313, 339-40, 342-46; Bouchier, *Life and Letters,* pp. 11-12, 118-26; Julien, *Histoire,* p. 180; Labriolle, *Histoire de la littérature,* II, 637; Lapeyre and Pellegrin, *Carthage,* pp. 98-99; Monceaux, *Les Africains,* pp. 99-121. See also, on Latin spoken in Africa, Augustine, *De Doctrina Christiana* 4.10.24 (*PL* XXXIV, 99-100), and *Enarrationes in Psalmos* 138.20 (*PL,* XXXVII, 1796). See below, Chs. II, n. 32, and VIII, n. 98.

[86] Augustine, *Confessions* 1.13-14 (*PL,* XXXII, 670); Bouchier, *Life and Letters,* pp. 39-41; Courcelle, *Les lettres grecques,* pp. 134-209; Thieling, *Der Hellenismus,* pp. 9-14; Warmington, *The North African Provinces,* p. 103. In addition, Punic was still spoken in the time of Augustine and may have been taught in the schools. Bardenhewer, *Geschichte der altkirchlichen Literatur,* IV, 491, says, "Sehr wahrscheinlich ist den ersten Lesern das Punische geläufiger gewesen als das Lateinische," but Mommsen, *The Provinces,* II, 328, declares that Punic was banished from the schools and from written use but remained as a popular dialect and was spoken by genteel ladies of Leptis Magna who were poor in Latin and Greek. See also Monceaux, *Les Africains,* pp. 37-38; Augustine, *Epistulae* 17.2.3 (*PL,* XXXIII, 83-84), *Sermones* 113.2 (*PL,* XXXVIII, 648), *Epistulae* 209.3 (*PL,* XXXIII, 953), "Quod ut fieret, aptum loco illi congruumque requirebam, qui et Punica lingua esset instructus," *Sermones* 167.34 (*PL,* XXXVIII, 910), "Proverbium notum est Punicum quod quidem Latine vobis dicam quia Punice non omnes nostis," *Sermones* 288.3 (*PL,* XXXVIII, 1305), "Invenit Punicum? Punicam vocem quaerit, qua procedat ad Punicum." When the Arabs overran North Africa at the end of the seventh century, Latin and Punic died out as spoken languages there, but Berber remained and is spoken today. See Albertini, *L'Afrique romaine,* p. 93, and Mommsen, *The Provinces,* II, 238.

[87] Augustine, *Confessions* 2.3.5 (*PL,* XXXII, 677); see also n. 7, above.

[88] *Florida* 20; see also B 8, above.

teach. Carthage, ancient teacher of our province, Carthage, heavenly Muse of Africa, Carthage, Camena of the people who wear the toga.

5. Boissier was not surprised to find no ruins of schools in the ancient cities of North Africa that he visited, for there, as elsewhere in the Roman world, classes were generally held beneath the porticoes or in the upper stories of private dwellings.[89] Schoolmasters also taught in booths and on balconies on the front of the house.[90] There were curtains (*vela*) at the entrances of some grammar schools, put there, Augustine sardonically remarks, not to assure privacy but to afford concealment to the folly (*tegimentum erroris*) being perpetrated within.[91] Augustine does not give a flattering picture of the schoolmasters of his day, whom he accuses of lack of understanding, of pedantry, and of cruelty. The schoolmaster portrayed by Luxorius in Poem 8 is also an unsavory type.

6. The passion of the Africans for learning is evidenced not only in literature but also in inscriptions.[92] The epitaph of a youth of seventeen of Mactaris (modern Maktar) tells us that he was beloved by his teachers, devoted to his studies, that at the age of fourteen he could read Greek shorthand (*notas Graecas*), and that he spoke, wrote, and painted well.[93] Another epitaph informs us that a young man knew the two learned languages remarkably well, that he was superior in the composition of dialogues, letters, and idylls, that he could improvise on any subject proposed to him, and that in spite of his youth he attracted a crowd when he declaimed.[94]

7. The study of poetry, as well as of rhetoric, was stressed. Special attention was paid to Vergil.[95] Although it has been said that Africa, home of celebrated grammarians, rhetoricians, and advocates, did not produce any truly great poets, the Africans were fond of poetry and

---

[89] Boissier, *L'Afrique romaine*, p. 267.

[90] Augustine, *Confessions* 1.16.26 (*PL*, XXXII, 672); Dionysius Halicarnassensis, *Antiquitates Romanae* 11.28; Suetonius, *De Grammaticis* 18.1, *Divus Augustus* 94.12; Livy, 3.44.6, "in forum—ibi namque in tabernaculis litterarum ludi erant." See Marrou, *Histoire de l'Éducation*, p. 549, n. 7, and p. 362, "le *magister* latin se contente, pour s'établir, d'une boutique, *pergula*; on aime en particulier utiliser celles qui s'ouvrent sur les portiques du forum; nous le constatons à Rome comme à Pompéi ou à Carthage."

[91] Augustine, *Confessions* 1.13.22 (*PL*, XXXII, 670).

[92] Boissier, *L'Afrique romaine*, pp. 268-69, 300-3; Graham, *Roman Africa*, pp. 128-30.

[93] *CIL*, VIII.1, 724.

[94] *CIL*, VIII.1, 5530; see also VIII.2, 8500, 9182; VIII, Supp. 1, 12152.

[95] See Augustine, *Confessions* 1.13.20-22 (*PL*, XXXII, 670-71). The famous mosaic of Vergil seated between two Muses and holding a *volumen* of the *Aeneid* was found in Sousse and is now in the Bardo Museum; see *MCAAT*, XV, 21, No. 266, Pl. 10.1.

many of their epitaphs are in verse.[96] Boissier cites the monument of T. Flavius Secundus at Cillium (modern Kasserine) in Byzacena, a monstrosity consisting of a pyramid with steps, columns, and bas-reliefs. At the summit is a cock flapping its wings, and on the sides there are holes in the stones to serve as homes for swarms of bees. To complete this monument, Secundus had somebody compose ninety hexameters and some distichs, which were duly inscribed on it.[97]

8. Not only rich men but also men of humble rank delighted in putting verses on their monuments. For example, an official messenger (*tabellarius*) of Carthage constructed his tomb while he was still alive and read his verses on the monument as he passed by.[98] The writers of such poetry were not content with simple meters; they also had a liking for trick forms of verse, such as acrostics. The Latin used in these inscriptions is of poor quality, but it was living Latin which shows how the language was developing and changing.

9. Nurtured by this tradition and the system of education, a long line of distinguished men of letters came from Africa during the period beginning with the first century A.D. and ending with the overthrow of the Vandals in 534. In their number are a few philosophers and poets, but emphasis must be placed upon the preponderance of orators, lawyers, grammarians, and rhetoricians, and especially of theological commentators and polemists.[99] A representative list is given in the following paragraphs.

10. Cornutus the philosopher, born in Leptis Magna *ca.* A.D. 20, teacher of Lucan and Persius; Septimius Severus, of the same city, friend of Statius (*Silvae* 4.5) and grandfather of the emperor, who was also a native of Africa; Publius Annius Florus, friend of Hadrian, and believed by some to have written the *Pervigilium Veneris,* sometimes identified with the historian Lucius Annaeus (or Julius) Florus;[100] Salvius Julianus (100-169), a great legal writer who drew up a code for Hadrian; his disciple, Caecilius Africanus (*fl.* 150); Fronto (*ca.*

---

[96] Boissier, *L'Afrique romaine,* p. 300; Mommsen, *The Provinces,* II, 343, "Significantly we do not meet in the whole field of African-Latin authorship a single poet who deserves to be so much as named." Exception taken here!

[97] Boissier, *L'Afrique romaine,* pp. 300-1; *CIL,* VIII.1, 212-13.

[98] *CIL,* VIII.1, 1027:
> Dum sum vitalis et vivo, ego feci sepulcrhum [*sic*]
> Adque meos versus, dum transseo [*sic*], perlego et ipse.

[99] Labriolle, *Histoire de la littérature,* I, 93, notes that for three centuries Africa gave to Christian literature most of its writers.

[100] Harvey, *The Oxford Companion, s.v. Florus* and *Pervigilium Veneris.*

100-166), a native of Cirta, orator, epistolarian, and teacher of Marcus Aurelius; Apuleius (born *ca.* 123 in Hadrumetum); Sulpicius Apollinaris (second century), born in Carthage, teacher of Aulus Gellius and the emperor Pertinax; Eutychius Proculus (second century) of Sicca Veneria (modern Le Kef), a grammarian; Terentianus Maurus (same century), the noted writer on meters.

11. Nemesianus of Carthage, author of the poem *Cynegetica,* and Gargilius Martialis of Numidia, who wrote on gardens, flourished in the third century. Later come Marcus Victorinus of Carthage, who opened a school of rhetoric in Rome *ca.* 340; Gaius Marius Victorinus (fourth century), writer on Cicero, rhetoric, and philosophy; Donatus, the celebrated grammarian of the fourth century, teacher of St. Jerome; Nonius Marcellus of Thubursicum (modern Khemissa), another grammarian of the same era; Martianus Capella of Madauros and Carthage, who wrote that strange medley of prose and verse, *Liber de Nuptiis Mercurii et Philologiae,* between 410 and 429; Caelius Aurelianus of Sicca Veneria (*fl.* 420), author of medical treatises; Fabius Planciades Fulgentius, mythographer of the fifth century; the historians Victor Vitensis (of Vita) and Victor Tunnunensis (of Tunnuna), who lived and suffered under the Vandals; Dracontius, the Christian poet who was imprisoned by King Gunthamund; Priscian the grammarian, born in Caesarea in the early part of the sixth century; and Corippus, who lived in Carthage and Constantinople and wrote epic poetry shortly after the fall of the Vandals.

12. Among the Christian writers, the best known are Tertullian (160-225), who spent most of his life in Carthage; St. Cyprian (200-258), bishop of Carthage; Arnobius of Numidia (*fl.* 284-305), author of *Adversus Nationes*; Lactantius, his pupil (*ca.* 250-317), the "Christian Cicero," a native of Proconsularis; Arnobius Junior, a commentator on Biblical topics; St. Optatus (*fl.* 366-90) of Milevis (modern Mila), author of works against the Donatists; St. Augustine (354-430); and Verecundus (died 552), bishop of Junca in Byzacena, author of the poem *De Satisfactione Poenitentiae.*[101]

Finally, there are the poets of the *Latin Anthology,* who will now be treated separately and in detail.

---

[101] The names of a few authors have been omitted from this list because it has not been established beyond doubt that they came from Africa. Among these are Minucius Felix, Commodian, Servius the grammarian, and Macrobius.

II. THE LATIN ANTHOLOGY

During the fourth century intellectual life had begun to decline in North Africa; supremacy in that respect passed over to Gaul.[1] However, Roman culture and education did persist, although yielding products inferior to those of the great period of Roman literature in Africa.[2] Even under the Vandals, whom they looked down upon as barbarians, a group of poets wrote for readers and listeners who loved poetry, whether or not their ears were attuned to the nuances of Latin pronunciation. These poets looked to the past for their models and wrote in the tradition of their predecessors; perhaps this was their refuge and fixed point in a changing world, as all was tottering and crumbling about them.

All alone is Blossius Aemilius Dracontius, advocate and poet, who wrote on mythology as well as on Christian themes. He was imprisoned by Gunthamund (484-96) for writing in honor of a foreign prince, probably the emperor at Constantinople.[3] The revolt of Dracontius did not last long, for he repented in prison and wrote a poetic apology, the *Satisfactio*.

The other poets who wrote during the Vandal occupation are actually a coterie whose slight pieces were collected in what has come down to us as the *Anthologia Latina*. It is not certain how many of these poets were contemporary, and little more than their names is known about almost all of them. These names follow: Avitus, Bonosus,

---

[1] Warmington, *The North African Provinces,* pp. 103-11.

[2] Procopius, *Bellum Vandalicum* 2.6.5-9; *CMH,* I, 321-22; Lapeyre and Pellegrin, *Carthage,* pp. 145-46.

[3] Julien, *Histoire,* p. 252.

[4] Riese, *Anthologia,* I, xxviii, identifies Felix, author of 210R-214R, with Flavius Felix, author of 254R.

[5] Audollent, *Carthage romaine,* pp. 691-700, 750.

Calbulus, Cato, Coronatus, Felix, Florentinus, Lindinus, Luxorius, Modestinus, Octavianus, Ponnanus, Regianus, Tuccianus, and Vincentinus.[4]

A new element was now added to Roman literature. For the first time it was being written to serve conquerors of Romans; the latter were no longer the masters whom writers among subject peoples extolled. For example, Josephus had praised the destroyers of his brethren; Polybius and Strabo had justified the mission and the destiny of the Romans to the Greeks; but now descendants of Roman settlers, living in a land that had once been a Roman province, wrote to please and honor barbarian overlords.

These poets did not seem to like the idea, as seen in the case of Dracontius.[5] The author of Poem 285R complains of his inability to write verse among the barbarians:

> *De conviviis barbaris*
> Inter "eils" goticum "scapia matzia ia drincan"
> Non audet quisquam dignos edicere versus.[6]

Although the poets of the *Latin Anthology* did write some poems praising the Vandal kings, they were not so abject as Martial was to Domitian, nor were they called upon to apotheosize their masters.[7] It is true, however, that the poets dealt almost exclusively with harmless topics; perhaps the lesson of Dracontius' punishment was a sufficient deterrent to bold expression. Moreover, the Vandals patronized a "classical revival, ready enough to divert the attention of their subjects."[8]

Boissier recreates what may have gone on in the minds of the poets.[9] According to him, they conceived a violent hatred of these intruders who had come to trouble them in their peaceful pursuits and literary enjoyments. However, since they were accustomed to wait upon the mighty and seek their favors, they wrote verses in favor of the Vandal

---

[6] "Among the Gothic 'to your health and orders to eat and drink,' no one ventures to write decent poetry." On the identification of the Vandals with the Goths, see above, Ch. I, n. 19. On the language and culture of the Vandals, see Courtois, *Les Vandales,* pp. 221, 228-29.

[7] Martial, *De Spectaculis* 17.4; 5.8.1; see also Suetonius, *Domitianus* 13.2, for the edict that Domitian should be addressed as *dominus et deus.*

[8] Bouchier, *Life and Letters,* p. 109.

[9] Boissier, *L'Afrique romaine,* p. 304.

kings just as they had celebrated the exploits of the proconsuls. In justice to the poets, they praised what was worthy of being praised, and they encouraged their new lords in their efforts to repair the damages of the invasion and to continue the work of the Romans. The Vandals had become soft and yielded to the charms of a more refined life: Carthage seemed to live again, and the poets were happy to sing of its resurrection. So, in Poem 376R Florentinus extols Thrasamund and pays a remarkable tribute to the new Carthage, which was still *Carthago studiis, Carthago ornata magistris.* In Poem 90L, a marvelous structure erected by Hilderic is praised; Felix wrote Poems 210R-213R in honor of the baths built by Thrasamund; 214R also deals with these magnificent baths.

The collection in which the poems of these authors appear is the only extant anthology of Latin poetry made in ancient times. It is now generally known as the *Anthologia Latina,* a title which is not found in the only manuscript of all the poems. In the Codex Salmasianus, the heading *Libri Epigrammaton* occurs before the entire African collection, although many of the poems in it are not epigrams.[10] The subscription *Liber Gramaton Explicit* appears at the end of Book 16 of this manuscript; Book 24, which contains all but two of the poems of Luxorius, is headed by *Liber Epigrammaton;* the subscription *Epigramaton Expli.Feliciter* follows Poem 379R. These are the only indications of a possible original title of the collection, but it is not known whether a title like *Liber Epigrammaton* was present in the archetype or whether it was later inserted by scribes.[11]

Any collection of Latin poetry may be called a *Latin Anthology* or *Anthologia Latina.*[12] However, in the absence of qualifying terms, this title, by convention, refers to a specific anthology, the one made in Africa. The name is due to Burmann, who first included (1759-73) most of the African poems in his work, which he entitled *Anthologia Veterum Latinorum Epigrammatum et Poematum.*[13] In 1835 Meyer, using Burmann's book as a basis, called his own collection *Anthologia Latina.* Although Riese (in 1869 and 1894) realized that the title was misleading, he nevertheless named his book *Anthologia Latina,* but

---

[10] See Ch. IX, A.

[11] For the credence to be given to the titles, see Ch. VII.

[12] For example, A. M. Cook, *A Latin Anthology* (London, 1924) or J. B. Hutter, *Lateinische Anthologie für die fünfte Classe der Lateinschule* (Munich, 1857).

[13] For a fuller treatment of this edition and other editions, see Ch. IX, B.

added the saving *sive Poesis Latinae Supplementum*.[14] In 1882 Emil Baehrens also used the title *Anthologia Latina*.

From the prominence given to Africa and the Vandals, it is most likely that the *Anthologia Latina* was compiled there.[15] Since Poem 90L praises Hilderic, who began to rule in 523, and since the rule of the Vandals was brought to an end in 534, Riese had set these dates as the *termini* for the compilation of the *Anthologia Latina*.[16] Later he considered Schubert correct in thinking that the *termini* are 532 and 534 on the basis of Poem 55L.[17] Both he and Schubert conclude that a collection praising the Vandals would probably not have been made after their defeat by the forces of Belisarius. Because of Poems 55L and 56L, which attack a minister of Gelimer, the last Vandal king, Schubert thinks that the poet could not very well have made these poems public until the last days of Vandal power, after Gelimer had been driven from Carthage, but before he was captured by Belisarius. He reasons therefore that the date of compilation is between 532, before which year Poems 55L and 56L could not have been published, and 534, after which date there would not have been much point in praising the Vandals. Moreover, the *Anthologia Latina* contains only the poems of poets who wrote before or during the Vandal occupation of North Africa—none of poets who flourished after the expulsion of the Vandals in 534.

Schubert's pinpointing of the dates is universally accepted by later commentators on the *Anthologia Latina*. No tangible evidence exists against his arguments. One may merely conjecture that there were earlier editions of the anthology compiled before 532 and that the poems used by Schubert and Riese to set the exact dates may have been included subsequently. Likewise, the poems praising the Vandal kings could have been included, even if the collection were made after 534.

---

[14] This title can cause confusion, since it may refer to Riese's entire collection or only to the African part. I use *Anthologia Latina* to refer to the collection made in Africa, unless otherwise noted. See Boissier's review of Riese's 1869 edition in *Revue critique d'histoire et de la littérature*, 4th Part (Paris, 1869), p. 199, "C'est à Burmann qu'est dû ce nom d'anthologie qui donne une si fausse idée de l'ouvrage." Burmann first used the term *Anthologia* to include not only the African poems but also a host of others. Boissier points out that Scaliger, Pithou, Burmann, and Meyer had compiled anthologies, and argues that Riese, to justify *Supplementum* in his title, should have included only poems not used by them and should have culled only the best Latin poems, properly to call his collection an anthology.

[15] Schubert, *De Luxorio*, p. 17.

[16] Riese, *Anthologia Latina*, I, xxv.

[17] Schubert, *De Luxorio*, pp. 17-19.

These rulers had no political significance in later times; poems about them could have been put in for historical interest.

Birt speculates along these lines concerning the manner and time of the composition of the *Anthologia Latina*.[18] He believes that at the close of ancient times (*am Ausgang des Alterthums*) there existed a large collection of epigrams, totaling more than twenty books that must have been similar to the books of Martial. Later, many non-epigrammatic poems were added. In its present form, therefore, the *Anthologia Latina* would be an abridgment of an earlier work from which the inscriptions had been almost completely eliminated, and in which additional poems had been interspersed. On the basis of present evidence, Birt's assumptions cannot be proved or disproved beyond all reasonable doubt.

Poem 285R raises certain questions. It is derogatory of the Vandals. When was it written? If early in the period of Vandal rule, was it made public as soon as written? If so, was it then safe to cast aspersions upon the Vandals? If publication was withheld, is it possible that the *Anthologia Latina* was published before 532 and that this poem, together with 55L and 56L, was added in a later edition? It would have been pointless to write such a poem when Vandal power was tottering. It shows that cultured Romans were not happy under the Vandals, partly because of the horrid sound of their language (just as Ovid in exile felt about Getic and Sarmatian), partly because of the barbarian devotion to eating and drinking, and partly also, as is natural, because the poets, formerly of the ruling people, were now the underdogs. Probably it was safe enough to publish the poem after the Vandals had consolidated their power and after some of them had achieved culture. There is no evidence that they persecuted anybody for this type of remark (Dracontius' offense may have been considered political). Moreover, the quasi-cultured Vandals who owned Roman statues and who had studied Latin might have smiled and agreed with the poet.

It is not possible to establish definitely who compiled the *Anthologia*

---

[18] Birt, *Das antike Buchwesen,* p. 387. He feels certain that the long poems, 21R, 83R, 200R, and 253R, were inserted later, and—with varying degrees of probability—that 7R-18R and 198R-199R were also added. He thinks that the riddle book of Symphosius and the complete book of Luxorius were joined to an existing collection. However, see Roberts, "The Codex," in *Proceedings of the British Academy,* XL (1954), 169, n. 1, on Birt's book, "As a collection of the literary material it is indispensable . . . , but the eccentricity of its interpretation makes it an unsafe guide even to these sources."

Latina. In what Ohl calls "one of his less likely flights of imagination," [19] Baehrens proves to his own satisfaction that the compiler was Octavianus, a stripling of sixteen, designated in the *Anthologia* as *vir inlustris annorum XVI, filius Crescentini viri magnifici.* This boy is the author of Poem 20R; Baehrens credits him with the authorship of the prose *Praefatio,* 19R.[20]

This preface is written in a language all its own formed from words and phrases taken from the glosses of Placidus, a grammarian of the fifth or sixth century.[21] Baehrens translates this into more familiar Latin, and then, on the basis of his own translation, weaves a romantic story telling how Octavianus received orders from a Vandal prince to compile an anthology. With rich inventiveness Baehrens proceeds to read the mind of Octavianus and tell how the latter went about his task, even describing the deference the young poet felt toward men of higher poetical pedigree! Riese falls upon Baehrens for this demonstration, proving that the latter's interpretation of many of the strange words in the preface is faulty. Moreover, Riese argues, a priori, it is true, that a child of sixteen would not have been entrusted with the labor of compiling such an anthology.[22]

However, Baehrens had and still has his followers. Audollent calls Octavianus the supposed compiler, and then, joining in the fanciful flights of Baehrens, asks whether Octavianus treated Luxorius generously because of the older poet's *notoriété*.[23] Bouchier writes, "A certain Octavianus of Carthage, on the invitation of a Vandal prince, formed an anthology of poems...."[24] The same refrain is heard in Allen, "that fifth-century revival of Carthaginian society which, on the invitation of a Vandal prince, Octavianus came afterwards to record,"[25] and in Haight, "produced ... by a certain young noble named Octavianus, apparently at the request of a Vandal overlord."[26] Finally, under *Anthologia Latina* in the *OCD,* R. Mandra says that it is the title of a collection "made by a certain Octavianus in 532-534."

[19] Ohl, "Some Remarks on the Latin Anthology," *CW,* XLII (February 21, 1949), 150.
[20] Baehrens, *PLM,* IV, 3, 28-33; Haupt, *Opuscula,* I, 217-18.
[21] On the *glossemata,* see Duebner, *RhM,* III (1835), 471-78; G. Loewe, "Beiträge zu Placidus," *RhM,* XXXI (1876), 55-75; and W. M. Lindsay, "The Shorter Glosses of Placidus," *JP,* XXXIV (1918), 255-66.
[22] Riese, *Anthologia Latina,* I, xxx-xxxi.
[23] Audollent, *Carthage romaine,* pp. 693, 750, 753.
[24] Bouchier, *Life and Letters,* p. 109.
[25] Allen, *The Romanesque Lyric,* p. 307.
[26] Haight, *Aspects of Symbolism,* p. 1.

Discussing whether a Roman or a Vandal compiled the *Anthologia Latina,* Schubert contends that no Vandal could have compiled it after 534, since the leaders of the Vandals were either killed or exiled.[27] Actually, some Vandals did remain in North Africa (see above, Ch. I, A, 22), and it is not absolutely certain that a leader had to be the compiler. It might just as well have been a scholarly young man of humbler rank who had learned Latin. Schubert also argues that no Vandal could have put the *Anthologia* together, although many Vandals were educated. He simply believes that a Vandal would not have known enough. Yet, one may argue, there might have been a genius among the Vandals who could absorb the language, literature, and mythology of the Romans, and who was of such independent spirit as to include a few poems against his own ruler and people. This is indeed a most remote possibility; there is no record of such a person. Probability therefore favors Schubert; the most likely and reasonable inference is that a Roman was the anthologist.

In spite of Baehrens, it is not definitely known who was the compiler. Certainly, says Riese, it was Luxorius or one of his friends.[28] To attribute the anthologizing to Luxorius because he has such a large place in the *Anthologia Latina* is mere guesswork. Another poet or an editor who thought highly of him may have honored him by including so many of his poems. There are some scholars, Riese avers, who prefer to call Faustus the compiler, but it is his opinion that this, although probable per se, is not supported by Poem 1L.

It is tempting, nevertheless, to think of Faustus as the one who put together the *Anthologia Latina* in the light of Luxorius' dedication to him in that poem. At the beginning, Luxorius alludes to the collection of poems made in his youth which he is sending to Faustus at the latter's urgent and repeated requests. Then, *post veteres* in line 1 could imply that Faustus was making a collection of poems old and new. Luxorius replies that he is now emboldened to send along his feeble *juvenilia,* even though Fautus has the work of older authors from which to choose. Luxorius later sent more recently written poems when Faustus was ready to complete the anthology. All of this may have an element of truth in it but there is no proof whatever that this

---

[27] Schubert, *De Luxorio,* pp. 17-19, 24.
[28] Riese, *Anthologia Latina,* I, xxv; see also Ehwald, "Curae Exegeticae," *Phil,* XLVI (1888), 636-37.

is what actually took place. And there the question of compilation must rest until further evidence is brought to light. (See Commentary, note to 1.1.)

The occasion for which the anthology was composed is also unknown. If Baehrens' conclusion is acceptable, it was put together at the request of a Vandal overlord, probably some one who had learned Latin and who wished to be further acquainted with Latin poetry. If so, it is a very poor compilation for such a purpose; it may also be the first example of a *liber manualis,* the type of collection so popular in the Middle Ages.

It is believed that the manuscript of the *Anthologia Latina* was brought over from Africa to Europe soon after 534 and that from that archetype, no longer extant, stem the manuscripts we now have.[29] The leading manuscript, the basis of any edition of the *Anthologia Latina,* is the Codex Salmasianus, now in the Bibliothèque Nationale, Paris.[30] As contained in this codex, the *Anthologia Latina* consisted of twenty-four books, of which the first five are now missing. There are 387 poems and a prose preface (19R) to Book 7. The codex also contains some other passages of prose, but we are concerned here only with the poems which, taken together, comprise the *Anthologia Latina.* This consists of centos, poems by Vergil, Propertius, Ovid, Petronius, Seneca, and Martial, a book of riddles by Symphosius, another book almost entirely devoted to Luxorius, poems by other African poets, the *Pervigilium Veneris,* light and occasional verse, and trick forms of poetry: serpentine, anacyclical, and epanaleptic poems, and acrostics.

The *Latin Anthology* was compiled, and a great part of it written, during a period when poets had run out of inspiration.[31] The poets living under Vandal rule wrote for an audience that was not too demanding. The African poets themselves asked no more, says Boissier, than that the line of poetry which they wrote should seem like a verse, and end in something that resembled a dactyl and a spondee. Their ears, which were not hard to please, heard the line as an echo of the beautiful hexameters of Vergil, which these poets had been taught

---

[29] Baehrens, *PLM,* IV, 3.

[30] See Riese, *Anthologia Latina,* I, xviii-xxv, for division into books and contents; also Birt, *Das Antike Buchwesen,* p. 386; Omont, *Anthologie,* pp. 3-8; Peiper, "Zur Anthologie des Luxorius," *RhM,* XXXI (1876), 198-99. See also below, Ch. IX, for a detailed study of the manuscripts.

[31] Audollent, *Carthage romaine,* pp. 750ff.; Dunlop, *Selections,* p. ii.

to admire in school, and which they were proud to imitate as best they could.[32]

Boissier, who is very harsh in his judgment of the African poets, asks whether they purposely disregarded quantities because they were using some new system, such as replacing quantity by accent. He feels that this would seem to do them too great an honor; he asseverates that the African poets used false quantities because they did not know any better. However, he admits that there were some poets living in this land where studies were pursued with such zeal who had succeeded in mastering quantities and who could write verse correctly. Since this ability came from hard work and not from inborn talent, and was acquired only with plodding effort, the production of these poets lacks ease and grace; it seems derived, stiff, and artificial, like the work of students who write Latin verse painfully with the aid of a dictionary. Yet, says Boissier, these authors were held in esteem and their works were prized.

In certain respects Boissier is not correct. He spends a great deal of time discussing the writers of sepulchral inscriptions as if they were the criteria to be used in judging poetry written in Africa. It is just as if one were to treat seriously the writers of jingles, commercials, greeting cards, and verse in graduation albums. These African poets, whose works are to be considered a contribution, no matter how insignificant, to Latin literature, were not ignorant of quantities, and actually were very skilled in metrical techniques.[33]

The *Latin Anthology* suffers by comparison with the better known *Greek Anthology* or *Anthologia Palatina*. The former does not have the traditions and dimensions of the latter, which developed from the compilation of Meleager, a most charming poet, and which was re-

---

[32] Audollent, *Carthage romaine*, p. 706; Boissier, *L'Afrique romaine*, pp. 302-4; Bouchier, *Life and Letters*, pp. 118-26. See Monceaux, *Les Africains*, pp. 108-10, on the poetry and the sounds of Latin of this period, especially the shortening of vowels. Augustine remarks that the Africans could not distinguish between long and short syllables: *De Doctrina Christiana* 4.24 (*PL*, XXXIV, 99-100), "Afrae aures de correptione vel productione non iudicant"; also *Enarrationes in Psalmos* 138.20 (*PL*, XXXVII, 1796). Brittain, *Medieval Latin Lyric*, p. 2, traces the breaking down of the distinction between long and short vowels, pointing out that poets began to hesitate about the length of syllables. By the end of the fourth century, there was probably no distinction made between unstressed long and short syllables in ordinary speech. Brittain notes that the distinction may have survived in stressed syllables for another century or more—to about the time when Luxorius wrote. See also Koster, *Traité*, pp. 316-17; above, Ch. I, n. 85, and below, Ch. VIII, n. 98.

[33] Luxorius, for example. See below, Ch. VIII, C.

vised, rearranged, and reedited through the centuries. Moreover, the *Greek Anthology,* although it does contain a few books of insipid, offensive, and worthless poetry, has this advantage over the *Latin Anthology*: it contains some of the most lovely poems of their kind ever written.

Nevertheless, the *Anthologia Latina* is worthy of study, not only for its own sake but also for the part it played in the development of Latin poetry. The continuity of that poetry was not cut off by the downfall of the Empire or the breaking up of classical Latin into a language that formed the basis of the Romance languages. The *Anthologia Latina* establishes a link between classical and medieval Latin, and is a living proof of the continuity of Latin and its literary tradition. In the *Anthologia* are found poems that paved the way for the Romanesque poems of the ninth and tenth centuries.[34] ". . . In the anthologies of the Codex Salmasianus and the lost Beauvais manuscript of Isidore, as well as in Ausonius, the secret romantic quality of Latin, *'praeclusi viam floris,'* is unsealed."[35]

Poets of the eleventh and twelfth centuries were familiar with the *Anthologia Latina.* Manutius cites about twenty authors or anonymous works where its influence can be traced.[36] Among them are the author of *Liber de Recuperatione Ptolimaidae* (*ca.* 1190), who used 256R.1; Petrus Pictor of St. Omer (twelfth century), who used the next line of the same poem; Giraldus Cambrensis (*ca.* 1147-1223), who used Poem 263R; and Donizo of Canossa (early twelfth century), who used Poems 256R, 257R, and 261R. Lines taken from the *Anthology* were employed in various literary genres: drama, sacred and historical poems.

The *Anthologia Latina* has never been translated in its entirety. Naturally, poems by Vergil, Propertius, Ovid, Petronius, Seneca, and Martial found in it have been translated because of the reputation of these poets. The anonymous *Cupido Amans* (240R) and poems by Reposianus, Modestinus, and Pentadius have been translated into prose in the Loeb Classical Library.[37] John Dunlop translated a number of

---

[34] Allen, *The Romanesque Lyric,* pp. 107-9, 307.

[35] Waddell, *Mediaeval Latin Lyrics,* p. v; see also Haight, *Aspects of Symbolism,* p. 21, "yet in the Latin Anthology there are love poems full of vivacity and spontaneity."

[36] Manitius, *Geschichte,* III, 87, 135, 299, 342, 398, 411, 633, 635, and Index, p. 1089. Sanford, "Classical Latin Authors in the Libri Manuales," *TAPA,* LV (1924), 190-248, listing collections made from the ninth to the thirteenth centuries, says (p. 201), "Almost all the literary collections involve some selections from the Anthology."

[37] J. Wight Duff and Arnold M. Duff, *Minor Latin Poets* (London, 1934), pp. 519-51.

the poems into verse more than a century ago.[38] More recently Helen
Waddell included a charming translation of *Amans Amanti* (24R) in
her *Mediaeval Lyrics*.[39] Elizabeth H. Haight wrote a free metrical
adaptation of 78L.[40] Howard Mumford Jones translated not only the
Pervigilium Veneris, but also poems 23R-25R.[41] The *Pervigilium
Veneris* has received due attention because of its beauty; notable is the
allusion to it in Walter Pater's *Marius the Epicurean,* Chs. 6 and 7.
Finally, Jack Lindsay made a verse translation of about thirty poems
from the *Anthologia Latina,* ten of which are by Luxorius, who is
represented by more lines in the Codex Salmasianus than is any other
of the thirty-odd poets who are named there.[42]

[38] Dunlop, *Selections.* This contains some poems from the *Latin Anthology* but it goes
back to the *Carmen Fratrum Arvalium,* Livius Andronicus, Pacuvius, etc. Dunlop's introduction, especially pp. ii-iii, is worth reading.
[39] Waddell, *Mediaeval Latin Lyrics,* p. 25.
[40] Haight, *Aspects of Symbolism,* p. 21.
[41] Allen, *The Romanesque Lyric,* pp. 95-96, 108-9.
[42] Jack Lindsay, *Song of a Falling World,* pp. 215-24. See his survey of the African poets
of the fifth and sixth centuries, pp. 205-14.

III. THE LIFE OF LUXORIUS

A. His Name

1. Little is known about Luxorius, either from the internal evidence of his own writings or from the testimony of other authors. We do not know his parentage, place of birth, or marital status. His poems reveal only a few details about his character, tastes, daily life, or occupation; he does not give us any direct clues about his own writings and literary predilections as Martial did. Except for Poem 37R there is no reference to Luxorius in any of the other poems of the *Anthologia Latina*. There is only one other mention of his name by a contemporary, which is found in a letter of Coronatus, the poet and grammarian to whom Poems 223R, 226R, and 228R are attributed.[1] Later writers do not allude to Luxorius at all, unless he is to be identified with a grammarian called Lisorius.[2]

2. In his thesis on Luxorius published in 1875, Otto Schubert declared that he knew no other instance of the name *Luxorius*.[3] Since that time, however, other examples of the name have come to light. Forcellini cites not only the name of the poet but also that of a martyr killed in Sardinia during the persecution by Diocletian.[4] The name was also spelled *Luxurius*.[5] Forcellini lists related names: a woman named Luxuria[6] and a horse called Luxuriosus.[7] An inscription from

---

[1] See below, Appendix III, A.
[2] See below, Appendix V; also Ch. IV, 8.
[3] Schubert, *De Luxorio*, p. 5.
[4] Forcellini, *Lexicon*, VI, 153.
[5] *CIL*, X.1, 593, found near Ravello, Italy.
[6] *CIL*, III, Supp. 1, 2113, full name *Aurelia Luxuria*, found at Split, Yugoslavia (formerly Spalato, Italy, site of Diocletian's palace); erroneously listed as 2143 in Forcellini. See also *CIL*, X.1, 3107, for the name *Vivia Luxuria*, on an inscription from Pozzuoli (ancient Puteoli), Italy.
[7] *CIL*, II, 5129 (erroneously numbered 5429 in Forcellini), p. xlviii, and Supp., p. 1195 (*s. v. equi*). This name, written as *Lucxuriosus* appears on a mosaic now in Barcelona (ancient Barcino), Spain, showing racing scenes, the spina of a circus, and the names of horses.

Dougga (modern Thugga) records the name *L. Terentius Luxurius.*[8]
Another inscription, from Auzia (modern Aumale) in Mauretania
Caesariensis, bears the name *Luxurus Secund. Fil.*[9] Luxorius is often
called the African Martial; by a marvelous coincidence, a most fascinating inscription links the two names. MARTIALICUS QUI / ET
LUXURIUS VIXIT / is part of this inscription found in the necropolis
of Hadrumetum.[10] Used as a *signum* or nickname, *Luxurius* occurs on
an inscription found in Lyon and dating several hundred years before
the time of the poet Luxorius.[11]

3. Forcellini derives the name from the noun *luxuria.* From its
derivation and the evidence of the inscriptions, the name should be
written *Luxurius.* However, *o* and *u* are frequently interchanged in the
manuscripts of the period to which those of the *Anthologia Latina*
belong.[12] For example, the reading of the second word of 64L.10 is
luxuriat but the reading of the first word of 33L.4 is *luxoriam.* Two
manuscripts attribute 90L to Luxorius through the heading *Luxuri* but
the spelling *Luxorius* is used in the name of the martyr and in that
of the poet as written in the letter of Coronatus and in four places in
the Codex Salmasianus. The spelling *Luxorius* is now used because it
is established by tradition.[13]

4. In Poem 37R (see below, B1), the *o* of *Luxori* is long. However,
the second *u* in *luxuriam* (33L.4) and *luxuriat* (64L.10) is short.
Luxōri may be explained on the ground that the poet lengthened the *o*
out of metrical necessity or that it is in the syllable bearing the accent.[14]
The possibility also exists that *Luxorius* may be a corruption of
Lusōrius,[15] but there does not seem to be any occurrence of this name.
The *o* in *Luxorius* is therefore to be considered short.

---

[8] *CIL,* VIII, Supp. 4, 26505. The *L*'s are in Greek script.

[9] *CIL,* VIII, Supp. 3, 20793. See also, VIII.5.1, Supp., Index, p. 98.

[10] *CIL,* VIII, Supp. 4, 22975; *qui et* is a formula for a nickname; see Sandys, *Latin Epigraphy,* pp. 213-14.

[11] *CIL,* XIII.1.1, 1916, and XIII.5, p. 38. The name is in Greek, Λου[ξ]ουριος. This inscription is also IG, XIV, 2528. Here the nickname refers to a woman. Λουξούριος is not listed as a Greek name in W. Pape, *Wörterbuch der griechischen Eigennamen,* ed. by G. E. Benseler (3rd. ed., Braunschweig, 1875-80), or as a Latin name in B. Meinersmann, *Die lateinischen Wörter und Namen in den griechischen Papyri* (Leipzig, 1927). See also Hélène Wuilleumier, "Etude historique sur l'emploi et la signification des signa, *MPAI,* XIII (1933), 569.

[12] Riese, *Anthologia Latina,* I, xxvii, xliii; Schubert, *De Luxorio,* p. 6.

[13] On variations of spelling in the manuscripts, see Riese, *Anthologia Latina* (1869), I, xli-xlviii, and 1894 ed., I, xlii-xlvi. In the former, Riese writes (p. xlv), "Nihil itaque ad pristinam formam restituendam hinc redundat lucri." This applies to any attempts to alter *Luxorius* to *Luxurius.*

However, the name *Lisorius* is found. Lisorius is the author of an *Orthographia* (or *Ortographia*) mentioned in a Latin glossary of the twelfth century. Robinson Ellis thinks "there is little doubt that the Lisorius of the glossary is the Luxorius of the Anthologia."[16] The same Lisorius appears in other manuscripts of the twelfth to the fourteenth centuries.[17]

5. The identification of Luxorius with Lisorius cannot be established with absolute certainty, but there is no strong reason to deny it. The name is unusual; the letter of Coronatus indicates that Luxorius was a *grammaticus*. In addition, one of the excerpts in the glossary provides an unusual bit of testimony. The meter of

Nec fronditura pinus
Nec floritura ficus

is the same as that of Poem 23.[18]

6. In the absence of any other evidence, it will be assumed here that Luxorius and Lisorius are the same person; moreover, the conjecture that *Lusorius* was the poet's name is rejected in the belief that *Lisorius* is a corruption of *Luxorius*.

B. His Reputation

1. The letter of Coronatus to Luxorius indicates that the latter was held in high esteem by a contemporary who paid tribute to Luxorius' knowledge and to his castigation of the foolish and the absurd.[19] Luxorius is also highly complimented in a poem which may explain why he has almost an entire book to himself in the *Anthologia Latina*. Poem 37R praises Luxorius in these words:

Priscos, Luxori, certum est te vincere vates;
Carmen namque tuum duplex Victoria gestat.

[14] See Ch. VIII, B 1, entry for *gula*, 17,1.
[15] See Ehwald, "Curae Exegeticae," *Phil*, XLVI (1888), 632.
[16] Ellis, "Some New Latin Fragments," *JP*, VIII (1879), 124. See below, Ch. IV, 8, and Appendix V, A.
[17] Manitius, *Geschichte*, III, 181-82, 790-91. He equates Lisorius and Luxorius in his index, pp. 1127-28. Thurot, *NE*, XXII.2 (1868), 435, n. 6, says, "Je ne connais pas ce poète [Lisorius] que par cette citation et par celles qu'en fait l'auteur du traité *De arte lectoria*." This was written before the appearance of Riese's first edition and before the article written by Ellis. Thurot must have known the Codex Salmasianus by virtue of his work in the Bibliothèque Impériale, but he did not connect Lisorius with Luxorius. See below, Appendix V, B-E.
[18] See Ch. VIII, Meter 9, for the meter of this fragment.
[19] See Mueller, "Sammelsurien," *NJbb*, XCIII (1866, Part 1), 555, on the friendship of Luxorius and Coronatus. For the text of the letter, see below, Appendix III, A.

It is certain that you are superior to the poets
of old, for a double Victory bears your
poetry.

2. The author of this laudatory gem is unknown, although Meyer
would identify him with Luxorius himself.[20] The anonymous poet
must have had an extremely high opinion of Luxorius to place him
above the poets of old; Luxorius himself was more diffident about his
early poems. What the double victory refers to is not clear. Meerman
conjectures that on the title page of Luxorius' poems, the poet himself
had allowed a scribe or an artist to paint a picture of Victory holding
a book in each hand.[21] Schubert dismisses this as nonsense. However,
Meerman may be right, or there may have been two figures of Victory
on the title page.[22] The problem would still remain, for it goes beyond
the graphical representation of Victory. No matter how depicted, what
does the double victory signify?

3. Schubert's idea is that it refers to the excellence of Luxorius'
poems in two ways: because he wrote them as a young man and because
they have charm and grace. But surely this is farfetched. Luxorius
did not write all of his poems in his youth. *Duplex* may refer to his
accomplishments as a youth and as an older man. In the *Anthologia*
are contained poems of both periods; of this Schubert himself was
aware. The double victory may also mean that Luxorius was superior
both to the poets of old and to his contemporaries.

C. Honorary Titles

1. From the writings of others one more thing about Luxorius is
learned. The superscription of Poem 1 contains the words *viri clari*
[*ssimi*] *Luxori et spectabilis*; that of 91, *a Luxorio VC* [*viro clarissimo*]
et spectabili. Illustris [or *inlustris*], *spectabilis,* and *clarissimus* were
titles of honor under the late emperors. Constantine (*ca.* 330) estab-

[20] See below, Ch. IX, B 2.
[21] Burmann, *Anthologia,* II, 579.
[22] Schubert, *De Luxorio,* pp. 26-27. He supports his supposition with a quotation from
Ennodius, *Epistola ad Boethium* 7.13 (*PL,* LXIII, 120A), "In cuius manibus duplicato igne
rutilat, qua veteres face fulserunt. Nam quod vix maioribus circa extremitatem vitae
contigit, hoc tibi abundat in limine." See Ehwald, "Curae Exegeticae," *Phil,* XLVI (1888),
632-39, and "Miscellen," *Phil,* XLVII, n.F.1 (1889), 764-65, for a dicussion of the
meaning of this double victory and a similar symbol found in codices. Baehrens, *PLM,* IV,
46-47, thinks it refers to a customary symbol of the times and to the beginning and end of the
verses doubling on themselves.

lished the rank of *clari viri* to be applied to the senators at Constantinople; later the rank of *clarissimus* was established. Eventually, senators of the first rank were called *illustres*; of the second, *spectabiles*; and of the third, *clarissimi*. The titles *clarissimus* and *spectabilis* were often coupled.[23]

2. Still later, these titles were held by others than senators, and new titles were invented. For example, ten *viri clarissimi* and two *viri perfectissimi* head the list in the *Album of Thamugadi* (modern Timgad), which gives in detail the composition of the council of that African town (*ca.* 363).[24] According to Warmington, the *viri clarissimi* and the *viri perfectissimi* may have been persons who had passed through all the grades in the council or who had reached positions in the imperial service carrying these titles.

3. If Luxorius was a *vir clarissimus et spectabilis*, did he necessarily have to be in public service to earn this title? Not at all, since *grammatici* were also entitled to special honors, according to a provision of the Theodosian Code.[25] It was as if some recognition was being given to underpaid teachers—they were rewarded with honorary degrees in lieu of higher wages:

De professoribus qui in memorato auditorio professorum fungantur officio, hi quoque cum ad viginti annos observatione iugi ac sedulo docendi labore pervenerint, isdem quibus praedicti dignitatibus perfruantur.

In re teachers who are performing the duties of teachers in a noted school, when they have reached twenty years of service in "the wearing of the yoke" and in the unremitting task of teaching, they may also be entitled to the same honors as the aforenamed.

4. Luxorius could therefore have received his honorary title without ever having held a public office. Incidentally, such titles were held without reference to age or sex. We have already seen that the youthful poet Octavianus was called *inlustris*; the titles occur in inscriptions bearing the names of girls, women, boys, and young men.[26] An in-

[23] Isidore, *Origines* 9.4.12 (*PL*, LXXXII, 349C); see also *RE*, IIIA.2, 1552, 1555ff., on *spectabilis*.

[24] *CIL*, VIII.1, 2403, and Supp. 2, 17903; see also Warmington, *The North African Provinces*, pp. 41-42.

[25] *Codex Theodosianus* 6.21.1, in T. Mommsen and P. M. Meyer, *Theodosiani Libri XIII*, ed. by L. Kruger (2nd ed., 2 vols. in 3, Berlin, 1944), 1.2, 268; cf. on the same page *Codex Justinianeus*. Ennodius refers to a certain Deuterius as a *vir spectabilis grammaticus* in the poem entitled *Dictio Data Deuterio V.S. Grammatico Ipsius Eugeneti V.I. Mittenda* (*PL*, LXIII, 310C, or *MGH*, VII, 170, No. 213).

[26] *CIL*, VIII.2, Index, p. 1063.

scription found near Sétif, dating to Vandal rule, honors Cypriana, who is called *clarissima* and *spectabilis*.[27] Audollent implies that the titles were hereditary, for in one of his imaginative turns he writes that the poor African poets were left with no worldly goods by the Vandals, that the titles borne by their ancestors were all that the poets retained of their patrimony.[28] Of course, Audollent does not prove that the poets' ancestors had either property or titles when the Vandals came.

5. How did it happen that subjects of the Vandals held titles set up by the laws of Roman emperors? As noted above, Genseric kept the framework of Roman administration.[29] Town and city councils functioned as before, with the retention of titles. Evidence of this is seen in a decree of Huneric (477-84), who fined "heretics" according to their rank: *inlustres* paying fifty pounds of gold and *spectabiles*, forty.[30]

6. In the superscriptions of Poems 37R and 90L, the titles of honor are not affixed to the name of Luxorius. Disregarding 90L, Schubert says that the titles are omitted from the name of Luxorius only once in the *Anthologia*—before Poem 37R.[31] His belief is that when 37R was written Luxorius had not yet received the honor. However, to deserve the praise given him in this poem, Luxorius must already have written some of the poems in whose superscription he is honored with a title. The greater likelihood is that the honorary title is omitted before 37R because Luxorius is not named there as the author of the poem. In those places where the title of honor is affixed to his name, he is definitely given as the author, but 37R is about him and not by him. Moreover, not much reliance can be put on the validity of the superscriptions and the titles of the poems.[32] Many of them could have been changed, altered in part, or affixed by later scribes. Therefore, the fact that the title of honor is omitted before 37R is not absolute proof that Luxorius did not have such a title when this poem was written.

[27] *CIL,* VIII, Supp. 3, 20410; see Courtois, *Les Vandales,* p. 371, who dates it October 19, 454.

[28] *Audollent,* Carthage, p. 752, but see *RE,* III.A, 2, 1553, about inheritance of titles and indication of rank when such titles were held by women.

[29] See Chapter I, A 19.

[30] Victor of Vita, *Historia Persecutionis* 4.3 (*PL,* LVIII, 237); see also Leclercq, *L'Afrique,* II, 190-95, for the text of this edict.

[31] Schubert, *De Luxorio,* pp. 24-27. Poem 90 may not be by Luxorius; see Schubert, pp. 8-9, and below, Ch. IV, 1, 2.

[32] See below, Ch. VII, A 2-4, 6-9; also Birt, *Das antike Buchwesen,* p. 387.

7. Luxorius is not the only poet in the *Anthologia Latina* who bears some distinctive title. Coronatus, Felix, and Flavius Felix are each called *vir clarissimus*; Octavianus is called *vir inlustris*; Symphosius, *scholasticus*; Calbulus, *grammaticus*; and Petrus, *referendarius*.[33] Riese propounds the theory that all the poets honored with such titles were either alive at the time of the compilation of the *Anthologia* or had died so recently that their memory was still fresh.[34]

8. Riese sets up the straw-man argument that he will not take as an objection the fact that manuscripts of later centuries gave titles of honor to earlier writers like Vegetius (fourth century) and Macrobius (*fl. ca.* 400). This only strengthens his case, he avers, since simple scribes perpetuated the titles of Vegetius and Macrobius, for example, copying only what they saw in an original edition, whereas the compiler of the *Anthologia* had a special reason for keeping the titles. That special reason is, of course, Riese's theory—a beautiful case of circular reasoning.

9. Finally, Riese declares that no poet of old was given such a title in the Codex Salmasianus. He does not consider the possibility that such poets may not have had a title. Baehrens agrees with Riese and adds that the titles were omitted in the case of poets long dead, like Lindinus (28R), Avitus (29R), and Porphyrius (81R).[35] However, it is not known exactly when these poets lived; the implication by Riese and Baehrens seems to be that if no title is given to them in the *Anthologia* they must have been long dead when it was compiled.

10. Objections arise to Riese's theory. It is impossible to prove that the ascription of titles was made only to living contemporaries. Finally, Symphosius, to whom all of Book 23 is assigned in the Codex Salmasianus, is called *scholasticus*. He may have lived long before the compilation of the *Anthologia Latina*: Ohl cites a wealth of authorities to prove that Symphosius lived in the late fourth century or in the fifth.[36] If this is so, Riese's theory is untenable. All this argument and counterargument indicates how difficult it is to establish facts for the life of Luxorius. Brilliant scholars propound theories to fill in gaps and then

---

[33] *Referendarius*, according to Souter, *Glossary*, p. 345, is a "referendary, a court or papal official whose business is with reports, petitions, etc. [saec. V on]."

[34] Riese, *Anthologia*, I, xxvi-xxvii.

[35] Baehrens, *PLM*, IV, 31.

[36] Ohl, *The Enigmas of Symphosius*, pp. 14-15.

use these theories to transform mere conjectures into supposedly incontrovertible facts.

11. In summation, all that can be learned about Luxorius with some degree of certainty from the inscriptions and the *testimonia* is that (1) his name may have been *Luxurius*; (2) he had a friend named Coronatus; (3) the latter held him in high esteem; (4) he was a *grammaticus*; (5) at least one poet, anonymous, thought that he surpassed the ancient poets; (6) he was called a *vir clarissimus et spectabilis*; (7) he may be the person referred to as Lisorius, author of books on spelling, vocabulary, and usage, of which a few fragments survive in citations by grammarians of the twelfth to the fourteenth centuries.

D. Evidence in Luxorius' Poems

1. Now Luxorius' own writings will be examined for information about his life and character. Except for the fact that he says he was a *puer* when he wrote the poems that he later sent to Faustus, Luxorius does not refer to his age. However, some of the poems do offer evidence about the period in which he lived. Schubert sets Luxorius' date of birth between 480 and 490.[37] On the other hand, Ellis thinks that the belief that Luxorius lived during the reign of Thrasamund (496-523) rests on insufficient evidence.[38] However, Schubert rightly argues that Luxorius lived in the later years of Vandal rule because of his description of their luxurious way of life, which was restrained at first by Genseric but flourished after his death in 477.

2. If Luxorius wrote Poem 90, he must have been alive during the reign of Hilderic (523-30). Poems 55 and 56 can be cited as evidence that Luxorius lived during the rule of Gelimer (530-34), since the two poems most probably refer to Boniface, Gelimer's minister.[39] The date of the event celebrated in Poem 44 is uncertain, but it may have taken place in the reign either of Hilderic or of Thrasamund.[40] References in Poems 59 and 83 to Oageis, who has been identified with some certainty as a historical character living at the time of Gelimer, help to fix the period in which Luxorius lived: during the latter half of Vandal rule in Africa.[41]

[37] Schubert, *De Luxorio*, p. 24.
[38] Ellis, "Some New Latin Fragments," *JP*, VIII (1879), 124.
[39] See below, Commentary, note on Poem 55.1.
[40] Schubert, *De Luxorio*, pp. 10-16; see below, Commentary, note on Poem 44.
[41] See below, Commentary, note on Poem 59.T.

3. Schubert says it is established that Luxorius lived in Carthage, and offers these lines in proof:[42]

> Reddita post longum Tyriis est mira voluptas (44.1),
> Heu nunc tam subito mortis livore peremtum
> Iste capit tumulus, quem non Carthaginis arces
> Amphitheatrali potuerunt ferre triumpho! (68.9-11)

and

> Atque tuum nomen semper Carthago loquetur (68.14).

4. These lines, however, do not at all prove that Luxorius was actually a resident of Carthage. They are merely references to the city and its people, and there is not enough information in them to enable us to draw any incontrovertible conclusions about Luxorius' residence. He may just as well have lived in a town in Proconsularis and visited the city to attend the games and races in the Circus and Amphitheater, for he also wrote about gardens and baths outside the city.

If, as is likely, *in foro* (1.5) refers to the Forum in Carthage, that would be better proof that Luxorius spent part of his life in Carthage. At first glance, the mention of the Forum would seem to indicate that Luxorius engaged in public life when young, and this would lead one to speculate about what kind of service he performed, but Luxorius nowhere hints about any public career. *In foro,* I am tempted to believe, refers only to his activities as a student and teacher.[43] In Poem 3 Luxorius again mentions the Forum, to which his little book had fled. Although this might again lead one to believe that Luxorius lived in Carthage, it is not beyond possibility that he lived in the country or in a little town, and that the book naturally gravitated to the center of intellectual life. Luxorius may have lived in Carthage, but this cannot be proved on the evidence of the lines quoted by Schubert.

5. In the same poem (No. 1) in which Luxorius says that he wrote poetry when young, it is learned that he was the dear friend of Faustus, a grammarian. Nothing more is known about Faustus than this, except for one line quoted in the Latin glossary mentioned above.[44] Luxorius makes no other specific references to his friends.

[42] Schubert, *De Luxorio,* p. 7.
[43] See above, Ch. I, n. 90.
[44] The line is "De lavacro redeunt, numerantur et inde videntur." See below Chs. IV, 8, IX, C 8; and Appendix V, A.

6. Schubert thinks that Poem 3.4 informs us that Luxorius was poor:

> Nostri defugiens pauperiem laris.

However, this may be merely a literary expression, a commonplace of poets. Persius, for example, implies that lack of money drove him to write (*Prologue* 10-12), but Suetonius reports in *Vita Auli Persi Flacci* that he left two million sesterces to his mother and sister. Tibullus (1.1.5) wrote:

> Me mea paupertas vita traducat inerti,
>
> Let my slender means lead me along
> a humble walk of life,

but "notwithstanding his complaints of 'paupertas,' not to be taken seriously, he had enough left to lead a comfortable existence in Rome or on his estate between Praeneste and Tibur."[46] Of course, the proverbial poverty of most ancient schoolmasters may have applied to Luxorius, but he does not refer to his financial state, as Martial does.

7. From a detailed study of the poems something more definite can be deduced about Luxorius as a personality. He had an eye for beauty and works of art; he attended the Circus and the Amphitheater. He is unduly occupied with perverts and abnormal types, toward whom he is bitter, and is most unkind to persons with physical defects, especially when these are linked with moral vices. On the other hand, he shows tenderness and feeling in the poems on Damira (No. 59) and on his pet dog (No. 73). How much this reveals of his true character, and how much is only literary convention cannot be ascertained. Bouchier calls Luxorius servile, declaring that he "rivals the coarseness and servility, but not the wit, of Martial."[47] Coarseness, yes; servility, no. His scurrility is truly an ingrained part of the epigram, in which he followed Martial, his master.[48]

E. Luxorius' Religion

1. Finally, there is the question of his religion. Most writers who refer to it call Luxorius a Christian, with little or no substantiating

---

[45] Schubert, *De Luxorio*, p. 30.
[46] *OCD, s. v. Tibullus.*
[47] Bouchier, *Life and Letters*, p. 111.
[48] See Ch. V, C 2, and Commentary, note on Poem 91.

evidence.[49] Only Schubert expatiates, arguing from every shred that he can interpret as proof, drawing every inference on no matter how tenuous grounds.[50]

2. First, Schubert correctly concludes that the use of mythology and pagan religious expressions by Luxorius does not prove that he was a pagan.[51] Even Christian poets and churchmen wrote about gods and goddesses or used words like *numina* and *superi.* Corippus and Ennodius are cited as cases in point. Employing a peculiar form of guilt by association, Schubert equates fallaciously. He seems to argue that since Corippus and Ennodius, who used pagan terms, were Christians, then Luxorius, who also used such terms, must have been a Christian like them. However, one factor is missing: affirmative and corroborative evidence must be presented for Luxorius as it can be for Corippus and Ennodius.[52]

3. Schubert proceeds to supply such evidence. He sees it in the use of *dei* instead of *Iovis* in 56.8; in the word *iustis* in 59.14; and in his own emendation of *almina* of the Codex Salmasianus in 17.4 to *almi.* Finally, he argues that even if these proofs were not present, Luxorius must have been a Christian, for the Vandals would not have honored or tolerated a pagan, since as Arians they persecuted Catholics.

4. These alleged proofs will be considered briefly. Pagan writers also used *deus* to mean a supreme deity.[53] *Iusti* is used in the Bible

[49] Mueller, *De Re Metrica,* p. 2, and *passim,* includes Luxorius among the Christian poets but he uses the term *Christian* to mean "late." Ebert, *Allgemeine Geschichte,* I, 431, says there is little doubt that Luxorius was a Christian, citing 59L.13-14. Jack Lindsay, *Song of a Falling World,* p. 213, and Raby, *Secular Latin Poetry,* I, 114, call him a Christian; Ohl, "Some Remarks on the Latin Anthology," *CW,* XLII (February 21, 1949), 151, refers to Luxorius as "a professed Christian." However, Weyman, although writing a book on Christian Latin poetry, omits Luxorius in the section devoted to the *Anthologia Latina.*

[50] Schubert, *De Luxorio,* pp. 27-30.

[51] He demolishes the conclusion of Teuffel that the use of myths and of *numina,* 83L.7, proves Luxorius a pagan. Schubert refers to Teuffel, *Geschichte,* p. 1082, § 467.3 (1st ed.), but in the 5th ed. (1890), p. 1226, § 467.3, the position is reversed and Luxorius is called a Christian in spite of his numerous allusions to the myths.

[52] *SchH,* IV.2, p. 81, § 1039, and p. 131, § 1065. Likewise, Nonnus wrote a pagan epic, *Dionysiaca,* but he also wrote a paraphrase of the Gospel of John in hexameters. The case of Boethius might also be cited; he has been held to be a Christian although he uses the arguments of pagan philosophy in his *De Consolatione Philosophiae;* see *OCD,* p. 139, and *SchH,* IV.2, pp. 149, 159, 161-66. However, for a contrary view, see Jourdain, "De l'origine des traditions sur le christianisme de Boèce," *MPAI,* First Series, VI (1860), 330-60.

[53] See, for example, Cicero, *De Republica* (*Somnium Scipionis*) 6.13, 15, 16, 17. Likewise, pagan writers expressed sentiments that are hardly distinguishable from Christian ideals. See the prayer of Simplicius, tr. by S. Angus, *The Religious Quests of the Graeco-*

and by early Christian writers to denote those who have lived *religioseque humaneque*.[54] But just as the use of pagan expressions does not prove a writer a pagan, so the use of a Christian term, no other testimony being present, does not establish that a writer was a Christian. Since Luxorius wrote an epitaph on a child, who, for the purposes of the argument, was concededly a Christian, why should he not have used an appropriate term like *iustis*? God was often called *almus* by Christian writers, Schubert declares; therefore the poet was a Christian. Tortuous and strained reasoning, if it has to depend upon an emendation; is it certain that Luxorius did use *almi*? Schubert's final argument does not hold water. The Vandals might have been more unlikely to persecute pagans than Catholics. We have seen in our own day that during political wars dissidents from an extremist group are treated with great severity, whereas nonbelievers are tolerated and even wooed.

5. Luxorius never mentions Jesus, salvation, sin, the Holy Spirit as the Paraclete, the crucifixion, or other tenets and beliefs of the Catholic Church. Had he mentioned some of these, even if only casually, it would be easier to determine whether he was a Christian. Nor does he use the standard phrases, the neologisms, or the old words put to new uses that distinguish the language of the early Christian writers, except in so far as Christian Latin and medieval Latin coincided.[55] If one were to rely on this negative evidence, then Luxorius was surely not a Christian.

6. The positive evidence is certainly scanty: the use of *dei* and *iustis*. The former can be countered by the expression *mors invida fatis* in line 1 of the same poem (No. 56) and by *ad Manes* in 68.12. *Dei* is balanced by *superi*, 81.6, *superos*, 33.2, *numina*, 28.7 and 83.7. There is surely little enough to prove that Luxorius was a Christian; certainly, practically nothing to show that he was a "professed"

Roman World (New York, 1929), p. 9, and Cleanthes' *Hymn to Zeus,* tr. by James Adam, in Hadas, *Greek Literature,* p. 188.

[54] See Poem 92R, *De Christiano infante mortuo,* line 3, "Sed quia regna patent semper caelestia iustis," and cf. 59L.13-14. *Iustus* and *iusti* are, of course, extensively used in the Vulgate, e.g., Matthew, 25.37, 46; Mark, 2.17, and 6.20; Luke, 5.32, and 14.14; John, 7.24; Acts, 10.22, 24; I Corinthians, 15.34; etc.

[55] See Mohrmann, *Latin vulgaire,* and *Vigiliae Christianae,* I, No. 1 (January, 1947), 1-12; II, No. 2 (April, 1948), 89-101; II, No. 3 (July, 1948), 163-84; III, No. 2 (April, 1949), 67-106; III, No. 3 (July, 1949), 163-83; IV, No. 4 (October, 1950), 193-211. See also Dwyer, *The Vocabulary of Hegesippus,* p. 35.

Christian. Pagan or Christian: in either case the verdict must be "Not proven."

7. If, however, Luxorius was a Christian, his being one merely proves that a Christian could write poetry that had little to do with his beliefs. If Luxorius was a pagan, the opposite is proved, that a pagan could employ a few words and phrases used by the Christians. Actually, as far as an understanding of his poetry is concerned, it does not matter whether Luxorius was a Christian or a pagan. His writings do not illuminate what was going on deep in the minds and souls of the men and women of his day; they do not reveal any inner beliefs and struggles of a people subjugated by "barbarians."

IV. CORPUS LUXORIANUM

1. Ninety-one poems are assigned to Luxorius in this book; some editors and commentators have attributed more to him. On the evidence of the superscriptions in the Codex Salmasianus, Poems 1-89 and 91 may safely be ascribed to Luxorius. This manuscript does not give the name of the author of Poem 90, but two other manuscripts (Parisinus 8071 and Voss Q.86) contain the name *Luxuri* above the poem.[1]

2. Schubert raises a number of interesting questions concerning the placing of this poem by itself, far apart from the body of poems by Luxorius.[2] Assuming that it was together with them in the archetype and was at some time omitted by a careless scribe, why was it not incorporated in the book devoted to Luxorius when later copies were made? Why was so prominent a name as that of Luxorius omitted in the chief manuscript? Why are no titles of honor affixed to his name in the two manuscripts that do name him as the author? It is Schubert's theory that a reader or scribe added *Luxuri* because it was easy for him to suppose that Luxorius had written this poem, since the poet lived in the time of Hilderic and he was the most popular of the African poets of the *Anthologia*.

3. If Poem 90 (203R) formed part of a group of poems treating a similar topic, it would be easy to understand its isolation. For example, Poem 91 (18R) is also detached from the book devoted to Luxorius in the *Anthologia*. But there is an apparently good reason —it is a cento, differing in genre from all his other poems and forming part of a collection of centos by different authors. As it is, the position of Poem 90 and the spelling *Luxuri* instead of *Luxori* present a problem

[1] For these manuscripts, see below, Ch. IX.

[2] Schubert, *De Luxorio,* pp. 7-9; see also Levy, *RE,* XIII.2, 2102, on Poem 90, "ist dazu die Autorschaft des L. ganz unsicher."

that cannot be solved on the basis of present knowledge. The ascription of Poem 90 to Luxorius may be an error, but until the evidence of the two manuscripts can be definitely disproved, Luxorius will have to be tentatively considered the author of this poem—*magno cum dubio* and with reservations.

4. Baehrens also credits Luxorius with the authorship of forty-odd couplets, which are anonymous in the manuscripts.[3] These are serpentine or epanaleptic verses, in which the last half of the pentameter line contains the same words as the first half of the hexameter line. In one of his two books on Latin poetry, Raby, discussing the epigrams of the African poets, dismisses Luxorius with a single sentence, "Luxorius, to whom a number of these poems is attributed, shows a vicious taste for the cento and epanaleptic verse."[4] In his other book, calling Luxorius "a prolific poet," he declares that these distichs "are almost certainly to be assigned to Luxorius."[5] Audollent believes that Baehrens attributed them to Luxorius *avec vraisemblance*.[6] Haight, also relying on Baehrens, cites 54R, one of these poems, as the work of Luxorius.[7]

5. However, there is no justification in any of the manuscripts for attributing these poems to Luxorius. His authorship cannot be established on the basis of style, subject matter, choice of words, or similar criteria. There are ten elisions in these couplets, only 12 percent, whereas in the poems of Luxorius the percentage is much higher.[8] No editor before Baehrens assigned all of these serpentine verses to Luxorius. Baehrens asseverates most vehemently that Luxorius did write these verses, contending that Poem 37R proves it and that the conclusions he draws from it have escaped others, etc., etc.[9] Furi-

---

[3] Baehrens, *PLM*, IV, 46-47; Poems 227-68 in his edition are 38R-80R. For the text of 37R, see above, Ch. III, B 1. I agree with Riese, *Anthologia*, I, xxiv, n. 1, "Cave autem ex hoc de Luxorio carmine [37R] id sumas quod Baehrens inde sumendum putavit, versus illos serpentinos (c. 38-80) a Luxorio scriptos esse: quae sententia neque argumentum habet ullum neque per se probabile est." See also Levy, *RE*, XIII.2, 2109, on 37R.

[4] Raby, *Christian-Latin Poetry*, p. 96.

[5] Raby, *Secular Latin Poetry*, I, 114-15.

[6] Audollent, *Carthage romaine*, p. 754.

[7] Haight, *Aspects of Symbolism*, p. 20.

[8] See below, Ch. VIII, 1 E.

[9] Meyer, *Anthologia*, I, note on Poem 296, p. 124 of his notes; I, xxxiii, and note on Poem 384, p. 135 of his notes. Meyer thinks that 131R, 190R, 191R, 204R, 205R, 209R, 284R, and 864R are similar to poems by Luxorius. He also includes the poem numbered 1126 in his edition, but Riese, *Anthologia*, II, xlv (1869 ed.), rejects it as a poem of the Middle Ages.

ous sound by Baehrens, but little sound proof. I reject the serpentine poems as the work of Luxorius. Since it cannot be proved that he wrote any, there seems to be no justification for Raby's charge that Luxorius had a vicious taste for this kind of verse. Nor is there a strong basis for Raby's similar accusation about Luxorius' taste for the cento, since there exists only one example of such a *tour de force* by him.

6. Meyer seems to believe that Poems 80R and 90R were written by Luxorius and that at least ten other poems in the *Anthologia* ought to be credited to him because of their similarity to some of his known poems.[9] However, one cannot proceed to attribute other poems to Luxorius on such grounds; many of the poems in the *Anthologia Latina* resemble each other in theme and language, as other scholars have noted.[10] For example, one is tempted to ascribe 173R to Luxorius; the use of the phrases *docta manus* and *ab arte* is duplicated in 48L.1, 49L.2, and 73L.10. However, one must refrain unless there is additional testimony.

7. In conclusion, after consideration of the available evidence and arguments, I have fixed the corpus of Luxorius' poetry as identical with that determined by Riese: ninety-one poems in all, less than 800 lines, including the cento of sixty-eight lines. Since Luxorius began to write when a *puer* and apparently did not die when young, how can Raby be correct in calling Luxorius a prolific poet? His output would be singularly small even if one granted him the authorship of all the poems in dispute.

8. I have also subsumed, as it were, into the canon the verses on grammar attributed to Lisorius. The known titles of works by this Lisorius are *Orthographia* and *Cornicius*. Riese and Baehrens have listed the fragments discovered by Ellis, but in Appendix V, below, these lines and others publicized by Thurot and Paul Meyer have been added so that here for the first time all the known lines by Lisorius the grammarian and poet who may be the poet and grammarian Luxorius are assembled.[11]

---

[10] Mueller, "Sammelsurien," *NJbb*, XCV (1867, Part 1), 796; Schubert, *De Luxorio*, pp. 8-9.

[11] See below, Appendix V, A-E.

V. THE POETRY

A. The Material of His Poems

1. No ancient poet worked outside some literary tradition, and in his genre, the epigram, Luxorius had a noteworthy list of predecessors. The greatest is, of course, Martial, with whom Luxorius has been compared.[1] However, resemblances, parallels, and even borrowings can be found in the poems of Luxorius which indicate that he was familiar with the works of other poets.

2. Since he composed a cento from the poems of Vergil, it quite naturally follows that he had read Vergil thoroughly and possibly knew him by heart. Moreover, as a schoolboy he must have studied Vergil intensively, and as a *grammaticus* he must have drilled his pupils line by line in the poems of Vergil.[2] However, with the exception of the cento, his borrowing of *stellantis regia caeli* in 59.13 from the *Aeneid* 7.210, and the influence of *Bucolics* 3.16 on Poem 59.13, Vergilian echoes and inspiration in his poems are rather faint. This may argue in favor of his originality. Among other writers with whom Luxorius shows some familiarity are Horace, Propertius, Ovid, Phaedrus, Martial, Juvenal, Statius, and Ausonius.

3. Luxorius may be called the Carthaginian Martial, but his canvas is exceedingly small. As a word painter of life in Carthage he does not reveal to us a detailed view of his city comparable to the Roman scenes illustrated by the epigrams of Martial. We learn little about the everyday doings of the Carthaginians and even less about the poet's activities. We miss Martial's personal touch; we are not invited by Luxorius to accompany him on his daily rounds.

4. He is chiefly occupied with abnormal types, which form the

---

[1] Bouchier, *Life and Letters*, p. 111; *OCD, s.v. Luxorius.*
[2] See Ch. I, C 2, 7.

subjects of more than one third of his ninety epigrams—sexual perverts; deformed beings; amatory defectives; doctors, teachers, and philosophers gone astray; entertainers who do not entertain; old men and women who do not know enough to act their age. Luxorius also wrote on the things the Vandal overlords liked—the huge Roman structures and estates that they had taken over and were using, such as circuses, amphitheaters, and gardens; the hunt, either in the fields or staged in the Amphitheater or sublimated in the taming of animals; and horses and racing, for which the passion had always been strong in Africa.[3] Finally, Luxorius wrote two epitaphs and a few poems on other miscellaneous themes: flowers, morals, Janus, the Seven Wise Men, a jealous neighbor, a greedy host. Four of his poems have some social and historical significance: No. 51 on an informer and blackmailer, Nos. 55-56 on a rapacious royal official, and No. 90 on a building erected by Hilderic.[4]

5. Luxorius is by no means a slavish imitator. His themes may have been worked over many times before, but he develops them in his own way. Consider, for example, Poem 82, which may have been suggested by a poem by Martial. However, if one examines Martial, 4.22 and 11.21, one can see that Luxorius' treatment is different. Occasionally, but not often, Luxorius borrows a few words from another poet, but he does not do this beyond the limits of classical usage and custom.

6. Luxorius may have known Greek or been familiar with the works of some Greek authors, but the evidence is inconclusive. Although Greek had been taught in Africa in the days of St. Augustine (d. 430), we do not know to what extent it remained in the curriculum a century later.

7. Martial and Ausonius translated or adapted Greek epigrams, and the former inserted Greek words into his poems. Luxorius uses no Greek words, nor is there a single epigram by him which seems to be an adaptation of any poem in the *Greek Anthology*. For example, his poem on the Seven Wise Men (No. 65) is on the same theme as *Anthologia Palatina,* 9.366, but his treatment is very different. Other Latin writers had written on the same subject, so that Luxorius could

---

[3] See Ch. I, B 13-16.
[4] Poems 44, 59, and 83 might also be included here; see below, Commentary, notes on Poems 44 and 59.

have used their work as a source.[5] See also the note on Poem 79.2, below, concerning his reference to Aristotle.

8. Luxorius exhibits a wide knowledge of mythology and cites the names of Greek places, heroes, demigods, gods, and goddesses. These he might also have learned from Latin authors. It may be argued that he was ignorant of Greek because of his use of *Lacedaemona* (65.3) and *Laida* (88.1), but these forms can be explained as part of the Latin usage of his day.[6] On the other hand, he uses *Tempe* (18.3) correctly as a plural and knew enough to turn *Bonifacius* (*Bonifatius*) into *Eutychus* (55.1 and 56.2). There may even be an echo of Homer and Xenophanes in 65.8; some of his meters may depend on a knowledge of Greek originals.[7]

B. Style

In his style Luxorius is singularly conservative, when one considers the age in which he lived and the emphasis placed on rhetoric in the African schools. Except for the cento and one line, a palindrome (39.3), his poems are free from the tricks and mannerisms that debased the work of poets in a period of decadence. With the exceptions just noted, one does not find in Luxorius any of the artificial forms of verse structure that abound in Ausonius, the *Latin Anthology,* and the *Greek Anthology.* Acrostic poems; figure poems, whose outline represents an object; lipogrammatic poems in which a selected letter is not used at all; rhopalic verse, in which the number of syllables increases in each successive word; verses that begin and end with a monosyllable; *versus rapportati,* in which groups of words maintain a certain sequence of ideas (872R)—all these Luxorius avoids, and it is greatly to his credit.[8]

However, Luxorius does resort to various devices whereby his style is enlivened. Some of these are the product of his rhetorical training. A list of his chief mannerisms follows.

---

[5] See below, Commentary, notes on Poem 65; on Greek in the curriculum of North African schools, see Ch. I, C 2.

[6] See below, Commentary, notes on *Lacedaemona,* 65.3, and *Laida,* 88.1.

[7] See below, Commentary, note on 65.8, and Ch. VIII, Meters 12-13.

[8] See Commentary, note on 39.3, on the palindrome, and note on Poem 91, on the cento. See Curtius, *European Literature,* pp. 273-91, on medieval literary mannerisms; Strecker, *Medieval Latin,* pp. 68-71, on the influence of rhetoric on style. For examples of trick poetry through the ages, see W. S. Walsh, *Handy-Book of Literary Curiosities* (Philadelphia, 1892), *s.v. Acrostic; Emblematic, Figurate, or Shaped Poems; Palindrome;* and *Rhopalic Verse or Wedge Verse.* For examples of shaped poems, see *Anthologia Palatina* 15.21, 22, 24-27. See also Strecker, *Medieval Latin,* p. 75.

1. *Antithesis and paradox.* The chief characteristic of Luxorius' technique as an epigrammatist is his use of antithesis and paradox. This is seen in poem after poem: the wild boar that becomes gentle, changing from a follower of Mars to a devotee of Venus (No. 6); the charioteer who resembles Memnon in looks but not in his fate (No. 7); the mad grammarian who should be a model of restraint but who raves like Orestes (No. 8); the dwarf who has a small body but a giant voice (No. 10); the priest who should consecrate himself to holiness and not to drink (No. 18), etc. Occasionally Luxorius points up the contrast with an oxymoron like *pium facinus* 39.1, or a neat juxtaposition of words, as in *Ursa ferox, placido cum facit ore* (45.2); see also 4.5; 43.6; 59.5; 65.10; 67.14; 78.7; 81.9; 87.7; and 89.4.

2. *Asyndeton.* The practice of using long asyndeta became a poetic cliché of the Silver Age and an uninspired affectation of a later, effete period.[9] Statius resorts to extended asyndeta frequently; Dracontius, excessively. Examples are also found in Ausonius and in the *Anthologia Latina.* This piling up of words without connectives was highly recommended by medieval rhetoricians and became an important stylistic mannerism, adopted still later by baroque writers of the seventeenth century.

Luxorius composed two short asyndeta (2.8 and 20.7) and four long ones (47.7; 67.4-5; 68.2; and 90.2). One of them (47.7) effectively suggests the rapid motion with which a gambler sweeps off all the objects lying on a gaming board; another (67.4-5), which may really be considered as two asyndeta, is a display of cleverness and virtuosity by the poet, who collects a list of nouns in one line followed by a list of adjectives in the next.

3. *Tropes.* Luxorius occasionally uses a bold phrase like *amica ruinis* (41.3); a simile, as in 45.6; 59.12; 67.7-12; and metaphors, metonymy, and implied comparisons, as in 2.10; 10.2; 42.5-6; 53.6; 72.9-10; 77.1-3; 78.4; 80.4-5; *et al.*

4. *Apostrophe.* In addition to the use of a regular apostrophe, as in 38.5-6, Luxorius sometimes suddenly addresses the person about whom he has been writing, as in 24.7-8; 38.6; 43.3; 51.7; and 87.8, shifting from the third to the second person.

[9] See Curtius, *European Literature,* pp. 285-86, § 5, and nn. 39-42, for examples from Lucretius, Horace, Statius, and Dracontius. See also Juvenal, 1.85-86; Ausonius, 19, *Epigrams* 106.8-9; Poems 21R.59, 107-9, 175-77; 26R.7; 118R.24; 132R.3; 230R.1-2; 376R.6; Ennodius, *MGH,* VII, 135, No. 129, Poem 2.21 (*PL,* LXIII, 339B, Poem 21.1).

5. *Sententiae.* The use of maxims is discussed in the leading works on ancient rhetoric. Luxorius' poems contain a few *sententiae*: see 3.10-11; 4.5-6; 53.7-8; and 58.9-10.

6. *Hyperbaton.* Some examples of unusual word order may of course be due to metrical needs; notable examples, however, are found in 1.14; 64.1; and 65.5.

7. *Alliteration.* Alliteration in the manner of *O Tite, tute, Tati, tibi, tanta, tyranne, tulisti* became popular in late Latin and served as a model for the exercise of poetic ingenuity in the Middle Ages.[10] About twenty examples of alliteration are found in the poems of Luxorius. Most of them involve only two words: *famulans furore* (6.4), *custodis clausas* (22.3), *plenam et patulam* (25.6), *futui furente* (31.3), and *futuit fervente* (82.1), etc. Occasionally he uses three words next or close to each other: *tam te talia* (1.18), *postulat . . . piscis parvolo* (5.2), which may suggest the opening of its mouth by a fish, *pro psalmis pocula* (17.2), *turpia tot tumulo* (33.1), *criminis ob causam carceris* (53.2), etc. From these examples it appears that Luxorius was fond of the repetition of *t, c,* and *p.* The letter *c* is favored in:

> Sic mea concinno si pagina displicet actu
> Finito citius carmine clausa silet (4.7-8)

and in:

> Alcides collo scapulis cervice lacertis (67.4).

Luxorius also liked the repetition of the sound of *p*:

> Postremum tanto populi pulcrescis amore (67.13).

Occasionally *c* and *p* are combined:

> Atque Agilis, pigro cum pede cuncta premas (38.2)

and:

> Qui licet ex propria populis bene laude placeres
> Praestabas aliis ut tecum vincere possent (68.5-6).

What special significance Luxorius attached to most of these sound effects is not obvious. We do not hear in them the vivid relationship between sound and sense that Juvenal worked out (as in 3.100-1, and 6.276-77), nor do we feel inspiration at play, as in the lines from Coleridge's *The Rime of the Ancient Mariner*:

[10] On alliteration, see Curtius, *European Literature,* pp. 283-84; Strecker, *Medieval Latin,* pp. 74-75; Walsh (cited above, n. 8), pp. 34-40.

The fair breeze blew, the white foam flew,
The furrow followed free.

But then Luxorius was writing a different kind of poetry.

C. Luxorius as an Epigrammatist

1. There is a certain cleverness in his poems, but in general he does not display a rapierlike wit. He is not the master of the sudden thrust; he does not dazzle the reader with an unexpected twist or overpower him with a rapid onslaught. He never gains his point with a single word like Martial's *tussit* (1.10.4). Too often his development is belabored, as in Nos. 16, 70, and 75; one sometimes has to ponder over the meaning, as in Poem 23. A few of the epigrams end rather tamely and weakly after a strong start, for example, Nos. 16, 30, 37, and 78. Moreover, a corrupt text makes some of the epigrams difficult to understand, such as Nos. 4, 13, 32, 36, 47, 70, 79, 85, and 88.

2. Obscenity and filth characterize a great number of the epigrams of Luxorius, as has already been noted (see above, Ch. III, D 7). Gaselee tries to explain this on the grounds that Christianity in North Africa had taken a somewhat puritanical form which may have induced a revulsion in secular life.[11] An explanation of this sort is not really necessary, nor does it sound convincing; obscenity was inseparable from the epigram, part of a literary tradition.[12] Its prevalence in Luxorius' poems stems from his model and master, Martial:[13]

> Nec per circuitus loquatur illam,
> Ex qua nascimur, omnium parentem,
> Quam sanctus Numa mentulam vocabat.
> Versus hos tamen esse tu memento
> Saturnalicios, Apollinaris:
> Mores non habet hic meos libellus.
>
> Let it [my little book] not beat around the bush in talking about the thing from which we are born, the common parent of us all, something that the revered Numa called the *mentula*. Only remember, Apollinaris, that these verses of mine are Saturnalian: this little book does not proclaim my own morals.

[11] Gaselee, *The Transition from Late Latin*, p. 7.
[12] Raby, *Secular Latin Poetry*, I, 114.
[13] Martial, 11.15.8-13; see also 7.25.

3. But in the midst of this filth there are some lovely and tender touches that have poetic feeling. I am reminded of a greater poet who injected a final note of beauty into his description of the sordid tenement inhabited by a Roman attic dweller: "molles ubi reddunt ova columbae." [14] Luxorius' poems on paintings and statuary (Nos. 26, 27, 48, 49, 61-63, 69, 70) are charming and contain pleasant conceits; an appreciation of beauty is disclosed in his poems on buildings and gardens (Nos. 18, 34, 46, 83, and 90).

4. On first reading, Luxorius seems to be a most inferior poet, but upon better knowledge of his work he improves in one's estimation. Allen has said of the entire *Anthology,* "It is safe to prophesy that a better understanding of the Latin anthology than is now current will show it to be a splendid thing and not a drab one." [15] I do not think it is safe to predict that anyone will ever consider the poems of Luxorius splendid things, but some anthologists have discovered that they are not all drab. [16] Luxorius has a marked virtuosity [17] and some of the darts in his last lines anticipate our modern brand of humor, as in Poems 11, 14, 21, 25, 40, and 52. He is worthy of study not only for his few good pieces of work but also for his place in the continuity of a literary genre and in the development and transformation of the Latin language. The Latin used by him and the other African poets of the *Anthologia* is not really barbaric. Although it reveals signs of the Latin of the future, it is chiefly the language of the past. [18] Luxorius illustrates the survival of a literary tradition in an age of transition and breakdown, when little that was original could be evoked. His choice of words and his deviations from classical norms of grammar and usage are a commentary on the history of the Latin language, showing trends that existed in the spoken tongue and tendencies that eventually prevailed in medieval Latin.

[14] Juvenal, 3.201.

[15] Allen, *The Romanesque Lyric,* p. 307.

[16] See Ch. IX, B 5.

[17] Audollent, *Carthage romaine,* p. 755, says, however, "Mais la virtuosité n'est pas la poésie; pour y atteindre, il faut une langue harmonieuse et riche au service de grandes pensées, deux conditions que remplissait nullement Luxorius. Il a donné une exacte définition de ses écrits, lorsqu'il les traite, dans sa préface au lecteur de ces 'bagatelles,' de 'propos legers.' " See also Addison, *The Tatler,* No. 163, April 25, 1710.

[18] On the language of the poets of the *Anthology,* SchH, IV.2, 70, § 1034, writes, "In der Sprache zehren unsere Dichter von der Lektüre klassischer Autoren."

VI. GRAMMAR AND LANGUAGE

Luxorius' literary antecedents were the classical authors, but he wrote at a time when Latin was evolving into medieval Latin. The latter did not spring into being in a day; some of its tendencies occur in the early writers and classical Latin, and are prominent in Silver Latin. No date can, of course, be set for the establishment of medieval Latin, although Mackail believes that if any definite point is to be fixed, the year 405, which marked the publication of the Vulgate and of the last of the poems of Claudian, may claim to be held "as marking the end of ancient and the complete establishment of mediaeval Latin."[1]

Vulgar Latin, the spoken tongue, influenced the written language; words, forms, and constructions of everyday speech entered the literary language, which lost its feeling for the formal and grammatical correctness of classical Latin.[2] So, Luxorius, although retaining most of the characteristics of classical Latin, foreshadows at times the trends of medieval Latin in his grammar and choice of words.

I shall now list some of the grammatical, morphological, and linguistic phenomena of medieval Latin which occur in the poems of Luxorius. It must be kept in mind, however, that some of these were not new, as noted above, and that there is no such thing as standard medieval Latin, for usage varied with the place and the writer.

A. Grammar

1. In medieval Latin *cum* is often replaced by *dum,* and since a sharp distinction between indicative and subjunctive was not observed in the Latin of the Middle Ages, these conjunctions govern either

---

[1] J. W. Mackail, *Latin Literature,* (London, 1895), pp. 278-79.
[2] Strecker, *Medieval Latin,* pp. 20-21. See also Beeson, *Medieval Latin,* pp. 1-28; Blaise, *Manuel, passim;* Browne, *British Latin,* pp. xiii-xxxii; Monceaux, *Les Africains,* pp. 99-121.

mood, even when they are used in a purely temporal sense.[3] Using *cum* nineteen times, Luxorius, for the most part, follows the rules of classical grammar, but he alternates between the indicative and the subjunctive in the present tense, even when expressing pure time.[4] He uses *dum* twenty times; in most instances he could just as well have used *cum*. Note, for example, *dum* adversative in 7.6.

2. The indicative is often used in medieval Latin in an indirect question.[5] Luxorius employs the subjunctive in an indirect question seven times, the indicative, four times: 23.11; 43.5; 51.6; 66.6. This use of the indicative is found even in classical Latin.

3. *Quod, quia, quoniam,* and even *qualiter,* with the subjunctive or indicative, introduce an indirect statement in medieval Latin.[6] This use of *quod* is also found in earlier Latin.[7] Luxorius employs *quod* in this manner six times, four times with the subjunctive (13.8, 9; 71.6; 75.6), twice with the indicative (81.6; 83.7).

4. The uses of the infinitive are extended in medieval Latin, a process that had been going on since Silver Latin.[8] The infinitive governed by *facio* to indicate "cause to happen" is often met in medieval Latin; Luxorius uses this once: *facit crescere* (45.6), a construction popular in French today (*faire croître*). Examples of a free and loose use of the infinitive in Luxorius are: *mori furit* (21.7); *aptasti pingere* (18.16); *defuncta est ferre* (52.7); *dixit te cernere* (65.2); *exquirere dixit* (65.6) to express a command; and *revocat esse* (88.4).

5. Differentiations of tenses, especially those denoting past actions, are not sharply made in medieval Latin.[9] For example, the pluperfect indicative is often used as a narrative tense where one might expect

---

[3] Beeson, *Medieval Latin,* p. 21, § 76; Blaise, *Manuel,* pp. 156, 160, 173-76; Browne, *British Latin,* pp. xxvi, xxix; Strecker, *Medieval Latin,* p. 66.

[4] Riese's emendation to *cum,* 64.3, and the insert from Claudian in Poem 64.13 are not counted here. Nor are the words in the titles; for these, see below, Ch. VII. For all the words treated in this section, consult the Index Nominum et Verborum and then turn to the appropriate notes on these words in the Commentary.

[5] Browne, *British Latin,* p. xxxii; see Kuehner-Stegmann, *Grammatik,* II, 488-93, on the use of the indicative in classical Latin.

[6] Beeson, *Medieval Latin,* p. 22; Blaise, *Manuel,* pp. 147-51; Browne, *British Latin,* pp. xxxi-xxxii.

[7] Browne, *British Latin,* p. xxxi; Kuehner-Stegmann, *Grammatik,* II, 544-45.

[8] Beeson, *Medieval Latin,* p. 21; Blaise, *Manuel,* pp. 181-82; Browne, *British Latin,* pp. xxvi-xxviii; Strecker, *Medieval Latin,* p. 40.

[9] Beeson, *Medieval Latin,* p. 21; Blaise, *Manuel,* pp. 134-37; Strecker, *Medieval Latin,* p. 67.

the imperfect or the perfect. Note in Luxorius *fuerat* (65.5) instead of *fuit* or *erat,* and his fondness for the pluperfect of *debeo* (14.4; 35.6; 50.2). This use of the pluperfect is also found in the poems of the elegiac poets of the Golden Age.[10] Luxorius does not adhere strictly to the rules of sequence; in 40.5-6, he shifts from the imperfect to the present subjunctive; in 23.15-18, *possit* depends upon a perfect, *cupivit.* In 68.3-4, the perfect subjunctive *advixeris* depends on *conplebas,* but in 1.5, *placeres* depends on an imperfect, *praestabas* (1.6), the normal construction. Other apparent oddities and inconsistencies of tense usage, some of which may be justified on logical rather than on grammatical grounds, are *rumpere* (58.5), where the future might be expected; the mixture of future and present, *instítues* and *canunt* in the same condition (30.6-8); the imperfect *haberes* with the present *retexis* (2.1-3); the use of *venient* with *necdum* (66.6).

6. In medieval Latin *proprius* often replaces the possessives *meus, tuus, suus, noster,* and *vester.*[11] Luxorius uses a form of *proprius* twelve times; except in one instance (68.5), it replaces a form of *suus.* Otherwise, once more illustrating the midway nature of his language, he uses forms of *suus* thirteen times, of *meus,* four times, of *tuus,* nineteen times, and of *noster,* thirteen times. *Proprius* is used fairly often by other poets of the *Anthologia Latina:* see 191R.3; 198R.6, 60; 213R.7; 215R.2; etc.

7. Degrees of comparison of adjectives are confused in medieval Latin, where the comparative may take the place of the positive or superlative.[12] *Satis* and *nimis* may impart an absolute superlative sense to the positive. In Luxorius, nine of the eleven uses of *nimis* may be translated as "very." Likewise, *nimium* (28.1) may be translated as either "too much" or "very much." Luxorius quite often uses the comparative for the positive. He is also fond of using words like *potior, potius, magis,* and *minus* to express preference, comparison, or negation. Even in classical Latin *bene* was used to intensify an adjective; in medieval Latin this use became very common, so that *bene felix* is a medieval locution meaning "very happy." Luxorius improves on this by comparing *bene* in such a phrase, using *melius grata* instead

---

[10] Platnauer, *Latin Elegiac Verse,* p. 112; see also Kuehner-Stegmann, *Grammatik,* I, 140-41.

[11] Blaise, *Manuel,* p. 116; Strecker, *Medieval Latin,* pp. 21, 63.

[12] Beeson, *Medieval Latin,* p. 20; Blaise, *Manuel,* pp. 97-100; Strecker, *Medieval Latin,* pp. 63-64. See Poems 1.19; 4.8; 5.2; 9.5; 16.7; 19.2; 28.3; etc.

of *gratiora* (37.5). Another odd use is the formation of a comparative *proximior* as if *proximus* were a positive (28.3); this, however, is found in other later writers.[13]

8. In medieval Latin *vel* is used alongside of *et, ac,* and *atque.*[14] Luxorius uses *vel* seven times; in four instances it clearly replaces *et* (8.3; 10.1; 79.4; 81.2). Similarly, *-ve* is used instead of *-que* or *et* (66.6).

9. Prepositions take on new meanings and uses in medieval Latin.[15] For example, *pro* came to mean "because"; twice it seems to have that meaning in Luxorius (19.8 and 75.8). Luxorius occasionally uses the ablative with *in* where one might expect the accusative, and vice versa, e.g., *in tabula das* (37.2) and *in statuam* (70.4). *Ad* is used peculiarly in 67.11 and 68.12. The phrase *a senio* (57.2) requires and has received extensive explanation.[16]

10. The ablative of the gerund replaces the present participle in medieval Latin.[17] This construction, without case distinctions, has persisted in Spanish, where it serves a number of uses, including the formation of a progressive periphrastic conjugation. Luxorius uses the ablative of the gerund four times: only once does it definitely replace the present participle, *spectat arando* (60.3); the other three occurrences—*sculpendo* (45.6), *rixando* (52.2), and *meditando* (65.12)—may better be considered as ablatives of means. A similar use of the gerund as a participle is found in Reposianus, *De Concubitu Martis et Veneris* (253R.166).

11. The gender of some words is changed in medieval Latin.[18] The only possible example of such a change in Luxorius' poems is *podium* (87.1), which may be construed as masculine there.[19]

12. In addition to the medieval usages mentioned above, some other grammatical and morphological anomalies are found in the poems of Luxorius. Apparently peculiar only to him is *bonis recenses* (1.18). The dative with *doceo* is never found in classical Latin, rarely in very

[13] See Commentary, note on 28.3.

[14] W. A. Baehrens, "Vermischtes," *Eranos,* XIII (1913), 23; Strecker, *Medieval Latin,* p. 65.

[15] Beeson, *Medieval Latin,* p. 18, § 40; Browne, *British Latin,* pp. xxiii-xxiv; Strecker, *Medieval Latin,* pp. 64-65.

[16] See Commentary, note on 57.2.

[17] Browne, *British Latin,* pp. xxix-xxx; Kuehner-Stegmann, *Grammatik,* I, 752-53.

[18] Beeson, *Medieval Latin,* p. 16, § 17; Strecker, *Medieval Latin,* p. 61.

[19] Klapp, *Quaestiones,* pp. ii, iii, xiv, thinks that *amphitheatralem* here agrees with *iuvenem,* not with *podium,* or that *amphitheatrale* is necessary.

late or even medieval Latin, but one instance does occur in Luxorius, *nobis docet* (29.7). Unusual forms met in his poems are: *mare,* ablative (82.4); *frondis,* nominative (46.8); *Marcie,* vocative (28.1, 8); *Olympie,* vocative (67.2); *Laida,* nominative (88.1); and *Lacedaemona,* nominative (65.3), but precedents for all of these exist. A noteworthy grammatical mannerism of Luxorius is the use of the nominative with the vocative, as in 68.1-2.

B. Vocabulary

Luxorius' vocabulary is mainly classical, but a few new and rare late Latin words are contained in his poems. He also imparts a special meaning to some words.

1. New words are: *baudus* (21.5); *placessit* (67.12); *praemedicante* (83.4); *praememores* (19.7); *resordet* (25.3); and *subaptat* (46.14)—all unique with Luxorius.

2. Late Latin words are: *fulgidulus* (an emendation, 70.1); *offuscant* (59.9); *pulcrescis* (67.13). Luxorius first used *incubus,* a popular medieval word, in poetry instead of the classical *incubo* (72.9). Jerome and Augustine had used *incubus* before him in prose. Luxorius also uses *pronubus* in its late Latin meaning of "bridegroom's attendant" or "witness" instead of *auspex* (51.2), and *praestare* to mean "help" (68.6).

3. He gives a new meaning to *consessus,* "an assembly" in classical Latin. In 18.6, *consessum* means "a seat." He extends the meaning of *fama* to "famous name" (65.11). *Zelor* as a deponent means "be zealous" in the Vulgate, but Luxorius uses it instead of the active *zelo* to mean "be envious" (28.1). *Gratum* is used adverbially in 28.5 with *ferimus* instead of *grate ferimus* or *nobis est gratum.* Luxorius writes *praevaleat* for *possit* (21.6), anticipating the use of *praevaleo* as a synonym of *possum* in medieval practice. To be noted also is his use of *exquirere* for *operam dare* (65.6), of *trivio* (see note to 30.2), and of *moecha* (see note to 33.4).

4. To the distress of a modern translator, Luxorius uses a few words loosely and vaguely. He may be accused here of not caring enough to bestir his mind in the quest of *le mot juste.* Examples are: *tenentur* (1.13); *roscidi* applied to a river (5.4); *retexis paginam* (2.3), "you turn the page," an unparalleled usage. He is very partial to the use

of *ars* and *locus* with different shades of meaning and relies greatly on *aptus,* the verb *apto,* and especially on *famulus* and *famulor.*

5. One word deserves special mention—*populus.* Even in classical times, it could mean not only "a nation," "a political entity," but also "people," "the public." Cf. Horace, *Satires* 1.1.66, Populus me sibilat. In classical Latin the plural means "nations," "population," or "mankind." A shift of meaning began in the Silver Age; Lucan uses the plural at least 113 times. In his *Pharsalia, populi* often approaches the meaning of "a multitude." For example, in *Pharsalia* 10.505, *populos* designates the Egyptian mob besieging Caesar in the palace at Alexandria. This use of *populi* to mean "the people, a crowd" is frequently found in medieval Latin.[20] Luxorius uses a singular form of *populus* only once (67.13), the plural four times (20.2; 41.1; 68.5; and 75.6). In each instance the plural denotes the people of Carthage or the crowd of spectators in the Circus and the Amphitheater.

---

[20] Monceaux, *Les Africains,* p. 112; Strecker, *Medieval Latin,* p. 54. For use by Lucan, see G. W. Mooney, *Index to the* Pharsalia *of Lucan* (Dublin and London, 1927), p. 205.

VII. THE TITLES OF LUXORIUS' POEMS

A. Their Authenticity

Further material for grammatical and linguistic commentary is contained in the titles of Luxorius' poems. Because these titles may not be entirely or even partly the work of Luxorius, they are considered separately here.

1. Every one of Luxorius' poems bears a title, even if it is no more than the word *Aliter* (No. 27), and in fact most of the other poems in the *Anthologia Latina* have some superscription. Luxorius himself testifies that his poems had titles:

> Discretos titulis quibus tenentur (1.13).

2. Are the present titles the same as the ones to which Luxorius alludes or are they the invention of copyists and editors? Riese retains the titles and headings found in the manuscripts but he makes it clear that he does not consider that these titles are the same as the ones given by the poets themselves.[1] He calls attention, without further comment, to the title of 269R. This poem of four lines is made up, with a slight change in the third line, of two distichs from Ovid, *Ars Amatoria* 65-66 and 73-74. It bears the title *De Aetate.* Obviously, this title is not to be attributed to Ovid. Similarly, the famous couplet on Vergil (264R) is entitled *De Vergilio*; the lines are excerpted from Propertius, 2.34.65-66 (3.32.65-66 in some editions). Once again the obvious inference is that this title was assigned to the poem by an anthologist, scribe, or reader. It is clear that not every title in the *Anthologia* is the poet's own; what is difficult to establish, however, is which titles originally written by the poet have survived.

3. Speaking of the entire *Anthology*, Birt, as noted before, thinks that the titles and superscriptions were appreciably shortened and

---

[1] Riese, *Anthologia,* I, xlvi.

practically eliminated in the course of successive copyings and editings.[2] Discussing only Luxorius, Klapp, on the other hand, believes that certain titles are the work of the poet or of a contemporary because they refer to persons and ideas not specifically mentioned in the poem itself, e.g., Nos. 13, 26, 38, 46, 54, 61, 64, 70, 83, 85, and 88.[3] Klapp contends that the writer of these titles, if he was not Luxorius, must have known what to write either because he actually saw the original titles or because he heard them from the lips of Luxorius himself. Otherwise, Klapp reasons, this anonymous writer could not have known enough from the poem itself to put in a specific word or name in the title. For example, although Poem 46 does not mention Eugetus, the title is *De laude horti Eugeti*. Similarly, the title of Poem 17 contains *diaconum*, although the poem mentions only *sacerdos*. Klapp's argument carries weight for some of the poems, but even if what he says is true, there is always the possibility that a scribe altered the original titles, retaining only part of the first version.

4. Klapp's deduction, moreover, would account for only about a dozen titles. On other grounds, it is reasonable to suppose that many of the remaining titles are not the invention of Luxorius. It is hard to believe that a poet, even an uninspired one, would use titles like *Aliter* (Poem 27), *Aliter unde supra* (Poem 49), *De eodem aliter* (Poem 56), or those given, for instance, to Poems 58 and 76. Such superscriptions are met frequently in the *Anthologia Latina*; they look like the headings made by copyists. Some of them are inaccurate. For example, Poem 262R is headed by *Eiusdem*. This poem is taken from Ovid, *Tristia* 2.33-34, and it is the first appearance of Ovid in the Codex Salmasianus. The poems immediately preceding it are attributed to Vergil (Poems 256R-261R).

5. At this point a digression is in order concerning *l'affaire Etemundes*. The ninth poem on page 65 of the Codex Salmasianus is headed by *Etemundes*; Riese wrote *Etemundis*, the genitive form of a supposed poet's name.[4] In 1882 Emil Baehrens made out a good

---

[2] Birt, *Das antike Buchwesen*, p. 387, "Aus ihnen ist dann Excerpt mit sehr bedeutener Verkürzung und fast gänzlicher Tilgung der Inscriptionen hergestellt." See above, Ch. II, nn. 18 and 30.

[3] Klapp, *Quaestiones*, pp. v-vi.

[4] Riese, *Anthologia* (1869 ed.), I, 92, Poem 78R. Meyer, *Anthologia*, I, xxxiii, lists Etemundus among the poets of the *Anthologia Latina*, "Nomen indicat, poetam fuisse Vandalicum." In his text (I, 192, Poem 547), *Etemundis*, however, appears. See also Duebner, *RhM*, III (1835), 470, and Peiper, "Zur Anthologie des Luxorius," *RhM*, XXXI (1876),

case for throwing Etemundes or Etemundus out of the brotherhood of poets on the grounds that this supposed name was nothing more than *item unde s̄., with s̄* equaling *supra.*[5] Acting upon Baehrens' suggestion, Riese replaced *Etemundis* in his 1894 edition of the *Anthologia Latina* with *Item unde supra* (Poem 78R).

6. Some other observations cast doubt upon the authenticity of the titles. The names of the meters are given in the titles of Poems 1-3, 5-6, 8-9, 11, 13, and 23. Is it poetic practice to specify the meter unless there is a specific reason?[6] If the poet did point out the meters of these poems, why did he not do the same in the titles of poems written in unusual meters, such as Nos. 19 and 36?[7] Still another point to be made is that Luxorius uses first person possessive adjectives in Poems 2-4, but in the titles of these poems the possessives are in the third person or the poet is referred to in that person, as if somebody else were talking about him. Also to be noted is the change in the number of a noun used first in the title and later in the poem itself: *stabulo,* 26.T, *stabulis,* 26.2; *simiis,* 44.T, *simia,* 44.2.

7. The use of *de* and *in,* "concerning," varies in the titles, as if the latter were written by different hands. Another variation is the use of *ad* in the title of Poem 32 instead of the usual *de,* or of *in* taken in the sense of "to," "against," or "concerning."[8] Although *in* meaning "concerning" or "about" does occur in classical writing, *de* was generally used in titles.[9] However, in late, medieval, and modern Latin, *in,* "about," is often found in titles of poems, books and articles.[10] It is possible, therefore, that a scholar or scribe who looked

---

185, n. 1, on Etemundes, The solution of the Etemundis-Etemundes problem and the discovery by Klapp of the palindrome in Luxorius should be warning signs to those who lightly bandy *sine dubio* and *ohne Zweifel* about when asseverating what they think Luxorius wrote; see above, Preface, fourth paragraph, and below, Commentary, note on 39.3.

[5] Baehrens, *PLM,* IV, 47.

[6] For example, "Elegiac Stanzas" by Wordsworth, "Elegiacs" or "Leonine Elegiacs" by Tennyson, and "Sapphics" by Swinburne. The names of the meters in these titles have special implications: they set the mood or give a historical background.

[7] See below, Ch. VIII, Meters 7 and 13.

[8] *Ad* in the titles of Poems 1-3 is different because there *in* or *de* would be inappropriate.

[9] Kuehner-Stegmann, *Grammatik,* I, 566, 3b.

[10] Cf. *In Laudem Regis,* 376R; *Elegiae in Maecenatem; Enarrationes in Psalmos* by Augustine; *Commentarium in Isaiam Prophetam* by Jerome; *In Laudem Justini Augusti Minoris* and *De Laude Justini* by Corippus; *In Anthologiae Latinae Librum IV* by Conrads, etc. The different meanings of *in* appear in the titles of poems by Claudian: "against," *In Rufinum* and *In Eutropium;* "on, about, concerning," *In Sepulcrum Speciosae,* 51(58), and *In Sphaeram Archimedis* 51(68); and "about" or "against" or even "to" in *In Podagrum,* 13(79). In translating the titles of Luxorius' poems, I have used all three possibilities

backward to classical usage wrote one set of titles with *de,* and another who turned to the present or future wrote the titles containing *in.* Although this line of reasoning points to different authors of the titles, a supporter of the argument that one man wrote all the titles might contend that such a writer, whether the poet himself or somebody else, was fond of variety. For example, Poems 75 and 76 are on the same topic, yet *in* is used in the title of the former and *de* in that of the latter; in each poem a person is addressed, so that *in* and *de* really mean "to," as in Poem 30.

8. Still another variation may be indicative of divided authorship of the titles, with the same arguments obtaining as in par. 7, above. A relative or causal clause is used in the titles of Poems 4, 5, 7, 11, 12, 19, 22-24, 29, 30, 32, 36, 38, 40, 43, 51-55, 57, 58, 70, 71, 74, 76, 79, 81, 84, 85, 87, and 89 to describe the subjects of the poems, but a participle is used in the titles of Poems 6, 15, 17, 20, 21, 25, 26, 35, 37, 41, 44, 47, 48, 50, 60-63, 72, 73, 77, 78, and 86.

9. The imperfect is used in the title of Poem 84, although the time of the poem is the present, as proved by *inest,* line 4. This would indicate that the writer of the title lived in a later period than the poet and was looking backward. A final point: some titles, as of Poems 57, 81, and 83, to take a few at random, seem to be not the creation of a poet but rather the product of a cataloguer summarizing the contents.

B. *Syntax and Vocabulary*

The syntax and vocabulary of the titles show the same trend toward medieval Latin as the poems themselves. However, in proportion to the small number of words in the titles, the tendency is more marked in the titles, as if they were written much later than the poems.

1. The imperfect tense is used freely in the titles, twice where the perfect would be the normal tense (Poems 12 and 87). This is medieval usage.[11] Luxorius uses *satis* only once (16.14) and with the usual meaning of "enough." In the title of Poem 77, it means "very," which is medieval usage.[12]

2. The use of the moods in the titles is generally regular. *Cum*

---

according to the sense of the poem, but in almost all instances "about" could be used to translate *in.*

[11] Strecker, *Medieval Latin,* p. 61.

[12] Strecker, *Medieval Latin,* p. 64; cf. 196R.6.

occurs in four titles (Poems 11, 57, 79, and 89), properly with the subjunctive—*dum* is not used at all. *Quod* is followed by the indicative in 76.T but in 58.T it is followed by the subjunctive, although the sense is the same. However, as noted before, this lack of differentiation between indicative and subjunctive is characteristic of both Luxorius and medieval Latin.[13]

3. Some other peculiarities of syntax and usage are: *pingere* followed by the accusative and the infinitive (18.T), analogous to *facere* and the infinitive in 36.T; *ad* used with *domum* (19.T); *ludere* followed by *in* and the ablative instead of the accusative (37.T); *salire* followed by the accusative (87.T), as if it were transitive.[14] Note also the tense of *mori* (58.T); see note on this word.

4. Unusual words, some of them found nowhere else, are: *acceptorarium* (14.T), unique; *medicolenonem* (16.T), also unique; *tablista* (47.T), rare, but also found in 196R.7; *paranympho* (51.T), late Latin for *auspex*, cf. *pronubus* (51.2); *concubas* (57.T), for *concubinas*, a late usage; *centumfoliae* (86.T), unique as one word for *centum foliae* or as a variant of *centifoliae*; *populante* (86.T), in its medieval Latin meaning of "growing"; *menetrix* (88.T), a late variant of *meretrix* (88.1). The different spellings of this last word may indicate once more that the title is by a different hand. Noteworthy also is the use of *distichi* instead of *disticha*; see note on this word, 65.T.

---

[13] Ch. VI, A 1.
[14] Each of the words discussed here and in the following paragraph is discussed more fully in the Commentary, below.

VIII. METERS AND PROSODY

A. Meters

Luxorius uses thirteen different meters in the ninety poems (exclusive of the Vergilian cento) attributed to him in this text. These meters are:

1. Elegiac—in 49 poems, 331 lines:[1] Poems 4, 7, 10, 17, 18, 20, 22, 24, 26, 27, 32-35, 38, 42-45, 47-49, 51-58, 60-64, 66, 73, 76-80, 82-85, 88-90.

2. Dactylic Hexameter—in 9 poems, 96 lines: Poems 14, 39, 41, 59, 65, 67, 68, 81, 87.

3. Phalaecean—in 10 poems, 104 lines: Poems 1, 11, 15, 16, 21, 31, 46, 50, 69, 86.

4. Lesser Asclepiad—in 6 poems, 48 lines: Poems 3, 28, 30, 37, 70, 75.

5. Lesser Sapphic—in 4 poems, 33 lines: Poems 8, 25, 40, 72.

6. Iambic Trimeter (Senarius) Acatalectic—in 3 poems, 30 lines: Poems 2, 29, 74.

7. Anapaestic—in 3 poems, 28 lines: Poems 13, 36, 71.

8. Anacreontic (Dimeter Ionic a minore with Anaclasis)—1 poem, 8 lines: Poem 12.

9. Anacreontic (Iambic Dimeter Catalectic or Dimeter Catalectic Ionic a minore)—1 poem, 18 lines: Poem 23.

10. Glyconic—1 poem, 11 lines: Poem 9.

11. Trochaic Tetrameter Catalectic—1 poem, 8 lines: Poem 5.

12. Elegiambic (Archilochian)—1 poem, 8 lines: Poem 6.

13. Iambelegiac—1 poem, 8 lines: Poem 19.

Luxorius exhibits great versatility and a willingness to try various

---

[1] Four lines (Poem 64.9-10, 13-14) are not taken into account because they are inserted from Claudian 26 (49), *Aponus* 19-22, and three lines (4.1; 47.14; and 66.2) are missing.

metrical forms in a limited area, for there are only 731 lines in the ninety poems. Martial used only eight meters in 1,561 poems, of which 1,235 are elegiacs, 238 Phalaeceans, and 77 choliambics or scazons.[2] It is interesting to observe that Luxorius, although considered an imitator of Martial, has not left any poems written in scazons.

Mueller attributes the variety of meters used by the later poets to a love of glitter and show. According to him, they hoped to overwhelm the minds of their readers with this metrical display or charm them with a spectacular exhibition.[3] Among such poets, Mueller names Septimius Serenus of the early second century, Ausonius, Prudentius, Martianus Capella, Boethius, and Luxorius. In the case of Luxorius, it may also be that as a *grammaticus* he was exhibiting his knowledge and skill.

According to Riese, Luxorius "in re metrica et prosodiaca poeta nimium quantum neglegens est."[4] On the other hand, Bouchier thinks that "he is on the whole a correct writer, displaying real metrical knowledge...."[5] Careless or correct, which was Luxorius? One must examine his handling of meters in detail to learn the answer.[6]

Luxorius did not experiment with a new kind of poetry based on accent instead of quantity, nor did he break away from the rules of meter observed by the classical poets. It is necessary, therefore, to study his meters and prosody at length to see how faithfully he followed his predecessors, notably Catullus, Vergil, Horace, Tibullus, Propertius, Ovid, and Martial.

1. ELEGIAC

First, Luxorius' treatment of the pentameter line of the elegiac distich will be examined. The rules for this line were rather standardized and strict in the work of the Augustan poets.[7] Any necessary

---

[2] Friedlaender, *Martial,* I, 26-27.
[3] Mueller, *De Re Metrica,* p. 94.
4 Riese, *Anthologia,* I, 247; an opinion often alluded to by him—see also pp. 144, 160, 162, 163, 173, and 179 of his edition.
[5] Bouchier, *Life and Letters in Roman Africa,* p. 111.
[6] Klapp, *Quaestiones,* pp. i-v, has a short survey of the meters and prosody of Luxorius. Mueller, *De Re Metrica,* mentions Luxorius 52 times, but unfortunately the index of his book lists only 8 allusions. A complete list is given here: pp. 3, 94, 104, 117, 118, 155, 158, 166, 180, 182(*bis*), 183, 224, 230, 232, 256, 260, 262, 264, 269, 272, 288, 289, 297, 316, 342, 351, 360, 362, 363, 370, 371, 373, 375, 382, 395, 408, 411, 422, 437, 441, 443, 445, 453, 455, 462, 473, 478, 480, 484, 493, 509.
[7] Koster, *Traité de métrique,* pp. 327-29.

comparions between Luxorius and non-Augustan poets will also be made.

a. In the pentameters of the Augustan poets, monosyllables are avoided at the end of the first member. *Es* and *est,* however, are regarded as enclitics. Luxorius ends the first member with one of these words seven times: in 7.4, 6; 42.6; 64.6; 73.8; 80.6; and 88.6. *Te* is the last word of the first member three times: in 10.2; 22.2; and 76.2. In the last example, *te* forms a hiatus with *oderis,* the first word of the second member:[8]

> Da pretium, ne te oderis ipsa simul!

Instances of caesural hiatus are found in Propertius and even in Ovid, but the correct reading of the lines is often in dispute.[9] Catullus allowed a hiatus twice at the end of the first member.[10] Monosyllables frequently come at the end of the first member of his pentameters: *se,* 66.52, 70.2, 76.2; *mens,* 68A.8; *haec,* 68B.46; *qua,* 68.B.156; *te,* 71.4, 76.8; *et al.* Monosyllabic endings are also found in Martial, e.g., 1.6.6.

b. The next rule applied by Augustan poets is that the second half of the pentameter must not end in a monosyllable, *es* and *est* excepted. Luxorius follows Augustan practice, ending only one line with a monosyllable, the allowable *est* (58.10).

c. Disyllables are preferred at the end of the line in Augustan pentameters. Ovid followed this rule without exception before his exile, but in his later poems he ended six lines, all of them in *Ex Ponto,* with a trisyllable. There are 165 pentameter lines in the poems of Luxorius; twenty of these, about 12 percent, end in words of more than two syllables. Ten of these words, about 6 percent of the total number of line endings, are trisyllabic. The figures for trisyllabic endings are 2 percent in Propertius, $3\frac{1}{2}$ percent in Tibullus, and $4\frac{1}{2}$ percent in Martial.[11] Catullus freely uses words of more than two syllables at the end of the pentameter; a heptasyllabic name, *Amphitryoniades,* is the complete second member of 68B.112.[12]

[8] Mueller, *De Re Metrica,* p. 375, denies this hiatus, emending to *Da pretium, ne te viderit ille* (vel *ipse*) *simul.* See below, A 2, on *superi animas.*

[9] See Platnauer, *Latin Elegiac Verse,* p. 58.

[10] In readings adopted by Koster, *Traité,* p. 327, for Catullus, 67.44, and 99.8.

[11] G. A. Wilkinson, "The Trisyllabic Ending of the Pentameter, Its Treatment by Tibullus, Propertius, Martial," *CQ,* XLII (1948), 68-75. See also Friedlaender, *Martial,* p. 30; Platnauer, *Latin Elegiac Verse,* pp. 15-17.

[12] Merrill, *Catullus,* p. xlvi, par. 76.

One trisyllabic ending in Luxorius is a tribrach, *senior* in 57.6. (There may be an additional one in 4.10, if Luxorius wrote *vitia*, my suggested emendation of *vitio*.) For this type of line ending, cf. Tibullus, 1.1.72.

A few lines in Luxorius end with a tetrasyllabic word: 4.2; 24.4; 49.4; 52.8; 54.2; 73.4. Examples of pentasyllabic words are found in 22.6; 79.2; 82.1. Such endings occur in the pentameters of Tibullus, Propertius, and Ovid; in fact, 166 tetrasyllabic endings are found in Propertius.[13]

d. In the Augustan poets, if the last word of a pentameter ends in a vowel, this vowel is usually long.[14] In Luxorius, every vowel at the end of a pentameter is long.

e. In Augustan poetry, elision is less frequent in the pentameter than in the hexameter line of the distich. There are 34 elisions in the 165 pentameter lines of Luxorius and 41 in the 166 hexameter lines of his couplets. Only two elisions are found in the second member of the pentameter: *diu est*, 58.10, and *atque elephans*, 58.2. In five instances, the elided vowel is long: *facie es*, 7.6; *proavi atque*, 35.2; *diu est*, 58.10; *nulli est*, 79.2; and *docto externum*, 84.2. In Martial such elisions are found through Book 12; Catullus elided freely, as in 73.6:[15]

> Quam modo qui me unum atque unicum amicum habuit.

f. The Augustan poets often kept the grammatical connection between the words in the two members of the pentameter.[16] To achieve a symmetrical arrangment, the adjective at the end of the first member agrees with a substantive at the end of the second, as in Ovid, *Ex Ponto* 1.2.48:

> Et dare captivas ad fera vincla manus.

Luxorius occasionally has this effect, as in:

> Si quis hoc nostro detrahit ingenio (4.2),
> Talem te nostris blanda referto iugis (26.2),

---

[13] Platnauer, *Latin Elegiac Verse*, p. 17; on polysyllabic endings, see also Hardie, *Res Metrica*, p. 54.

[14] Postgate, *Prosodia Latina*, pp. 86-87, "As in the Hexameter, the last syllable of the verse may be short, the pause completing the quantity...." Postgate points out, however, that this is far rarer in the pentameter than in the hexameter. See also Platnauer, *Latin Elegiac Verse*, pp. 64-66.

[15] Friedlaender, *Martial*, I, 33; Merrill, *Catullus*, p. xlix, par. 86.*a*; see also Platnauer, *Latin Elegiac Verse*, pp. 86-90.

[16] Hardie, *Res Metrica*, p. 54; Koster, *Traité*, pp. 328-29.

and in 18.14; 20.4; 54.2; 60.2. Cf. similar effect in hexameters, 48.1; 53.3.

A similar effect, with the genitive of a noun replacing the adjective, is seen in:

> Memnon, Pelidae conruit ille manu (7.2).

g. The pentameters of the Augustan poets generally end with a verb or a substantive.[17] About 80 percent of the pentameters of Tibullus, Propertius, and Ovid end in this way; about 17 percent end with a pronoun or—more often—with a possessive adjective, chiefly forms of *meus*, *tuus*, and *suus*. Other parts of speech, including ornamental adjectives especially, make up the rest. Luxorius ends Poem 10.6 with an adjective other than the possessives listed—most effectively, to point a contrast:

> Cum sit forma levis, clamor et ira gravis.

Only three pentameters in Luxorius end with a word which is not a verb, substantive, or adjective: 38.8; 55.4; and 76.2. Tibullus, Propertius, and Ovid also ended the pentameter with adverbs, conjunctions, and numerals.

From this detailed study of the pentameter in Luxorius, it can be seen that he adhered rather closely to the rules observed by the poets of the Augustan Age or to the practices of the best Latin poets before and after that time.

2. DACTYLIC HEXAMETER

The dactylic hexameter is actually Luxorius' favorite, for he uses it in 9 poems written entirely in that meter and in 49 elegiac poems, a total of 58 out of 90, or about 65 percent of his poems. Of the 731 lines in the 90 poems, 262, or about 36 percent, are dactylic hexameters.

In the composition of his hexameters Luxorius adheres strictly to the general rules.[18] With the exception of a few apparent false quantities, all the lines are mechanically correct, although not distinguished by elegance or grace.[19]

Elision takes place 71 times: 31 times in the 96 lines of the 9 hexameter poems, and 40 times in the 166 hexameters of the elegiac distichs,

---

[17] See Platnauer, *Latin Elegiac Verse*, pp. 40-48.

[18] See Koster, *Traité*, pp. 320-27, for rules of the dactylic hexameter.

[19] See below, B 1-4, for a listing and treatment of changes of quantity in Luxorius' poems.

[20] Some emendations, such as *zelo agitas*, 22.1, are not counted here.

or about 27 percent in all.[20] Corresponding figures for elisions in dactylic hexameter lines are 26 percent in Ovid, 29 percent in Vergil's *Bucolics,* and 33 percent in Horace.[21] These percentages indicate the total number of elisions in each 100 lines.

In the type of elision used by Luxorius, that of a short vowel ranks first, followed by the elision of the *-um* type. There are comparatively few elisions of an enclitic, and not many occur before *es* and *est.* A long vowel or diphthong is elided 13 times, or about 19 percent of the total number of elisions.[22] Here the practice of Luxorius resembles that of Horace and Vergil, whose elisions of long vowels or diphthongs amount to 24 percent and 22 percent respectively, rather than that of Ovid, in whom such elisions come to only 4 percent.

Poems 59 and 65 contain 9 elisions each; three are found in a single line (65.14):

> Omne, inquit, magnum est, quod mensura optima librat.

No hiatus is found in the dactylic hexameters of Luxorius, unless we accept Riese's emendation of *superis animas,* the reading of the Codex Salmasianus, to *superi animas* (81.6):

> Credo quod aut superi ‖ animas post funera reddunt.

Burmann, Meyer, and Baehrens follow the manuscript reading; Mueller emends to *animas superi.*[23] However, as Riese notes, "Sed hiatus tolerandus est."[24] A precedent for such a hiatus before the caesura exists in Vergil, *Aeneid* 4.235:

> Quid struit aut qua spe ‖ inimica in gente moratur.

There are no hypermetric lines in Luxorius' hexameters. Nor are there any spondaic lines: every fifth foot is a dactyl. There are 20 lines in which every foot but the fifth is a spondee, like the famous Vergilian line:[25]

> Ibant obscuri sola sub nocte per umbram (*Aeneid* 6.268).

---

[21] For some of these statistics and the five types of elision, see R. G. Kent, "Likes and Dislikes in Elision, and the Vergilian Appendix," *TAPA,* LIV (1923), 86-97, and E. H. Sturtevant and R. G. Kent, "Elision and Hiatus in Latin Prose and Verse," *TAPA,* XLVI (1915), 129-55.

[22] Count may vary from 12 to 15 because some final vowels in Luxorius may be considered long or short, as *vero aetherias,* 18.3; see below, B 3.

[23] Mueller, "Sammelsurien," *NJbb,* XCV (1867, Part 1), 784.

[24] Riese, *Anthologia,* I, 284.

[25] Poems 4.9; 14.5; 18.3; 22.3; 39.3; 41.7; 45.5; 49.5; 59.7; 65.2, 8, 14; 67.3, 10; 78.3; 79.5; 81.4; 85.3, 5; 87.8. Depending on the scansion of *parietibus,* 83.1 may be included (see below, B 1, entry for this word).

However, unlike Vergil, Luxorius does not seem to have written such lines for special effects.

Following the preference of the classical poets, Luxorius ends his dactylic hexameters with a disyllable or a trisyllable, but unlike them he never uses a monosyllabic ending.[26] As in the case of the pentameter, the classical poets generally ended the hexameter with a verb or a substantive, a practice upheld by Luxorius. Only 12 of his hexameters end with an adjective, and 3 with an adverb.[27]

In most of his hexameters Luxorius places the caesura after the arsis of the third foot (penthemimeral).[28] In the remaining lines he puts the caesura after the arsis of the fourth foot (hephthemimeral), with a secondary caesura after the arsis of the second foot (trithemimeral), a combination called *recherchée* by Koster, who quotes an example from Vergil:[29]

> Quidve dolens ‖ regina deum ‖ tot volvere casus (*Aeneid* 1.9).

The penthemimeral caesura occurs most frequently in Vergil; in Luxorius it occurs about 90 percent of the time. Once (in 83.5), the latter wrote a line containing a hephthemimeral caesura without the accompanying trithemimeral:

> Nil Phoebi Asclepique tenet ‖ doctrina parandum.

He also divided the line improperly in:

> Chilon quem patria egregium Lacedaemona misit (65.3).

These flaws may be due to the difficulty of fitting proper names into the meter.[30]

Nevertheless, in his handling of the hexameter, as well as the pentameter, it appears that Luxorius was acquainted with the rules of writing technically correct lines and that he did not noticeably deviate from them.

3. PHALAECEAN

Following the example of the Greeks, Catullus allowed a trochee

[26] As in Vergil, *Aeneid* 1.105, and Juvenal, 10.268.
[27] Ending with an adjective: 14.2, 3; 22.3; 24.5; 35.1; 67.5; 73.7, 9; 76.3, 79.1, 3; 83.1. Ending with an adverb: 24.1; 58.7; 73.1.
[28] As used here, *arsis* denotes the rise in voice at the long syllable of an anapaest, iambus, dactyl, etc., *thesis*, the fall of the voice at the short syllable—corresponding to the German *Hebung* and *Senkung*; see Hardie, *Res Metrica*, p. 262.
[29] Koster, *Traité*, p. 323.
[30] See Klapp, *Quaestiones*, p. v.

or an iambus in the first foot. The base is always a spondee in Petronius, Martial, and the *Priapea*—it is almost always a spondee in later writers.[31] Of the 104 lines in this meter by Luxorius, 97, or 93.2 percent, begin with a spondee. *An hoc* at the beginning of 15.12 may be an iambus, but it can also be considered a spondee, since *h* can make position in Luxorius.[32] *Mori* at the beginning of 21.7 is an iambus. Five lines (11.1, 5; 31.2; 46.3, 4) begin with a trochee, but *plura* (11.5) is an emendation of *plora*, a spondee.[33] Although Luxorius did not observe the extreme rigidity of Martial in the base of the Phalaecean, nevertheless, in comparison with Catullus, he did not take undue liberties.

In classical poets, the caesura in Phalaecean verse usually comes after the fifth or sixth syllable.[34] There are only two exceptions to this in Luxorius: in 1.22 and 86.2. Similar caesuras occur frequently in Catullus (6.11), Martial (1.104.3), and Statius (*Silvae*, 2.85).

Elision is common in Catullus, but rare in Martial and Statius.[35] There are ten elisions in the Phalaeceans of Luxorius.

There are a few examples of a monosyllabic ending other than *es* and *est* in Catullus and many in Martial.[36] In Luxorius only one hendecasyllabic line ends with a monosyllable: 31.7, *sis*.

For the purpose of clarifying the observations made in the next paragraph, I have considered this the metrical scheme of the Phalaecean: $\underline{\;}\,\underline{\;} \mid \underline{\;}\,\cup\cup \mid \underline{\;}\,\cup \mid \underline{\;}\,\cup \mid \underline{\;}\,\cup$.[37] Luxorius not only allowed variations in the basis, but he also substituted or seems to have substituted spondees in the third or fourth foot.[38] The length of the syllables concerned is marked in the following examples of such substitutions:

    (1) Versus ex variis locīs dēductos (1.6).
    (2) Plura ne futuas, petō, Lūcine (11.5).
    (3) Novi quid libeat tuūm, chīrurge (16.11).

---

[31] Ellis, *A Commentary on Catullus*, p. xli; Friedlaender, *Martial*, I, 28; Hardie, *Res Metrica*, p. 116; Lane, *Latin Grammar*, p. 482, § 2664; Merrill, *Catullus*, p. xlvii, par. 81.

[32] See below, B 1, entry for *quis*, 4.2.

[33] A reading kept by Baehrens. See Mueller, *De Re Metrica*, p. 180, "Luxorius in hendecasyllabis admisit interdum trochaeum et iambum."

[34] Hardie, *Res Metrica*, pp. 114-17; Koster, *Traité*, p. 336.

[35] Hardie, *Res Metrica*, p. 117.

[36] Friedlaender, *Martial*, I, 29-30.

[37] On the scanning of Phalaeceans, see Friedlaender, *Martial*, I, 29; Hardie, *Res Metrica*, pp. 115-17; Koster, *Traité*, p. 336; also B. L. Gildersleeve and G. Lodge, *Latin Grammar*, p. 477, and Allen and Greenough's *New Latin Grammar*, p. 421.

> (4) Umquam vincere pōssīs ut quadrigis (50.4).
> (5) Suspensis reficīt līber pharetris (46.6).
> (6) Praecedis, Vico, nec tamēn prǣcedis (50.1).
> (7) Corruptor tibi sit retrō pōnendus (50.5).

Lucine (2) may be subject to the practice of changing quantities in proper names.[38] The *i* in *chirurge* (3) should be short to make the line metrically perfect. Possibly Luxorius so considered it, for in the only other use of this word by him (23.6), the *i* must be short to make the line scan.[40] The *i* in *possis* (4) may also have been thought to be short by Luxorius.[41] *Liber* (5), the reading of A, was changed to *puer* by *a* and the Codex Leidensis, which is better, metrically. For 6, cf. 28.7, *quĕsumus,* but *praecedis* with the proper quantities is the first word of this same line, 50.1. No case can be made out for (1) and (7).

In 1.9, the *u* in *ut* must be lengthened; see entry for this word, below, B 1, for an explanation.

4. LESSER ASCLEPIAD

In Horace the basis of this meter is regularly a spondee.[42] Luxorius begins every Asclepiad in this way. In classical writing, the diaeresis, the break in the line, comes after the sixth syllable; this holds true in the Asclepiads of Luxorius. Monosyllabic endings are rare in the poets before him; there is only one example in Luxorius: *sunt* in 37.5.

There are 12 elisions in the 48 lines: 3.9, 11; 28.8; 30.2, 4, 5, 7; 70.2, 4; 75.2, 7, 8. Two of these sound awkward: *pro exequiis* in 3.9, and *te ut* in 75.8.

Luxorius knew the structure of the meter, but he has allowed a few apparently false quantities. The words in which they occur are: *proximiōr,* 28.3; *quĕsumus,* 28.7; *vĭvis,* 28.8; *Zenōbi,* 30.2; *indoctāque,* 30.3; *cuperē,* 37.8. These words are considered at the end of this chapter.

[38] This is found only in Luxorius among the Latin poets. Apparent changes of vowel quantity in Luxorius can be regarded in two ways. On the one hand, we may consider that Luxorius actually altered a vowel quantity to fit the word into the meter, or, on the other hand, we must assume that he violated the strict rules of a metrical scheme. Thus, in (1), he either considered the *ē* of *deductos* short or he knowingly used a long syllable where the meter requires a short one.

[39] See below, B 4.

[40] Klapp, *Quaestiones,* p. iv, compares with *cheragra,* Martial, 1.98.2, and 9.92.9, where the antepenult is short. However, in the sole instance in which Martial uses *chirurgus* (1.30.1), the *i* is properly long.

[41] See below, B 2, entry for *quamvis,* 7.1.

[42] Hardie, *Res Metrica,* p. 255; Koster, *Traité,* p. 344.

In addition, *an tabulae* (37.5), the reading of A, does not scan; this has been changed to *an tali* by Mueller and to *an tablae* by Schubert.[43] These emendations scan properly. *Candenti* (70.1) seems corrupt; *a* suggests *candidulo,* which fits the meter.[44]

5. LESSER SAPPHIC

Luxorius did not put his four Sapphic poems in stanza form, for he omits the Adonic fourth line. This was a tendency among later poets; they abstained from metrical systems but used consecutive single lines.[45] Both systems are found in Seneca: strophes in *Medea,* 579-606; single lines with an Adonic after every eight lines in *Medea,* 607-69.

Luxorius follows the classical rules for Sapphic verse, which are given as the first sentence of each of the following six paragraphs:[46]

Every third foot is a dactyl. Luxorius observes this without exception.

The second foot is generally a spondee. Catullus occasionally uses a trochee (as in 11.6), in the manner of Sappho and Alcaeus; Horace, never. Luxorius uses only spondees there.

Frequent elision is permissible. There are numerous instances of elision in Catullus; in Horace elision occurs once in every ten lines. Luxorius has four elisions in 33 lines: 8.1, 6, 9; 72.1.

Monosyllabic endings are rarely used. Horace ends a Sapphic verse with a monosyllable three times; some of Seneca's Sapphics also have monosyllabic endings. Luxorius has none.[47]

The last syllable of the final word of a line, if it ends in a vowel, is long. Only two of Luxorius' Sapphics end in a short vowel: *docere,* 8.2, and *patrare,* 72.5.

The caesura regularly comes after the fifth syllable. This is called the Horatian caesura.[48] Luxorius observes this rule except in 8.8;

---

[43] Mueller, *De Re Metrica,* p. 182; Schubert, *De Luxorio,* pp. 34-35; see below, Commentary, note on 37.5-6.

[44] Riese, *Anthologia,* I, xliv, n. 1, is so firmly convinced that Luxorius is *neglegens* that he prefers to keep *candenti* of A. However, *candidulo* makes sense and scans; Riese did accept a similar emendation, *fulgiduli* for *fulgidi,* 69.1. See below, Commentary, notes on 69.1 and 70.1.

[45] Mueller, *De Re Metrica,* p. 125.

[46] Hardie, *Res Metrica,* pp. 250-53; Koster, *Traité,* p. 347; Gildersleeve and Lodge, *Latin Grammar,* pp. 477-78; Postgate, *Prosodia Latina,* pp. 111-12.

[47] Mueller, *De Re Metrica,* pp. 263-64.

[48] Hardie, *Res Metrica,* p. 251.

precedents for deviations from this rule are found in Catullus.[49] In Luxorius, the caesuras after *si* in 40.7 and after *cum* in 72.7 are awkward.

Two irregularities of quantity occur: *dĕtur*, 40.6, and *Catō*, 72.10.

6. IAMBIC TRIMETER ACATALECTIC

Only one pure iambic line is found in Luxorius' three poems in this meter:

> Velut iocosa si theatra pervoles (2.10).

Luxorius does not substitute dactyls or anapaests, nor is there any resolution of long vowels. The caesura invariably comes after the fifth syllable; in Horace it is sometimes found in the fourth foot also. Luxorius follows the rule that only the odd feet may be spondees;[50] therefore, he either has a metrical fault or has used a false quantity in the fifth foot of Poem 29.6, where the *o* of *moveas* must be considered long to scan as a spondee:

> Tace parentes, ne quietos moveas.

7. ANAPAESTIC

Latin poets had their troubles with the composition of anapaests, and Luxorius is no exception.[51] In the judgment of Mueller, "Luxorii anapaesti et duri nimis et satis feruntur mendosi."[52] He substitutes spondees and dactyls freely and indulges in false quantities, among which the most startling examples are the shortening of *e* in *diei* (13.1) and of the same letter in *fame* (13.6).

Luxorius' anapaests are acatalectic dimeters, with the caesura coming after the fifth syllable. In Riese's text the caesura comes after the sixth syllable in Poem 36.4 (322R), for he has accepted the emendation by *a* of *spurcos* in A to *spurios*. The full line in A is:

> Pariat spurcos ut tibi natos.

Klapp considers *spurcos* the correct reading, pointing out that the first and third feet of all the lines in Luxorius' three anapaestic poems

---

[49] Hardie, *Res Metrica*, p. 251, cites Catullus, 11.6, *Seu Sacas sagittiferosque Parthos.*
[50] Hardie, *Res Metrica*, p. 234.
[51] *Ibid.*, p. 251; see also Christ, *Metrik*, pp. 248-49, for a discussion of anapaests, especially dimeters.
[52] Mueller, *De Re Metrica*, p. 158.

consist of three syllables, and the second and fourth, of two syllables.[53] This would not be true if *spurios* were kept, unless it is read as a disyllable. Baehrens and I retain *spurcos*, which is metrically sound and makes practically as good sense as *spurios*.

The lines of Poem 36 break neatly into two parts, and there is no hiatus at any of the divisions. Metrical parallels can be found in the poem by Seneca in *Apocolocyntosis* 12.3.3, which he clearly labels anapaestic, "nenia cantabatur anapaestis." In Luxorius' poem, line 6, there is an apparently false quantity in *forsan*. The final syllable may be *anceps*[54], or may be considered long before the caesura (see the entry for this word in B 1, below). Another problem in Poem 36 is the emendation of *coniugis* in A to *coiugis,* made by Klapp and accepted by Baehrens and Riese. The manuscript reading makes the first foot a cretic. If *coniugis* is retained and scanned as a dactyl, one must assume that Luxorius considered the *s* silent.[55] Otherwise, he is metrically at fault here in a meter in which other Roman poets were also guilty of irregularities.

This is true of Seneca and of the few later poets who wrote anapaests, such as Ausonius and especially Boethius.[56] Speaking of the latter's different types of poetry, Migne (*PL,* LXIII, 634) says something that can be applied to his anapaests—that he cared for only one thing, "ut sint quattuor pedes." Incidentally, Luxorius seems to have been the only Latin poet who wrote epigrams in anapaests.

8. ANACREONTIC (DIMETER IONIC A MINORE WITH ANACLASIS)

Poem 12 contains eight syllables in each line with anaclasis (an exchange of place between a short syllable and a preceding long one)

---

[53] Klapp, *Quaestiones,* p. iv.

[54] Hardie, *Res Metrica,* pp. 66-67, 269. Instead of *syllaba anceps* some modern authorities use *syllaba brevis in elemento longo* or *brevis in longo* to denote that the final syllable of a verse of independent series may be long or short indifferently in spite of the demands of the meter. See *OCD,* p. 564, lower right-hand column, one line from the bottom; Maas, *Griechische Metrik,* p. 35, addendum to § 45, and Snell, *Griechische Metrik,* pp. 1-3.

[55] Mueller, *De Re Metrica,* pp. 427-29, gives examples from Ennius, Lucretius, etc. On the elision of final *s,* see Cicero, *Orator* 48.161; for an example, see Catullus, 116.8. Klapp, *Quaestiones,* p. ii, reasons that Luxorius wrote *coiugis* in imitation of *coiugare* and then shortened the *o* on the false analogy of *biugus, quadriiugus,* etc. This is rather complicated; did all this go through Luxorius' mind? See below, n. 81.

[56] Mueller, *De Re Metrica,* p. 104.

in the second and third feet. The metrical scheme is ⏑⏑|⏓⏑|⏓⏑|⏓⏓,
which is the same as that of a fragment of Anacreon:[57]

Φέρ' ὕδωρ, φέρ' ὄινου, ὦ παῖ.

There is one fault in line 7—the *o* in *cogente* must be considered short
to make the line scan properly.

9. ANACREONTIC (IAMBIC DIMETER CATALECTIC OR DIMETER CATALECTIC IONIC A MINORE)

The metrical scheme of Poem 23 differs from that of Poem 12,
although both are Anacreontic. Poem 23 has only seven syllables to
a line and there is no anaclasis. The verse pattern resembles that of
another fragment of Anacreon:[58]

'Ο μὲν θέλων μάχεσθαι,
πάρεστι γάρ, μαχέσθω.

The writer or writers of the collection known as the *Anacreontea*
(written probably four centuries after Anacreon, who lived in the sixth
century B.C.) used this meter in some of the lines and actually incorporated this fragment in one of the poems.[59] Another name for
this meter is the *hemiambus*. As used by Anacreon in its pure form,
its pattern is ⏑⏓|⏑⏓|⏑⏓|⏓.
Luxorius did not have to know Greek to find models, since some
form of Anacreontics had been used by Roman writers—first by Laevius
(born *ca.* 129 B.C.), later by Seneca and Petronius.[60] Both Anacreontic
meters treated here are found in the fragments of Petronius:[61]

[57] Fragment 62, T. Bergk, *PLG, Poetae Melici*, ed. by J. Rubenbauer (4th ed., Leipzig,
1914), *Pars* III, p. 271. See also Hephaestion, *Enchiridion*, ed. by M. Consbruch (Leipzig,
1906), p. 39 [76] 40 (5). For a discussion of this meter, see Hardie, *Res Metrica*, p. 158;
Thomson, *Greek Lyric Metre*, pp. 8-9, 153. Klapp, *Quaestiones*, p. iv, calls it ithyphallic
with double anacrusis; on this, see Christ, *Metrik*, pp. 284-86, 496-99; Hardie, *Res
Metrica*, pp. 158-65; Koster, *Traité*, pp. 23, 96-97, 133.
[58] Fragment 92, Bergk (cited above, n. 57), p. 279; Hephaestion, *Enchiridion* (cited
above, n. 57), p. 16 [32] 18 (3). See also Koster, *Traité*, pp. 96-99.
[59] *Anacreontea* 45.8-9 (Bergk, *PLG*, p. 324), with a change to πάρεστω. Antipater of
Sidon (2nd century B.C.) may be the compiler; see Hadas, *Greek Literature*, p. 219.
[60] Mueller, *De Re Metrica*, p. 107.
[61] Buecheler, *Petronius*, p. 118, Fragments 20 and 21; Sage, *Petronius*, pp. 139-39.
Fragments 20 and 21. Fragment 20 is contained in Terentianus Maurus, *De Metris*, 2865;
Fragment 21 in Diomedes, *De Arte Grammatica*, Book 3 (Keil, *GL*, VI, 409, and I, 518,
respectively).

> Rapidum pererret orbem

and

> Anus recocta vino
> Trementibus labellis.

In Poem 23 Luxorius uses a spondee at the beginning of the line and a short syllable at the end, so that his metrical scheme is $\_\_|\:\cup\_|\:\cup\_|\:\overset{\cup}{\_}\,$. A precedent for the use of an initial spondee is found in a fragment of Laevius:*Lasciviter ludunt.*[62] It exists also in Prudentius, *Hymnus ante Somnum* 39 and 51 (in *Liber Cathemerinon,* 6):

> Per quas repente currens

and

> Hunc lux serena vibrans.

Three quantities in Poem 23 require comment: the short *o* in *ergo,* line 13, the short *i* in *chirurge,* line 6 (cf. 16.11), and the short *u* in *lugubrem,* line 14. Since Luxorius correctly uses only iambics in the second and third feet of this poem, it would appear that he considered the vowels in question as short.

10. GLYCONIC

In No. 9, a poem of eleven lines, Luxorius uses the meter of the odd lines of Horace, *Odes* 3.1, without committing any technical errors. There is one elision, *agnovi ut,* in line 9. Although elision of a long vowel in this meter is rare in Horace, it does occur, as in *Nil mortalibus ardui est (Odes* 1.3.39). In Horace the base is always a spondee: $\_\_|\:\cup\cup\:|\:\cup\:|\:\_$. Luxorius also begins very Glyconic verse with a spondee. Catullus used Glyconics only as part of a system, as in his Poems 17 and 34, and he allowed variations in the basis. Only Luxorius seems to have used continuous Glyconics.

11. TROCHAIC CATALECTIC TETRAMETER (SEPTENARIUS)

This meter is represented by one poem, No. 5, consisting of eight lines. This is the meter of the *Pervigilium Veneris.* The only technical flaw in Luxorius' poem is in line 5, *lībet,* but this word is an emendation by Maehly (see entry for this word, below, B 1).

---

[62] Fragment 5, E. Baehrens, *Fragmenta Poetarum Romanorum* (Leipzig, 1886), p. 292.

12. ELEGIAMBIC

Among later poets Luxorius is the only one to have used this meter.[63] This form of verse, designated as Archilochian in the title of Poem 6, is asynartetic, consisting of a dactylic penthemimeris (the first half of a dactylic hexameter up to the penthemimeral caesura), also known as a *hemiepes,* and an iambic dimeter acatalectic. An example in Archilochus is:[64]

’Αλλά μ’ ὁ λυσιμελής, ὦ ταῖρε, δάμναται πόθος.

Its metrical scheme is: $\_\cup\cup|\_\cup\cup|\_||\_\_|\cup\_|\cup\_|\cup\bar{\cup}$. Archilochus was fond of composing asynartetic verses. Horace adopted some of his meters, using a slightly different form of the elegiambus in the even lines of *Epode* 11. Luxorius is closer to the Greek poet in his work with this meter.[65] There are no technical faults in his poem. As in his Sapphics and Glyconics, Luxorius wrote continuous lines without forming stanzas.

13. IAMBELEGIAC OR IAMBELEGUS

This is the reverse of the elegiambus. In the iambelegus the iambic colon precedes the dactylic penthemimeris. The eight lines of Poem 19 contain twelve syllables each, however, as in:

Monstrent volatu praememores famulo (line 7).

The even lines of Horace's *Epode* 13 are called iambelegiacs; they have fifteen syllables each. According to Koster, the name *iambelegus* is not properly aplied to these verses of Horace; he cites as an example of a true iambelegus this Pindaric fragment:[66]

Κείνων λυθέντες σαῖς ὑπὸ χερσίν, ἄναξ.

[63] See Mueller, *De Re Metrica,* pp. 117-18, on asynartetic verses from Archilochus to Luxorius. He calls the ingenious combinations of the later poets "facetias."

[64] Hephaestion, *Enchiridion* (cited above, n. 57), p. 50 [94] 51 (9); Fragment 85, Bergk, *PLG, Poetae Elegiaci et Iambographi* (5th ed., Leipzig, 1914), Pars II, p. 706. On this meter, see Christ, *Metrik,* p. 569; Juret, *Principes de Métrique,* p. 51; Mueller, *De Re Metrica,* p. 81; Postgate, *Prosodia Latina,* p. 107.

[65] Koster, *Traité,* p. 340, n. 1, thinks that the name *elegiambus* is not at all adequate for these verses of Horace, *Epode* 11. He considers the Greek originals the true form (pp. 192-93).

[66] *Ibid.* The Pindaric fragment is in T. Bergk, *PLG,* I.1, *Pindari Carmina,* ed. by O. Schroeder (5th ed., Leipzig, 1900), p. 396, Fragment 35(10); or Hephaestion, *Enchiridion* (cited above, n. 57), p. 51[95]52(11). Hephaestion calls this meter *iambelegus* and names it as the opposite of the elegiambus, which he calls *encomiologicum.* See also Christ, *Metrik,* p. 568. Koster, p. 193, notes a striking use of the iambelegiac in Euripides, *Ion* 769-70, where a change of speakers is effected at the end of each colon.

Its metrical pattern, which is exactly matched by Luxorius' poem, is: $\_\_\,|\,{\rm u}\_\,|\_\,\|\,\_{\rm u\,u}\,|\_{\rm u\,u}\,|\,\overset{\rm u}{\_}$. If Luxorius had not read the Greek poets, where then did he find the meter of his poem, which no other Latin poet seems to have used? Most probably he made his own combination. The second half of the line, the dactylic part, is nothing more than part of a pentameter line. Luxorius had used it in his elegiacs and, of course, in the elegiambus. The first part may have come from the first half of the first two lines of the Greater Alcaic, as in Horace, *Odes* 1.9.9, Permitte divis.

Late Roman poets indulged in the practice of making odd combinations in a line, following the lead of Seneca. Like the creation of acrostics and other bizarre types of poetry, this joining of different meters in a line gave them one more method of exercising their versatility and virtuosity.

In whatever way Luxorius arrived at his combination, he worked it out without any metrical faults. However, there is no variety in the lines—every first foot is a spondee, every second, an iambus. The last syllable of the first member is always long; there is no hiatus or elision. The result looks like an exercise well-tailored to a set pattern, as if the author had placed before himself a diagram of the metrical scheme and had decided to follow it mechanically and undeviatingly.

This completes the examination of the meters used by Luxorius. Judgment on his accuracy and proficiency must be reserved until more evidence has been assembled relating to his prosody, with careful attention directed toward quantities.

B. *Changes of Quantity*

All apparent changes of vowel quantity in the poems of Luxorius will now be listed. These are grouped in four categories:

1. Lengthening of short vowels.
2. Shortening of long vowels.
3. Final *o*.
4. Proper names.

Where a change of quantity appears in an emendation, the fact that the word has been emended will be noted, for Luxorius is not to be held responsible for the conjectures of his correctors. Unless the original readings are hopelessly corrupt, changes of quantity in the manuscript readings of the emended words themselves will also be noted.

1. LENGTHENING OF SHORT VOWELS

(A macron over a vowel in the words listed indicates that the quantity of that vowel, properly short, is to be considered long to avoid a metrical fault. Thus, the entry "1.9. *ūt*" means a change from *ŭt* in Poem 1, line 9, to *ūt*.)

1.9. *ūt*. Luxorius frequently lengthens the short vowel of a syllable in the arsis. See below, entries for 18.4; 28.3; 29.6; 30.3; 32.3; 36.6; 37.8; 39.2; 42.3; 46.2, 12; 54.2; 55.5, 6; 63.1; 68.1.

4.2. *quīs*. H is often considered a consonant, especially by the late poets.[67] It can make position either when it is inside a word or when it is the first letter of a word. In the second instance, elision can be avoided if the preceding word ends in a short vowel plus *m*. Sometimes the vowel involved can be lengthened for other reasons, such as the position of the syllable in the arsis or before a caesura. Cf. Vergil, *Bucolics* 6.53:

> Ille latus niveum molli fultūs hyacintho

and Vergil, *Aeneid* 9.610:

> Terga fatigamūs hasta, nec tarda senectus.

See also below, entries for 16.6; 47.13; 52.7; 55.5; 63.1; 79.3; 80.5; 81.2, 4; 86.6.

5.6. *lībet*. The reading of A is *liber esse,* which fits metrically but is difficult grammatically. Riese accepts Maehly's emendation to *libet,* but Baehrens keeps *liber* in conjunction with Duebner's emendation of *esse* to *esset.* Elsewhere, Luxorius uses forms of *libet* with a short *i*: *libebit,* 1.12, and *libet,* 78.5. The *i* is short also in *libeat,* 16.11, and *libitum,* 75.2—both emendations by Burmann. If Luxorius actually wrote *lībet,* he may have lengthened the *i* because of accent or arsis. See below, entry for 17.1.

16.6. *mēthodicis*. The reading of A is *metodicis,* which may be a scribal mistake or part of the tendency in later times to drop an aspirated *h* after a consonant.[68] See above, entry for 4.2.

---

[67] Mueller, *De Re Metrica,* pp. 14, 289, 370, 382, 391, 426; Strecker, *Medieval Latin,* p. 72. Dracontius often used *h* as a consonant; ten examples are found in *De Laudibus Dei,* Book I, and eight in the *Satisfactio.* See Irwin, *De Laudibus Dei,* pp. 103-4; Saint Margaret, *Satisfactio,* p. 102.

[68] Strecker, *Medieval Latin,* p. 60, gives an example of *Talia* for *Thalia.*

17.1. *gūla*. Lengthened because of the accent.[69] Cf. entries for 5.6, above, and 29.6, below.

18.4. *-quē*. This is an emendation by Riese. It is strange that Riese, who calls Luxorius careless in prosody, should saddle him with an apparently false quantity. However, *-quē* can be justified as a syllable in the arsis. There were many precedents for the lengthening of the enclitic, but late poets did not often take this liberty.[70]

28.3. *proximiōr*. In arsis and before the caesura.

29.6. *mōveas*. In arsis, like *ut* in 1.9, and because of accent, like *gula* in 17.1.

30.3. *indoctāque*. Meyer emended to *indocta atque,* presumably to avoid the lengthening. Clever, but unnecessary, for a short vowel before *qu* was often lengthened by the later poets.[71] Cf. 55.1 and 84.1, below; also 198R.71:

> Parte miser, forma brevior mentēque fugaci.

32.3. *vīgilias*. In arsis, but cf. *invĭgilat,* 54.3.

36.6. *forsān*. See above, A 7. In arsis and before the caesura. Lengthening before the caesura was a license enjoyed by the classical poets. Cf. Vergil, *Aeneid* 2.563:

> Et direpta domūs et parvi casus Iuli.

See also below, entries for 37.8; 39.2; 42.3; 55.6; 71.6; 80.5; 81.2, 4; 84.4.

37.8. *cuperē*. See above, entry for 36.6.

39.2. *datūr*. A triple combination: in arsis, before the caesura, and before *h.* Cf. Florentinus, *In Laudem Regis,* 376R 18·

> Contulit et soli tribuīt haec cuncta potiri.

Examples of the lengthening of a syllable with a closed short vowel in a verb ending before the caesura are found in Vergil, *Aeneid* 2.411, and 5.284; Tibullus, 1.4.27, and 1.10.13; Propertius, 1.10.23; 2.8.8; 2.23.1.

42.3. *regerē*. *Regere metas* is the reading of A; *et* was added after *regere* by *a.* This eliminates the need of considering the final *e* of *regere* as long. The addition of *et,* which makes for smoother reading, is retained in my text. However, there can be no objection

---

[69] Mueller, *De Re Metrica,* p. 443.
[70] *Ibid.,* p. 392.
[71] *Ibid.,* pp. 382, 443.

to the original reading of the manuscript on the grounds of meter, if the example of *cupere,* 37.8 above, is followed.

46.2. *chŏro.* In arsis and bearing the accent; see entry for 17.1. The margin of the Codex Leidensis and *a* have the reading *viretque Chloris,* which fits metrically. Baehrens transposes *virente choro* of A to *choro virente,* which eliminates the necessity of lengthening the first *o* in *choro.* Riese, who keeps the reading of A (as does my text), directs attention to p. 247 of his edition, where he informs the reader that Luxorius is a most careless poet. The reading of A does not have to be altered, since Luxorius has similar changes of quantity. Moreover, Luxorius, like the medieval poets, did not observe the correct quantities in words of Greek origin.[72] Cf. *phĭlosophum,* 88.4.

46.12. *dulcīs.* In arsis.[73] See entry for 1.9.

47.13. *iăm.* Before *h*; see above, entry for 4.2. Baehrens' transposition of *iam huic* to *huic iam* is not necessary; see also entry for 52.7. *Huic* may be disyllabic;[74] then the entry for 86.6 below would apply.

52.1. *tandēm.* In arsis, before the caesura, and followed by *h.* See entries for 4.2 and 39.2.

54.2. *nēgotii.* In arsis. Here Luxorius also shortened the long *o,* although it bears the accent, so that the word is to be read *nĕgŏtii* instead of *nĕgōtii.*[75] However, he showed that he knew the correct quantities when he wrote *nĕgōtia* in 9.7.

55.1. *noctēque.* Riese emends *nocteq;* of A to *noctuque,* but Baehrens and my text keep *nocteque.* See entry for 30.3, above. Inconsistently, Riese also emends *nocte* to *noctu* in 32.T but allows *nocte* to remain in 72.2.

55.5. *gravīŭs.* In arsis and before *h.* See entry for 4.2.

55.6. *domĭnūs.* In arsis and before the caesura. See entry for 46.12. This is not a case of *syllaba anceps,* since Luxorius ends the first half of his pentameters with a long syllable. Cf. Florentinus, *In Laudem Regis,* 376R.6:

> Virtus forma decūs animus sensusque virilis.

63.1. *quĭs.* According to A, the first two words of this line are *Quis*

---

[72] Strecker, *Medieval Latin,* pp. 58-59.
[73] Mueller, *De Re Metrica,* pp. 407-8.
[74] *Ibid.,* p. 318.
[75] Mueller, *De Re Metrica,* p. 441, explains the drastic changes on the plea of metrical necessity.

hunc, which were transposed both by Riese and Baehrens. However, on the basis of 4.2, the original reading can be kept, since the *h* of *hunc* will make position.

63.1. *credāt.* In arsis and before the caesura. See entries for 1.9; 36.6; 39.2; and 55.6.

68.1. *nimīs.* In arsis and before the caesura. See 1.9, above.

71.6. *illē.* Riese again makes the allegation that Luxorius was careless. However, *ille* is at the end of a line division; Luxorius may have considered the final syllable *anceps.* Moreover, this poem is in anapaests.[76]

73.1. *brēvis.* This lengthening is necessary only if the text of A is followed. It would then have to be explained on the grounds of accent. However, *est* was inserted after *brevis* by *a*, a most commendable addition, which preserves the correct quantity of the *e* in *brevis.*

77.2. *sūperior.* In arsis. Note, however, short *u* in *superet,* 7.5; *superis,* 13.8; *superos,* 33.2.

77.4. *horridiūs.* In arsis and before the caesura. See 55.6.

79.3. *sōphismate.* See above, entries for 4.2 and 46.2.

80.5. *sidūs.* In arsis, before the caesura, and followed by *h.* See above, entries for 39.2 and 52.7.

81.2. *Phrygiūs.* Like 80.5, above.

81.4. *fictūs.* Like 80.5, above.

83.1. *pariētibus.* The full line, a hexameter, is:

> Constructas inter moles parietibus altis.

For the line to scan, *parietibus* must be a pentasyllable. This word is a tetrasyllable in Vergil, *Aeneid* 2.442, and 5.589. There, the first *i* is consonantal, so that the *a* is naturally long; the *e* is short. Luxorius' line will also scan if *parietibus* is considered a tetrasyllabic word, but the *e* will still have to be lengthened—as well as the *a.* Since *pariēs* is trisyllabic in 28.4, it is more likely that Luxorius considered *parietibus* a pentasyllabic word.[77]

84.1. *cunctāque.* The complete line in A is:

> Pica hominum voces cunctaque animalia monstrat.

There is no need of emending to correct a metrical fault, since *-que* makes position; see above, 30.3. However, Klapp's emendation to

---

[76] On the liberties taken in the writing of anapaests, see above, A 7.
[77] See Mueller, *De Re Metrica,* p. 13, on *parietibus;* pp. 299-301, on synizesis.

cuncta ante is such an improvement that it has been adopted by Riese and Baehrens.[78]

84.4. *erāt.* In arsis and before the caesura. See above, entries for 36.6; 39.2; 55.6; and 63.1.

86.6. *quam horto.* There is no vowel change here, but these words are listed to complete the remarks made in the entry for 4.2. *H* can avoid elision without changing the preceding short closed vowel into a long one.

88.8. *phĭlosophum.* In arsis; see also 46.2 and 79.3 for other words of Greek origin.

2. SHORTENING OF LONG VOWELS

(See explanation under "1. Lengthening of Short Vowels," above. In this section, a breve indicates a change from long to short.)

7.1. *quamvĭs.* Many late Latin poets shortened a final long syllable ending in *s.*[79] Cf. Dracontius, *Romulea,* 8.603:

Quamvĭs Alexander si viribus Herculis esset.

9.5. *făcundior.* No explanation except that of metrical necessity. Schubert emends to *fēcundior,* which does not help, metrically; Baehrens to *sĕcundior,* which does.

10.4. *alterĭus.* A vowel before another vowel inside a word could be shortened. The genitive singular of words like *alter, ille, ipse, ullus, unus,* etc. was written with a short or long *i* according to metrical necessity.[80] Cf. *ipsĭus,* 24.4, below; *alterĭus,* Vergil, *Aeneid* 2.667; *illĭus,* Ovid, *Amores* 1.13.44, but *illĭus, Amores* 1.4.34. Cf. *alterĭus,* 20L.5.

12.7. *cŏgente.* Mueller points out that it was forgotten that a prefix had been added to a word beginning with *a,* as *co* plus *ago,* and words like *copulare* (*co-apulare*) and *coperire* (*co-operire*) were used by late poets as if the *o* were short.[81]

---

[78] Klapp, *Quaestiones,* p. iii, argues cogently that the magpie does not imitate the voices of other animals and that the implication of the title and of the poem is that the magpie surpasses all other animals in its vocal imitation of human beings.

[79] Mueller, *De Re Metrica,* p. 422.

[80] See Kuehner, *Grammatik,* I, 587, § 131c, on the shortening of this *i* early in Latin literature; Mueller, *De Re Metrica,* pp. 285-86; Platnauer, *Latin Elegiac Verse,* pp. 54, 64.

[81] Mueller, *De Re Metrica,* p. 453; cf. *coiugis,* n. 55, above.

13.1. *dĭĕi.* Of this, Mueller says that only Luxorius and Venantius dared to shorten the penult of *diei* without precedent.[82]

13.6. *fămĕ.* Mueller reports his inability to find *fame* used in any other way than as an iambus before Luxorius and Corippus (in *Johannis* 6.308); see Commentary, note to 28.3. He adds that even in their time *famĕ* was considered a solecism.[83]

16.11. *chĭrurge.* See below, entry for 23.6, and above, this chapter, A 3 (3).

20.5. *altĕrĭus.* See above, entry for 10.4.

23.6. *chĭrurge.* See above, entry for 16.11.

23.14. *lŭgubrem.* See above, this chapter, A 9.

24.4. *ipsĭus.* See above, entry for 10.4.

28.7. *quĕsumus.* The *e*, although it replaces *ae*, must be considered short to fit the meter. In 39.3 *cedis* is written for *caedis*, but the *e* is properly long there. However, a diphthong was sometimes shortener by poets.[84] Cf. 21R.235, *pĕnitudo,* and 205R.6, *obscĕnitas.*

28.8. *vĭvis.* Elsewhere Luxorius shows that he knew that the *i* is long: e.g., *vīvus,* 23.8, *vīvere,* 32.4, *vīvas,* 32.6.

32.6. *vivăs.* *Vivas* is the reading of A, *vivus* of a, better for the meter but not for the sense. Baehrens emends to *vivas antipodas,* remarking that *vivăs* "nec apud Luxorium ferendum."[85] Elsewhere, Luxorius considered the *a* of the *-as* subjunctive ending long, as in *vincās,* 37.7. If he did write *vivăs* here, perhaps he did this by analogy with *quamvĭs,* 7.1. Mueller declares that *as* is never shortened "in Latinis."[86] However, in 382R.3, *reddas* must have a short *a* to scan, and there is no doubt about the text:

> Viribus ut propriis mollem tu reddăs, ab alvo.

36.3. *cŏiugis.* See above, A 7, and entry for 12.7.

40.6. *dĕtur.* The *e* is shortened, although it bears the accent, a disregard of quantity to fit the word in. Cf. above, B 1, entry for 54.2. Dracontius treats this word in the same way in *Romulea* 8.314, and 9.226.

54.2. *negŏtii.* See entry for this word above, B 1, 54.2.

---

[82] *Ibid.,* p. 288.

[83] *Ibid.,* p. 480. Kuehner, *Grammatik,* I, 486, § 1098, finds it is always *famē* in the classical poets.

[84] Mueller, *De Re Metrica,* p. 445.

[85] Baehrens, *PLM,* IV, 401.

[86] Mueller, *De Re Metrica,* pp. 423-24.

59.8. *verĕcundo*. Mueller observes that the Christian (that is, late) poets occasionally shortened an *e* when it was not in the penult and when it was followed by a long syllable.[87]

71.8. *cuĭ*. The complete line is:

Cui dedit plures docta libido.

If the *i* is long, the first foot of this anapaestic verse would be a cretic. Riese returns to his refrain, "Neglegens." However, Mueller reports a number of examples in which *cui* is a monosyllable with a short *i*.[88]

73.8. *cătis*. See below, Commentary, note on this word.

75.2. *libĭdo*. Libido is the reading of A, emended by Burmann to *libitum*, which has been accepted by Riese and Baehrens. *Libitum* is more appropriate to the meter and sense. If Luxorius wrote *libĭdo*, he shortened a syllable bearing the accent, as he did elsewhere; see above, entry for 40.6,

On possible changes in *deductos*, 1.6; *liber*, 46.6; *praecedis*, 50.1; *possis*, 50.4; and *ponendus*, 50.5, see above, end of A 3, this chapter.

3. FINAL *o*

The final *o* of many words had been shortened by poets long before Luxorius wrote.[89] For example, the final *o* of the adverb *modo*, originally long, was shortened by Plautus, the Augustan poets, and Seneca. *Egŏ* is invariably found in classical poetry. Likewise, the final *o* of the present indicative active, future, and future perfect, and of the future imperative was shortened. The final *o* of the ablative of the gerund became *ŏ*, especially after Seneca.

Luxorius occasionally exhibits this tendency to shorten the final *o*, although not to the extent of Dracontius, who did this twenty-six times in a single book while keeping the long *o* only four times.[90] Florentinus, a poet of the *Anthologia Latina*, felt free to alternate between

[87] *Ibid.*, p. 455.

[88] *Ibid.*, p. 319; cf. Klapp, *Quaestiones*, p. ii, who says that *cui* cannot fit the verse as a long monosyllable or as a disyllable, but that Luxorius wanted to use it with a short *i*.

[89] Kuehner, I, 112-13, § 15.8-9; W. M. Lindsay, *Latin Language*, p. 422; Mueller, *De Re Metrica*, pp. 34-36; Platnauer, *Latin Elegiac Verse*, pp. 50-53; Strecker, *Medieval Latin*, p. 72; see also Haskins, *Lucani Pharsalia*, p. ci, § 49h, for examples in Lucan.

[90] Irwin, *De Laudibus Dei*, pp. 102-3; Saint Margaret, *Satisfactio*, p. 103, reports fourteen examples in the *Satisfactio*.

Carthagō and *Carthagŏ,* sometimes in the same line, to meet the demands of the hexameter:

> Carthagō regimen; victrix Carthagŏ triumphat (376R.29)

and

> Carthagō populis pollet, Carthagŏ refulget (376R.33).

Luxorius keep the *o* of *Carthago* short (68.14).

An alphabetical list of the words in which Luxorius shortened the final *o* follows (for proper names ending in *o,* see below, "4. Proper Names":

arando: 60.3. The four gerunds used by Luxorius in the ablative all end in *ŏ*.

ergo: 21.6; 23.13; 38.7; 56.5. Cf. Ovid, *Heroides* 5.59, and *Tristia* 1.1.87.

homo: 79.3; 84.4. Cf. Ovid, *Ibis* 408.

meditando: 65.12.

modo: 33.3. Cf. *modō,* 49.3.

nemo: 53.7; 56.7; 59.6. Cf. Ovid, *Amores* 1.8.43, *Tristia* 1.9.44, and *Fasti* 6.324.

nescio: 28.2; 35.5; 81.5. Cf. *sciŏ,* Ovid, *Tristia* 5.4.46.

puto: 1.8; 9.11; 13.9; 37.7; 80.1; 83.7. Ovid has 24 cases of *putŏ*.

referto: 26.2. Cf. *datō,* 1.14. Ovid also varies the quantity of the *o* in the future imperative: e.g., *estŏ, Tristia* 4.3.72, but *estō, Heroides* 20.66.

rixando: 52.3, a necessary emendation.

sculpendo: 45.6.

4. PROPER NAMES

The problem of fitting proper names into fixed metrical patterns troubled greater Latin poets than Luxorius. For example, any school text of Vergil calls attention to his treatment not only of Greek names but also of Roman names.[91] It is obvious that some names could not be used in verse unless the poet took liberties with them. It is possible also that in Luxorius' time the pronunciation of some names that he used was not fixed. Therefore, it is not to be wondered at that Luxorius

[91] See, for example, Charles Knapp, *The Aeneid of Vergil* (Chicago, 1923), p. 80, § 251: *Dīana (Aeneid* 1.499), *Dĭana (Aeneid* 11.582); *Lāvina (Aeneid* 1.2), *Lăvini (Aeneid* 1.258); *Sȳchaeus (Aeneid* 1.343), *Sȳchaeus (Aeneid* 1.348).

allowed himself the same freedom in the metrical treatment of proper names that other poets had used before his day.

(Except in the name *Fridamal,* a macron over a vowel in the list of names below indicates that the quantity of the vowel so marked was changed from short to long; a breve denotes the opposite.)

11.5. *Lŭcine*: Only a possibility; see above, A 3 (2).

18.14. *Frĭdamal*: Must be a dactyl here, but see the next entry.

19.1. *Frĭdămāl*: Must have these quantities here to scan as the end of the second half of an iambelegus.

20.1. *Cȳriāce*: See below, Commentary, note on 20.1.

24.1. *Macedōnia.* Ovid, on the other hand, lengthened the *e*: *Metamorphoses* 12.466:[92]

> Qui clipeo gladioque Macĕdoniaque sarisa.

30.2. *Zenōbi*: *Zenobia,* the name of the celebrated queen of Palmyra, although pronounced *Zenōbia* in English, has an omicron in Greek and a short *o* in Latin.[93]

65.1. *Sōlon*: The remarks on arsis and accent might apply here; see above, B 1, entries for 1.9 and 17.1.

65.7. *Thāles*: See above, entry for 65.1.

65.9. *Bīas*: According to Mueller, short vowels followed by a vowel in a Greek word are sometimes lengthened by Christian (that is, late Latin) poets, a license that even the Greeks allowed themselves in the Golden Age.[94] However, see above, entries for 65.1 and 65.7.

65.11. *Perīander*: See above, entry for 65.9.

65.13. *Clēobŏlus*: Luxorius here shifts two quantities, as he did in *Cyriace,* 20.1, above; and in *negotii,* 54.2 (see above, entries for this word, B 1, B 2). Commenting on the changes of quantity in this word, Riese, as if speechless with horror, forgets to refer the reader to page 247 of his edition but can only exclaim, "*Luxorius!*" Why was he so shocked? Other poets had also changed quantities in names, if the exigencies of the meter so demanded. Calmer and more rational about such changes, Mueller merely emends to *Cleubulus* and cites similar changes in other words of Greek provenance made

---

[92] See Mueller, *De Re Metrica,* p. 437, on this change; also pp 418, 487-89, on names in Latin poetry.

[93] See H. Wuilleumier, "Étude historique sur l'emploi et la signification des signa," *MPAI,* XIII (1933), 568, on Ζηνόβιος.

[94] Mueller, *De Re Metrica,* p. 289.

out of metrical necessity "et apud nostros Latinos," e.g., Ovid, *Ibis*
466, *Theudotum*.[95] However, the reading *Cleobulus* can be retained,
for it is consonant with other liberties taken by Luxorius; and, when
a name like *Cleobulus* is involved, some freedom may be granted
to the poet. If he did write *Cleubulus,* the change of *u* to *o* would
be due to a scribe's idiosyncrasy (see below, Chapter IX, C 3).

72.10. *Catō*: Here Luxorius breaks away from the trend to final *ŏ*
which he followed elsewhere.[96]

81.2. *Phrygĭūs*: Listed again because it is a proper adjective. See above,
B 1, entry for this word.

88.1. *Dīogenem*: Change necessary, since this name begins a dactylic
hexameter. Cf. entry for *Cleobulus*, 65.13, above.

C. An Estimate of Luxorius' Metrical Qualities

Now it is possible to frame a reply to the question asked earlier in
this chapter: Careless or correct, which was Luxorius? It is obvious
after this detailed examination of Luxorius' meters and prosody that
he is not a polished craftsman. However, one may also conclude that
his alleged metrical defects were not due to ignorance. Little fault can
be found with his technical knowledge of the many meters that he used.
A poet who could put together the meters used by Luxorius in Poem 19,
for example, without committing any mechanical errors, is not to be
judged ignorant of the demands of Latin verse structure.

For the most part Luxorius adheres to the classical rules of meter.
Mueller points out some failings in his verse, but on the other hand
he includes him many times in lists of poets who refrained from taking
certain liberties. In the matter of pentameter endings, for example,
Mueller says of Luxorius and Maximianus that they come quite close
to the principles of the best poets.[97]

In reference to the vowel changes made by late poets, Mueller asserts
that these poets often hoped to find a ready pardon for their trans-
gressions, for they were most likely to find readers and listeners whose

---

[95] *Ibid.,* p. 316.

[96] *TLL, Onomasticon* II, 266, quotes Censorinus (grammarian, third century A.D.),
13.2, to the effect that *Cato* is a pyrrhic of two short syllables, but that the *o* is long at
the caesura in Vergil, *Aeneid* 6.841. However, it is *Catŏ* in Juvenal, 2.40, and in Lucan,
Pharsalia 2.247, 285; 3.164; 9.166, 221, 227, 250, 734, 761.

[97] Mueller, *De Re Metrica,* pp. 256, 260, 262, 264, 272, 342, 351, 360, 362, 363, 395.

ears were not keenly attuned to differences in vowel quantities.[98] Luxorius must be set against the background of his era and his audience. What has been said earlier about the language of Luxorius also applies to his metrics. Just as authors who preserved the feeling of classical modes of expression "did not shy away from using colloquial expressions in order to be understood," [99] so poets became less strict in their use of quantities and broke away from the more rigid rules of an earlier period.

Surely Luxorius knew what the quantities were as used by the classical poets, especially Vergil, whose poems he may have known practically by heart. Luxorius may have a false quantity in a word in one poem but he shows by his use of the correct quantity in another poem that he was not totally ignorant of the classical pronunciation of the word. Moreover, a glance at the list of changes reveals that very few such changes were made by Luxorius alone. Much greater poets, including some masters of the Golden Age, exercised similar freedom.

The answer to the questions about Luxorius' faultiness as a poet involves a matter of degree. Luxorius is not to be regarded as absolutely and utterly careless. He did not violate the rules of quantity with almost total abandon; he merely took a few liberties too many. Whether he acted pardonably because he obeyed the laws of metrical necessity or because he yielded to the trends of his time, it may still be argued that an excess of license is a perversion of metrical standards. A more resourceful poet, a more skilled workman might have rearranged the line or found the correct word to fit the meter, or he might have expressed his ideas in some other way.

One of the features of Luxorius' technique is the paradox. He himself is a literary paradox—a classicist in many respects, but also a phenomenon reflecting his own times. He modeled himself upon classical authors, but he could not or would not write in pure, classical Latin, probably agreeing with another poet of the Vandal age that it was difficult to write good verse amid the carousals of barbarians.[100]

---

[98] *Ibid.*, p. 441, "Sane facilem veniam delictorum licuit sperari eis, qui haud dubie nacturi essent auditores lectoresve ipsis multo minus suptiles ad mensuras verborum." See above, Chs. I, n. 85, and II, n. 32.

[99] Strecker, *Medieval Latin*, p. 30. See above, Ch. IV, D 4.

[100] See Poem 285R, *De conviviis barbaris*, cited above, Ch. II, n. 6.

IX. TEXTUAL TRADITION

A. The Codex Salmasianus

No separate manuscript of the poems of Luxorius is known to exist. They are included in manuscripts containing other material, and in only one of them are all his extant poems found. This is the Codex Salmasianus, Parisinus 10318, now in the Bibliothèque Nationale, Paris.[1] (See Pl. I.)

It consists of 290 large quarto parchment pages; the size of most of them is 320 × 245 mm., or about 12.6 × 9.6 inches. The smaller pages measure 230-245 × 190 mm., or about 9.5-9.6 × 7.5 inches. The first eleven quaternions are missing. The script is uncial; there are generally 29 lines on a page—pages 33-48 and 81-84 have 28. The titles are written in mixed angular red capitals; the initials are formed with a plait motif, fishes, and reptiles' heads in green, yellow, and red. The first letter of each second line is also in red.

This manuscript was written in the late seventh or early eighth century. Riese believes that it is in the handwriting of a single scribe, but Lowe thinks it is in the work of several scribes with a similar handwriting.[2] The place where it was written is unknown (possibly Italy or France, or even Spain), nor is its whereabouts known from the time when it was written until it became public in the seventeenth century. In 1615 Jean Lacurne, bailiff of Arnai le Duc, presented it to the renowned scholar Claude Saumaise (Salmasius), who allowed scholars to use it. How and where Lacurne came across it is a mystery. Upon

---

[1] For descriptions and the history of this manuscript, see Baehrens, *PLM*, IV, 4-8; Burmann, *Anthologia*, I, xlvi-lvi; Lowe, *Codices Latini*, V, 22, No. 593, reproduction of page 262 of the manuscript; Omont, *Anthologie*, pp. 1-8; Riese, *Anthologia*, I, xii-xiv, xviii-xxv. All the 290 pages of the manuscript are reproduced in a reduced facsimile in Omont, where page 137 is also reproduced full size; page 246 of the manuscript is given in full-sized reproduction in Zangemeister and Wattenbach, *Exempla codicum*, Pl. 46. I have inspected the original in Paris.

[2] Lowe, *Codices Latini*, V, 22; Riese, *Anthologia*, I, xiii.

Saumaise's death in 1653 his eldest son, also named Claude, inherited the manuscript. After his death, in 1661, the Codex passed into the possession of some citizens of Dijon, and eventually, between 1744 and 1756, reached the Bibliothèque Royale, now the Bibliothèque Nationale.

The Codex Salmasianus contains the complete corpus of the poems of Luxorius. His name is found in the superscriptions of poems 1L and 91L; the attribution of poem 90L is based on two other manuscripts, Parisinus 8071 and Vossianus Q.86.[3]

Riese assigned the siglum A to the Codex Salmasianus.[4] On the pages of the manuscript itself there are two sets of major emendations, one in what is presumably the handwriting of the original scribe, based on the codex from which he was copying, the other set by Saumaise himself. Riese's sigla for these are A^1 and a, respectively. There are also corrections by others.

The archetype is presumed to have been made in 532-34, as has been noted above, and to have reached Europe from Africa shortly thereafter.[5] If, however, the archetype did not cross over so early or actually never came to Europe, a copy of the complete original collection or of parts of it must have been in Europe in the seventh or eighth century, available to the scribe of the Salmasian codex.

Birt feels that the Codex Salmasianus is not a true copy of the archetype, but that the *Anthologia Latina*, as we have it, consists of two main parts: an original collection of epigrams, and poems like 7R-18R, 21R, 83R, 198R-200R, and 253R, which are of different genres from the other poems. The present *Anthologia*, he thinks, belongs to a later period, possibly to the time of the Codex Salmasianus itself.[6]

The internal evidence must be weighed to decide on the basis of probability whether the Codex Salmasianus is a true copy of an archetype which we do not possess. The Codex Salmasianus contains some passages in prose as well as poems. Poem 379R is on page 188 of the manuscript; pages 189-95 are devoted almost entirely to a work on the calendar and tables by Bishop Dionysus, but Poems 382R and 383R

---

[3] See above, Ch. IV, 1-3.

[4] Riese's sigla are used in this book; for others of major importance, see table at the end of this chapter.

[5] Baehrens, *PLM*, IV, 3-4; see also above, Ch. II.

[6] Birt, *Das Antike Buchwesen*, p. 387.

are strangely placed at the bottom of pages 192 and 193, respectively. Pages 196-273 are all in prose. Poems 383R-388R, which end the African portion of the *Anthologia Latina*, begin at the bottom of page 273 and continue for another page. Pages 275-90, all in prose, are misplaced between pages 266-67 of the manuscript.

If the compilation made in Carthage consisted only of poetry, somewhere and at some time somebody added prose pieces. The arrangement of the poems referred to in the previous paragraph seems haphazard; it is odd to find a poem placed at the bottom of a page containing a work in prose that continues on to the next page. It does not seem that the Codex Salmasianus is a true copy of the archetype.[7] It is also possible that only the African poems were contained in the archetype. Many other poems might have been added by copyists; there is no direct testimony concerning which poems were put into the collection made in Carthage. New discoveries of manuscripts or papyri are needed to settle the problem definitely.[8]

Soon after Saumaise disclosed his acquisition to scholars, handwritten copies were made of parts of the Codex Salmasianus, sometimes by the scholars themselves, who wrote notes in them and made useful emendations. Copies valuable for the study of Luxorius are:

1. Catalectorum et epigrammatum veterum schedae Salmasianae N. Heinsii manu scriptae, made between 1631 and 1649 by Nicholas Heynse (Heinsius). This is one of a collection of various copies forming a single fasciculus of 267 pages now called Heidelberg 46. These copies, which Burmann used, were bought by the University of Heidelberg in 1867 at the request of Riese, who used Heynse's copy. It contains Poems 1L-89L and 91L. In the margin Heynse added emendations by Saumaise, and Burmann wrote material taken from the Codices Leidenses (Voss. O. 16 and Voss. O. 63).[9]

2. Schedae Divionenses, another part of Heid. 46, also listed as Epigrammata antiqua ex Codice Divionensi descripta. This manuscript, copied between 1651 and 1756 from a copy of the Codex Salmasianus, contains 82 poems by Luxorius and many valuable emendations by an

---

[7] Baehrens, *PLM*, IV, 3-4, and Riese, *Anthologia*, I, xlv, think that the Codex Salmasianus was copied from a copy of the archetype.

[8] Baehrens, who did not hesitate to offer dogmatically and most assuredly conjectures as incontrovertible facts, nevertheless humbly expresses the hope that the future will bring to light new material and that others after him will carry on the work (*PLM*, IV, 52).

[9] Riese, *Anthologia*, I, xv-xvi, n. 2. I have inspected a microfilm of this collection.

unknown scholar. Burmann often used the Schedae in preference to the Codex itself.[10] The nine poems by Luxorius missing from the Schedae are 10L, 49L, 60L-63L, 78L, 90L, 91L. Riese's siglum for the Schedae is α.

3. Vossianus O. 16 (one of the Codices Leidenses), now in the Library of the Royal University (Bibliotheek der Rijks-Universiteit te Leiden). It contains poems 1L-89L and emendations made by Saumaise in the Codex Salmasianus.[11]

4. Vossianus O. 63 (another of the Codices Leidenses). It is in the handwriting of Isaac Voss (1618-89) and contains only the cento, Poem 91L.

5. Codex Guelferbytanus, Gudianus 187, in the Library of Duke August (Herzog August Bibliothek), now a public library, Wolfenbüttel, Brunswick, Germany. This copy was made by Marquard Gude (1635-89), a collector of manuscripts, who wrote in the lower left-hand corner of folio 1: "Ex Msto Cod. vetutissimo Philiberti de la Mare Senatoris Divionensis." In it are all the poems of Luxorius except the cento and 90L.[12]

---

[10] Mueller, "Sammelsurien," *NJbb*, XCV (1867, Part 1), 801-2; Riese, *Anthologia*, I, xii, n. 1; xvi, n. 2; xxxii; and "Zur lateinischen Anthologie," *NJbb*, XCVII (1868), 698. I have received additional information in personal communications from Dr. E. Jammers, November 9, 1956, and from Mlle Jeanne Vielliard, January 24, 1957, and March 4, 1957. (See acknowledgments in the Preface, above, for the identification of correspondents referred to in the notes to this chapter.)

[11] On 3 and 4, see Riese, *Anthologia*, I, xii, n. 1. Further information on these was supplied to me in personal communications by K. A. de Meyïer, August 10, 1956, and February 27, 1957. On p. xvi, n. 2, Riese refers to "cod. Voss. oct. 15"; this is an obvious misprint. The correct number is 16; see Riese, *Anthologia* (1869 ed.), I, xvi, n. 10. The punctuation of line 1, n. 2, p. xvi (1894 ed.) is misleading—a parenthesis should follow *addidit* to show that Burmann added only poems 99-106, not 107-198, to Heynse's copy. Riese also says that Burmann copied poems 83R-89R and others "cod. Vossiano," which Heynse followed in writing 277R-285R and 287R-379R. Riese does not give the number of this codex; the assumption is that he is still talking about Voss O. 16. There is some discrepancy here, for Voss O. 16 does not contain 88R or 277R-285R.

On p. xxxv, n. 1, Riese refers to Voss. Oct. 15 as a manuscript of the thirteenth century. Some confusion exists here, also. Voss. Gr. Oct. 15 contains, imbedded among material from Greek authors, some poems of the *Anthologia*, but this manuscript is entirely in the handwriting of Voss himself. There is no Leiden manuscript Voss. Oct. 15 belonging to the thirteenth century and containing poems from the *Anthologia Latina*. Voss. Lat. Oct. 15 contains one folio of the thirteenth century, notes on the history of Limoges by Bernardus Iterius, librarian of St. Martialis, Limoges, 1221. The rest of the manuscript dates from the tenth and eleventh centuries, and does contain a few poems from the *Anthologia Latina*. Riese must have confused these manuscripts or been misinformed, he admits he did not use Oct. 15. A description of Voss. Gr. Oct. 15 by K. A. de Meyïer is found in "Codices Vossiani Graeci et Miscellanei,' in *Codices Manuscripti* (Bibliotheca Universitatis Leidensis), VI (Leiden, 1955), 215 ff.

[12] Riese, *Anthologia*, I, xii, n. 1. He is in error when he says that it contains only about

6. Parisinus 17904, the oldest copy, made by François Juret (1553-1626), now in the Bibliothèque Nationale, Paris, formerly in the library of Jean Bouhier (1673-1746). Folio 1 bears the title "Epigrammata latina vetera, inedita, Fr. Jureti manu exscripta," and also contains a charming paragraph giving its provenance and its history until its purchase in 1708. It contains only four poems by Luxorius, 1L, 2L, 90L, 91L, and the title of 3L. For many of the other poems Juret merely refers his readers to the collections of Pithou and Scaliger.[13]

B. *Other Manuscripts*

A few of Luxorius' poems are found in the following manuscripts:

1. Parisinus 8071, formerly Codex Thuaneus, now in the Bibliothèque Nationale, Paris. It dates from the end of the ninth or the beginning of the tenth century and contains five poems by Luxorius: Nos. 10, 17, 24, 32, and 90.[14] Riese gives it the siglum B.

2. Codex Vossianus Q. 86 (another of the Codices Leidenses), first half of the ninth century, now in Leiden. It contains four poems by Luxorius: Nos. 10, 17, 32, and 90.[15] Riese assigns to it the siglum V.

3. Codex Parisinus 8069, tenth or eleventh century, now in Paris. It contains only one poem by Luxorius, No. 65, which appears twice.[16] Riese's siglum for it is C.

Still another manuscript, whose age and present whereabouts are unknown, seems to have contained some poems by Luxorius. This manuscript is called Codex Bellovacensis, for it is presumed to have been in the library of Beauvais Cathedral. Its former existence is deduced from a reference to it in the preface of a collection of poems of Petronius and of epigrams which was compiled by Claude Binet and printed at Poitiers in 1579. Binet mentions that he took a good part of the selections from the library of the cathedral of Beauvais. One copy of this rare book is now in Heidelberg; two others are in Paris

sixty poems of Luxorius. See also von Heinemann, *Die Handschriften*, IX, 184, No. 4491. Riese believes that de la Mare did not own the codex but that J. B. Lantin did. I am indebted to Dr. Erhart Kästner for information on the inscription (letter of July 7, 1956), and have also seen it in a photostat of the manuscript.

[13] Information from letters of Mlle Marie-Thérèse d'Alverny, November 3, 1956, and Mlle J. Vielliard, November 14, 1956. Claude Lantin (1661-1756), son of J. B. Lantin mentioned in n. 12 above, is named in the charming paragraph.

[14] Baehrens, *PLM*, IV, 9; Riese, *Anthologia*, I, xxxiv-xxxvii.

[15] Baehrens, *PLM*, IV, 11-12; Riese, *Anthologia*, I, xxxvii-xli.

[16] Baehrens, *PLM*, IV, 17-19; Riese, *Anthologia*, I, xli-xlii.

(listed by the Bibliothèque Nationale as YC 922 and Réserve M.YC 656). Poems 60L-63L and 78L are contained in Binet's collection. Riese's siglum for the lost manuscript is S.[17]

C. A Comparison of the Manuscripts

1. Manuscripts B, V, and C, and Binet's book contain only eleven different poems of Luxorius in fifteen entries.[18] Pithou and Voss used V and C, whose readings they occasionally emended, and later editors have profited by their suggestions.[19] Moreover, these two manuscripts supply the name of Luxorius, missing in A, as the author of poem 90L.[20] However, the chief value of B, V, C, and of the evidence of S in Binet's collection is their relation to the rest of the *Anthologia Latina*: the reconstruction of parts missing in A and the establishment of the text of many poems in it. This last manuscript is indispensable for a study of Luxorius. If all the other manuscripts mentioned above did not exist, the loss would have slight bearing on Luxorian scholarship, but if A had not been brought to light, there would be little to write about Luxorius on the basis of what there is of his poems in other manuscripts.

2. Between the assumed date of the compilation of the *Anthologia Latina*, A.D. 532-34, and the probable date of A, seventh or early eighth century, the text became more and more corrupt in the course of successive copying and recopying. Copious emendations were required; much work in that respect still remains.[21] We have no way of knowing whether any of Luxorius' poems were omitted, but three lines (4.1; 47.14; 66.2) have definitely dropped out.

3. The spelling in A is not uniform; certain letters, such as *i* and *e*, *o* and *u*, *b* and *v*, etc., are often interchanged.[22] *F* is almost always

---

[17] For a description of this book, see Baehrens, *PLM*, IV, pp. 13-14; Riese, *Anthologia*, I, xxxiii-xxxiv; and see below, C 1.

[18] Another manuscript, not related to the Codex Salmasianus, is reported by Baehrens, *PLM*, IV, 24, and Riese, *Anthologia*, I, xlii. This is Casanatensis B. IV 18, ninth century, in the Dominican Convent of Santa Maria sopra Minerva, Rome. Poems 224R, 232R, and 318R (32L) are written in the margin of folio 74, but the text of the poem by Luxorius is almost entirely faded.

[19] Riese, *Anthologia*, I, xxxv-xxxvii.

[20] See above, Ch. IV, 1-3.

[21] Levy, in *RE*, XIII.2, 2109, "Für die Emendation und Einzelklärung bleibt noch sehr viel zu tun."

[22] For a detailed study of such changes, see Riese, *Anthologia*, I, xlii-xlv.

used for *ph,* as in *faretris, epitafion,* etc.[23] In his text Riese is inconsistent, keeping *elefans* (15.5; 58.2; 67.11), *fialas* (17.4), and *sarcofagus* (34.7), but changing to *sarcophago* (33.T) and writing all other words of this kind with *ph* where A has *f.* F appears in African inscriptions for *ph,* and it is possible to argue that using *f* for *ph* preserves the flavor of the linguistic background of the original anthology and of the Codex Salmasianus. But this produces results that look outlandish to our eyes: *Zefyri, Saficum, Flegethon,* etc. Therefore, in my text *ph,* not *f,* is uniformly used in words like *sarcophagus.*

4. However, in another instance it is possible to retain the peculiarity of the scribe or scribes who inconsistently did not assimilate the final *n* of the prefix *in* in some words but did change it in others. So, we find *inplere* (11.T) but also *impleret* (54.2) and *implet* (55.5). Here the practice of the scribes may be followed. Not much is gained by uniformity, for some modern editors of other authors use *in-,* others, *im-.*

5. A belongs to one family of manuscripts; B and V to another.[24] S, the lost manuscript, does not appear to have belonged to either of these two families, according to Riese. Baehrens believes, however, that if we did have a copy of S, we could show by more definite proofs than the few paltry ones we now possess that it had a kinship with ABV. C is not connected with ABV.

6. B and V are not twins, but were copied from two different manuscripts.[25] Each of the latter was a copy of a collection of excerpts made from the original anthology. Riese calls the manuscript from which a scribe copied the Codex Salmasianus, A[1]. This in turn had been copied from X, a copy of the original compilation.

7. On the other hand, Baehrens believes that the many manuscripts containing parts of the *Anthologia Latina* were once closely related, that they are descended either from the same parent as A or from a twin of A. In his opinion, B has the same parent as A.

8. To round out the study of the manuscripts containing the

---

[23] See Mueller, *De Re Metrica,* p. 593. The scribe was inconsistent, writing *limphis* in 124R.1, using *ph* and *f* in the same word, *philosoforum,* 65.T, but two *f*'s in *filosofum,* 72.T, and alternating between *f* and *p* in two words on the same line; *anfiteatrali* and *triumpho,* 68.11.

[24] On the relationship of the various manuscripts, see Baehrens, *PLM,* IV, 4-5, 8-9, 14; Riese, *Anthologia,* I, xiii, xxxviii, xlii.

[25] Riese, *Anthologia,* I, xxiii, "duae codicum familiae ortae sunt." Riese's stemma for X, A[1], A, B, and V appears in I, xlv of his 1869 edition but is omitted in the 1894 edition.

writings of Luxorius, there remain those in which the fragments of Lisorius are found. These manuscripts are listed below, Appendix V, A-E.

D. Editions

Hitherto there has been no separate edition of the poems of Luxorius. They are all found, however, in each of four large anthologies.

1. The *editio princeps* of a complete Luxorius forms part of a collection made by Peter Burmann (Burman in Dutch) the Younger or Petrus Burmannus Secundus (1714-78), nephew of the renowned scholar Peter Burmann the Elder. The younger Burmann was a professor and head of the public library in Amsterdam. He edited Aristophanes, Vergil, Propertius, and Claudian, and compiled an anthology in two volumes, the huge work in which the poems of Luxorius are included.

This was published in Amsterdam by Schouten (Officina Schouteniana), Volume I appearing in 1759 and Volume II in 1773. Its full title is *Anthologia Veterum Latinorum Epigrammatum et Poematum sive Catalecta Poetarum Latinorum in VI Libros Digesta.* Book VI contains *Priapeia* and most of the poems of Luxorius; the rest of his poems are scattered throughout the other five books, where they either are attributed to Petronius or remain anonymous.[26]

Burmann's anthology is based on collections made by some of his great predecessors, notably Joseph Justus Scaliger, Claude Binet, and Pierre Pithou (Petrus Pithoeus), who are named here chiefly *honoris causa,* for they included little or nothing by Luxorius, since they did not know A. Scaliger (1540-1609) did know V, which contains four poems by Luxorius.[27] However, he did not put these into his *Catalecta Poematia,* first published in a book containing the *Appendix Vergiliana* in 1573 at Lyon, and reprinted in 1596 and 1617 at Leiden. Pithou (1539-96) enlarged Scaliger's work and included the four poems by Luxorius found in V in his *Epigrammata et Poematia Vetera,* published in Paris in 1590, in Lyon in 1596, and in Geneva in 1619. In 1579 Binet included five poems by Luxorius in his collection *Petronii Arbitri itemque veterum Epigrammata hactenus non Edita Cl. Binetus con-*

---

[26] See below, Collation, Appendix I, for the order of the poems in the different editions.
[27] Riese, *Anthologia,* I, xiv, n. 2, xl.

quisivit et nunc primum publicavit, presumably taking them from the lost manuscript S.[28] This is apparently the first appearance in print of any poem of Luxorius.

Burmann enlarged the work of his predecessors, including poems from all sources, sometimes without regard for their dates of composition. He relied heavily upon the Schedae Divionenses and the Codices Leidenses. His notes—in Latin, of course—are remarkable for their wealth of literary parallels and for his exploration of geographical, historical, botanical, and zoological material. He called upon other scholars for occasional commentary, especially the amazing Gerhard Meerman of Leiden (1722-71), diplomat, politician, traveler, author, and collector of manuscripts, whose long notes amounting to miniature essays enliven parts of Burmann's volumes.[29]

Burmann concerned himself greatly with variant readings and did not hesitate to make suggestions and emendations. However, he did not often try to clarify the poet's ideas or to explain the meaning of a difficult passage. Possibly he felt that his contemporaries understood Luxorius as well as he did, and that they needed no such aids. Nevertheless, he annotated much more amply than did his successors.

2. The next anthology containing all the poems of Luxorius was compiled by Heinrich Meyer and published in two volumes by Gerhard Fleischer in Leipzig in 1835 under the title *Anthologia Veterum Latinorum Epigrammatum et Poematum.* It is a reworking of Burmann, as admitted on the title page: *Editionem Burmannianam Digessit et Auxit Henricus Meyerus.* In his introduction Meyer wrote that Burmann had so perfected the *Anthologia Latina* that a future editor would have to be concerned not so much with increasing its contents as with putting them into better order and excluding poems that were not ancient enough.

In general, Meyer follows Burmann's arrangement of the poems of Luxorius. In both collections three poems (37R, 80R, and 90R) preface the main body of Luxorius' poems. Meyer, but nor Burmann, says that these three are by Luxorius. Both compilers place the cento (91L),

---

[28] Riese, *Anthologia,* I, xxxiii-xxxiv.

[29] Meerman, like Gude, is neglected by modern encyclopedists, but these scholars received full treatment in older books like *Biographie universelle, ancienne et moderne,* ed. by J. F. and L. G. Michaud (53 vols., Paris, 1811-1862). They were polymaths and polyglots, men of action as well as scholars, equally at home in the turmoil of public life, the acquisition of private gain, and the supposed seclusion of the study. Meerman compiled thesauri, and wrote on the Vandals, travel, printing, antiquarianism, and the law.

which is separated in A from the other poems of Luxorius, together with them at the end. Six other poems (10L, 60L-63L, and 89L), which form part of the 89 poems of Luxorius arranged as a consecutive group in A, are detached and scattered by Burmann and Meyer. They do not attribute these poems to Luxorius, although they mention him in the notes to a few of these six poems. Otherwise, they name Petronius as the author of some of them and give no author for the others.

Meyer's edition is less detailed and less ponderous than Burmann's. His notes, written in Latin with occasional lapses into German, are meager; many of the poems are not annotated at all. His comments vary in quality from good to poor, mistaken, and naive. At times he explains the obvious, as in his note on *priscorum* (42L.2) in Vol. I, 129 (second section, Poem 339 of his edition), "priscorum aurigarum similis." Sometimes he reveals ignorance or a *lapsus memoriae,* as in his note on *mitellam* (12L.3) in Vol. I, 126 (as above, Poem 309), "mitella sive mitra est tegumentum capitis virginum deo sacratarum atque pontificum" (*mitella* or *mitra* is the headdress of virgins consecrated to a god and of priests). This may be, but had Meyer forgotten:

> Copa Surisca, caput Graeca redimita mitella?

The Syrian hostess of a tavern with her head wrapped in a Greek turban was no virgin or maid dedicated to the service of the gods.

Meyer was severely castigated by Conrads a century ago:[30]

Qui cum nullo nomine Burmanno superior esset, in multis ei inferior, spernanda asciscendis antetulit non semel, nonnulla felicissime emendavit, multa imperite mutavit, plurima inutiliter aut perperam coniecit vel potius iecit, non nisi levissima explevit, perplexa et obscura vel non intellegere se fassus est vel corrupta iudicavit, permulta quae explicatione non egerent, curiose interpretatus est quin etiam interdum falso.

Although he was in no respect superior to Burmann, and in many ways inferior to him, more than once he preferred readings that should have been rejected to those that should have been allowed. He made some very felicitous emendations but he ignorantly made many changes. He tossed forth an extremely large number of useless and erroneous conjectures—or rather, he merely tossed words about. He either admitted that he did not understand difficult and obscure points, or he judged the text involved to be corrupt. He assiduously—wrongly at times, I should rather say—explained many things that appeared to need no explanation.

[30] Conrads, *In Anthologiae Latinae Librum IV,* p. 4.

Credit is properly given to Meyer for some of his emendations, which are truly felicitous. However, it is no sin to confess that one cannot understand what is dark and difficult or to decide that a text is corrupt, for how can one explain the unexplainable?

3. The third anthology containing the full text of the poems of Luxorius was compiled by Alexander Riese, and is entitled *Anthologia Latina sive Poesis Latinae Supplementum*.[31] The first edition and all subsequent printings, revisions, and additions bear the imprint of Teubner in Leipzig. Part I consists of two fasciculi; the first was published in 1869, the second in 1870. In the first are found the poems of the Codex Salmasianus and related manuscripts; in the second, poems from other manuscripts. In 1894 a new and revised edition of Part I was published, in which Riese enlarged his introduction, made some textual changes, and corrected the *apparatus criticus*.[32]

Discarding the somewhat confusing arrangement of Burmann and Meyer, Riese arranged the poems in his text to conform with their positions in the manuscripts.[33] He threw out poems that in his judgment had been written too late to be part of the *Anthologia Latina*. In this way he fulfilled the duties foreseen by Meyer for future editors.

Riese's introductions (in Latin) are thorough and valuable, reviewing the work of his predecessors and describing the various manuscripts. His notes are almost all critical, but among them are interspersed a few literary and historical references and an occasional explanatory aid. Riese's emendations are more conservative than those of Baehrens, the fourth and last editor of a collection containing all the poems of Luxorius.

4. *Poetae Latini Minores* was first published in 1882 by Teubner in Leipzig.[34] Volume IV is entitled *Anthologia Latina*. Baehrens arranged the poems of Luxorius according to their order in A, but

---

[31] On this title, see above, Ch. II, n. 14; see also Riese, *Anthologia*, I, iii-v.

[32] A new edition of Fasciculus 2 appeared in 1906; Supp. 1, *Damasi Epigrammata*, ed. by M. Ihm, had appeared in 1895. F. Buecheler, joint editor of the second edition, edited Volume II, *Carmina Latina Epigraphica*, in 1897 (reedited in 1930); E. Lommatzsch saw Volume III (Supplement of II) through publication in 1926, thereby bringing the total number of poems in Riese's *Anthologia Latina* up to 2,299.

[33] For his reasons, see *Riese, Anthologia*, I, iv-v.

[34] *PLM*, originally published in 1879-83, and again in 1910-23, with Volume I reedited by F. Vollmer in 1930, consists of five volumes (six, if one includes *Fragmenta Poetarum Romanorum*). Volume I contains the *Appendix Vergiliana*, Volume II, Ovid, *Nux* and *Consolatio ad Liviam*, and the *Priapea*, Volume III, *Homerus Latinus*, Volume IV, *Anthologia Latina*, and Volume V, Dracontius.

elsewhere he differs from Riese. In his long introduction (in Latin) Baehrens gives reasons for his arrangement, describes the codices, and argues with great vehemence about the supposed compiler of the *Anthologia* and about the attribution of serpentine poems to Luxorius.[35] Baehrens was strong-willed and dogmatic, possessing powerful convictions and a fertile imagination. Consequently, he emended rather freely.

5. A few poems of Luxorius have found their way into modern anthologies. For example, J. W. Basore and S. H. Weber include 61L and 80L in *Latin Poetry* (Boston, 1925), p. 135; H. W. Garrod includes 2L, 46L, 80L, 61L, and 3L, in that order, in *The Oxford Book of Latin Verse* (Oxford, 1912), pp. 439-40.

Sigla

Riese	*Baehrens*		
A	S	olim Salmasianus, nunc Parisinus 10318	s. VII vel VIII init.
A¹	ex... corr. S'	manus A ipsius librarii	s. VII vel VIII init.
a	*Salm.*	emendationes Salmasii ipsius	s. XVII
B	T	olim Thuaneus, nunc Parisinus 8071	s. IX f. vel X init.
C	Y	olim Thuaneus, nunc Parisinus 8069	s. X vel XI
S	W	codex Bellovaciensis	s. IX vel X (?)
V	V	Vossianus Q.68	s. IX init.
α	*schedae*	schedae Divionenses, Heid. lat. 46	ab a. 1651 ad a. 1756

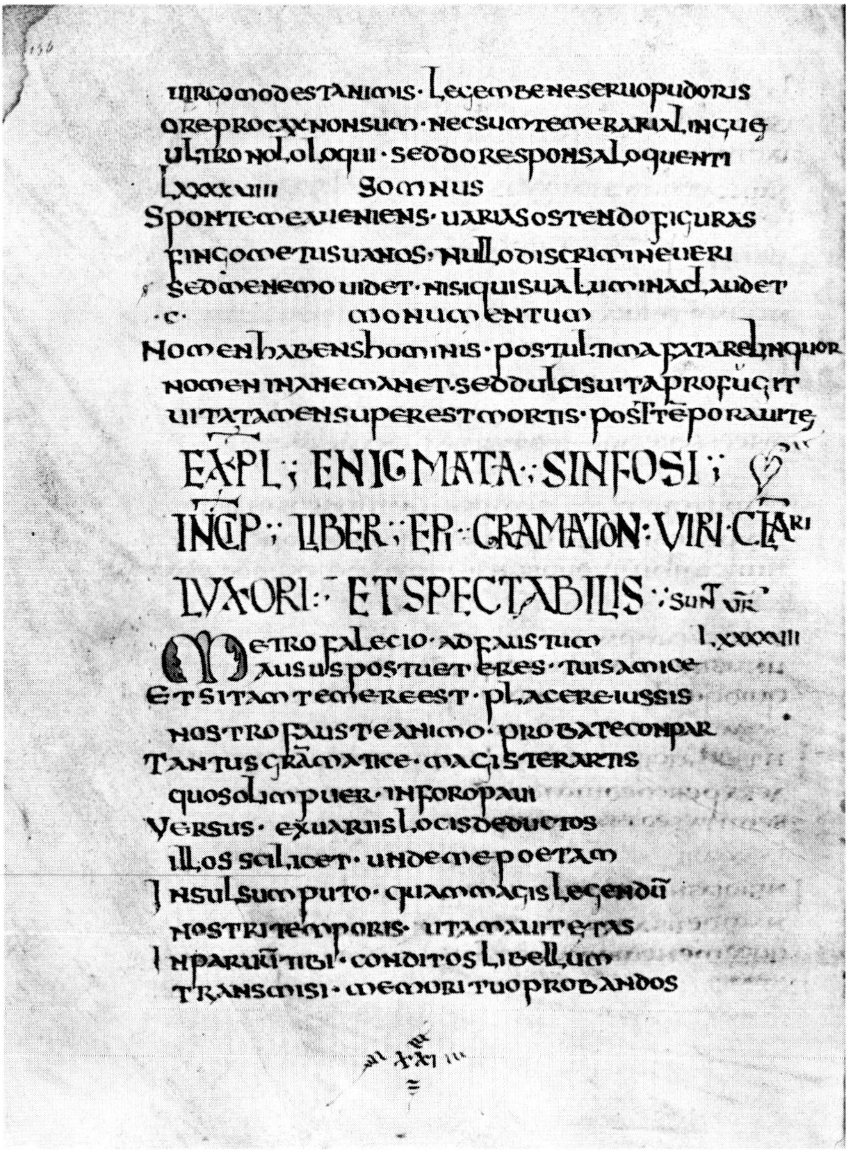

VIRGO MODESTA NIMIS· LEGEM BENE SERVO PUDORIS
ORE PROCAX NON SUM· NEC SUM TEMERARIA LINGUE
ULTRO NOLO LOQUI· SED DO RESPONSA LOQUENTI
LXXXVIIII   SOMNUS
SPONTE ME A VENIENS· VARIAS OSTENDO FIGURAS
FINGO ME TIS VANOS· NULLO DISCRIMINE VERI
SED ME NEMO VIDET· NISI QUI SUA LUMINA CLAUDET
·C·   MONUMENTUM
NOMEN HABENS HOMINIS· POST ULTIMA FATA RELINQUOR
NOMEN IN HAEC MANET· SED DULCIS VITA PROFUGIT
VITA TAMEN SUPEREST MORTIS· POST TEMPORA VITAE

EXPL; ENIGMATA· SINFOSI;
INCP; LIBER; ER· GRAMATON· VIRI CLARI
LUXORI· ET SPECTABILIS ·SUNT VR

METRO PALECIO· AD FAUSTUM   LXXXIIII
AUSUS POSTUET ERES· TUIS AMICE
ET SI TAM TEMEREEST· PLACERE IUSSIS·
NOSTRO FAUSTE ANIMO· PROBATE COMPAR
TANTUS GRAMATICE· MAGISTER ARTIS
QUOS OLIM PUER· IN FORO PAUL
VERSUS· EX VARIIS LOCIS DEDUCTOS
ILLOS SCILICET· UNDE ME POETAM
INSULSUM PUTO· QUAM MAGIS LEGENDU
NOSTRI TEMPORIS· UT AM AUIT ETAS
IN PARUUM TIBI· CONDITOS LIBELLUM
TRANSMISI· MEMORI TUO PROBANDOS

Page 156 of the Codex Salmasianus, now in the Bibliothèque Nationale, Paris, showing the superscription of the poems of Luxorius.

PLATE I

A: A *viridarium* or garden is mentioned in the title of Poem 18. The outline of an octagonal *viridarium* is still visible on the grounds of the Aviary House in Carthage.

B: At the entrance to the ruins of the Amphitheater in Carthage, to which Luxorius refers in Poems 68 and 87.

PLATE II

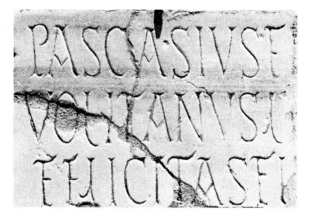

A: Pascasius, the name of a charioteer in Poem 41, is found in many North African inscriptions, as in this one now in the Lavigerie Museum, Carthage.

B: "Giace l'alta Cartago" (Here lies great Carthage), Tasso sang. The ornate capital of a huge broken column in the area of the Baths of Antoninus is a reminder of the splendor of Carthage under the Roman emperors.

C: Mosaics were abundantly used to decorate the private and public buildings of North Africa. The Naron Synagogue at Hammam Lif (ancient Ad Aquas), about ten miles from Tunis, has yielded a large number of beautiful examples. The one pictured, showing the Menorah, the sacred seven-branched candelabrum, and ritualistic symbols, is now in the Brooklyn Museum.

PLATE III

A: An example of the ornate mosaics found in the North African villas, now in the Bardo (Alaoui) Museum, Tunis: a marine scene of a Nereid attended by Cupids, birds, and dolphins.

B: In Poems 48 and 49 Luxorius describes a striking use of the eye as a symbol. Modern examples of this symbol are seen on small boats in southern Europe, such as this fishing boat at Cascais, Portugal.

PLATE IV

PART TWO: THE POEMS

LIBER EPIGRAMMATON
VIRI CLARISSIMI
LUXORI ET SPECTABILIS

1. *Metro Phalaecio ad Faustum*

Ausus post veteres, tuis, amice,
Etsi iam temere est, placere iussis,
Nostro Fauste animo probate conpar,
Tantus grammaticae magister artis,
Quos olim puer in foro paravi   5
Versus ex variis locis deductos
(Illos scilicet unde me poetam
Insulsum puto quam magis legendum),
Nostri temporis ut amavit aetas,
In parvum tibi conditos libellum   10
Transmisi memori tuo probandos
Primum pectore; deinde, si libebit,
Discretos titulis quibus tenentur,
Per nostri similes dato sodales.
Nam, si doctiloquis nimisque magnis   15
Haec tu credideris viris legenda,
Culpae nos socios notabit index—
Tam te, talia qui bonis recenses,
Quam me, qui tua duriora iussa
Feci nescius, inmemor futuri.   20
Nec me paeniteat iocos secutum
Quos verbis epigrammaton facetis
Diversos facili pudore lusit
Frigens ingenium, laboris expers.
Causam, carminis unde sit voluptas,   25
Edet ridiculum sequens poema.

THE BOOK OF EPIGRAMS
OF THE MOST DISTINGUISHED
AND EMINENT LUXORIUS

1. In the Phalaecean Metre to Faustus

Daring, after the poets of old, to obey your orders, even if it is now
a rash act, dear friend and comrade Faustus, great teacher of literature
and grammar, whose friendship has long been tested in my heart,
I have collected the poems which I wrote on different occasions as a
youth in the Forum. They appealed to the tastes of our generation but
actually they are such as to make me think of myself as a bungler
rather than as a poet worth being read.

I have gathered them into a little book and sent them on so that
remembering the past you may be the first to judge them with your
knowledge and understanding. Then, if such is your pleasure, pass
them along distinguished by the titles attached to them among friends
like ourselves. For, if you believe that they deserve to be read by
learned and eminent men, evidence will be given equally against us
as partners in guilt—against you, who class such trifles with good
poetry, and against me, who in my ignorance and lack or regard for the
consequences carried out your commands that were so difficult to
fulfil.

I hope I shall not regret having aimed at a variety of jokes, which,
with little effort and light morality, my frozen wit has playfully
uttered in the humorous words of epigrams.

The following piece of light verse will reveal the source of pleasure
to be found in my poetry.

2. Iambici ad lectorem operis sui

Priscos cum haberes quos probares indices,
Lector, placere qui bonis possent modis,
Nostri libelli cur retexis paginam
Nugis refertam frivolisque sensibus,
Et quam tenello tiro lusi viscere?   5
An forte doctis illa cara est versibus,
Sonat pusillo quae laboris schemate,
Nullo decoris, ambitus, sententiae?
Hanc tu requiris et libenter inchoas,
Velut iocosa si theatra pervoles.   10

3. Asclepiadei ad librum suum

Parvus nobilium cum liber ad domos
Pomposique fori scrinia publica
Cinctus multifido veneris agmine,
Nostri defugiens pauperiem laris,
Quo dudum modico sordidus angulo   5
Squalebas, tineis iam prope deditus,
Si te despiciet turba legentium
Inter Romulidas et Tyrias manus,
Isto pro exequiis claudere disticho:
"Contentos propriis esse decet focis   10
"Quos laudis facile est invidiam pati."

4. Epigrammata parva quod in hoc libro scripserit

[Parva quod exiguo sint scripta epigrammata libro]
   Si quis hoc nostro detrahit ingenio,
Adtendat modicis condi de mensibus annum,
   Et graciles hiemis, veris et esse dies;
Noverit in brevibus magnum deprendier usum.   5
   Ultra mensuram gratia nulla datur.
Sic mea concinno si pagina displicet actu,
   Finito citius carmine clausa silet.
Nam, si constaret libris longissima multis,
   Fastidita forent plurima vel vitia.   10

2. *Iambics to the Reader of His Work*

Although, dear reader, you had the works of writers of old whom you esteemed highly and who could please you with their excellent harmonies, why do you turn the pages of my little book, pages filled with trifles and frivolities that I wrote as a novice when my talents were undeveloped?

Can it be that you are fond of that kind of book whose versification is skillful but whose structure is limited, with not a whit of elegance, ostentation, or serious thought? This book of mine is what you are looking for and eagerly begin to read, as if hurrying to a theater dedicated to fun and laughter.

3. *Asclepiads to His Book*

When you, my little book, have come to the homes of the great and to the public bookshelves of the stately Forum, so that you are surrounded by a multifarious throng, after fleeing from the poverty of my household, where for a long time you lay covered with dust in a tiny nook and almost completely devoured by bookworms,—if the multitude of readers looks down upon you with scorn among the crowd of Romans and Carthaginians, end your days with this distich as your funeral oration:

"Let those be content to stay at home who easily endure their envy of fame."

4. *On the Reason Why He Wrote Short Epigrams in This Book*

If anybody belittles this talent of mine [because short epigrams are the material of my slender book], let him consider that the year is composed of short months and that the days of winter and spring are brief. Let him take notice also that great use is found in small things. No pleasure is given beyond measure. If, therefore, my book displeases anybody because of its brevity, the sooner the poem is finished, the sooner the book is shut and silent. If, on the other hand, the work were very long and contained many parts, it would be an exceeding bore and numberless would be its faults.

5. *Trochaicum de piscibus qui ab hominibus cibos capiebant*

Verna clausas inter undas et lacunas regias
Postulat cibos diurnos ore piscis parvolo
Nec manum fugit vocatus nec pavescit retia.
Roscidi sed amnis errans hinc et inde margine,
Odit ardui procellas et dolosi gurgitis,   5
Ac suum quo libet esse transnatans colit mare.
Sic famem gestu loquaci et mitiori vertice
Discit ille quam sit aptum ventris arte vincere.

6. *Archilochium de apro mitissimo in triclinio nutrito*

Martis aper genitus iugis inesse montium
Frangere et horrisonum nemus ferocius solens,
Pabula porticibus capit libenter aureis
Et posito famulans furore temperat minas.
Nec Parios lapides revellit ore spumeo   5
Atria nec rabidis decora foedat ungulis,
Sed domini placidam manum quietus appetens
Fit magis ut Veneris dicatus ille sit sacris.

7. *De auriga Aegyptio qui semper vincebat*

Quamvis ab Aurora fuerit genetrice creatus
   Memnon, Pelidae conruit ille manu.
At te Nocte satum, ni fallor, matre paravit
   Aeolus et Zephyri es natus in antra puer.
Nec quisquam qui te superet nascetur Achilles.   5
   Dum Memnon facie es, non tamen es genio.

8. *Sapphicum in grammaticum furiosum*

Carminum interpres meritique vatum,
Cum leves artem pueros docere
Diceris vel te iuvenes magistrum

5. Trochaic Poem about Fish That Used to Take Food from Human Hands

A homebred fish enclosed in the sheltered waters of the royal pool asks for its daily food with its tiny mouth. When summoned, it does not fear the hand of the feeder nor does it dread the nets, but wandering here and there along the border of the moist stream, it hates the storms of a swift and treacherous current, and swimming across, it lives in its own sea, where it is happy to be.

So, by an expressive gesture and a gentle movement of its head, the fish learns how easy it is to conquer hunger with craftiness taught by the stomach.

6. Archilochian Poem about a Very Tame Boar Fed in the Dining Room

A warlike boar, born to live on mountain ridges and accustomed to break down with ferocity the reechoing grove, willingly takes his food among gilded colonnades, and becoming tame, obediently controls his threatening nature. He neither tears down the Parian marble with his foaming mouth nor does he mar the beautiful rooms with his raging feet, but gently taking food from the calm hand of his master, he becomes something more likely to be dedicated to the rites of Venus.

7. About an Egyptian Charioteer Who Always Won

Although Memnon was the son of Aurora, he fell at the hands of Achilles. Unless I am mistaken, Night is your mother and Aeolus your sire, and you, their son, were born to occupy Zephyr's cave. However, no Achilles will arise to conquer you. Although you are a Memnon in looks, you are not like him in your fate!

8. Sapphic Poem to a Mad Teacher

Interpreter of poetry and of the merits of poets, when you are said to be teaching your subject to tender striplings, and when young men listen to you as if you were a learned teacher of literature, why do you

Audiunt verbis veluti disertum
Cur in horrendam furiam recedis   5
Et manu et telo raperis cruentus?
Non es, in quantum furor hic probatur,
Dignus inter grammaticos vocari
Sed malos inter sociari Orestas.

9.   *Glyconeum in advocatum effeminatum*

Execti species viri,
Naturae grave dedecus,
Usu femineo Paris,
Foedae cura libidinis,
Cum sis ore facundior,   5
Cur causas steriles agis
Aut corrupta negotia
Et perdenda magis locas?
Agnovi. Ut video, tuo
Ori quid bene credier   10
Non vis sed, puto, podici.

10. *In clamosum Pygmaeum corpore et furiosum*

Corpore par querulis es vel clamore cicadis—
   Hinc potior quod te tempora nulla vetant.
Dum loqueris, quaerunt cuncti vox cuius oberret,
   Atque sonum alterius corporis esse putant.
Miramur, tantum capiant qui membra furorem,   5
   Cum sit forma levis, clamor et ira gravis.

11. *Phalaecium in moechum quod debriatus plorabat*
      cum coitum inplere non posset
Saepius futuis nimisque semper,
Nec parcis, nisi forte debriatus
Effundis lacrimas quod esse moechus
Multo non valeas mero subactus.

fall into a horrifying fit of madness and why are you carried away with your hand and weapon bloodstained? To the extent proved by this insane raging, you are not fit to be enrolled among teachers, but you should rather be put into the company of evildoers like Orestes.

9. Glyconic Poem to an Effeminate Lawyer

Likeness of a castrated man, foul disgrace of nature, a Paris treated like a woman, an instrument of shameful lust, although you have an eloquent mouth, why do you by preference plead weak cases or contract to handle debased and desperate affairs?

I know the answer. As I see it, you do not wish anything good to be entrusted to your mouth but, so I think, to your backside.

10. To a Noisy and Raging Dwarf

In size of body and noise you are the equal of chirping crickets, even more so because no seasons restrain you. When you speak, everybody asks whose voice is flying about and everybody thinks that the sound is coming from some other person. I wonder how your body can give vent to so much rage; although your frame is frail, your cries and anger are robust.

11. Phalaecean Poem to a Debauchee Because He Wept When Drunk Since He Could Not Fulfil His Desire

Too often and always too much you give free rein to your desire and you do not stop unless you happen to be drunk and shed tears because you can no longer play the part of a rake when you are overcome by

Plura ne futuas, peto, Lucine,   5
Aut semper bibe taediumque plange,
Aut, numquam ut futuas, venena sume.

12. *In spadonem regium qui mitellam sumebat*

Rutilo decens capillo
Roseoque crine ephebus
Spado regius mitellam
Capiti suo locavit.
Proprii memor pudoris,   5
Bene conscius quid esset,
Posuit, cogente nullo,
Fuerat minus quod illi.

13. *Anapaesticum in magum mendicum*

Tibi cum non sit diei panis,
Magicas artes inscius inples.
Ire per umbras atque sepulcra
Pectore egeno titubans gestis.
Nec tua Manes carmina sumunt,   5
Fame dum pulsus Tartara cantu
Omnia turbas, aliquid credens
Dare quod possit superis Pluton
Pauperibus. Qui puto quod peius
Egeas totum semper in orbem,   10
Mage, si posces membra perempta.

14. *In acceptorarium obesum et infelicem*

Pondere detracto miseras, Martine, fatigas
Pressura crudelis aves. Pinguedine tanta
Ut tu sis, frustra maciem patiuntur iniquam.
Debuerant, fateor, magis has tua pascere membra,
Ut numquam possent ieiuna morte perire.   5

wine. I beg of you, Lucinus, in order that you may never make love again, either drink all the time and bewail your sickness, or in order that you may never make love again, drink—poison!

12. *About a Royal Eunuch Who Put on a Turban*

A youthful eunuch of the royal household, resplendent in his reddish hair and flame-colored locks, placed a turban on his head. Mindful of his own modesty, knowing well what he was, he put on, with nobody forcing him, what had not been appropriate to him.

13. *Anapaestic Poem to a Mendicant Magician*

Because you do not have your daily bread, you practice the art of magic, though ignorant of it. Staggering with hunger and need, you eagerly desire to go among the shades and tombs. But the spirits of the dead do not listen to your incantations, as, driven by hunger, you throw all Tartarus into turmoil with your chanting in your belief that Pluto can give something to the destitute in the upper world.

I believe, magician, that you will always go about in greater want throughout the wide world, if you demand the limbs of corpses.

14. *To a Fat and Unlucky Falconer*

By reducing their weight, Martinus, you cruelly torment your poor birds with suffering. In vain do they endure undeserved hunger that you may be so corpulent. Your body should rather have fed them, I admit, so that these birds could never starve to death.

15. *In vetulam virginem nubentem*

Virgo, quam Phlegethon vocat sororem,
Saturni potior parens senecta,
Quam Nox atque Erebus tulit Chaosque,
Cui rugae totidem graves quot anni,
Cui vultus elephans dedit cutemque,   5
Mater simia quam creavit arvis
Grandaeva in Libycis novo sub orbe,
Olim quae decuit marita Diti
Pro nata Cereris dari per umbras—
Quis te tam petulans suburit ardor,   10
Nunc cum iam exitium tibi supersit?
An hoc pro titulo cupis sepulcri,
Ut te cognita fama sic loquatur,
Quod stuprata viro est anus nocenti?

16. *In medicolenonem*

Quod te pallidulum, Marine noster,
Cuncti post totidem dies salutant,
Credebam medicum velut peritum
Curam febribus et manum pudicam
De pactis logicae parare sectae   5
Aut de methodicis probare libris.
At tu fornice turpius vacabas,
Exercens aliis quod ipse possis
Lenatis melius tibi puellis
Scortandi solito labore ferre.   10
Novi quid libeat tuum, chirurge,
Conspectos animum videre cunnos.
Vis ostendere te minus virum esse:
Arrectos satis est mares videre.

17. *In diaconum festinantem ad prandium cauponis*

Quo festinus abis, gula inpellente, sacerdos?
    An tibi pro psalmis pocula corde sedent?

15. To an Aged Virgin Who Is Getting Married

Virgin whom Phlegethon calls his sister, you who are probably old enough to be the mother of Saturn, you whom Night and Erebus and Chaos brought into the world, you whose deep wrinkles are as numerous as your years, you to whom an elephant gave his looks and his hide, you whose mother was an aged ape that gave birth to you in Africa when the world was young, you who long ago could fittingly have been given instead of Ceres' daughter to Pluto as his bride among the dead, with what impetuous passion do you now burn when you are on the point of death?

Can the reason be that you crave the following epitaph so that widespread report will speak of you thus:

"Old lady raped by a sex criminal"?

16. To a Medical Procurer

Because you look so pale, my good Marinus, when everybody is greeting you after an absence of many days, I had the idea that, like a skilled doctor, you were busy preparing a cure for fevers or you were lecturing to a respectful little group on the principles of the medical profession or you were weighing the truth of scientific books.

But, on the contrary, you were disgracefully loose in a brothel, procuring for others something that, because of your long practice with courtesans, you could submit to more easily than the prostitutes.

I know why, my medical friend, you are so happy to look on exposed bodies. You wish to show that you are not a man; it satisfies you to see men excited with desire.

17. To a Deacon Hurrying to an Innkeeper's Luncheon

Where are you hurrying, my good priest? Where is your gullet driving you? Can it be that cups are on your mind instead of psalms? Frequent

Pulpita templorum, ne pulpita quaere tabernae,
Numina quo caeli, non phialas referas.

18. *De turre in viridario posita, ubi se Fridamal*
aprum pinxit occidere

Extollit celsas nemoralis Aricia sedes,
Sternit ubi famulas casta Diana feras.
Frondosis Tempe cinguntur Thessala silvis
Pinguiaque Nemeae lustra Molorchus habet.
Haec vero aetherias exit quae turris in auras,
Consessum domino deliciosa parans,
Omnibus in medium lucris ornata refulget
Obtinuitque uno praemia cuncta loco.
Hinc nemus, hinc fontes extructa cubilia cingunt
Statque velut propriis ipsa Diana iugis.   10
Clausa sed in tanto cum sit splendore voluptas
Artibus ac variis atria pulcra micent,
Admiranda tuae tamen est virtutis imago,
Fridamal, et stratae gloria magna ferae,
Qui solitae accendens mentem virtutis amore   15
Aptasti digno pingere facta loco.
Hic spumantis apri iaculo post terga retorto
Frontem et cum geminis naribus ora feris.
Ante ictum subita prostrata est bellua morte,
Cui prius extingui quam cecidisse fuit.   20
Iussit fata manus telo, nec vulnera sensit
Exerrans anima iam pereunte cruor.

19. *De avibus marinis quae post volatum ad domum remeabant*

Felix marinis alitibus Fridamal,
Felix iuventa, prosperior genio,
Quem sponte poscunt aequoreae volucres.
Nec stagna grato frigida concilio
Pigris strepentes gurgitibus retinent,   5
Sed quo tuorum temperiem nemorum
Monstrent, volatu praememores famulo
Pro te relictam non repetunt patriam.

temple benches, not tavern bars, so that you may carry the will of heaven, not bottles.

18. *About a Tower Situated in a Pleasure Garden, Where Fridamal Had a Picture of Himself Painted Killing a Boar*

Wooded Aricia lifts up its lofty abodes where chaste Diana shoots down wild beasts, her servants; Thessalian Tempe is begirt with leafy forests, and Molorchus holds the rich woods of Nemea.

But truly this tower rising into the very heights of heaven, a delightful place providing a resting place for its owner, is richly adorned and shines out far and wide, excelling all other places in beauty.

On one side a grove and on the other side fountains surround the rooms built there, and a statue of Diana stands just as if she were on her own mountaintops. But, although things that give pleasure have been enclosed in such splendor and although the beautiful rooms are resplendent with varied artistry, yet must be admired the picture of your brave deed, Fridamal, and the great and glorious feat of slaying a wild boar.

Excited by love of your characteristic courage, you set your mind upon picturing your exploits in a worthy setting. Here, drawing back and aiming the spear from behind your back, you are striking the foaming boar straight on its forehead and two-nostriled face. Even before the blow penetrated, the beast was laid low by sudden death and suffered the fate of dying before it fell. Your hand decreed the beast's destiny with your spear and its dripping lifeblood did not feel the wounds as its spirit was leaving its body.

19. *About Sea Birds That Used to Return Home after a Flight*

Happy Fridamal, happy in your birds of the sea, happy in your youth, fortunate in your guardian spirit!

Of their own accord the birds of the sea come to you. Cool pools and slow-moving waters do not detain them as they whirr about in joyful flocks, but in order that they may show to the world the coolness of your glades, they remember you in their obedient flight and do not head for their native habitat which they left behind on account of you.

20. *In aurigam senem victum crimina in populos iactantem*

Te quotiens victum circus, Cyriace, resultat,
   Crimine victores polluis et populos.
Non visum quereris senio languente perisse
   Castigasque tuae tarda flagella manus.
Sed quod in alterius divulgas crimina nomen,   5
   Cur non illa magis credis inesse tibi?
Es meritis inpar, virtute, aetate relictus.
   Haec cum habeant alii, crimina vera putas.
Sola tamen falsis surgat tibi poena loquellis,
   Ut victus semper nil nisi crimen agas.   10

21. *In podagrum venationi studentem*

Apros et capreas levesque cervos
Incurvus rapidis equis fatigat.
Tantum nec sequitur capitque quicquam.
Esse inter iuvenes cupit, vocari
Baudus, dum misero gemat dolore   5
Et nil praevaleat. Quid ergo gestit?
Mori praecipiti furit caballo,
Cum lecto melius perire possit.

22. *In supra scriptum, quod multa scorta habuit et eas custodiebat*

Zelo agitas plures, Incurvus, clune puellas,
   Sed nulla est quae te sentiat esse virum.
Custodis clausas, tamquam sis omnibus aptus.
   Est tamen internus Iuppiter ex famulis.
Si nihil ergo vales, vanum cur arrigis inguen   5
   Et facis ignavus mentis adulterium?

23. *Anacreontium in medicum inpotentem qui ter viduam duxit uxorem*

Post tot repleta busta

20. To a Charioteer Who Is Old and Who Finds Fault with the Spectators When He Is Beaten

Whenever the Circus resounds with cries that you have been beaten, Cyriacus, you besmirch the winners and spectators with accusations. You do not complain that your eyesight is gone because of your feeble old age and you do not blame the slow whips you hold in your hands. But, as to the faults you impute to the name of somebody else, why do you not rather believe that those faults lie in you? You are not equal to the task of winning prizes, you have been abandoned by strength and youth. When others have these qualities, you consider them real crimes.

However, may this be the sole punishment for your false accusations:

Always a loser, may you drive nothing but charges!

21. On a Sufferer from the Gout Who Wants to Hunt

Incurvus tires out boars and does and fleet stags with his swift horses. Yet he neither overtakes nor captures anything. He likes to be in the company of young men and to be called their dashing chief, but in the meantime he groans in wretched pain and accomplishes nothing. What then is he so passionate about? He is in a fever to die on a galloping horse when he could be better off dying in bed.

22. Written against the Above Because He Had Many Girls and Guarded Them Closely

Vigorously you make love to many wenches, Incurvus, but not one of them feels that you are a man. You keep the girls shut in and watch them closely as if you were a match for all of them. But within your household there is a Jupiter—one of your slaves. If therefore you get nowhere, why do you heat yourself up in vain and impotently satisfy your desires in your mind alone?

23. Anacreontic Poem to an Impotent Doctor Who Married a Woman Thrice a Widow

After so many tombs have been filled, after the horde of funerals,

Et funerum catervas
Ac dispares maritos
Rugosa quos peremit
Fatis anus sinistris,   5
Tu nunc, chirurge, quartus
Coniunx vocate plaudis.
Sed vivus es sepultus,
Dum parte qua decebat
Nil contines mariti.   10
Iam nosco cui videtur
Nupsisse Paula rursus.
Nulli! Quid ergo fecit?
Mutare mox lugubrem
Quam sumpserat cupivit   15
Uxor nefanda vestem
Ut quartus atque—quintus
Possit venire coniunx!

24. *In pantomimam Pygmaeam quae Andromachae fabulam*
     frequenter saltabat et raptum Helenae

Andromacham atque Helenam saltat Macedonia semper
   Et quibus excelso corpore forma fuit.
Haec tamen aut brevior Pygmaea virgine surgit
   Ipsius aut quantum pes erat Andromachae.
Sed putat illarum fieri se nomine talem,   5
   Motibus et falsis crescere membra cupit.
Hac spe, crede, tuos incassum decipis artus.
   Thersiten potius finge, quod esse soles!

25. *In ebriosum nihil comedentem sed solum bibentem*

Dum bibis solus pateras quot omnes,
Saepe nec totis satiaris horis
Et tibi munus Cereris resordet
Ac nihil curas nisi ferre Bacchum,
Nerfa, iam te non hominem vocabo,   5
Sed nimis plenam et patulam lagonam.

after so many husbands ill-fatedly brought to their deaths by a wrinkled old woman, you, my medical friend, are pleased with yourself because you are now called her fourth husband. But, although alive, you too have been buried, for you do not possess the power properly to exercise your right as a husband.

But I know whom Paula seems to have married again. Nobody! Why then did she do this? An abominable wife, she wanted to change in a hurry the mourning garb that she had put on so that a fourth husband might come along—and even a fifth!

24. *About a Female Pantomimist, a Dwarf Who Often Acted the Story of Andromache and the Rape of Helen*

Macedonia always dances the part of Andromache and of Helen and of others who had a tall figure. However, she rises up shorter than a Pygmy or than Andromache's foot. But she thinks she can become like them by playing their roles and she wants her body to grow by her make-believe movements.

Believe me, vainly do you deceive your limbs with this hope. Pretend rather that you are Thersites—which is more like you in real life!

25. *To a Drunkard Who Eats Nothing but Is Forever Drinking*

Since you alone often drink as many bowls of wine as all other men put together, and you never have enough at any hour, and scorn bread and care to take nothing but wine, Nerfa, I am no longer going to call you a man, but a wide-mouthed flagon filled to the brim.

26. De Fama picta in stabulo circi

Qualem te pictor stabulis formavit equorum
    Talem te nostris blanda referto iugis.
Semper et adsiduo vincendi munera porta
    His quorum limen fortis amica sedes.

27. Aliter

Verum, Fama, tibi vultum pictura notavit,
    Dum vivos oculos iuncea forma gerit.
Tu, quamvis totum velox rapiaris in orbem,
    Pulcrior hoc uno limine clausa sedes.

28. In vicinum invidum

Zeleris nimium cur mea, Marcie,
Tamquam si pereas, limina, nescio,
Cum sis proximior, una velut domus,
Et nostros paries dimidiet lares.
Sed gratum ferimus. Talis es omnibus,   5
Nec quemquam nisi te vis miser aspici.
Contingat—quesumus, numina,—quod cupis!
Te solum ut videas, Marcie, dum vivis.

29. In gibberosum qui se generosum iactabat

Fingis superbum quod tibi patrum genus,
Nunc Iuliorum prole te satum tumens,
Nunc Memmiorum Martiique Romuli,
Prodesse gibbo forte quid putas tuo?
Nil ista falso verba prosunt ambitu.   5
Tace parentes, ne quietos moveas.
Natura nobis unde sis natus docet.

30. De eo qui se poetam dicebat quod in triviis cantaret et a pueris laudaretur

Conponis fatuis dum pueris melos,

26. *About a Painting of Fame on a Circus Stable*

Just as the artist has painted you on the horses' stables, in that same pose alight favorably on our teams. Always and unfailingly carry the prize of victory to those on whose portal you are seated as such a powerful friend.

27. *Another Poem on the Same Theme*

Your true features, Fame, have been delineated in the painting, which shows your slender body and your sparkling eyes. Although you fly with speed over the whole world, you are so much more beautiful when you sit here permanently fixed on this portal.

28. *To a Jealous Neighbor*

I do not know, Marcius, why you are so bitterly and desperately envious of my house, although you are my next-door neighbor and we live practically in one and the same house, with only a wall separating our homes. But I do not take offense; you are like that to everybody. You wish, poor man, that nobody but yourself should be looked at. I pray, O gods, that you, Marcius, should get what you want; that you should look only upon yourself as long as you live!

29. *Against a Hunchback Who Boasted That He Was of Noble Birth*

In what way perchance do you think it helps your humpback to imagine that yours is a noble line of ancestors, puffing yourself with pride at one moment as a descendant of the Julii, at another, of the Memmii and of Romulus, son of Mars? Useless are such words with their false ambition. Keep quiet about your ancestors lest you disturb the dead. Your nature tells us from whom you are descended.

30. *About a Man Who Called Himself a Poet Because He Sang in the Streets and Was Praised by Boys*

When you are composing poetry for foolish boys, Zenobius, and you

Zenobi, et trivio carmine perstrepis,
Indoctaque malis verba facis locis,
Credis tete aliquid laudibus indere
Famamque ad teneros ducere posteros?   5
Hoc nostrae faciunt semper et alites.
Ni rite institues, sibila tum canunt.

31. *In puellam hermaphroditam*

Monstrum feminei bimembre sexus,
Quam coacta virum facit libido,
Quin gaudes futui furente cunno?
Cur te decipit inpotens voluptas?
Non das, quo pateris facisque, cunnum.   5
Illam, qua mulier probaris esse,
Partem cum dederis, puella tunc sis.

32. *Ad eum qui per diem dormiens nocte vigilabat*

Stertis anhelanti fessus quod corde, Lycaon,
  Exhorrens lucis munera parta die,
Et tibi vigilias semper nox tetra ministrat,
  Iam scio te nostro vivere nolle die.
At si tale tibi studium natura paravit,   5
  Vivas ad antipodas—sis vel ut inde, redi!

33. *De sarcophago ubi turpia sculpta fuerant*

Turpia tot tumulo defixit crimina Balbus,
  Post superos spurco Tartara more premens.
Pro facinus! Finita nihil modo vita retraxit!
  Luxuriam ad Manes moecha sepulcra gerunt.

34. *Item unde supra scriptum: ubi equi circi hihehant*

Crevit ad ornatum stabuli circique decorem

make a loud noise with your street songs and utter words of ignorance in low quarters, do you think that you are doing anything worthy of praise and that you are establishing your fame among the younger generation? Our birds always do the same thing also; if you do not instruct them properly, they do not sing but merely whistle.

31. To a Hermaphroditic Girl

Two-organed monster of the female sex, whom enforced lust turns into a man, why do you not enjoy the normal way of making love? Why does violent, vain pleasure deceive you? You do not give that with which you are passive and also active. When you offer that part of you which proves that you are a female, then you may be a girl.

32. To a Person Who Slept by Day and Stayed Awake by Night

Because, worn-out and with your chest heaving, you snore and dread the blessings of daylight, Lycaon, and you are always awake during the dark night, I now know why you do not want to live in our daylight. But if nature has given you such a desire, go live in the antipodes; or rather, that you may really be among your own kind, go back to them!

33. About a Stone Coffin on Which Foul Deeds Had Been Sculptured

Balbus had a great many disgraceful deeds carved on his coffin, overwhelming first the gods above and then Tartarus with his filthy way of life. For shame! His recent death altered nothing; his bawdy coffin bears his licentiousness to the very shades!

34. On the Same Theme as a Preceding Poem: Where Circus Horses Drank

A fountain of pure water has been provided and has appeared in a

Purior egregio reddita nympha loco
Quam cingunt variis insignia clara metallis
    Crispatumque super scinditur unda gradum.
Excipit hanc patuli moles miranda sepulcri,   5
    Corporibus vivis pocula blanda parans.
Nec iam sarcophagus tristis sua funera claudit,
    Sed laetos dulci flumine conplet equos.
Fundit aquas duro signatum marmore flumen,
    Falsa tamen species vera fluenta vomit.   10
Plaudite vos, Musae, diversaque, plaudite, signa,
    Quae circum docili continet arte decor,
Et dum palmiferis post praelia tanta quadrigis
    Garrula victores turba resolvit equos,
Praebete innocuos potus potusque salubres,   15
    Ut domino proprius gaudia circus agat.

35. *In cinaedum bona sua corruptoribus dantem*

Divitias grandesque epulas et munera multa,
    Quod proavi atque atavi quodque reliquit avus,
Des licet in cunctos et spargas, Becca, maritos,
    Plus tamen ille capit cui dare saepe cupis.
Nescio quid miserum est quod celas, Becca. Talento   5
    Vendere debueras, si bona membra dares.

36. *De eo qui uxorem suam prostare faciebat*
pro filiis habendis

Stirpe negata patrium nomen,
Non pater, audis; carus adulter
Coiugis castae viscera damnas,
Pariat spurcos ut tibi natos,
Inscia quo sint semine creti.   5
Fuerant forsan ista ferenda
Foeda, Proconi, vota parumper,
Scire vel ipsam si tuus umquam
Posset adultus dicere matrem.

remarkable location to adorn a stable and to beautify a circus. Resplendent statues of different metals surround this fountain and the fall of the water is broken over a curving step. A marvelous massive open coffin catches this water and gives pleasant draughts to the living. No longer does the grim coffin enclose its dead, but it fills the happy horses with fresh water. A stream flowing in a channel cut into the hard marble pours forth its waters; although its appearance is artificial, nevertheless real flowing rivulets issue from it.

Applaud, you Muses, applaud, you different statues, surrounded by beauty wrought with skillful art. And, while the chattering crowd unhitches the victorious horses from their chariots decorated with the palms of victory after so many races, supply safe drinks and drinks that are healthful so that his own circus may bring joy to the owner.

35. To a Catamite Giving Away His Property to His Seducers

Riches and sumptuous feasts and lavish gifts—whatever your great-great-grandfathers and your great-grandfathers and your grandfather left you—although you give them away and squander them among all your "husbands," Becca, still there is a favorite who takes more and to whom you often wish to give more. I do not know what foul thing it is, Becca, that you are hiding; you could have sold it for a talent, if you were giving away a sound body.

36. About a Man Who Made His Wife Prostitute Herself for the Sake of Having Sons

Although you cannot sire children, you, without being a father, still hear yourself called a father. A beloved adulterer, you put the organs of your chaste wife to illicit use so that she may bear you basely born offspring, herself ignorant from what seed they have sprung. Perhaps these shameful pretensions of yours might have been bearable for a little while, Proconius, if ever your son when grown-up could say that his mother herself knew.

37. De aleatore in pretio lenocinii ludente

Ludis, nec superas, Ultor, ad aleam,
Nec quicquam in tabula das nisi virginem,
Spondens blanditias et coitus simul.
Hoc cur das aliis quod poteras tibi?
An tablae melius praelia grata sunt?   5
Aut prodest vitium tale quod impetras?
Si vincas, ego te non puto virginem
In luxum cupere sed mage vendere.

38. In nomen Aegyptii quo equi circi infortunium capiebant

Icarus et Phaethon, Veneto nolente, vocaris
    Atque Agilis, pigro cum pede cuncta premas.
Sed tamen et Phaethon cecidit super aethera flammis,
    Dum cupit insolitis nescius ire plagis.
Tu quoque confractis defectus in aequore pinnis,   5
    Icare, Phoebeo victus ab igne cadis.
Digna his ergo tibi praebentur nomina fatis,
    Per te iterum ut pereant qui periere prius.

39. De Romulo picto ubi in muris fratrem cecidit

Disce pium facinus—percusso, Romule, fratre,
Sic tibi Roma datur. Huius iam nomine culpet
Nemo te c(a)edis, murorum si decet omen.

40. De eo qui amicos ad prandium clamabat ut plura exposceret xenia

Gaudeo quod me nimis ac frequenter
Ambitu pascis, Blumarit, superbo.
Unde sed pascor? Mea sunt per omnes
Sparsa convivas bona. Nec volebam

37. *About a Diceplayer Gambling with Pandering as the Stakes*

You play at dice, Ultor, but you do not win and you never lay any bet on the board except a girl, pledging caresses and intercourse with her at the same time.

Why do you give away to others what you could have had for yourself? Can it be that the thrill of gambling is more pleasant? Or is such a vice useful to you because you get what you want? If you should win, I do not think that you desire the girl for pleasure but rather for sale.

38. *On the Name of an Egyptian That Brought Misfortune to the Horses of the Circus*

With the Blues in opposition you are called Icarus and Phaethon and Speedy, although you tread on everything with sluggish feet. However, even Phaethon fell in flames through the upper air when in his ignorance he wanted to traverse unaccustomed regions. You also, Icarus, with your wings broken and yourself exhausted in the sea, fall, conquered by the sun's fire.

Therefore, names fitting the fate of these are being given to you so that in your own person those who perished before may perish once again!

39. *About a Painting of Romulus Showing Him Killing His Brother on the Walls*

Realize that yours was a virtuous crime, Romulus. When you struck down your brother, Rome was given to you by that act. Let no one now accuse you of this deed as murder, if the omen of the walls proves that what you did was right.

40. *About a Man Who Used to Invite His Friends to a Meal That He Might Ask for Many Gifts*

I am happy that you feast me sumptuously and frequently with proud extravagance, Blumarit. But what am I to live on? Whatever I own has been scattered among your guests. I did not want you to feed and

Pasceres quemquam peteresque mecum, 5
Ne tibi quicquam detur unde pascas.
Hoc tamen sed si vitio teneris,
Me precor numquam iubeas vocari.

41. *De auriga elato frequenter cadente*

Pascasium aurigam populi fortem esse fatentur
Ast ego non aliud quam turgida membra notabo
Inflatumque caput papulis et amica ruinis
Brachia quae numquam recto moderamine frenant.
Mox cadit et surgit, rursum cadit, inde resurgit 5
Et cadit ut miseris frangantur crura caballis.
Non iste humano dicatur nomine natus;
Hunc potius gryphum propium vocet Africa circo.

42. *De laude aurigae Prasini*

Iectofian, prasino felix auriga colore
 Priscorum conpar, ars quibus ipsa fuit,
Suetus equos regere et metas lustrare quadrigis
 Et quocumque velis ducere frena manu,—
Non sic Tantalides humero stat victor eburno. 5
 Una illi palma est, at tibi multa manet.

43. *In eum qui foedas amabat*

Diligit informes et foedas Myrro puellas.
 Quas aliter pulcro viderit ore, timet.
Iudicium hoc quale est oculorum, Myrro, fatere,
 Ut tibi non placeat Pontica, sed Garamas.
Iam tamen agnosco cur tales quaeris amicas. 5
 Pulcra tibi numquam, se dare foeda potest.

44. *De simiis canum dorso inpositis*

Reddita post longum Tyriis est mira voluptas,
 Quem pavet ut sedeat simia blanda canem.

invite anybody else with me lest anything be given to you for feeding us. But if you are addicted to this failing, I beg of you never to invite me.

41. About a Much-Praised Charioteer Who Often Falls

People say that Pascasius is a stalwart charioteer, but I shall mention only his bruised limbs and his head puffed up with swellings and his arms that favor falls, arms that never curb the horses that they may go in a straight line. He falls at the very beginning and rises, falls again, then rises again, and falls so that the legs of his unlucky horses are broken. Let it not be said that this man was born a human being; let Africa rather call him her own special circus griffin.

42. In Praise of a Charioteer of the Green Faction

Iectofian, charioteer happy in the wearing of the green, equal to the charioteers of old, who embodied the art of racing, skilled in controlling your horses and in flying over the course in your four-horse chariot, and in guiding the reins with your hand wherever you wish,— not so does ivory-shouldered Pelops stand out as a victor; he won only one prize, but many a prize still awaits you.

43. Against a Lover of Ugly Girls

Myrro loves hideous and ugly girls. On the other hand, he fears any beautiful girls he sees. In this way, Myrro, you reveal what kind of judgment it is that your eyes have so that a Pontic girl does not please you, but a Garamantian does! Yet I now know why you seek such lovers. A beautiful girl can never give herself to you, an ugly one may.

44. About Monkeys Placed on the Back of Dogs

After a long interval a wonderful pleasure has been granted to the Carthaginians: a gentle monkey is sitting on the back of a dog that it fears.

Quanto magna parant felici tempora regno,
  Discant ut legem pacis habere ferae!

45. *De partu ursae*

Lambere nascentis fertur primordia prolis
  Ursa ferox, placido cum facit ore genus.
Expolit informes labris parientibus artus
  Et pietas subolem rursus amore creat.
Attrito truncum formatur corpore pignus,   5
  Ut sculpendo facit crescere membra faber.
Officium natura suum permisit amanti—
  Formam post uterum lingua magistra parit.

46. *De laude horti Eugeti*

Hortus quo faciles fluunt Napaeae,
Quo ludunt Dryades virente choro,
Quo fovet teneras Diana Nymphas,
Quo Venus roseos recondit artus,
Quo fessus teretes Cupido flammas   5
Suspensis reficit liber pharetris,
Quo sese Aonides ferunt puellas
Cui numquam minus est amoena frondis,
Cui semper redolent amoma verni,
Cui fons perspicuis tener fluentis   10
Muscoso riguum parit meatu,
Quo dulcis avium canor resultat—
Quidquid per varias refertur urbes,
Hoc uno famulans loco resultat.

47. *De tablista furioso quasi tesseris imperante*

Ludit cum multis Vatanans sed ludere nescit,
  Et putat imperio currere puncta suo.
Sed male dum numeros contraria tessera mittit,
  Clamat et irato pallidus ore fremit.

What great things the times presage for the happy kingdom when wild animals learn to observe the ways of peace!

45. About the She-Bear's Parturition

The fierce she-bear is said to lick the shapeless body of her young at birth when she fashions her cub with her gentle mouth. She moulds the formless limbs with maternal lips and her devotion once again creates her offspring with love. An imperfect whelp is given shape by the rubbing of its body just as an artisan makes limbs appear by his sculpturing. Nature has entrusted its own duty to a loving mother. First her womb and then her skillful tongue gives birth to the cub's shape.

46. In Praise of the Garden of Eugetus

Garden where the wood nymphs gently flit about, where the dryads frolic in a verdant troop, where Diana cherishes the tender nymphs, where Venus hides her rosy limbs, where tired Cupid, now free after hanging up his quivers, restores his smooth flames, where the Muses retreat, Garden whose beautiful foliage never grows thinner, whose spring balsam is always fragrant, whose delicate fountain of clear water gives rise to a spot well watered by a mossy stream, Garden where the sweet singing of birds resounds,—

Whatever is carried to other cities, this garden obediently supplies in this one spot.

47. About an Angry Diceplayer Who Thinks He Can Rule the Dice

Vatanans plays with many other gamblers, but he does not know how to play and he thinks that the points will come at his bidding. But when the die perversely turns up losing numbers, he shouts, becomes

Tum verbis manibusque furens miserandus anhelat,   5
  De solitis faciens proelia vera iocis.
Effundit tabulam, mensam, subsellia, pyrgum,
  Perditaque Harpyacis aera rapit manibus.
Hic si forte unam tabulam non arte sed errans
  Vicerit aut aliam, nil bene dante manu,   10
Mox inflat venas et pallida guttura tendit
  Plusque furit vincens quam superatus erat.
Non iam huic ludum sapientum calculus aptet,
  [Qui possit potius ludere cum furiis.]

48. *De venatore picto in manibus oculos habente*

Docta manus saevis quotiens se praebuit ursis,
  Numquam fallentem tela dedere necem.
Hinc etiam digitis oculos pictura locavit,
  Quod visum frontis provida dextra tulit.

49. *Aliter unde supra*

Venatori oculos manibus pictura locavit
  Et geminum egregia lumen ab arte manet.
Hic quocumque modo venabula fulgida pressit,
  Signatum veluti contulit exitium.
Naturae lucem vicerunt fortia facta.   5
  Iam visus proprios coepit habere manus.

50. *In aurigam effeminatum numquam vincentem*

Praecedis, Vico, nec tamen praecedis,
Et quam debueras tenere partem,
Hac mollis misero teneris usu.
Umquam vincere possis ut quadrigis,
Corruptor tibi sit retro ponendus.   5

51. *De paranympho delatore qui se ad hoc officium omnibus ingerebat*

Hermes cunctorum thalamos et vota pererrat,

pale, grumbles, and rages. Then his tongue and hands become abusive and the miserable wretch puffs hard, making real battles out of normal games. He overturns the diceboard, table, chairs, and dicecup, and seizes the lost money with Harpy-like hands.

If he happens to win a game or two, not by skill but by mistake, while his hand does nothing well, he soon puffs up with pride and stretches out his pale neck, and he becomes more violent as a winner than he had been as a loser.

No longer should the game of Wise Men be suitable for him, [but he can rather play with the Furies.]

48. About the Painting of a Hunter Having Eyes on His Hands

No matter how many times his skilled right hand opposed savage bears, his weapons never failed to deal out death. Therefore the painting has put eyes even on his fingers because his all-seeing right hand had his forehead's power of sight.

49. Another Poem on the Same Topic as Above

The painting has put eyes on the hunter's hands, and his two eyes remain there because of remarkable art. In whatever way he held the gleaming hunting spear, the hunter dealt out death as if it were fore-ordained. His brave deeds outshone natural vision and now his hand has begun to have its own power of sight.

50. To an Effeminate Charioteer Who Never Wins

You go ahead to the races, Vico, but you never go ahead in the races. By the part over which you should hold the reins tight, you are held back, made soft through wretched abuse. In order that you may ever be able to win with your four-horse team, you must put your corruptor on his back.

51. About an Attendant at Weddings, an Informer Who Used to Offer Himself to Everybody for This Function

Hermes flits to the marriages and wedding ceremonies of everybody

Omnibus ac sponsis pronubus esse cupit.
Hunc quisquam si forte velit contemnere dives,
    Mox eius famam rodit iniqua ferens.
Nec tutum obsequium nuptis. Famulatur amicis,   5
    Indicet ut potius quae videt, ille nocens.
Non sua sortitur te qui facit auspice vota,
    Sed tua, cui multum conferet ut taceas.

52. De funere mulieris formosae quae litigiosa fuit

Gorgoneos vultus habuit Catucia coniunx.
    Haec dum pulcra foret, iurgia saepe dabat.
Fecerat atque suum semper rixando maritum,
    Esset ut insano stultius ore tacens.
Et quotiens illam trepido cernebat amore,   5
    Horrebat, tamquam vera Medusa foret.
Defuncta est tandem haec iurgia ferre per umbras
    Cumque ipsa litem reddere Persephone.

53. De duobus qui se conpedibus quibus vincti erant ceciderunt

Conpedibus nexi quidam duo forte sedebant
    Criminis ob causam carceris ante fores.
Hi secum subitae moverunt iurgia rixae.
    Ebrietatis opus gessit iniqua fames.
Nec caedem pugnis aut calcibus egit uterque;   5
    Vincla illis telum, vincla fuere manus.
Nemo truces posthac debet pavitare catenas,
    Si reus e poenis ingerit arma suis.

54. De causidico turpi qui concubam suam Charitem vocabat

Esset causidici si par facundia nervo,
    Impleret cuncti viscera negotii.
Ac tamen invigilat causis quae crimina pandunt—
    Cum Veneris famula iure Priapus agit.

and he wants to be a groom's attendant at all betrothals. If by chance any rich man should wish to scorn him, he immediately blackens his reputation by bringing false charges against him.

Neither is compliance safe for those who are getting married. He waits upon his friends rather to reveal what he sees in order to do them harm.

The person who pledges his troth with you as a witness does not direct his prayers for his own welfare but for yours, since it will be greatly to his interest to have you keep silent.

52. About the Death of a Beautiful Quarrelsome Woman

A married woman named Catucia had the looks of a Gorgon. Although she was beautiful, she was often involved in quarrels. By her constant bickering she had caused her husband to remain stupidly silent because of her raving talk. As often as he looked upon her with frightened love, he shuddered as if she were the real Medusa.

At last she died, to carry these wrangles into the lower world and to dispute with Persephone herself.

53. About Two Men Who Killed Themselves with the Chains with Which They Were Bound

It happened that two men bound together with chains because of some crime were sitting before the doors of a prison. Suddenly a quarrel flared up between them. Cruel hunger accomplished the work of intoxication. Neither man fought with fists or feet; chains were their weapon, chains were their hands.

Henceforth nobody ought to fear cruel chains, if a prisoner turns his own punishment into weapons.

54. About an Infamous Lawyer Who Called His Concubine Grace

If this lawyer's eloquence equaled his manhood, it would penetrate the vitals of every case. However, he is awake all night on obvious cases. Priapus pleads when he goes courting with the handmaiden of Venus.

55. *In ministrum regis, qui alienas facultates vi extorquebat*

Bella die nocteque suis facit Eutychus armis,
    Divitias cunctis e domibus rapiens.
Huic si forte aliquis nolit dare sive repugnet,
    Vim facit et clamat, "Regis habenda," nimis.
Quid gravius hostis, fur, aut latrunculus implet,   5
    Talia si dominus atque minister agit?

56. *De eodem aliter*

Cum famulis telisque furens penetralia cuncta
    Eutychus inrumpit divitiasque rapit,
Hunc nullus vetat ire parens, non forsan amicus;
    Deterior precibus redditus ille manet.
Quae sunt ergo manus aut ferrea tela ferenda,   5
    Quisve aries talem quodve repellat opus?
Huic si nemo potest ullas opponere vires,
    Obvia sint illi fulmina sola dei.

57. *In eum, qui, cum senior dici nollet, multas sibi concubas faciebat*

Accusas proprios cur longo ex tempore canos,
    Cum sis phoenicis grandior a senio,
Et quotiens tardam quaeris celare senectam,
    Paelicibus multis te facis esse virum?
Incassum reparare putas hac fraude iuventam—   5
    Harum luxus agit, sis gravior ut senior.

58. *Item in supra scriptum quod se mori numquam diceret*

Quantum tres Priami potuissent vivere mundo
    Aut quantum cornix atque elephans superest,
Tantam dum numeres longaeva aetate senectam,
    Te numquam firmas Tartara posse pati
Et credis Lachesim numquam tua rumpere fata   5
    Aeternoque putas stamine fila trahi.

55. *Against a Royal Official Who Took the Property of Others by Force*

Night and day Eutychus makes war with his weapons, seizing property from all homes. If perchance anybody should refuse to hand over anything to him or should fight back, he uses force and shouts in a very loud voice, "All belongs to the king."

What worse act does an enemy, thief, or highwayman perpetrate, if a lord and his official do such things?

56. *Another Poem about the Same Person*

With his attendants and his weapons Eutychus madly breaks into all homes and carries away property. No relation, no friend perchance prevents him from going in. He becomes even worse if anybody tries to hold him back by entreaties. What hands, therefore, what iron weapons are to be used against him, what ram or engine of war would beat back such a man? If nobody can oppose him with any force, may the thunderbolts of God alone bar his way!

57. *Against a Man Who, Because He Did Not Wish to Be Called an Old Man, Kept Many Mistresses for Himself*

Why do you find fault with your hair that has long been white, since you are older than the phoenix, and why, whenever you seek to hide your doddering old age, do you play the part of a man with many mistresses?

In vain do you think that you are regaining your youth by this deception. Pleasure with these ladies reveals that you are a sick and decrepit old man.

58. *Another Poem on the Person Mentioned Above, Because He Said That He Would Never Die*

While you count off for yourself a prolonged old age which is as long as the time three Priams might have spent on this earth, or as long as the span of life of a crow or an elephant, you declare that you can never suffer Tartarus, and you believe that Lachesis will never break your fates, and you think that the threads of your life are being drawn out with eternal spinning.

Quamvis tarda, tibi veniet mors ultima tandem,
  Cum magis oblitus coeperis esse tui.
Nam poena est potius morbis producere vitam—
  Quod non semper habes, tristius, esse diu, est.   10

59. *Epitaphion de filia Oageis infantula*

Heu dolor! Est magnis semper mors invida fatis,
Quae teneros artus inimico sidere mergit!
Damira hoc tumulo regalis clauditur infans,
Cui vita innocua est quarto dirupta sub anno.
Quam facile offuscant iucundum tristia lumen!   5
Nemo rosam albentem, fuerit nisi quae bona, carpit.
  Haec parvam aetatem cuncta cum laude ferebat.
Grata nimis specie, verecundo garrula vultu
Naturae ingenio modicos superaverat annos.
Dulce loquebatur, quidquid praesumpserat ore,   10
Linguaque diversum fundebat mellea murmur,
Tamquam avium verna resonat per tempora cantus.
  Huius puram animam stellantis regia caeli
Possidet et iustis inter videt esse catervis.
At pater Oageis, Libyam dum protegit armis,   15
Audivit subito defunctam funere natam.
Nuntius hic gravior cunctis fuit hostibus illi,
Ipsaque sub tali flevit Victoria casu.

60. *De amphitheatro in villa vicina mari fabricato*

Amphitheatrales mirantur rura triumphos
  Et nemus ignotas cernit adesse feras.
Spectat arando novos agrestis turba labores
  Nautaque de pelago gaudia mixta videt.
Fecundus nil perdit ager, plus germina crescunt,   5
  Dum metuunt omnes hic sua fata ferae.

61. *De sigillo Cupidinis aquas fundentis*

Igne salutifero Veneris puer omnia flammans
  Pro facibus propriis arte ministrat aquas.

Although it will come late, nevertheless your death will finally come when you have begun no longer to be aware of your own existence. For it is torture, all the more, to prolong life through sickness; it is sadder for that which cannot last forever to last too long.

59. Epitaph for the Little Daughter of Oageis

Alas, Grief! Death is always envious of those born with promising fates, death which lays tender bodies to rest under an unfriendly star! The royal child Damira lies in this tomb, her innocent life ended in its fourth year. How easily sadness darkens a joyous light! No one plucks the white rose unless it is good.

She fulfilled her short life with every kind of merit. Most pleasing in appearance, chattering, and of modest mien, she had a natural talent far beyond her few years. She spoke sweetly, no matter what she said, and her honeyed tongue poured forth a wealth of sound like the singing of birds in the springtime.

Now the starry realm of heaven possesses her pure soul and sees her dwelling among the just. But while her father Oageis was defending Libya by force of arms, he heard that his daughter had died a sudden death. This news weighed upon his heart more than all the forces of the enemy, and Victory herself wept over such a calamity.

60. About an Amphitheater Built on a Country Estate Near the Sea

The countryside marvels at the triumphs of the amphitheater and the forest notices that strange wild beasts are there. The many farmers look at new struggles while plowing and the sailor sees varied entertainments from the sea. The fertile land loses nothing, the plants grow in greater abundance while all the wild beasts fear their fates here.

61. About a Little Statue of Cupid Pouring Forth Water

The son of Venus, who inflames everything with health-giving fire, provides water in place of his own torches through the medium of art.

62. *De Neptuno in marmoreo alveo aquas fundente*

Quam melior, Neptune, tuo sors ista tridente est.
    Post pelagus dulces hic tibi dantur aquae!

63. *De puteo cavato in monte arido*

Quis hunc non credat ipsis dare Syrtibus amnes,
    Qui dedit ignotas viscere montis aquas?

64. *De aquis calidis Cirnensibus*

Ardua montanos inter splendentia lucos
    Culmina et indigenis nunc metuenda feris,
Quo deserta prius solum nemus atra tenebat
    Tetraque inaccessam sederat umbra viam,
Qua vos laude canam quantoque in carmine tollam,   5
    In quibus extructa est atque locata salus?
Hic etiam ignitus tepet ad praetoria fervor,
    Plenior et calidas terra ministrat aquas.
[Quis sterilem non credat humum? Fumantia vernant
    Pascua; luxuriat gramine cocta silex.]   10
Innocuos fotus membris parit intima tellus
    Naturamque pio temperat igne calor.
[Et cum sic rigidae cautes fervore liquescant,
    Contemtis audax ignibus herba viret.]

65. *De sententiis septem philosophorum distichi*

Solon praecipuus, fertur qui natus Athenis,
Finem prolixae dixit te cernere vitae.

Chilon, quem patria egregium Lacedaemona misit,
Hoc prudenter ait te ipsum ut cognoscere possis.

Ex Mitylenaeis fuerat qui Pittacus oris,   5
Te, ne quid nimis ut cupias, exquirere dixit.

Thales ingenio sapiens Milesius acri
Errorem in terris firmat non caelitus esse.

62. About Neptune Pouring Forth Water in a Marble Trough

What a better lot is this than waving your trident, Neptune! After the salt waters of the sea sweet waters are given to you here.

63. About a Well Dug in a Dry Mountain

Who would not believe that he makes rivers flow through the Syrtes themselves who drew unknown streams from the bowels of a mountain?

64. About the Hot Springs of Cirne

Lofty building tops gleaming among the mountain thickets, now dreaded by the wild beasts of the region, where formerly only forests covered the gloomy uninhabited area, and where a dark shadow had settled upon an inaccessible road, with what praise shall I sing about you, with what mighty song shall I extol you, in which a monument to health has been erected?

This glowing heat spreads its warmth in the magnificent palace also, and the rich earth supplies warm waters.

[Who would not believe the ground to be unproductive? The smoking pasture land grows green, the heated flint abounds in grass.]

The bowels of the earth bring forth harmless warmth for the body and the heat regulates nature with nourishing fire.

[And although the hard cliffs boil with heat in this way, the grass, disregarding the fire, boldly flourishes.]

65. Distichs on the Sayings of the Seven Wise Men

The renowned Solon, who is said to have been born in Athens, ordered you to look to the end of a long life.

Chilon, a renowned citizen of Sparta, wisely said this: that you can know yourself.

Pittacus, who was from the shores of Mitylene, said that you should seek to wish for nothing in excess.

Thales the Milesian, a philosopher of keen intellect, declared that blind folly on earth is not due to the gods.

Inde Prienaea Bias tellure creatus
Plures esse malos divina voce probavit.   10

Urbe Periander genitus, cui fama Corintho est,
Omnia constituit tecum ut meditando revolvas.

Cleobolus, proprium clamat quem Lindia civem,
Omne, inquit, magnum est quod mensura optima librat.

66. *De Ianuario mense*

Lucifer annorum et saeclis Sol, Iane, secundus,
   [Principium faciens, omnia tu renovas.]
Est rota certa tui tecum sine fine laboris;
   Itque reditque tibi, quidquid in orbe venit.
Omnia perpetuis praecedis frontibus ora;   5
   Quae necdum venient quaeve fuere vides.

67. *De Olympio venatore Aegyptio*

Grata voluptatis species et causa favoris,
Fortior innumeris, venator Olympie, palmis,
Tu verum nomen membrorum robore signas,
Alcides collo, scapulis, cervice, lacertis,
Admirande, audax, velox, animose, parate.   5
Nil tibi forma nocet nigro fuscata colore.
Sic ebenum pretiosum atrum natura creavit;
Purpura sic parvo depressa in murice fulget;
Sic nigrae violae per mollia gramine vernant;
Sic tetras quaedam conmendat gratia gemmas;   10
Sic placet obscuros elephans inmanis ad artus;
Sic turis piperisque Indi nigredo placessit;
Postremum tanto populi pulcrescis amore,
Foedior est quantum pulcher sine viribus alter.

68. *In epitaphion supra scripti Olympii*

Venator iucunde nimis atque arte ferarum
Saepe placens, agilis, gratus, fortissimus, audax,
Qui puer ad iuvenes dum non advixeris annos,
Omnia maturo conplebas facta labore.

Thereupon Bias, born in the land of Priene, in a divine voice showed that most men are evil.

Periander, born in the city that bears the famous name of Corinth, decided that you can settle all things by thought.

Cleobolus, whom Lindus proclaims as her own citizen, said that everything is great which moderation balances.

66. *About the Month of January*

Morning star of each year, Janus, second sun of the ages, [who causes the beginning and restores all things,] the wheel of your toil is fixed and endless, whatever takes place upon the earth goes and returns with you.

You go ahead of all other faces with your eternal faces: you see what has not yet happened and what has already been.

67. *About Olympius, an Egyptian Hunter*

Pleasing sight of joy and reason for popular acclaim, stronger by your countless victories, animal fighter Olympius, you bear a fit name because of your bodily strength, a Hercules by virtue of your neck, shoulders, back, and limbs. O wonderful, O bold, O swift, O spirited, O always ready! Not at all does your swarthy body harm you because of its blackness. So did nature create black precious ebony. So does the purple deeply placed in the tiny murex gleam, so do violets of deepest shade bloom in the soft grass, so does a certain grace set off gems of somber hue, so does the huge elephant please because of its dusky limbs, so do black Indian incense and pepper give pleasure. Finally, you are as beautiful in the great love the people bear you as another man, handsome without strength, is ugly.

68. *Epitaph of the Above-mentioned Olympius*

Animal fighter who brought us great joy and often delighted us with your skill against the wild beasts—quick, pleasant, most brave, daring —who, as a boy that had not yet reached the age of young men, used to perform all feats with mature effort, who gave to others the privi-

Qui licet ex propria populis bene laude placeres,   5
Praestabas aliis ut tecum vincere possent.
Tantaque mirandae fuerant tibi praemia formae
Ut te post fatum timeant laudentque sodales.
Heu nunc tam subito mortis livore peremtum
Iste capit tumulus quem non Carthaginis arces   10
Amphitheatrali potuerunt ferre triumpho!
Sed nihil ad Manes hoc funere perdis acerbo.
Vivet fama tui post te longaeva decoris
Atque tuum nomen semper Carthago loquetur.

69. *De Chimaera aenea*

Aeris fulgiduli nitens metallo
Ignes pertulit, ante quos vomebat,
Et facta est melior Chimaera flammis.

70. *De statua Veneris in cuius capite violae sunt natae*

Cypris candidulo reddita marmore
Veram se exanimis corpore praebuit.
Infudit propriis membra caloribus,
Per florem in statuam viveret ut suam.
Nec mendax locus est. Qui violas feret,   5
Servabit famulas inguinibus rosas.

71. *In caecum qui pulcras mulieres tactu noscebat*

Lucis egenus, viduae frontis,
Iter amittens, caecus amator
Corpora tactu mollia palpat
Et muliebres iudicat artus
Nivei cui sit forma decoris.   5
Credo quod ille nolit habere
Oculos per quos cernere possit,
Cui dedit plures docta libido.

lege of winning with you, although you could give great pleasure to the spectators and win acclaim by yourself—so great were the rewards of your remarkable physique that after your death your companions are still awed by you and praise you.

Alas, now this tomb contains you carried off so unexpectedly by envious death, you whom the walls and towers of Carthage could not bear when you triumphed in the arena! But you lose nothing among the shades because of this bitter death. The fame of your glory will live everlastingly after you, and Carthage will always say your name!

69. About a Bronze Chimera

Shining in gleaming bronze, she has endured the flames that she formerly spewed forth, and the Chimera has been improved by her own fires.

70. About a Statue of Venus on Whose Head Violets Grew

A Venus made of bright marble, though lifeless, by her body proved herself real. She spread her own warmth into her limbs so that she came to life through the flowers on her statue.

Neither is the place deceptive. If it bears violets, it will also keep roses to serve other parts of the body.

71. On a Blind Man Who Knew Beautiful Women by Touch

Bereft of light, with forehead widowed, losing his way, the blind lover strokes soft bodies and judges the limbs of women, deciding by touch which one has a body of snow-white beauty.

I believe that he to whom skilled lust has given several eyes does not want to have eyes with which he can see.

72. *In philosophum hirsutum nocte tantum cum puellis concumbentem*

Hispidus tota facie atque membris,
Crine non tonso capitis verendi,
Omnibus clares Stoicus magister.
Te viris tantum simulas modestum
Nec die quaeris coitum patrare   5
Ne capi possis lateasque semper.
Fervidus sed cum petulante lumbo
Nocte formosas subigis puellas.
Incubus fies subito per actus,
Qui Cato dudum fueras per artes.   10

73. *De catula sua brevissima ad domini sui nutum currente*

Forma meae catulae brevis est sed amabilis inde,
  Hanc totam ut possit concava ferre manus.
Ad domini vocem famulans et garrula currit,
  Humanis tamquam motibus exiliens.
Nec monstrosum aliquid membris gerit illa decoris;   5
  Omnibus exiguo corpore visa placet.
Mollior huic cibus est somnusque in stramine molli.
  Muribus infensa est, saevior atque catis.
Vincit membra nimis latratu parvola torvo.
  Si natura daret, posset ab arte loqui.   10

74. *De pardis mansuetis qui cum canibus venationem faciebant*

Cessit Lyaei sacra fama numinis
Lynces ab oris qui subegit Indicis.
Curru paventes duxit ille bestias
Mero gravatas ac minari nescias
Et quas domarent vincla coetu garrulo.   5
Sed mira nostri forma constat saeculi;
Pardos feroces saeviores tigribus
Praedam sagaci nare mites quaerere
Canum inter agmen et famem doctos pati,

72. To a Hairy Philosopher Who Sleeps with Girls Only at Night

Hairy all over your face and body, with the hair of your respected head unshorn, in the eyes of everybody you are a distinguished Stoic philosopher.

You merely pretend to men that you are sexually virtuous and you do not seek intercourse by day in order that you may not be caught and that you may always escape notice. But at night with heat and passion you overwhelm beautiful maidens. By your actions you will suddenly become a lecher, you who in your teachings had long been a Cato.

73. About His Tiny Puppy That Runs to Her Master's Bidding

My puppy has a tiny frame, but she is lovable for that very reason, inasmuch as I can hold all of her in the hollow of my hand. Obedient and chattering she runs toward the sound of her master's voice, leaping with almost human movements. Her body does not have any ill-formed strangeness that passes for beauty; when looked at she pleases everybody by her diminutive size. Her food is soft and so is her sleep on her soft mattress. She is a bane to mice and cruel to cats. By her mighty, fierce barking she overcomes her small body. If nature permitted, she could speak with eloquence.

74. About Trained Leopards That Hunted with Dogs

The sacred fame of the divine power of Bacchus, who drove lynxes from the shores of India, has been surpassed. He yoked to his chariot terrified wild beasts that, being overcome by wine and unable to threaten, were held in restraint by the reins, although a noisy team.

But a marvelous sight appears in our times—fierce leopards more savage than tigers become gentle and with keen nostrils hunt their prey in the company of a pack of dogs, and trained to endure hunger

Quidquid capessunt ore ferre baiulo.   10
O qui magister terror est mortalium,
Diros ferarum qui retundit impetus,
Morsum repertis ut cibis non audeant!

75. *In psaltriam foedam*

Cum saltas misero, Gattula, corpore
Hoc cuiquam libitum est, horrida, quod facis,
Insanam potius te probo psaltriam
Quae foedam faciem motibus ingraves
Et, dum displiceas, quosque feras iocos.   5
Credis quod populos cymbala mulceant?
Nemo iudicium tale animi gerit
Pro te ut non etiam gaudia deserat.

76. *Item de ea quod ut amaretur praemia promittebat*

Quid facis ut pretium promittens, Gattula, ameris?
  Da pretium ne te oderis ipsa simul!
Praemia cur perdis? Cur spondes munera tantis?
  Accipe tu pretium ne mihi dona feras!
Non est tam petulans pariterque insanus amator   5
  Qui te non credat prodigiale malum.
Sed si forte aliquis moechus surrexit ab umbris,
  Cui talis placeas, huic tua dona dato!

77. *In ebriosam et satis meientem*

Quod bibis et totum dimittis ab inguine Bacchum,
  Pars tibi superior debuit esse femur.
Potabis recto—poteris, Follonia,—Baccho,
  Si parte horridius inferiore bibas.

78. *In mulierem pulcram castitati studentem*

Pulcrior et nivei cum sit tibi forma coloris,

they submissively carry in their mouths whatever they seize.

Oh, what a master is the fear of human beings! It blunts the fierce attacks of ferocious animals so that they do not dare to take a bite when they have found food!

75. *To an Ugly Cymbalist*

Whenever you dance with your repulsive body, Gattula, and, my frightful one, what you are doing gives pleasure to nobody, I really think that you are a mad musician making your foul face worse by your gyrations. As long as you displease, you would put up with every gibe. Do you believe that your cymbal playing appeases the public? Nobody has such critical judgment that he would not run away from even such pleasures on account of you.

76. *Another about the Same Musician Because She Offered a Price to Be Loved*

What are you doing, Gattula, offering a price to be loved? Give a reward that you should not hate yourself at the same time. Why do you waste your bonuses? Why do you promise gifts to so many men? Take a present from me, and do not offer me any money! There is no lover so passionate and equally insane who does not believe that you are a monstrous evil. But if it should happen that some debauchee arises from the dead whom somebody like you pleases, give your largesse to him!

77. *To a Drunken Woman Who Passes Water Copiously*

Because you drink wine and discharge all of it from your loins, your upper region should have been your thigh.

You will drink holding your wine in (you will be able to do this, Follonia), if you should grossly imbibe with your lower part.

78. *To a Beautiful Woman Devoted to Chastity*

Although you have a beautiful snow-white body, you desire to observe

Cuncta pudicitiae iura tenere cupis.
Mirandum est quali naturam laude gubernes
' Moribus ut Pallas, corpore Cypris eas.
Te neque coniugii libet excepisse levamen;   5
Saepius exoptas nolle videre mares.
Haec tamen est animo quamvis exosa voluptas:
Numquid non mulier conparis esse potes?

79. *De eo qui, cum Burdo diceretur, filiae suae Pasiphaae nomen inposuit*

Disciplinarum esse hominem risusque capacem,
Quod nulli est pecudi, dixit Aristoteles.
Sed cum Burdo homo sit, versum est sophismate verum.
Nam et ridere solet vel ratione viget.
Surrexit duplex nostro sub tempore monstrum: 5
Quod pater est burdo Pasiphaeque redit.

80. *De laude rosae centumfoliae*

Hanc puto de proprio tinxit Sol aureus ortu
Aut unum ex radiis maluit esse suis.
Sed si etiam centum foliis rosa Cypridis extat,
Fluxit in hanc omni sanguine tota Venus.
Haec florum sidus, haec Lucifer almus in agris.   5
Huic odor et color est dignus honore poli.

81. *De statua Hectoris in Ilio, quae videt Achillem et sudat*

Ilion in medium Pario de marmore facti,
Stant contra Phrygius Hector vel Graius Achilles.
Priamidae statuam sed verus sudor inundat
Et falsum fictus Hector formidat Achillem.
Nescio quid mirum gesserunt Tartara saeclo.   5
Credo quod aut superi animas post funera reddunt
Aut ars mira potest legem mutare barathri.
Sed si horum nihil est, certe extat marmore Hector
Testaturque suam viva formidine mortem.

all the rules of chastity. It is wonderful how gloriously you control nature, inasmuch as you pass for a Minerva in your way of life and for a Venus with your body. You find no happiness in taking to yourself the comfort of a husband, and you often choose to shun the sight of men.

Nevertheless, you have a fancy for this pleasure, hateful though it may be to you!

Is it not possible for you to be the wife of somebody like yourself?

79. *About a Man Who Gave the Name Pasiphae to His Daughter When His Own Name Was Burdo (Mule)*

Aristotle has said that man is capable of learning and laughing, gifts that no other animals have. But since Mule is a man, truth has been turned about by a fallacy, for he can laugh and waxes strong in reasoning.

A two-fold monstrosity has arisen in our time—a mule is a father and Pasiphae has returned to earth!

80. *In Praise of the Hundred-leafed Rose*

I think that the golden sun has dyed this flower with the colors of its own rising or has wished it to be one of its own rays. But if it is also the rose of Venus with a hundred leaves, Venus has entirely flowed into it with her blood. This is the star of flowers; this is the gracious morning star over the fields; its fragrance and hue are worthy of heavenly honor.

81. *About a Statue of Hector in Troy That Sees Achilles and Sweats*

Trojan Hector and Greek Achilles, statues of Parian marble, face each other in the middle of Troy. But real sweat pours down the statue of Hector, and a likeness of Hector dreads a make-believe Achilles. Tartarus has wrought a strange wonder in this age. I believe that either the immortals restore dead souls to life after death or a wondrous art can change the laws of the lower world. But if neither of these is true, it is a fact that Hector stands there in marble and attests his death by his living fear.

82. *De muliere Marina vocabulo*

Quidam concubitu futuit fervente Marinam;
    Fluctibus in salsis fecit adulterium.
Non hic culpandus, potius sed laude ferendus,
    Qui memor est Veneris quod mare nata foret.

83. *De horto domni Oageis, ubi omnes herbae medicinales plantatae sunt*

Constructas inter moles parietibus altis
    Hortus amoenus inest aptior et domino.
Hic vario frondes vitales semine crescunt
    In quibus est Genio praemedicante salus.
Nil Phoebi Asclepique tenet doctrina parandum: 5
    Omnibus hinc morbis cura sequenda placet.
Iam puto quod caeli locus est ubi numina regnant,
    Cum datur his herbis vincere mortis onus.

84. *De pica quae humanas voces imitabatur*

Pica hominum voces cuncta ante animalia monstrat
    Et docto externum perstrepit ore melos.
Nec nunc oblita est quidnam prius esset in orbe;
    Aut haec Picus erat aut homo rursus inest.

85. *De rustica in disco facta, quae spinam tollit de planta satyri*

Cauta nimis spinam satyri pede rustica tollit,
    Luminibus certis vulneris alta notans.
Illum panduri solatur voce Cupido,
    Inridens tali vulnere flere virum.
Nil falsum credas artem lusisse figuris: 5
    Viva minus speciem reddere membra solent.

86. *De colocasia herba in tecto populante*

Nilus quam riguis parit fluentis

82. *About a Woman Named Marina*

Somebody made love passionately to Marina in the salty waves. He is not to be blamed but rather to be praised, for he remembers Venus because she was born in the sea.

83. *The Garden of Lord Oageis, Where All Medicinal Herbs Have Been Planted*

Set among buildings erected with high walls, there is a garden that is beautiful and also useful to its owner. Here from different seeds grow life-giving plants in which there is health dispensed by a guardian spirit.

The science of Apollo and Asclepius contains no recipe that has to be obtained from the outside; from this place the treatment to be followed satisfies all ailments.

Now I believe that this is a heavenly spot where the will of the gods rules, because with these plants it is possible to overcome the burden of death.

84. *About a Magpie That Imitated the Human Voice*

A magpie imitates the human voice better than all other animals and with its skillful mouth loudly sings a song not native to it. Nor is it now forgetful of what it previously was in the world. Either this bird was Picus or there is a human being inside it again.

85. *About a Country Girl Pictured on a Plate, Removing a Thorn from a Satyr's Foot*

A country girl is very carefully removing a thorn from a satyr's foot, while peering at the deep wound with great concern. Playing a pandora, Cupid is consoling him but also mocks him because he, a man, is crying over such a wound.

You would believe that art has not given a single false touch to the figures; living beings are usually less lifelike.

86. *About a Lily Plant Growing in a House*

Spreading its broad branches, flourishing in pleasant surroundings, the

Extendens colocasia ampliores
Ramos, per spatium virens amoenum,
Haec nostris laribus creata frondet.
Naturam famulans opaca vertit					5
Plus tecto ut vigeat solet quam horto.

87. De eo qui podium amphitheatri saliebat

Amphitheatralem podium transcendere saltu
Velocem audivi iuvenem nec credere quivi
Hunc hominem, potius sed avem, si talia gessit.
Et posui huic, fateor, me Dorica vina daturum
Conspicere ut possem tanti nova facta laboris.			5
Aspexi victusque dedi promissa petenti
Atque meo gravior levis extitit ille periclo.
Non iam mirabor sumtis te, Daedale, pinnis
Isse per aetherios natura errante meatus.
Hunc magis obstipui coram qui plebe videnti			10
Corpore, non pinnis, fastigia summa volavit.

88. De Diogene picto, ubi lascivienti menetrix barbam evellit et Cupido mingit in podice eius

Diogenem meretrix derisum Laida monstrat
	Barbatamque comam frangit amica Venus.
Nec virtus animi nec castae semita vitae
	Philosophum revocat turpiter esse virum.
Hoc agit infelix, alios quo saepe notavit.			5
	Quodque nimis miserum est: mingitur arte sophus.

89. De catto, qui, cum soricem maiorem devorasset, apoplexium passus occubuit

Inmensi soricis cattus dum membra vorasset
Deliciis periit crudior ille suis.

colocasia, which the Nile gives birth to in its moist waters, puts forth its leaves when it is planted in our house.

Serviceable and shady, it reverses the laws of nature, in that it grows better under our roof than it generally does in a garden.

87. About a Man Who Leaped Above the Balcony of the Amphitheater

I heard that a speedy young man leaped above the balcony of the amphitheater and I could not believe that he was a man, but I thought rather that he was a bird if he accomplished such a feat. And I bet him, I admit, that I would give him Greek wine to see him repeat such a strenuous and strange achievement. I saw, and, beaten, I gave what I had wagered when he asked me for it, and though weighed down by my wager he turned out to be light enough.

No longer shall I wonder, Daedalus, that by putting on wings you went over the course of heaven through an aberration of nature. I am more amazed at this man who in front of the spectators flew over a great height, not with wings, but with his body.

88. About a Painting of Diogenes, in Which a Harlot Plucks His Beard as He Is Frolicking and Cupid Drenches His Backside

The harlot Lais reveals Diogenes as an object of derision and she, his companion in love, is plucking his beard. Neither a virtuous mind nor the path of an upright life deters the philosopher from acting disgracefully as a man.

The ill-fated Diogenes is doing the very thing for which he often found fault with others. And, what is most disgraceful—the wise man is being artistically befouled!

89. About a Cat That Suffered an Apoplectic Stroke and Died When It Devoured Too Big a Mouse

When a cat had devoured the body of a huge mouse, it suffered a cruel death because of this dainty morsel.

Pertulit adsuetae damnum per viscera praedae:
Per vitam moriens concipit ore necem.

90. *In Anclas; in salutatorium domini regis*

Hildirici regis fulget mirabile factum
    Arte, opere, ingenio, divitiis, pretio.
Hinc radios sol ipse capit quos huc dare possit.
    Altera marmoribus creditur esse dies.
Hic sine nube solum; nix iuncta et sparsa putatur.   5
    Dum steterint, credas mergere posse pedes.

91. *Epithalamium Fridi a*
LUXORIO,
viro clarissimo et spectabili, dictum centone

Sol, qui terrarum flammis opera omnia lustrat,
Extulit os sacrum caelo tenebrasque resolvit.
Laetitia ludisque viae plausuque fremebant,
At Venus aetherios inter dea candida nimbos
Aurea subnectens exertae cingula mammae,   5
Dona ferens, pacem aeternam pactosque hymenaeos
Atque omnem ornatum, Capitolia celsa tenebat,
Punica regna videns, Tyrios et Agenoris urbem.
Hinc atque hinc glomerantur Oreades et bona Iuno.
Incedunt pariter pariterque ad limina tendunt.   10
Tectum angustum, ingens, centum sublime columnis,
Hae sacris sedes epulis, atque ordine longo
Perpetuis soliti patres considere mensis.
Una omnes, magna iuvenum stipante caterva,
Deveniunt faciemque deae vestemque reponunt.   15
Dant signum, fulsere ignes et conscius aether
Conubiis, mediisque parant convivia tectis.
Fit strepitus tectis vocemque per ampla volutant
Atria, ubi adsuetis biforem dat tibia cantum.
At tuba terribilem sonitum procul aere canoro   20
Increpuit mollitque animos et temperat iras.

It paid the supreme penalty on account of the vitals of its customary prey. Dying through the means of living, it met death through its own mouth.

90. *About Anclae; about the Audience Chamber of the King*

The remarkable edifice of King Hilderic gleams, erected with skill, toil, talent, riches, wealth. From it the sun itself takes its rays which it can spread to this place. Another dawn is believed to arise from the marble. Here the flawless pavement is thought to be thick snow spread about. When your feet stand upon it, you would think they could sink into it.

91. *Epithalamium of Fridus Written as a Cento by the Most Distinguished and Eminent Luxorius*

The sun, that with its rays makes bright all the works of earth, lifted up its sacred head in heaven and dispelled the darkness. With joy and games and shouts the streets resounded, and Venus, a goddess resplendent among the clouds of heaven, binding a golden belt beneath her naked breast and bearing gifts, everlasting peace and the marriage covenant and every kind of splendid ornament, stood upon the lofty Capitol, looking down upon the Punic realm, the Carthaginians, and the city of Agenor.

All about assemble the Oreads and kindly Juno; they walk side by side and keeping close to each other they go toward the portals. A stately and huge house, rising high with a hundred columns—this was the scene of the sacred feast, and in long array the elders used to sit at the long tables. With a great throng of youths in attendance, they all come down together and the goddesses lay aside their divine appearance and garments.

The signal is given, lightning and the upper air flash, witnesses of the wedding, and the feast is prepared within the palace. There is a sound of revelry in the palace and voices roll through the spacious halls where the double-mouthed flute gives forth music to accustomed ears. But the trumpet blared forth far and wide its terrifying call with sounding brass and softens passion and calms anger.

It clamor caelo, cithara crinitus Iopas
Obloquitur numeris septem discrimina vocum,
Iamque eadem digitis, iam pectine pulsat eburno.
Nec non et Tyrii per limina laeta frequentes   25
Convenere, toris iussi discumbere pictis.
   Tunc Venus aligerum dictis affatur Amorem:
"Nate, meae vires, mea magna potentia solus,
"Huc geminas nunc flecte acies, illam aspice contra.
"Quae vocat insignis facie viridique iuventa,   30
"Iam matura viro, iam plenis nubilis annis,
"Cui genus a proavis ingens clarumque paternae
"Nomen inest virtutis et nota maior imago.
"Hoc opus, hic labor est; thalamos ne desere pactos!
"Credo equidem, nova mi facies inopinave surgit.   35
"Nonne vides, quantum egregio decus enitet ore?
"Os humerosque deo similis, cui lactea colla
"Auro innectuntur, crines nodantur in aurum,
"Aurea purpuream subnectit fibula vestem.
"Qualis gemma micat, qualis Nereia Doto   40
"Et Galatea secant spumantem pectore pontum.
"Cura mihi comitumque foret nunc una mearum!
"Hanc ego nunc ignaram huius quodcumque pericli est,
"Cum tacet omnis ager, noctem non amplius unam
"Conubio iungam stabili propriamque dicabo.   45
"Hic Hymenaeus erit monumentum et pignus amoris.
"Incipe si qua animo virtus, et consere dextram.
"Occultum inspires ignem paribusque regamus
"Auspiciis: liceat Frido servire marito,
"Cui natam egregio genero dignisque hymenaeis   50
"Dat pater et pacem hanc aeterno foedere iungit."
Paret Amor dictis carae genetricis et alas
Exuit et gressu gaudens sic ore locutus:
"Mecum erit iste labor; si quid mea numina possunt,
"Cum dabit amplexus atque oscula dulcia figet   55
"Inmiscentque manus manibus pugnamque lacessunt,
"Nusquam abero, solitam flammam (datur hora quieti)
"Desuper infundam et, tua si mihi certa voluntas,
"Omnia praecepi atque animo mecum ante peregi.

The din rises to heaven; long-haired Iopas accompanies their measures on his lyre, using the intervals of the seven strings; now he strikes the notes with his fingers, now with his ivory pick. In great numbers also came the Carthaginians throughout the joyous palace, invited to sit down on the embroidered couches.

Then Venus speaks to winged Cupid:

"My son, my strength, the only source of my great power, now turn your eyes this way and look straight at her who is calling, so beautiful to look at, so young and blooming, now ripe for a husband, now of the right age for marriage. Her lineage is mighty, her father's reputation for valor is renowned, her appearance is greater than usual.

"This is your duty, this your task: do not forsake the plighted nuptial chamber! I believe indeed, a strange and unexpected shape is appearing before me. Do you not see what great beauty shines from her wonderful face? Her face and shoulders are goddess-like, her milk-white neck is entwined with gold, her hair is knotted with gold, and a golden brooch binds her purple dress. She glitters like a jewel, like Doto, daughter of Nereus, and like Galatea, who cut through the foamy sea with their breasts. Would that she were now dear to me and one of my band! In a single night, when all the world is still, I shall unite her now unaware of peril, whatever it may be, in a firm marriage and declare her his own.

"This marriage will be a testimonial and a pledge of love, Begin, if there is any courage in your heart, and come to close quarters; breathe hidden fire into her and let us rule with joint power. Let her be obedient to her husband Fridus, a splendid son-in-law to whom her father is giving his daughter in just and proper marriage and is confirming this peace with an everlasting compact."

Cupid obeys the commands of his dear mother, and taking off his wings he walks joyously forth and says:

"That task will be in my hands; if my divine powers can accomplish anything, when he embraces her and gives her sweet kisses and they battle hand-to-hand and begin the fray, I shall never be away from them and I shall pour over them the wonted fires of passion (the hour is given to rest) and, if I am sure of your good will, I have anticipated everything and gone over it in my mind. She will feel it!" And he cheers her spirit by his ready pledge.

The bride, however (for there is no longer any escape from her

"Sentiet!" atque animum praesenti pignore firmat.   60
Illa autem (neque enim fuga iam super ulla pericli est)
Cogitur et supplex animos summittere amori.
Spemque dedit dubiae menti solvitque pudorem.
Illum turbat amor; ramum qui veste latebat
Eripit a femine et flagranti fervidus infert.   65
It cruor inque humeros cervix conlapsa recumbit.
His demum exactis geminam dabit Ilia prolem,
Laeta deum partu, centum conplexa nepotes.

peril), is compelled humbly to submit her pride to love and she gave hope to her wavering mind and cast away her chastity.

Love arouses the groom; he pulls from his thigh the bough concealed in his cloak, and heated with desire he takes it to his passionate bride. Blood flows, her neck droops and sinks on her shoulder. When this is over, Ilia will bear twins and she will rejoice in the divine family to which she has given birth, embracing her hundred grandsons.

PART THREE: COMMENTARY

COMMENTARY

1

Meter: Phalaecean; see above, Ch. VIII, Meter 3.

Superscription: In A, between Book 23, which contains the riddles of Symphosius, and Book 24, the following appears (here it is given without abbreviations and with the original spelling): *Explicuerunt enigmata Sinfosi. Incipit Liber Epigramaton viri clarissimi Luxori et spectabilis. Sunt versus LXXXXVII.* For the title *vir clarissimus et spectabilis,* see above, Ch. III, 7. The heading indicates that there are 97 poems in this book of the *Anthologia Latina;* this number includes the 89 poems of Luxorius plus 376R-379R, with 378R consisting of five poems.

Title: See above, Ch. VII, A 6.

Metro Phalaecio: Riese omits these words in his 1894 edition. Baehrens does not retain them in the title, but in his critical apparatus he indicates that perhaps they should be kept and that Faustus may have added them. At any rate, they are in the manuscript. For the spelling of *Phalaecio,* see above, Ch. IX, B.

Faustum: Birt, *Das antike Buchwesen,* p. 348, sees in the relationship of Luxorius and Faustus a parallel to that of Synesius and his friends Nikander and Polyaemenes, to whom Synesius sent his book *In Praise of Baldness* for approval. Birt also refers to Cicero, *Ad Atticum* 1.14.2, in which Cicero calls Atticus the Aristarchus (Alexandrine critic of Homer) of his orations. However, Luxorius implies nothing about the entrusting of editorial duties to Faustus.

The dedication is unique in Latin poetry. Other poets, like Lucretius and Vergil, dedicated poems to friends or to distinguished patrons but none of them asked the person to whom the poem was dedicated to distribute it. Cf. the simple dedication in Catullus, 1, and the dedications of Martial in 5.1 and in his prefaces to Books 2 and 12.

1. post veteres: This phrase offers some difficulty because its idea does not seem to be explained or developed in the poem. At first glance *post veteres* appears to have a temporal meaning, "after the ancient poets." Cf. *post superos,* 33.2, and *post pelagus,* 62.2. Martial refers to the poets of old as *veteres:* 8.69.1-2; 10.78.14; 11.90.7. With his typical love of contrasts Luxorius may simply mean that he, a poet of his day, is now writing poetry after other poets have written before him. The phrase may refer to something in the exchange of messages between Faustus and Luxorius but these communications are unknown. If Faustus compiled the anthology, Luxorius might mean that he is now sending his poems after the poems of earlier poets have been chosen. *Iam* in line 2 would then be opposed to *post.* See Ch. II, p. 31; see also

Baehrens, *PLM* IV, 29, lines 10-13, and Riese, *Anthologia*, I, xxx, on *post veteres poetas Romanos. Post* may mean "inferior to," since Luxorius is diffident about his poems (*insulsum*, 1.8). That is the sense in which Riese takes *post* in *post artitum Nasonem* in 19R, the *Praefatio* of Octavianus (see Riese, I, xxxi). This idea is strengthened by *priscos . . . indices*, 2.1, where Luxorius in self-depreciation compares his poems with those of earlier poets. Another possibility remains. *Ausus* may be a noun; cf. Dracontius, *Satisfactio* 105 (*PL*, LX, 105), carminis illius ausu. The first comma in line 2 would then have to be omitted, making the sense, "After previous attempts, even if it is now rash to carry out your orders." Luxorius has tried to write some poems for Faustus, has failed, and now satisfies his friend's demands with the poems he has at hand, the poems of his youth. However, after due consideration, I think that *post* can be translated by "after," retaining the indefiniteness of Luxorius, or by "though inferior to." Cf. a similar idea expressed near the end of the letter of Coronatus, below, Appendix III, A, "qui audeat aliquid post veterum librorum doctrinam minuere vel superaddere," and "post peritissimum Sergium."

2. etsi iam temere est: Luxorius here deviates from idiomatic usage. *Temere est* is found in other writers with *haud* or *non*, "it is not meaningless," but not in the affirmative, as here.

2. iussis: For other examples of poems written *sur commande*, see Vergil, *Georgics* 3.41, tua, Maecenas, haud mollia iussa; Sidonius, *Carmina* 9.11, In formam redigi iubes libelli, and 12.1-2, Quid me, etsi valeam, parare carmen/ Fescenninicolae iubes Diones; Ausonius, 1, *Praefatiunculae* 4.9, scribere me Augustus iubet, and 17, *Cento Nuptialis,* prose introduction, iussum erat.

3-4. Fauste . . . tantus: *Tantus* modifies *magister,* which is in apposition with *Fauste,* a vocative. The vocative is occasionally replaced by the nominative in poetry, solemn prose, and sacred formulas, or when it is in apposition with a word like *tu* and a verb is expressed. See Vergil, *Aeneid* 8.72-77, Tuque . . . fluvius regnator aquarum; Horace, *Odes* 1.2.43-45, Filius Maiae . . . redeas; and Livy, 1.24.7, Audi tu, populus Albanus. The usual construction, however, is that when a vocative is used, a noun, adjective, or participle in apposition should also be in the vocative. See Kuehner, *Grammatik,* I, 447, § 103.8, and Kuehner-Stegmann, *Grammatik,* I, 255-56, Remark 3. Cf. 23L.6-7, 42L.3, 68L, 1-2, 190R.2, Bumbule parvus, and Dracontius, *Satisfactio* 107 (*PL* LX, 914A), summe Deus. For a full treatment of the linking of the nominative and the vocative, see J. Svennung, *Anredeformen,* Vol. XLII of *Acta Societatis Litterarum Humaniorum Regiae Upsaliensis* (Lund, Sweden, 1958), pp. 192-94, 271-79, 464-65.

5. puer: In its strictest sense, *puer* means a boy up to the age of sixteen or seventeen but it was also used of young men older than that. In the *Aeneid* 11.42, Vergil applied it to Pallas, son of Evander; Cicero, *Ad Familiares* 12.25.4, to Octavian, aged nineteen; Silius Italicus, *Punica* 15.33, to Scipio Africanus, aged twenty. In medieval Latin *puer* designates a man until at least the age of twenty-eight (Strecker, *Introduction to Medieval Latin,* p. 54).

5. in foro: See above, Ch. III, D 4.

8. insulsum: "without wit." Cf. Martial, 7.85.1, Quod non insulse scribes tetrasticha quaedam.

8. quam magis: inverted word order; cf. *solet quam,* 86.6, and *potius sed,* 82.3, and 87.3.

9. nostri temporis . . . aetas: may refer to Luxorius and Faustus when they were young or may mean "our generation." Cf. Ausonius, 5.2.6, aetas recentis temporis. Coronatus uses the words *temporis nostri lectores* in the first sentence of his letter to Luxorius; see below, Appendix III, A.

10. libellum: This small book was probably in the form of a codex, for "with the opening of the fourth century the codex is near its triumph" (Roberts, "The Codex," p. 199); see also Hall, *Companion to Classical Texts,* p. 24, and Schubart, *Das Buch bei den Griechen und Römern,* pp. 114-15. Birt, p. 118, calls the *libellus* of Luxorius "ein codex minimalen Umfanges."

11. memori: modifies *pectore,* ablative of means or manner governed by *probandos*; on the ending, see Kuehner, *Grammatik,* I, 359, § 78c. Cf. Martial, 6.25.4, Accipe et haec memori pectore vota tene, and Juvenal, 11.28, memori tractandum pectore. See also Burmann, *Anthologia,* II, 580, note to line 11.

12. deinde: synizesis.

13. tenentur: used loosely here; see above, Ch. VI, B 5. When *titulus* means an inscription on a tomb, then it bears (*tenet* or *habet*) a message: cf. Burmann, *Anthologia,* II, 84, Book IV, *Epigram* 129.2, Et lege quod nomen hic titulus teneat, and Ovid, *Metamorphoses* 9.793, Addunt et titulum: titulus breve carmen habebat. Possibly Luxorius had this epitaphic formula in mind, but in the matter of literary works, it would seem that the poem bears or has the title. When books were made in the form of rolls, the title was put on a parchment ticket and was fastened to one base of the roller (see DarSag, III.2, 1180). If however, Luxorius asked Faustus to distribute his poems by separate pages, and if he attached the titles by tickets to each page, then the pages could be held by their titles. Otherwise, the expression *titulis quibus tenentur* is a vague way of saying that the poems are separated or distinguished by their titles. In this case the titles may have been put at the head of each poem individually. (See Birt, *Buchwesen,* p. 118, on distribution of books by parts.)

15. nimis: See above, Ch. VI, A 7.

15-20. Cf. these lines with the ending of the letter of Coronatus to Luxorius, Appendix III, A.

17. index: There seems to be a play on words here. *Index* means a witness, which has a legal appropriateness vis-à-vis *culpae socios,* but it is also the word for a title (Birt, p. 66). Birt, p. 118, note 1, thinks that the *index* of Luxorius' *monobiblion* named Faustus—hence, his coresponsibility. Birt reconstructs the publication of the small book of poems in this way: (1) Luxorius puts the poems together in a book; (2) he sends them to Faustus; (3) Faustus judges them, separates them, and sends them to friends; (4) the poems are edited, probably by Faustus, and reach learned men; (5) the poems are published with the names of Luxorius and Faustus on the title page. Birt asks us to compare Quintilian, *Institutio Oratoria, Praefatio,* on the editorial responsibility assigned

to Trypho. One can agree with Birt on the first three steps only, for they are mentioned in this poem. See notes on *Faustum* and *post veteres,* above.

18. tam te talia: For the alliteration, see above, Ch. V, B 7.

18. bonis recenses: *Recenseo* is used here instead of *censeo*; a fondness for compound verbs is characteristic of late and medieval Latin; see Beeson, *Medieval Latin,* p. 14, § 6a, and Sage, *Petronius,* p. xxxii, D. 1. Whether *bonis* means "for their good points" or "as good works," the ablative is not found with the active of *(re)censere*; see Kuehner-Stegmann, I, 391, § 81, 10c. Cf. Sidonius, *Epistulae* 2.6.1, meruit inter personas nobis quoque caras devinctas censeri. Baehrens emends *bonis* to *bonus* on the analogy of 83R.3, Cerne bonus mentisque fidem probus indue iudex. However, Luxorius may not have said what Baehrens wanted him to say; the thought is more like that of Catullus, 1.3-4, namque tu solebas/ Meas esse aliquid putare nugas, than like that of the poem in the *Anthologia* cited by Baehrens. Luxorius' emphasis is on the judging of the poems as good rather than on Faustus as a kind judge.

19. duriora: On the use of the comparative, see above, Ch. VI, A 7.

25. causam: Luxorius explains in 2.4, 7-10, why pleasure will be derived from his poems.

26. edet: Baehrens prefers *edit* as the emendation of *egit,* the reading of A. The future seems better.

2

Meter: Iambic Trimeter (Senarius) Acatalectic; see above, Ch. VIII, Meter 6.

In 1.25-26 Luxorius tells Faustus that the next poem will reveal the source of pleasure in his poems. Schubert, *De Luxorio,* pp. 20-23, argues that Poem 2 is not *ridiculum* and that it does not show how the poems bring enjoyment. He points out that the *sodales* of 1.15 who were to pass judgment on the poems are forgotten in Poem 2, which is addressed to the *lector.* It is Schubert's contention that Poems 2 and 3 were not part of the collection Luxorius sent to Faustus but that they are the introductions to another set of poems written by Luxorius. Schubert believes that Poem 4 is the *ridiculum sequens poema* alluded to in 1.26 and that somebody put the two collections together at a later date. Schubert brushes aside blithely (and *sine dubio,* of course) any possible relationship between *quos olim puer in foro paravi* in 1.5 and *et quam tenello tiro lusi viscere* in 2.5. He tries (fruitlessly, in my opinion) to prove on the basis of composition and metrics that Poems 2 and 3 were written later than Poem 4.

Lector may be an address to any of the *sodales,* who became *lectores* the moment they looked at the poems. Schubert thinks that Poem 2 is not *ridiculum* but that 4 is, especially because of the contrast between small and great things in the latter. It all depends on one's sense of humor and the meaning of *ridiculum.* This word can mean "playful" or "light," as in "light verse." Poem 2 is light verse, especially in its description of Luxorius' poetry as *nugis refertam frivolisque sensibus.* Levy, in *RE,* XIII.2, 2107-8, cites Horace, *Epistles* 2.1.237-38, Idem ex ille, poema/ Qui tam ridiculum tam care prodigus emit. Here *ridiculum* describes a badly written poem by Choerilus on the exploits of Alexander. "Poor" or "bad" is another possible meaning of the word as used in 1.26, since Luxorius is self-depreciatory. Poem 2 seems to me to follow naturally after 1; it explains that the poems are trifles devised without heavy structural planning or deep thoughts—hence, easy and pleasant to read. Poem 4 is not so good an introduction as 2 but is rather a supplement and a development of the theme; the former gives the entire scope of the poems, the latter only one phase—brevity.

1. priscos . . . indices: See above, note to 1.1 Applied to books, *index* means "list," "catalogue," as well as "title." By a trope, Luxorius here uses it to mean "books" or "authors."

1. haberes: For the sequence of this verb and of *possent,* line 2, with *retexis,* line 3, see above, Ch. VI, A 5.

2. lector: The appeal to the "gentle reader," a favorite cliché of novelists of the past century, is a commonplace in Martial, a personal touch that Luxorius may have borrowed. Cf. Martial, 1.1.4; 1.113.4; 4.55.27; 5.16.2; 7.12.12; *et al.*

3. retexis: The meaning is obviously "read," "open," "turn to," but I have been unable to find any other example of *retexere* in this sense. *Texere* means "to compose" or "to write," and *retexere* applied to writing means "to alter" or "to repeat." Luxorius may have wanted to use figuratively a verb applicable to the unrolling of a *volumen* but *plicare, explicare, volvere,* and *revolvere,* not *retexere,* are the appropriate verbs for that action.

4. nugis: *Nugae* is a favorite word employed by the poets themselves to describe their lighter efforts. Cf. Catullus, 1.4; Sidonius, *Carmina* 9.9; and especially Martial, 4.10.4; 5.80.3; 6.64.7-8; 7.11.4; 10.17.4; *et al.*

5. tiro lusi: Cf. 90R.1, iunior aetas; Martial, 1.113.1, Quaecumque lusi iuvenis et puer quondam.

6-8. For an interesting alternate reading of these three lines, see *The Oxford Book of Latin Verse,* ed. by H. W. Garrod (Oxford, 1912), p. 439.

Luxorius gives three reasons why his poetry will please the reader:

(1) The poet uses learned meters; the versification is skillful.

(2) The book is framed in small artistic scope—its structure is slight.

(3) The book is without adornment or intellectual grandeur; it is more like a mime or a farce.

So Martial describes his own poems in about twenty-five places: 1. *Praefatio;* 1.16; 1.35; 2.8; 3.99; 4.49; 4.82; 5.16; 7.88; 8. *Praefatio;* 8.3; 9.50; *et al.* The only other poem of this kind in the *Anthologia* is 90R, which Burmann and Meyer use as part of an introduction to Luxorius' poems (see above, Chs. IV, 6, and IX, C 2).

7. sonat: Cf. Martial, 10.45.2, Si quid honorificum pagina blanda sonat.

7. pusillo: Cf. Martial, 9.50.1, ingenium pusillum. Baehrens emends *pusillo* to *pusilli* and freely changes many other words in this poem.

7. schemate: Riese's conjecture for *comute* in A. Baehrens emends to *scommate,* "a taunt" (cf. Macrobius, *Saturnalia* 7.3.13-14). *Schema* refers to a rhetorical figure or, in its original meaning, to an attitude or a plastic figure; synonyms for it are *habitus, ornatus,* and *conformatio.* By extension it may be taken to mean "a manner of speaking" or "structure" in this poem. Martial used the word once, in 3.68.7, to mean "a trope." *Schemate,* an emendation by *a,* oc-

curs in 377R.3, Curvavit canoris vario pro schemate conchas, where it means "pattern" or "design."

7. nullo: Mariotti, *"Congetture,"* pp. 346-48, emends to *nudo ("senza dubbio")*.

9. hanc: apparently takes up *illa* of line 6; both refer to *paginam*, line 3.

9. requiris: Cf. Martial, 1.1, Hic est quem legis ille, quem requiris. Riese puts a question mark at this sentence (line 10) but Baehrens and I do not. The interrogation is unnecessary, for lines 9-10 are a conclusion following upon lines 6-8; Luxorius has a way of compressing ideas in this manner; cf. especially 75.6-8.

10. theatra: So too Martial compares his poems to the theater. Cf. the end of the preface to his Book 1, Non intret Cato theatrum meum, and Cur in theatrum, Cato severe, venisti?

10. pervoles: Cf. Juvenal, 1.60-61, dum pervolat axe citato/ Flaminiam puer Automedon, and 6.398, totam pervolet urbem.

3

Meter: Lesser Asclepiad; see above, Ch. VIII, Meter 4.

The prototypes of Luxorius' advice to his book are found in Horace, *Epistles* 1.20, and Martial, 1.3. For other and varied addresses by an author to his book, see Ovid, *Tristia* 1.1; Martial, 3.2; 3.4; 3.5; 4.86; 8.72; 10.19; 10.104; 11.1; 12.2; Ausonius, 19.1; Sidonius, *Carmina* 3.19 (*Ad Libellum*); and 783R. In later days "Go, little book," became a favorite injunction, ranging from Chaucer's, "Go litel book, go litel myn tragedie" (*Troilus and Criseyde*, 5.1786) to Walt Whitman's, "Then falter not, O Book, fulfil thy Destiny" ("In Cabin'd Ships at Sea").

2. pomposi fori: See above, Ch. I, B 10.

2. scrinia publica: "The foundation of libraries became henceforth [after Caesar] an imperial habit" (Kenyon, *Books and Readers*, p. 80). The Vandals could not have been so destructive if they allowed a library to remain; see above, Ch. I, n. 31, and A 17.

4. pauperiem: See above, Ch. III, D 6, on the supposed poverty of Luxorius.

5. quo: used here instead of *ubi*, as in 46.1, 2, 3, 5, 12, and in 64.3. This use cannot be duplicated in classical Latin, certainly not in the written language where *quo* invariably denotes direction toward a place, and *ubi*, place where. See Fischer, *Latin Grammar*, II, 574-76, § 616; W. M. Lindsay, *Latin Language*, p. 568, and *Latin Grammar*, p. 141. This distinction was maintained in the written language, but there was confusion in the expression of other place relationships; note, e. g., *in mentem esse*. See Blaise, *Manuel*, p. 78, § 76; Blatt, *Précis*, p. 88, § 122; Ernout and Thomas, *Syntaxe latine*, pp. 112-14, § 134-35; and Woelfflin, "Die Lokalsätze in Lateinischen," *ALL*, IX (1896), 449.

In the spoken language the differences in showing place relationships were observed less sharply, to judge from Petronius, where *foris* and *foras* are exchanged, and a locative is used to show place to or from which. See Friedlaender, *Cena Trimalchionis*, p. 207; Nelson, *Petronius*, pp. 147, 183-84; and Sedgwick, *Cena Trimalchionis*, p. 21, § 5.IV.4.

This breakdown in the expression of place relationship is further exemplified in the *Itinerarium* (or *Peregrinatio*) *Aetheriae* (also known as *Sanctae Silviae Peregrinatio*), written between 400 and 539. This work may therefore have been written by a contemporary of Luxorius; on the date, see Pétré, *Ethérie*, pp. 14-16. In the *Peregrinatio* there are two examples of *quo* for *ubi* (*eo loco quo sunt*, 1, and *quo ... adparuit lapis*, 16) but the tendency was for *ubi* to replace *quo*, as witnessed by the fact that in the work cited *ubi* is used for *quo* 122 times. See Bechtel, *Peregrinatio*, pp. 108, § 5b; 109, § 7; 110, § 13; 148, §13; and Löfstedt, *Kommentar*, p. 227, n. 1. The prevalence of *ubi* over *quo* is evidenced in some of the Romance languages where there is no derivative from *quo*, but one from *ubi* does double service, as French *où*, Italian *dove*. Cf. also Hic quo natus fuerat, optans erat ille reverti, in E. Lommatzsch, *Carmina Latina Epigraphica* (Leipzig, 1926), p. 128, No. 2199.4.

It is also possible that Luxorius simply used *quo* for *in quo*; cf. the modern Latin phrase *status quo* or *in statu quo*.

6. tineis: Cf. Martial, 14.37, on this scourge of ancient books, Selectos nisi dat mihi libellos,/ Admittam tineas; and Ausonius, 78, *Epigrams* 1 [34].

8. Romulidas et Tyrias manus: Baehrens, *PLM* IV, 31, thinks that these words refer to the Roman and African poets in the *Anthologia Latina*. His argument resembles that of Schubert, *De Luxorio*, p. 19. However, cf. *Romulidas* in Dracontius, *Praefatio*, 1.13 (cited above, Ch. I, n. 39), a clear reference to the Carthaginians of Roman descent. *Romulidas*, etc. in Luxorius can be taken to mean the *turba legentium* who will pass judgment on the poems. Baehrens believes that Luxorius' *juvenilia*, after having been edited once before, were now sent on to Octavianus, who was asking for contributions for an anthology. It is just as possible, however, that Luxorius' youthful poems—hitherto unpublished—were gathering dust until the summons came from Faustus.

9. claudere: passive imperative.

10-11. Cf. Martial, 1.3.12, I fuge! sed poteras tutior esse domi, and Ovid, *Tristia* 1.1.49, Denique securus famae, liber, ire memento. Luxorius' lines appear to be an echo of Phaedrus, *Fables* 1.4.13-16:

> Contentus nostris si fuisses sedibus
> Et quod natura dederat voluisses pati,
> Nec illam expertus esses contumeliam,
> Nec hanc repulsam tua sentiret calamitas.

> If you had been satisfied with your home, and had been willing to endure what nature had allotted to you, neither would you have experienced that insult, nor would your misfortune feel this present rejection.

However, Luxorius does not apply this moral to his book. It could not suppress its envy of fame but bravely ventured forth and suffered. Defiantly it advises the weak of heart to long for the safety of the home. On the use of *sententiae*, see above, Chapter V, B 5.

4

Meter: Elegiac; see above, Ch. VIII, Meter 1.

Title. scripserit: On the mood, see above, Ch. VII, B 2.

1. There is a lacuna in A; the line is supplied by Burmann from the title and fits in well. Martial often refers to the smallness of his books and to the virtue of brevity: 1.45; 2.1; 4.29; 4.82; 8.24; 9. *Praefatio*; 9.50; 10.1; 10.59; 12.1.3. See also *Anthologia Palatina* 9.874 on the charm of small things.

4. graciles: an emendation by Meyer of *faciles* in A. For *gracilis*, "slender," cf. Horace, *Odes* 1.5.1, gracilis . . . puer, and Martial, 8.24.1, gracili libello.

5. brevibus: Cf. Martial's warmer and more poetic treatment of a similar theme (*rara iuvant*) in 4.29.

5. brevibus magnum: On Luxorius' use of contrasting words, see above, Ch. V, B 1.

5. deprendier: another emendation by Meyer. (The reading in A is *dependere*.) Cf. *credier*, 9.10; *conplerier*, 21R.124; and *succendier*, 21R.194. The -*ier* form of the present passive infinitive is often found in Plautus and in later writers: cf. *defendier*, Juvenal, 15.157; *dicier*, Persius, 1.28, and *fallier*, 3.50. Common in old Latin, this form was later confined to legal language and to poetry when the poet wished to impart an archaic flavor. Monceaux, *Les Africains*, p. 110, notes that there was a tendency to use the -*ier* form in Africa; see also Kuehner, *Grammatik*, I, 693, § 168E, Remark 2.

6. On the use of *sententiae*, see above, Ch. V, B 5.

7. concinno: unnecessarily emended to *continuo* by Baehrens. Luxorius is telling the reader that if his book is brief it has the advantage of being finished quickly. *Concinnus* generally means "elegant, pretty, felicitous," but *TLL*, IV, 52, gives *brevis* as a synonym. *Concinnus* is related to brevity in Nepos, *Epaminondas* 5.1, concinnus in brevitate, and in Caelius Aurelian, *Tardae Passiones* 3.4.62, brevi ac concinna oratione. Note the clicking sound in this line and the next. On the alliteration, see above, Ch. V, B 7, and cf. 182R.3, Corvus carbo cinis concordant cuncta colori.

9-10. libris longissima multis: Cf. Martial, 2.1, on the merits of a concise book, which, even if bad, will not be boring.

10. fastidita: Cf. Ovid, *Tristia* 1.7.31-32, Et veniam pro laude peto, laudatus abunde,/ Non fastiditus si tibi, lector, ero, and *Ex Ponto* 4.1.19-20, Idque sinas oro, nec fastidita repellas/ Verba. In Callimachus' opinion (Fragment 359) a big book is a big nuisance, in Luxorius' judgment it could be a big bore.

10. vel: used instead of *et*; see above, Ch. VI, A 3.

10. vitia: The reading of A is *vitio*. Riese conjectures *merito*; Petschenig, *ZöstG*, XXVIII, 488, suggests *bella cito* for *vel vitio*. *Vitia* is much closer to the manuscript reading and balances *fastidita* grammatically. *Fastidita* is used as a noun in Pliny, *Natural History, Praefatio* 15. No other pentameter line in Luxorius ends with a short open vowel, it is true, but such endings do occur

in other poets, e.g., *auxilia*, Propertius, 1.1.26, and *maria*, 2.18.38. (See Plat-nauer, *Latin Elegiac Verse*, p. 65.)

5

Meter: Trochaic Tetrameter Catalectic; see above, Ch. VIII, Meter 11.

Plato, *Politicus* 264, refers to fishponds in Egypt and Persia. Jennison, *Animals for Show and Pleasure*, pp. 121-25, traces the history of fishponds among the Romans. In the last years of the Republic the cultivation of fishponds was somewhat of a craze among the nobles. The ponds were both fresh- and salt-water. Martial writes about fishponds in 4.30 and 10.30.

1. verna: "domesticated, home-grown"; cf. Martial, 10.30.21, Piscina rhombum pascit et lupos vernas.

1. clausas: "imprisoned, walled-in"; cf. 27.4.

1. undas et lacunas: may be considered a hendiadys.

3. vocatus: Apparently the fish answer to a call or a given name; cf. Martial, 4.30.6-7, Quid quod nomen habent et ad magistri/ Vocem quisque sui venit citatus? and 10.30.23, Nomenculator mugilem citat notum.

4. roscidi amnis: Cf. Lucretius, 1.496, lympharum rore.

6. libet: On the scansion, see above, entry for this word, Ch. VIII, B 1.

7. gestu loquaci: refers to the open mouth of the fish.

7. mitiori vertice: refers to the tame head of the fish.

8. ventris arte: Cf. Persius, *Prologue* 10-11, Magister artis ingenique largitor/ Venter ... The reader may draw the inference that these fish are like courtiers who have learned to bow politely and so earn their board at the tables of their lords.

6

Meter: Elegiambic; see above, Ch. VIII, Meter 12.

1. Martis aper: Cf. Claudian, 42(53), *De Apro et Leone* 3, hunc [aprum] Mars, hunc [leonem] laudat Cybele. There is, however, no mythological allusion to the boar as the favorite animal of Mars; the relationship merely indicates the boar's martial qualities; cf. Valerius Flaccus, *Argonautica* 3.635, Martia tigris.

1. genitus ... inesse: late use of the infinitive; see above, Ch. VI, A 4.

2. ferocius: See above, Ch. VI, A 7.

4. famulans: See above, Ch. VI, B 4.

5. Parios lapides: See above, Ch. I, n. 45, on marble used in Carthage; cf. also 130R.4, Et vibret Parium nitens colorem.

7. domini placidam manum: Cf. 5.3, nec manum fugit. Martial has a number of poems on the theme of wild animals that have become tame; cf. *De Spectaculis* 18; also 1.14; 1.48; 1.104; 2.75; 5.31; and 9.71.

8. Veneris: A typical Luxorian contrast; the wild boar has become so tame that he is now like the gentle doves of Venus.

7

Meter: Elegiac; see above, Ch. VIII, Meter 1.

Title. Aegyptio: Here the charioteer is called an Egyptian but, from what is said about him in the poem, he was clearly a Negro. If the title goes back to Luxorius' time, this is further evidence of the ancients' hazy idea of anthropology (see note on *Garamas, 43.4*). The Romans used many names for the Negroes: Moors, Ethiopians, etc. See Snowden, *AJP,* LXVIII, 287-88, on Negroes as charioteers and hunters in the Roman world, and p. 272, on Negroes in Carthage. According to him, p. 290, there was no color bar among the Romans. Cf. also Poem 67.

1. quamvis: On the scansion, see entry for this word, above, Ch. VIII, B 2.

2. Memnon: See 189R for another poem on Memnon and 182R for a poem on an Egyptian. See also Philostratus, *Imagines* 1.7; Vergil, *Aeneid* 1.489.

3. paravit: Cf. Tibullus, 1.10.39, prole parata.

4. in antra: If this phrase means "in the cave," we should expect the ablative case. However, Luxorius sometimes uses prepositions with the accusative instead of the ablative "in miro modo"; see Klapp, *Quaestiones,* p. viii, and above, Ch. VI, A 9, and note on *quo, 3.5.* Cf. also *in statuam, 10.4.* Baehrens thinks that *latus* can be read instead of *natus.* This suggested correction can be tolerated. However, *natus* can be used with *in* and the accusative to mean "born to the cave," i.e., "born to occupy or live in the cave of Zephyr," and hence, by extension, "to be under Zephyr's care." This is another of Luxorius' bold and pregnant phrases. Cf. Cicero, *Tusculan Disputations* 1.5.9, in miseriam nascimur.

6. dum: For use in place of *cum* adversative, see above Ch. VI, A 1.

6. facie... genio: another Luxorian contrast. *Genio* is here equivalent to Τύχη, and *fatum, fors, fortuna,* or *sors;* see *TLL,* VI.2, 1827.65, and 1837.83; and Charisius, *Ars Grammatica,* in Keil, *GL,* I, 32.1, and I, 548.4.

Luxorius has paid great attention to structure in this poem. Each couplet expresses a different idea but the three are bound closely together, with the last in contrast to the first.

8

Meter: Lesser Sapphic; see above, Ch. VIII, Meter 5.

Title. in grammaticum furiosum: This poem again illustrates a paradox. The *grammaticus* should be wise and sane, but this one is evil and mad. Was Luxorius especially indignant because a fellow teacher was a disgrace to his profession? Other poems by Luxorius on the vices and failings of professionals are Nos. 9, 16, 17, 23, 54, 72, and 88. See above, Ch. V, A 4. Cf. Poem 96R, which is a more witty and pleasant poem on a teacher who is mildly remiss.

6. telo: The schoolmaster's weapon was the ferule, which was applied not unsparingly as a matter of course; cf. Juvenal, 1.15, et nos ergo manum ferulae subduximus. However, in his madness the teacher of this poem may have used an actual weapon like a sword.

6. raperis: Cf. *rapiaris, 27.3.*

7. in quantum: Schubert emends this to make the line read *Non es, inquam, dum furor hic probatur (De Luxorio,* p. 31). He reasons that only half of the comparison is present. But why force Luxorius to spell it out? This would

be contrary to his condensed, cryptic manner of expression. The comparison is implied, "To the extent that this fit of madness indicates, (to that extent) you are not fit to be called a *grammaticus*." *In tantum* can be understood with *non dignus es* as a correlative of *in quantum,* and the comparison becomes complete. *In quantum* equals *quantum* in Augustan poetry and post-classical prose; see Kuehner-Stegmann, *Grammatik*, I, 569, § 108e. Cf. also Velleius Paterculus, *Historiae Romanae* 2. 119.2, in quantum voluerant, and 2.43.4, viri in tantum boni, in quantum humana simplicitas intellegi potest.

9. Orestas: On the mad Orestes, see Aeschylus, *Libation Bearers* 1047-62; Euripides, *Orestes*, and *Iphigenia in Tauris* 83, 284-310; Persius, 3.118, non sanus iuret Orestes; and Juvenal, 14.284-85.

9

Meter: Glyconic; see above, Ch. VIII, Meter 10.

Title. Like the preceding poem this is directed against a professional who has gone astray. For other poems about lawyers who are perverts, see 148R and 149R.

3. usu femineo Paris: "handsome as Paris but treated as a woman," the darling of foul and lustful men. *Paris* is Burmann's emendation of *pares* in A; Baehrens corrects it to *patens*, which is also suitable.

5. facundior: On the scansion, see above, entry for this word, Ch. VIII, B 2; on the use of the comparative, see above, Ch. VI, A 7.

8. magis: Luxorius uses *magis, potior,* and *potius* to indicate the idea of preference; see above, Ch. VI, A 7, and consult the Index Nominum et Verborum for the occurrence of these words.

8. locas: *Locare* means "to hire out to somebody else" but here *locas* seems to mean "you hire out to yourself," "you contract to assume."

10. credier: Cf. *deprendier*, 4.5.

11. puto: Luxorius is fond of the parenthetical *puto* or *credo*, sometimes varied with *ut video*, as in line 9 of this poem, or with *ni fallor*, 7.3, a mannerism often found in Martial, e.g., 9.78.2; 10.104.19; 11.2.28; 11.101.2.

10

Meter: Elegiac; see above, Ch. VIII, Meter 1.

Title. Pygmaeum: For a literary reference to the size of the Pygmies, see Juvenal, 13.173, ubi tota cohors pede non est altior uno; for representations in ancient art, see *MCAAT*, VII, 173, No. 241; VIII, 110-111; XX, 217, Nos. 2040-43, and p. 310, No. 1159; also Reinach, *Répertoire de la statuaire*, II.2, 564-66, *Répertoires de peintures,* 161-62, 376-77; and *RE*, XXIII.2, 2064-74, *s.v. Pymaioi*.

Pygmaeus, as listed in Forcellini, *Onomasticon*, II, 541-42, is used as an adjective; *Pygmaei*, the plural, is a noun. The Greek words from which they are derived are similarly used. Here *Pygmaeum* may be a noun modified by *clamosum et furiosum*; cf. *longis Pygmaeus in armis,* 190R.3. It may be used in this title figuratively to emphasize the short stature of the noisy midget or dwarf; cf. 24.T, 3. The usual Latin words for a dwarf are *nanus* and *pumilio*; the figurative and singular substantive use of a form of *Pygmaeus* is rare.

However, *Pygmaeum* may be considered an adjective joined to *furiosum* by *et* and modifying *clamosum*, "a noisy fellow," used substantively, like *ebriosum*, 25.T, and *gibberosum*, 29.T. Another possibility is that *furiosum* is likewise a substantive connected with *clamosum* by *et*, with both modified by *Pygmaeum*. There is no direct reference to a Pygmy in the poem itself; the title may be the inferior production of a scribe or an editor (see above, Ch. VII, A 2-4).

In spite of the mosaics and statues of diminutive human beings listed above, it is problematical whether members of the tribe or ethnic group known as Pygmies were to be found in Carthage at the time of Luxorius, although there is evidence that many centuries earlier Pygmies had been captured and taken to Egypt. However, W. R. Dawson, in "Pygmies, Dwarfs, and Hunchbacks in Ancient Egypt," *Annals of Medical History*, IX (New York, 1927), 315-26, asserts that many of the small men depicted in ancient Egyptian art are really achondroplastic dwarfs, but that even authoritative scholars refer to them as Pygmies because they mistakenly consider dwarfs and Pygmies to be synonymous. *EB*, VIII (1960), 789, on the other hand, identifies the figures on the tombs at Saqqara, for instance, with true Pygmies. The ancients themselves were careless and unscientific in making ethnic identifications; see note on *Garamas*, 43.4. For a detailed account of ancient and modern Pygmies, see R. Verneau, "Les Pygmées," *Bibliothèque universelle at revue suisse*, CX (Lausanne, 1923), 273-86. See also Homer, *Iliad* 3.6; Herodotus, 2.32.6; 3.37; 4.43.5; and Pliny, *Natural History* 4.11.44; 5.29.109; 6.35.188.

corpore: This is found in A but is omitted in B, V, and by Burmann. Its use here does seem otiose, for *Pygmaeum* by itself refers to bodily size. A phrase like *Giganta voce* instead of *et furiosum* is needed in opposition to *Pygmaeum corpore* to point up the contrast between the boisterous fellow's tiny body and his tremendous voice, as in the use of the antonyms *levis* and *gravis* in line 6.

1. querulis: Cf. Vergil, *Georgics* 3.328, Et cantu querulae rumpunt arbusta cicadae.

1. vel: equal to *et*; see above, Ch. VI, A 8.

1. cicadis: Martial uses *cicada* as a comparison of smallness in 3.93.3, pectus cicadae, and 11.18.5, argutae tegit ala quod cicada.

2. potior: See above, Ch. VI, A 7.

3. vox: Suetonius, *Divus Augustus* 43.3, tells about a young man of respectable rank whom Augustus exhibited as a curiosity: quod erat bipedali minor, librarum septemdecim ac vocis immensae.

4. alterius: For the scansion, see above, entry for this word, Ch. VIII, B 2.

6. Another of Luxorius' contrasts and paradoxes: the loud voice in the small body. Cf. Giles the dwarf, brother of the hero, Gerard, in Charles Reade's *The Cloister and the Hearth*. He was only three feet high, but "Nature relenting at having made Giles so small, had given him as a set-off the biggest voice on record. His very whisper was a bassoon" (Modern Library edition, p. 14).

11

Meter: Phalaecean; see above, Ch. VIII, Meter 3.

Title. debriatus: a nonclassical word; see Souter, *Glossary,* p. 88, and Peiper, *NJbb,* CVII, 340, on *ebrius-debrius. TLL,* V, 1, 115, citing this occurrence and other late examples, as in Cassiodorus, Fulgentius, and the Vulgate, defines *debriare* as *valde ebrium facere.*

5. plura: For the scansion, see above, Ch. VIII, A 3.

6. taedium: may be used here in late meaning of "grief" or "illness." See Souter, p. 412. Cf. refrain in 83R.42-43, sua taedia solus/ Fallere nescit amor. For another study of the relationship between love and wine, see Ovid, *Ars Amatoria* 1.565 ff.

7. venena sume: Cf. Propertius, 2.17.14, Sumere et in nostras trita venena manus.

12

Meter: Anacreontic (Dimeter Ionic a Minore with Anaclasis); see above, Ch. VIII, Meter 8.

Title. mitellam: See above, Ch. IX, C 2. Cf. Juvenal 3.66, picta lupa barbara mitra. According to Cicero, *De Haruspicum Responsis* 21.44, Clodius wore a *mitra.*

2. roseoque crine: This seems repetitious after *rutilo capillo.* Petschenig, *ZöstG,* XXVIII, 488, suggests *roseaque carne.* Cf. Martial, 11.56.12, roseo ... ore puer.

4. capiti locavit: apparently a poetic use of the dative instead of *in* with the ablative or accusative; cf. *tumulo defixit,* 33.1; *manibus locavit,* 49.1; and see Kuehner-Stegmann, *Grammatik,* I, 589.

6. bene conscious: For use of *bene* with positive, see above, Ch. VI, A 7.

7. cogente nullo: Cf. Juvenal 8. 193, nullo cogente Nerone. On the scansion of *cogente,* see above, Ch. VIII, A 8, and entry for this word, Ch. VIII, B 2.

8. minus: "not"; see above, Ch. VI, A 7. The eunuch was donning (*sumebat*) what had been either wrong or absurd or inappropriate for him to wear before he became a *spado* (see line 5). But now he was like a woman; he knew his altered standards of propriety, and he accepted his new status.

13

Meter: Anapaestic; see above, Ch. VIII, Meter 7.

Title. magum: On the cult of magic in Carthage, see above, Ch. I, A 5 and B 15.

The beggar is not a true magician but a fraud (*inscius*). He is always starving and must do something desperate like stealing offerings left at funerals or raising the dead. Luxorius tells the magician that Pluto and the dead can give him no food; therefore, he will always go hungry if he seeks the limbs of corpses. See Petschenig, *ZöstG,* XXVIII, 488, on this poem.

There are numerous references in Latin poetry to the snatching away of these funerary offerings by the hungry poor who frequented the funerals and swooped down like vultures upon the food once the *Ave atque Vale* had been pronounced. These stolen morsels are called *dapes sordidae* by the anonymous author of *Epigram* 246.28 in Burmann, *Anthologia,* I, 434. See also Terence, *Eunuchus* 3.2.491, E flamma petere te cibum posse arbitror; Catullus, 59.2-5; Tibullus, 1.5.53-54; Calpurnius Siculus, *Bucolics* 3.82; and Martial, 11.54.2-5. An extensive list is given in E. Baehrens, *Catulli Veronensis Liber,* II (Leipzig, 1885), 289.

On witchcraft, magic rites at the graves, and the ceremony of the raising of the dead, see Tibullus, 1.2.45-46, Haec cantu finditque solum manesque sepulcris/ Elicit et tepido devocat ossa rogo; Lucan, *Pharsalia* 6.419-830, describing the activities of the witch Erichtho. For literary treatments of this theme in Latin and Greek literature, see Kirby F. Smith, *The Elegies of Albius Tibullus* (New York, 1913), pp. 216-17.

3. ire per umbras: Cf. Ovid, *Heroides* 6.89-90, Per tumulos errat passis discincta capillis,/ Certaque de tepidis colligit ossa rogis.

4. gestis: Cf. 21.6, Quid ergo gestit?

6. fame: On the short *e*, see above, entry for this word in Ch. VIII, B 2.

8. possit: For the mood, see above, Ch. VI, A 3.

8. superis: emendation by Klapp of *super his.* In 81.6 *superi* means "the gods above," but here it refers to human beings.

9. puto quod peius: Baehrens puts these words between parentheses, which, though awkward, is possible, but it is better to consider *egeas* the main verb of an indirect statement after *quod.*

10. egeas: For the mood, see above, Ch. VI, A 3.

10. orbem: For the use of *in* and the accusative, see notes on *quo,* 3.5, and *in antra,* 7.4. *Orbem* may here mean the beggar's rounds as in the expression *in orbem ire.*

11. membra perempta: The beggar does not confine himself to filching food but also takes away parts of the corpse. Note the variant spelling *peremtum,* 68.9; see above, Ch. IX, C 3.

11. posces: Note use of the indicative in a subordinate clause in an indirect statement; see above, Ch. VI, A 1.

14

Meter: Dactylic Hexameter; see above, Ch. VIII, Meter 2.

Title: accceptorarium: Souter, *Glossary,* lists *acceptatorius,* "falconer," citing the title of this poem but the word is not the same. *TLL,* I, 283, gives no other occurrence of *acceptorarius*; Du Cange, I, 46, gives *accipitrarius,* "accipitrum curator et domitor."

Riese did not include in his collection (*Anthologia Latina,* 1869 edition, II, xli) a poem entitled *Invitatio ad convivium,* which is found in Burmann (*Anthologia,* II, 412, Book V, *Epigram* 136) and in Meyer (*Anthologia,* II, 64, *Epigram* 1074), because line 11 contains a reference to falcony: Unguibus accipitris captam, rogo, percipe, praedam. (The next line is: Si non, scindaris unguibus accipitris.) Riese's opinion is, "Ab antiquitate alienum esse apparet." There is, however, a reference to falcons in Martial, 14.216, one of the *Apophoreta,* entitled *Accipiter:* Praedo fuit volucrum: famulus nunc aucipis idem/ Deicit et captas non sibi maeret aves. Schubert, *De Luxorio,* pp. 32-33, also cites Sidonius Apollinaris, *Epistles* 3.3 and 4.9, on falconry. Keller, *Die Antike Tierwelt*, II, 25-26, mentions neither Martial nor Luxorius, but he gives a long list of other allusions to falconry. Among the authors to whom he refers are Prosper of Aquitaine (*ca.* 430) and Paulinus of Pella (*ca.* 456). See T. H. White, *The Goshawk* (New York, 1951), on modern falconry.

1. pondere detracto: The hunter is starving the falcons and *their* weight is being reduced. According to Fletcher-Allen, *A Wayfarer in North Africa*, p. 55, falconry was still practiced in Tunis and Algeria twenty-five years ago, especially at Le Kef. He reports that the method of starving the birds was used, for "hungry birds take their work seriously." Cf. Shakespeare, *The Taming of the Shrew*, Act IV, scene 1:

> My falcon now is sharp and passing empty
> And till she stoop she must not be full-gorg'd,
> For then she never looks upon her lure.

1. Martine: The cognomen *Martinus* appears in *CIL*, VIII.2, 10583.

2. pressura: to be taken in its late and ecclesiastical sense, "suffering, oppression, torment, want" (see Souter, *Glossary*, p. 321). Cf. Tertullian, *Ad Uxorem* 1.5 (*PL*, I, 1282), quaecumque pressuram persecutionemque libere perferent.

4. magis: See note on this word, Poem 9.8.

4-5. Another of Luxorius' contrasts. The hunter is fat, the birds are thin—kept that way to go after food for him. The poet would reverse the situation—let the birds feed on the fat man before they die of hunger imposed on them by him.

15

Meter: Phalaecean; see above, Ch. VIII, Meter 3.

Title. For a similar theme treated differently, cf. Martial, 10.67. See Poems 57L and 58L for comparisons indicating great age.

1. Phlegethon: The parentage of this flaming infernal river, which unites with Cocytus to form Acheron, is not found in Hesiod's *Theogony*, Apollodorus' *Bibliotheca*, or Hyginus' *Fabulae* (*Genealogiae*). Mueller suggests that Phaethon instead of Phlegethon is meant because the former had sisters (*NJbb*, XCV, 783). Surely this is an unnecessary attempt to pin preciseness on Luxorius. He wrote figuratively, using names as symbols of old age without too much concern for the minutiae of genealogical details about which the ancient writers are in conflict. Moreover, Phaethon would be too young in this context—the virgin was as old as Earth herself.

Phlegethon may be a trope for Tartarus or the Styx. According to Hyginus (*Fabulae, Praefatio* 3) the Styx is the offspring of Nox and Erebus; Tartarus and Saturn are among the children of Terra and Aether; Nox, Dies, Erebus, and Aether are the children of Chaos and Caligo. In Hesiod's account (line 123) Erebus and Dark Night were born of Chaos; Cronos (Saturn) is the son of Heaven and Earth. Likewise, Apollodorus (1.1-3) says that Heaven and Earth are the parents of Cronos and the other Titans.

For a reference to Phlegethon as a divinity, see the argument put into the mouth of Cotta the Academician by Cicero, *De Natura Deorum* 3.17.43-44, Iovem et Neptunum deos numeras; ergo etiam Orcus frater eorum deus, et illi qui fluere apud inferos dicuntur, Acheron, Cocytus, Pyriphlegethon, tum Charon, tum Cerberus di putandi.

2. potior: See note on *magis,* Poem 9.8.

2. senecta: ablative of the noun or nominative singular of the adjective; better taken as an adjective here.

5. elephans: On the spelling, see above, Ch. IX, C 3.

7. novo sub orbe: "when the world was young"; cf. Juvenal, 6.11, tunc orbe novo caeloque recenti, and see Petschenig, *ZöstG,* XXVIII, 488, on this phrase.

8. quae decuit: *Decet* may be used personally with a passive infinitive; see Kuehner-Stegmann, I, 706.

12. pro titulo: reminiscent of Juvenal, 6.229-30, where the accomplishment of a woman who has had eight husbands in five years is considered *titulo res digna sepulchri.*

13-14: stuprata: Once again the paradox: this woman is so old that she cannot expect her marriage to be known as the fulfilment of love but rather as a sex crime. For other poems on aged hags in love, see Burmann, *Anthologia,* II, 488-89, Book V, *Epigram* 12, or *PLM,* I, 151, *Priapea* 12 (ed. by F. Buecheler, 1922), and Burmann, II, 529, Book VI, *Epigram* 58, or *PLM,* I, 162, *Priapea* 57, especially lines 3-4, Quae forsan potuisset esse nutrix/ Tithoni, Priamique, Nestorisque.

16

Meter: Phalaecean; see above, Ch. VIII, Meter 3.

Title. medicolenonem: a coined compound found only here; not listed in Du Cange, Forcellini, or Souter. Riese thinks it should be *medicum lenonem.*

Like Poems 8 and 9, this deals with the derelictions of a professional. (See note to 8.T.) Luxorius infers from the doctor's absence that he has buried himself in a library or a laboratory, doing research, practicing dissection, or discovering a new cure. Instead the doctor has been acting as a procurer in a brothel. This antithesis is intensified by another antithesis: the doctor is a homosexual and a *voyeur.* He could just as easily do the work of the girls because he has been accustomed to playing the part of the female, but he also derives satisfaction from watching the men in action.

1. Marine: *Marinus* is listed in the index of *CIL,* VIII.2, p. 1028, as a cognomen.

7. turpius: See above, Ch. VI, A 7.

11. libeat: Burmann's emendation of *liberat* in A.

11. chirurge: On the scansion, cf. 23.6, and see above, Ch. VIII, A 3, and entries for this word in Ch. VIII, B 2.

13. minus: used as a negative; cf. 12.8, and see above, Ch. VI, A 7.

17

Meter: Phalaecean; see above, Ch. VIII, Meter 3.

Title. diaconum: See above, Ch. VII, A 3. The office of deacon was established early in the history of the Church; at first deacons were servants at the love feasts (*agapae*) but later they became the helpers of bishops and presbyters; see *Catholic Encyclopedia* (New York, 1913) IV, 647ff.

For the relation of this poem to the question of Luxorius' religion, see above, Ch. III, E 3-4. See also note to 8.T.

1. gula: For the scansion, see above, entry for this word, Ch. VIII, B 1.

2. pro psalmis pocula: On the alliteration, see above, Ch. V, B 7; on the juxtaposition of contrasting words, see Ch. V, B 1.

2. corde sedent: In classical Latin *sedere* is followed by the ablative or by *in* and the ablative. In late Latin *sedere* may govern an accusative and it may be used in the passive; see Kuehner-Stegmann, *Grammatik*, I, 103, 264, 354; II, 634 (S. 354). Luxorius alternates between the ablative and the accusative, using the former in 17.2 and 27.4, the latter in 26.4; 44.2; and 64.4. Note especially *limen sedes* in 26.4 but *limine sedes* in 27.4, a singular variation in two poems closely related in thought and position. In English the verb *sit* may also be transitive or intransitive, "to sit on a horse" or "to sit a horse."

3. ne pulpita quaere tabernae: Cf. I Timothy 3.8, "deacons [must] . . . not [be] given to much wine." Lines 3-4 are a typical Luxorian antithesis in the contrast between *templorum* and *tabernae, numina caeli* and *phialas*.

4. quo: introduces a purpose clause; cf. 19.6.

4. phialas: On the spelling, see above, Ch. IX, C 3.

18

Meter: Elegiac; see above, Ch. VIII, Meter 1.

Title. viridario: See above, Ch. I, B 3-6, on these gardens and country estates, Ch. II, p. 27, and below; notes to Poems 60 and 64.T, on the Vandals' love of luxury.

Fridamal: Fridamal occurs in Poem 19 also. He is otherwise unknown to us except for the obvious fact that he was wealthy and that his name indicates that he was of Germanic origin. Meerman (in Burmann, *Anthologia*, II, 588) deduces that the name is formed from the roots *frod*, "prudent," and *amal*, 'bold, spirited." Meerman compares *Fridamal* with similar names in Gothic history, such as *Amalafrida, Amalaric*, etc. (Cf. also *Fridus*, 91L; *Fridi*, 82R.6; and *Fridila, CIL*, VIII, 21424.) Meerman refers to the Gothic version of the Bible, quoting Matthew, 7.24, *vaira frodamma*, which is *viro sapienti* in the Vulgate but which he equates with *virum prudentem*. Meerman compares *frod* with the Dutch *vroede*, "wise, discreet." Modern writers on the origin of names think of *frid (friede)* as the root of such names as Freda, Frieda, Frederick, Wilfred, Wilfrid, etc., and relate it to the old Germanic *frithu*, "peace." The element *amal*, which occurs also in *Amelia, Emmeline*, etc., may have the connotation of "industrious." Schoenfeld, *Wörterbuch, s.v. Freda* and *Fridamal*, pp. 93-94, considers *Fridamal* a turning around of *Amalafrida*. See also E. G. Withycombe, *The Oxford Dictionary of English Christian Names* (Oxford, 1947) and M. Nurnberg and M. Rosenblum, *Your Baby's Name* (New York, 1951), for the modern names listed in this paragraph.

pinxit: Note use of the infinitive instead of the participle; cf. Pliny, *Natural History* 3.5.92, [Apelles] pinxit Alexandrum magnum fulmen tenentem. (See Kuehner-Stegmann, I, 705, § 127.4b.)

This type of poem is found in Statius; see *Silvae* 1.3 on the villa of Manilius Vopiscus at Tibur, and *Silvae* 2.2 on the villa of Pollius Felix at Sorrento. It belongs to the genre known as ecphrasis or *descriptio,* an elaborate delineation of people, places, and works of art. "Late antique and medieval poetry used it lavishly," according to Curtius, who calls the ecphrasis one of the stylistic devices of the New Sophistic (or Second Sophistic) of the second to the fourth centuries *A.D. (European Literature and the Middle Ages,* p. 68, n. 28). See also Ziehen, *Neue Studien,* p. 9, for a list of similar gardens in later times, and notes on Poem 46, below.

1. Aricia: a town in Latium near Alba Longa, receiving its name, according to Vergil, *Aeneid* 7.762, from the wife of its founder, Hippolytus. Here was a grove dedicated to Diana.

2. famulas: See above, Ch. VI, B 4. Cf. Ovid, *Fasti* 1.286, tradiderat famulas iam tibi Rhenus aquas, and Juvenal, 14.81-82, famulae Iovis et generosae/ In saltu venantur aves.

4. Except for the last two words, this line is badly mangled in A; Riese has restored order and meaning.

4. lustra: "woods, forests, haunts of wild beasts"; cf. Vergil, *Aeneid* 4.151, invia lustra; 11.570, horrentia lustra. The land is now rich and no longer does *lustra* really apply to it, but the word is kept as if to mean "what once was the lair of savage animals."

4. Molorchus: a poor man living in Cleonae who entertained Hercules when the latter was on his way to kill the Nemean lion. As a reward Molorchus was enriched by Hercules with the gift of the fertile fields about Cleonae. See Vergil, *Georgics* 3.19; Tibullus (*Panegyricum Messalae*) 4.1.13; Statius, *Silvae* 3.1.29; and Martial, 4.63.30, Aut, facti modo divitis, Molorchi.

4. consessum: See above, Ch. VI, B 3. Cf. Milton, *Paradise Lost,* 4.247, "A happy rural seat of various view."

7. in medium: For the use of the accusative, cf. *Ilion in medium,* 81.1; see above, Ch. VI, A. 9, and see Kuehner-Stegmann, I, 569, § 107e, on the use of *in medium* meaning *in commune* and for similar late Latin phrases. There may be a brachyology here—the tower rises *in medium* and then shines; see Nelson, *Petronius,* p. 147, for parallel phrases, such as *videbo te in publicum.*

8. uno loco: Cf. 46.14, and see above, Ch. VI, B 4.

9. cubilia: This was apparently a retreat with sitting rooms and bedrooms. The house was very rustic, like its modern California counterparts: woods came up to one side and fountains played on the other.

9. extructa: A has *et structa,* emended by Riese to *exstructa;* in my text the *s* is dropped, as in 64.6 and 81.8.

10. propriis: See above, Ch. VI, A 6.

10. Diana: refers to a statue of the goddess.

11. clausa: Cf. 5.1.

12. artibus: one of Luxorius' favorite words; see above, Ch. VI, B 4.

13. imago: For a detailed study of an ancient picture of a boar hunt, see Philostratus, *Imagines* 1.28. The portrayal of a boar hunt in ancient art goes back to the fresco from Tiryns (1300-1200 B.C.), copy in the Metropolitan Museum of Art, New York (No. 12.58.4), photograph in *Greek Painting,* Metropolitan Museum of Art Picture Book (6th ed., New York, 1952), p. 5. The hunting of the Calydonian boar (Homer, *Iliad* 9.533ff.) provided vase painters with an often used subject; a notable example is the François vase, the work of Clitias and Ergotimus, now in the Archaeological Museum at Florence. This is illustrated in many books on Greek art, e. g., H. N. Fowler and J. R. Wheeler, *A Handbook of Greek Archaeology* (New York, 1909), pp. 474-76, and H. B. Walters, *The Art of the Greeks* (3rd ed., London, 1934), Pl. 72. Boar hunts were sculptured on Roman monuments; e.g., the Mausoleum of the Julii at St. Rémy in southern France has a bas-relief of a boar hunt on the southwest side; see also *MCAAT,* VI, 32, and Pl. 2, No. 1, for such a scene on a tomb. Finally, there are the innumerable mosaics with boar-hunting illustrations. The originals can be seen in the museums of Europe and North Africa; descriptions and photographs of them are contained in the museum catalogues, as *passim* in the *Inventaire des mosaïques de la Gaule et de l'Afrique* and in *Musées et Collections archéologiques de l'Algérie et de la Tunisie.* Noteworthy are *MCAAT,* VII, 24, No. 105, Pl. 6; XV, 13, No. 225, Pl. 3; and XXII, 81-82, for these resemble the scene described by Luxorius. See also above, Ch. I, B 3-5, 13.

Just as the Romans in Africa and in other colonies loved to have their hunting feats depicted in their villas, so the nobles of later times had the walls of their country homes or hunting lodges adorned with scenes of the chase. In the Villa Maser at Asolo near Venice there are frescoes by Veronese showing the master in hunting costume, and in the Casa del Labrador at Aranjuez near Madrid the hunts of Charles IV were painted on the walls of one of the rooms by Velázquez.

14. Fridamal: For the scansion, see above, entries for this name in Ch. VIII, B 4.

16. aptasti: used here with the infinitive as if by analogy with *aptus* and the infinitive, a poetic construction, or as a synonym of *facere.* See Kuehner-Stegmann, I, 685.

17-18. Fridamal is apparently drawing back, pulling the spear behind his back, a position illustrated in the mosaics mentioned in the note to line 13, above. On the position of the boar, cf. Homer, *Iliad* 13.470-75; see also *Odyssey* 19.428-54.

20. cecidisse: *Est* with the infinitive is generally a construction used by poets under Greek influence; see Kuehner-Stegmann, I, 669, § 124d. *Cecidisse* parallels *extingui,* analogous to constructions with verbs like *malo.*

The paradox in this poem is that instead of having the boar take the charge on his spear and letting it bleed to death, Fridamal hit the animal so hard that he concussed it to death. The boar dropped before the spear penetrated its body (*ante ictum*). Francis Yeats-Brown describes a modern boar hunt in *The Lives of a Bengal Lancer* (New York, 1930), p. 93, "My spear is well down this time. He throws himself on it. A fountain of blood jets up. He is dead . . ." Another modern account of boar hunting is found in Gavin Maxwell, *People of the Reeds* (New York, 1958), published in England as *A Reed Shaken by the Wind,* pp. 72-75, 105-8, 159-60, where the tracking of huge wild boars with spears, clubs, and rifles in the marshlands of the Tigris-Euphrates valley is related. Yeats-Brown hunted on horseback, Maxwell, on foot. Luxorius does not tell how Fridamal went to the chase—the mosaics show both methods. Xenophon, *Cynegeticus* 10.1-23, describes boar hunting on foot, giving a complete manual of instructions and a list of implements used, and attesting the strength of the boar. Jeeps are now used in India—a modern refinement. Jack Denton Scott (New York *Herald Tribune,* October 22 and 24, 1957), reporting on a chase in Florida with guns and dogs, declares that the boars are so formidable that not even bears will tangle with an old wild boar. "These boars are fast and killers," says the guide in Scott's story. "They cut you to pieces in seconds." Fridamal's pride is therefore understandable.

See also Jack Denton Scott, *Forests of the Night* (New York, 1959), pp. 47-52, 131-32.

19

Meter: Iambelegiac; see above, Ch. VIII, Meter 13.

Title. ad domum: The preposition with *domus* is found even in classical Latin; see Kuehner-Stegmann, I, 483, Remark 8.

This poem is concerned with the familiar theme of the reverence and obedience given to a lord and ruler by animals that apparently know their place and duty. Cf. Poems 5 and 6, also Martial, *De Spectaculis* 17, an extravagant treatment of the topic.

1. felix: Cf. Sidonius Apollinaris, *Carmina* 9.5 ff., Felix nomine, mente, honore, etc.

2. genio: Cf. 7.6.

3. sponte: generally found with an adjective like *mea, tua, sua,* but sometimes alone, as in Lucan, *Pharsalia* 4.642; 5.500; 8.98, etc.; Statius, *Silvae* 2.4.14; and Vergil, *Aeneid* 4.361.

6. quo: See above, note to 17.4.

7. praememores: late Latin word, translated by Souter as "remembering well"; see above, Ch. VI, B 1.

7. famulo: Cf. 18.2.

8. pro: approaches the idea of "on account of." Cf. 75.8, and see above, Ch. VI, A 9.

20

Meter: Elegiac; see above, Ch. VIII, Meter 1.

Title. crimina in populos iactantem: *adferre, inferre,* and especially *obicere* are generally the verbs used with *crimen* to mean "charge somebody with." Cf. Tacitus, *Annals* 2.30, se crimina obiecturum professus; and 3.12, obiecta crimina pro adprobatis accipiatis.

populos: See above, Ch. VI, B 5.

1. Cyriace: For the scansion, see above, entry for this name in Ch. VIII, B 4.

Cyriace is Burmann's emendation of *Quiriace.* The latter name occurs, however; see *Inventaire,* II, Supp. pp. 34-35, No. 334a, where it is found on the tomb of a three-year-old African boy. The name is derived from κυριακός, "belonging to a master, lord, or the Lord." Many bishops and martyrs bore that name (see *TLL, Onomasticon,* II, 805). Among the celebrated bearers of a form of the name *Cyriacus* are St. Cyriack of Iconium, infant martyr son of St. Julitta. In French the name was shortened to *Cyr* or *Cirgues*; cf. the military academy at St. Cyr. Milton addressed two sonnets to his friend Cyriack Skinner—Nos. 21 and 22 in *The Poetical Works of John Milton,* ed. by David Masson (Oxford, 1954).

2. crimine: Different forms of this noun are used four times in this poem; cf. repetition of *pretium* in Poem 76.

4. castigasque: -*Que* is carried over with negative force, a mannerism frequently found in Lucan, e.g., *Pharsalia* 1.77; 2.355, 373. Cf. also *capitque,* 21L.3.

4. tarda: a transfer of epithet to *flagella* from *manus.*

5. quod: "as to the fact that, in respect to"; see Kuehner-Stegmann, II, 277.

5. alterius On the short *i,* see note to 10.4; cf. *ipsius,* 24.4.

6. magis: See note to 9.8.

7. aetate relictus: Cf. Phaedrus, *Fables* 1.21.3, defectus annis et desertus viribus.

10. crimen agas: Cf. Martial, 1.79 and 5.61 for more extended puns on *agere.*

21

Meter: Phalaecean; see above, Ch. VIII, Meter 3.

2. Incurvus: He is suffering from the gout, as indicated by the title, and may be crooked or hunchbacked, if Luxorius chose this name aptly to describe him.

3. nec . . . -que: See note to 20.4.

5. baudus: a word of Germanic origin. *TLL,* II, 1791, listing only this occurrence, compares it with Gothic *anabiudan,* which equals *instruere, edicere, imperare.* Souter translates it by "ruler." Riese equates it with *audax, fortis.* It appears as an element in many old Germanic names; Schoenfeld, *Wörterbuch, s.v. Bauto,* defines it as "hunter, fighter, hero." Cf., for example, *Merobaudes,* the name of the fifth-century Spanish soldier and poet. The root appears in the names Archibald, "noble and bold," Baldwin, "bold friend," and Theobald (Tybalt, Thibaud), "bold for the people."

5. dum: subjunctive in a temporal clause; see above, Ch. VI, A 1.

6. praevaleat: used for *possit*; see above, Ch. VI, B 3, and cf. *valeas,* 11.4.

6. gestit: Cf. *gestis,* 13.4.

7. mori: For the scansion, see above, Ch. VIII, A 3.

22

Meter: Elegiac; see above, Ch. VIII, Meter 1.

1. The full line in A is *Zelotypus plures incurbas clune puellas.* I have followed Riese's changes; Baehrens doubts that *Incurvus* is a name. His text

reads *Zelaris plures incurva clune puellas,* which is quite striking but suitable. However, it is preferable to carry *Incurvus* over as a name from 21.2, above.

1. Incurvus: On nominative for vocative, see above, note on *Fauste,* 1.3; cf. *hortus,* 46.1.

3. clausas: Cf. 5.1 and 18.11.

3. aptus: Cf. 5.8 and 83.2; see above, Ch. VI, B 4.

4. internus Iuppiter: a reference to the story of Zeus and Amphitryon.

4. famulis: See note to 18.2.

5. vanum... inguen: A has *vacuo oge.* Riese keeps this but obelizes; in his 1869 edition he had emended to *orche* and changed *vacuo* to *vacua.* He refers to Martial, 10.91.1, Omnes eunuchos habet Almo nec arrigit ipse, which indicates that *arrigere* may be used intransitively but does not tell what word *oge* has replaced. In fact, *oge* does not exist as a Latin word and *orchis* is not used in Latin for *testis.* Burmann emended to *vacua arte,* which makes sense in the light of Luxorius' fondness for the word *ars.* Mueller, *De Re Metrica,* p. 182, changed the two words to *vana orge* (from Greek ὀργή, "passionate impulse"), comparing *orge* to Horace, *Satires* 1.2.71, mea cum conferbuit ira, a pretty parallel, but the unique use of *orge,* a Latinized Greek word, is foreign to Luxorius. I have accepted Baehrens' emendation, *vanum inguen.*

. 23

Meter: Anacreontic; see above, Ch. VIII, Meter 9.

6. chirurge: For the scansion, see note on this word in 16.11. On the failings of a professional, see note to 8.T.

6. quartus: predicate nominative of a vocative, *vocate,* line 7, together with *coniunx;* see note on *Fauste,* 1.3.

11. videtur: On the use of the indicative in an indirect question, see above, Ch. VI, A 2.

13. ergo: For the scansion, see above, Ch. VIII, B 3.

14. lugubrem: For the scansion, see above, Ch. VIII, A 9.

17. quartus atque—quintus: Paula married the doctor although he is impotent because she wanted to put aside her mourning clothes. However, she does not consider him a husband at all and therefore, although he is No. 4, he is also the means by which she will get No. 5. There is an intimation, especially in *peremit,* line 4, that he may not last long.

24

Meter: Elegiac; see above, Ch. VIII, Meter 1.

Title. pantomimam: See above, Ch. I, B 17, on the popularity of pantomimes at this time.

Pygmaeam: See note on *Pygmaeum,* 10.T. Here the word definitely refers to a girl of diminutive size, not to a true Pygmy, for she is compared with a Pygmy girl, *Pygmaea virgine,* line 3.

fabulam saltabat: Cf. Horace, *Satires* 1.5.63, saltaret uti Cyclopa, for a similar use of the accusative with *saltare;* see Kuehner-Stegmann, I, 278.

1. Andromacham: Andromache was noted for her height; cf. Ovid, *Ars Amatoria* 3.777-78, where she is called *longissima.* See also Juvenal, 6.502-7,

which may have suggested the theme to Luxorius, for in Juvenal's lines Andromache and a Pygmy are compared.

1. Macedonia: For the scansion, see above, entry for this word in Ch. VIII, B 4.

4. ipsius: For the short *i*, see note on *alterius*, 10.4.

4. quantum: Klapp, *Quaestiones*, p. vii, thinks *quantum* should be *quam*, saying, "Sed audacius *quantum* post comparativum positum est pro *quam*." But *quantum* is not to be construed with *brevior*; it belongs with *erat*; the entire clause, *quantum . . . Andromachae*, is a grammatical nexus equaling *pede Andromachae* and balancing *Pygmaea virgine*. On grammatical nexus, see O. Jespersen, *The Philosophy of Grammar*, (London, 1935), pp. 114-44, especially 124-25. The construction is bold, however, for Luxorius omits *quam*, which is required after a comparative and before a clause; see Kuehner-Stegmann, I, 299, § 194c.

7-8. On the change to the second person, see above, Ch. V, B 4.

8. Thersiten: Thersites was proverbially ugly; he was also lame and round-shouldered (*Iliad* 2.216ff.). Cf. the speech of Achilles in 198R.69-71:

> Quanto tolerabo pudore
> Me non ferre pedem, quo fert Thersites, in omni
> Parte miser, forma brevior menteque fugaci?

> With what feeling of shame shall I endure my not going where Thersites goes, who is completely a miserable being with a short body and an unstable mind?

Thersites appears as the standard by which to measure ugliness in a Greek inscription (*IG*, XIV, 2131) now in the British Museum. The legend accompanying a sketch of the tablet in the catalogue reads (*A Guide to the Select Greek and Latin Inscriptions in the Department of Greek and Roman Antiquities in the British Museum* [London, 1917], p. 36, No. [77] 1114): "Tablet of a recumbent skeleton. The spectator is asked if he can say whether the deceased was a Hylas (a beautiful youth) or a Therseites (an ugly clown)."

8. potius: See note on *magis*, 9.8.

Luxorius, who is most unkind to those afflicted with human failings and physical defects, does not understand the psychology of men and women striving to act as if they had attained what nature has denied to them. A short person may refuse to accept his "brevity" and will conduct himself as if he were tall. Charles Reade understood this better when he had the dwarf Giles utter these words of objection as he refused to ride a dwarf mule: "What would ye throw all in one scale? Put muckle to muckle, and little to wee? Besides I hate and scorn small things. I'll go on the highest horse here, or not at all" (*The Cloister and the Hearth*, Modern Library edition, p. 444; see also note to 10.6, above).

25

Meter: Lesser Sapphic; see above, Ch. VIII, Meter 5.

1. bibis solus: Cf. Martial, 1.11.2, Bis decies solus, Sextiliane, bibis, and 1.26.1-2, Sextiliane, bibis quantum subsellia quinque/ Solus ...

2. totis ... horis: Baehrens emends to *urnis,* to which Riese apparently takes exception with the remark, "quasi biberet aquam." However, there is no need of emending; it is not a question of what or in what Nerfa drank. A phrase of time can be kept to show that he drank all the time; cf. Martial, 10.56.1, totis diebus. Note the rhyme; cf. 26.2; 38.4; 65.2; and 80.4.

3. munus Cereris: almost like a metonymy; cf. *Bacchum,* line 4, and 77.1. On tropes in Luxorius, see above, Ch. V, B 3.

3. resordet: Luxorius has formed a new compound here; see above, Ch. VI, B 1, and note on *praemedicante,* 83.4. Souter lists only this occurrence and translates *resordeo* by "appear contemptible."

5. Nerfa: probably for *Nerva,* which is found in African inscriptions; see *CIL,* VIII.1, 69, and 7758.

6. nimis: See above, Ch. VI, A 7.

6. plenam ... lagonam: Note the rhyme, as in *totis ... horis,* line 2.

6. lagonam: Riese and Baehrens emend *lacunam* (corrected to *lucunam*) of A to *lagunam.* Variants found in the manuscripts of other authors are *lagena, lagaena, lagoena,* and *lagonam.* Riese is not consistent, for in 137R.1, he has *lagoenam,* his emendation of *agunam* of A, which α corrected to *lagenam.* Baehrens has *lagunam* again. Friedlaender, *Martial,* II, 444, always spells the word *lagona*—it occurs seventeen times in Martial—and this is the spelling preferred here.

According to an epigram of doubtful vintage (Burmann, *Anthologia,* I. 288, Book II, *Epigram* 78, 11-12) the people thought of Tiberius as a *cantharus* because of his drinking proclivities and called him Non Claudium Tiberium Neronem/ Sed Caldium Biberium Neronem. Even as a recruit Tiberius Claudius Nero became Biberius Caldius Nero to the soldiers because of his excessive desire for wine (Suetonius, *Tiberius* 42.1).

26

Meter: Elegiac; see above, Ch. VIII, Meter 1.

Title. stabulo: The plural *stabulis* is used in line 1, raising the question whether the title and the poem are by the same person; see above, Ch. VII, A 2, 4-6; see also note on *simiis,* 44.T.

circi: The stable (or stables) probably belonged to one particular team. See above, Ch. I, B 12-16, on the love of racing in Carthage.

This poem and the companion piece following are among Luxorius' more charming poems. For their genre as examples of ecphrasis, see note to 18.T.

2. nostris ... iugis: Note the rhyme. See note on *totis ... horis,* 25.2.

2. referto: On the short *o,* see above Ch. VIII, B 3.

4. limen sedes: On *sedere* with the accusative, see note to 17.2.

27

Meter: Elegiac; see above, Ch. VIII, Meter 1.

2. iuncea: "slender as a reed."

3. totum ... in orbem: Cf. 13.10.

3. rapiaris: Cf. *raperis,* 8.6.

4. limine sedes: See note on *limen sedes,* 26.4.

4. clausa: Cf. 5.1; 18.11; and 22.3.

28

Meter: Lesser Asclepiad; see above, Ch. VIII, Meter 4.

Title. vicinum invidum: Variations on the theme of the envious man are found in Martial, 1.40 and 9.97. The jealous neighbor appears in Martial, 1.86, but Luxorius' treatment of the two subjects is his own.

1. zeleris: a deponent here in its late and ecclesiastical meaning of "to envy, be jealous of"; Souter, *Glossary, s.v. zelor,* cites a number of examples from the Vulgate and late Latin authors.

1. nimium: See above, Ch. VI, A 7.

1. Marcie: For the vocative ending, see above, Ch. VI, A 12, and cf. *Olympie,* 67.2; *filie* and *Laertie,* Livius Andronicus, *Odissia* 2, 5. See also Mueller, *De Re Metrica,* p. 473. The name *Marcius* is common in African inscriptions; see *CIL,* VIII.2, pp. 1007-8.

3. proximior: For the form and scansion, see above, Ch. VI, A 7, and entry for this word, Ch. VIII, B 1. Cf. Corippus, *Johannis* 6.21 and 7.11 (Books 6 and 7 are numbered 7 and 8 by M. Petschenig, *BSCP,* IV [1886], 161, since he divides Book 4 into two parts). For further examples of *proximior,* see Kuehner, I, 571.

5. gratum ferimus: *Grate ferre* is the classical expression; *gratum habere* is also found, as in Plautus, *Mercator* 3.1.527. The closest to Luxorius' phrase is *Iovi ... gratum referens,* in *CIL,* VIII. 2, 9324.

7. quesumus: On the scansion, see above, entry for this word, Ch. VIII, B 2.

7. numina: Cf. 83.7, and see above, Ch. III, E 6.

8. solum: Cf. 64.3.

8. videas: Marcius does not want to see anyone living near him; therefore he casts the eye of *invidia* upon his neighbor. Luxorius wishes Marcius to see only himself henceforth so that he may cast the evil eye upon himself only—a typical Luxorian twist.

8. vivis: For the scansion, see above, Ch. VIII, B 2.

29

Meter: Iambic Trimeter (Senarius) Acatalectic; see above, Ch. VIII, Meter 6.

Title. qui se generosum iactabat: A treatment of pride of ancestry is found in Juvenal, 8.40ff., tumes alto Drusorum stemmate; in Martial, 5.17.1, Dum proavos atavosque refers et nomina magna; and in 156R.1, Cum te Barbati referas de sanguine cretum. Cf. also Ausonius, *Epigrams* 45. Once again, however, Luxorius is individual in his development of the theme.

3. Memmiorum: For the supposed origin of the gentile name *Memmius,* see Vergil, *Aeneid* 5.117. Lucretius dedicated the *De Rerum Natura* to C. Memmius, a member of the *gens.*

4. prodesse: Cf. Juvenal, 8.1-2, Stemmata quid faciunt? Quid prodest, Pontice, longo/ Sanguine censeri ... ?

5. ambitu: dative with *prosunt* or ablative of means, "with their false ambition."

6. moveas: For the scansion, see above, Ch. VIII, A 6, and entry for this word, Ch. VIII, B 1.

7. nobis: For the use of the dative with *doceo,* see above, Ch. VI, A 12. Cf. Augustine, *Contra Cresconium Donatistam* 4.58.69 (*PL,* XLIII, 586), Proinde, ut plurimum valeatis, et nunc mihi haec vera esse doceatis; *Evangelium Thomae* 6.6, Ego scio litteras quas tu vis docere mihi. For other examples, see *TLL,* V.1, 1711, lines 3-5; 1715, line 55; and 1733, lines 62-78; for remarks on this construction, see W. A. Baehrens, *Eranos,* XIII, 19-21, and Löfstedt, *Kommentar,* p. 152.

30

Meter: Lesser Asclepiad; see above, Ch. VIII, Meter 4.

Title. cantaret, lauderetur: On the use of the subjunctive, see above, Ch. VI, A 1, and VII, B 2.

2. Zenobi: For the scansion, see above, entry for this name, Ch. VIII, B 4.

2. trivio carmine: Cf. Justin, *Historiarum Philippicarum Epitoma* 21.5, pueros in trivio docebat, said about Dionysius, tyrant of Syracuse. Luxorius' use of the adjective *trivio* with *carmine* is unusual, for *trivius* was used only as an epithet of Diana or Hecate: cf. Lucretius, 1.84, Triviai virginis, and Propertius, 2.32.10, Triviae... deae. The proper word for "trivial" is *trivialis,* as in Juvenal, 7.55, carmen triviale.

3. indoctaque: On the long *a,* see above, entry for this word, Ch. VIII, B 1.

6-7. The poet is proud because the schoolboys know his verses. Luxorius, however, insists that this does not make him a poet; even parrots can be taught to utter words that they do not understand. Moreover, when the boys recite or sing the badly taught songs of the poet, they sound just like birds emitting a thin, unmelodious whistle (*sibila*), which is not real music but is more like an odious hiss. A filler in the *New Yorker* (October 20, 1956), p. 204, refers to "the mute swan, which can hiss but cannot sing." This was placed directly under an item about a rock 'n' roll singer.

31

Meter: Phalaecean: see above, Ch. VIII, Meter 3.

Title. hermaphroditam: The physical attributes of such a girl are admirably described by Casanova in *Mémoires de J. Casanova de Seingalt écrits par lui-même* (n. éd., Garnier Frères, Paris, [1924]), IV, 379-80. For representations in ancient art, see M. Bieber, *The Sculpture of the Hellenistic Age* (New York, 1955), Figures 623, 625, 626; Reinach, *Répertoire de la peinture,* pp. 98-99; *Répertoire de la statuaire,* V.2, 584; and *MCAAT,* VIII, 110-11.

On sexual abnormalities and failings as a fertile field for satire in the poems of Martial and Luxorius, see above, Chs. III, D 7, V, A 4, and below, note on Poem 91. Cf. also poems of Luxorius, 9, 11, 12, 15, 16, 22, 23, 33, 35-37, 43, 50, 54, 71, 72, and 82. With the present poem, cf. Martial, 1.90; Ausonius, *Epigrams* 102 and 103; and Poems 786R and 912R.

5. das: *Dare* is regularly used by Martial to denote participation in the act of love; see especially 7.75.2, where he puns on the verb: *vis dare nec dare vis.*

7. partem: Cf. 23.9. A similar idea is expressed by Martial, 11.22.9-10, Divisit natura marem: pars una puellis,/ Una viris genita est. Utere parte tua, and 12.96.11-12, Scire suos fines matrona et femina debet:/ Cede sua pueris, utere parte tua. Cf. also 129R.6, Femina cum non sis, vir tamen esse nequis.

32

Meter: Elegiac; see above, Ch. VIII, Meter 1.

Title. nocte: See above, entry for *nocteque,* 55.1, Ch. VIII, B 1.

Lycaon: The name means "wolflike." Lycaon was the king of Arcadia who was turned into a wolf by Jupiter: see Ovid, *Metamorphoses* 1.198ff., and Hyginus, *Fabulae* 176ff. Our term for the subject of Luxorius' poem would be a night owl. Seneca describes an ancient specimen in *Epistulae Morales* 122.10ff., a certain Buto on whom morning calls were paid at night. Historically, there is also Petronius as sketched by Tacitus, *Annales* 16.18, Nam illi dies per somnum, nox officiis et oblectamentis vitae transigebatur.

2. die: Riese's emendation of *dei* in A. Baehrens changes *parta* (found in ABV) *dei* to *grata piae,* a bold figure and a bold change.

3. vigilias: For the scansion, see above, entry for this word, Ch. VIII, B 1.

6. vivas: For the scansion, see above, entry for this word, Ch. VIII, B 2.

6. ad antipodas: See above, note on *in antra,* 7.4, and Ch. VI, A 9, on Luxorius' use of prepositions. The use of *ad* to express place where is not unusual in late Latin; see Bechtel, *Peregrinatio,* p. 103.IV, for examples.

6. antipodas: Cf. Seneca, *Epistulae Morales* 122.2, Sunt quidam in eadem urbe antipodes, qui, ut M. Cato ait, nec orientem umquam solem viderunt nec occidentem.

6. sis vel ut inde: For the inversion *sis ... ut,* cf. 57.6. There is a faint reminiscence here of Martial, 7.18.14, disce vel inde loqui, and 12.68.6, redeo, si vigilatur et hic, not in the meaning but in the choice of words.

Petschenig, *ZöstG,* XXVIII, 489, thinks that line 6 means, "Since you came here from the antipodes, go back again."

Klapp, *Quaestiones,* p. ii, interprets the line thus, "Si per diem dormis et per noctem vigilas, nos, quibuscum vivis, antipodes tui sumus, itaque hinc ad tuos redi." This is essentially the idea, but Klapp does not account for *vel ut,* nor are *hinc* and *inde* equal.

Vel is here used with corrective or even intensive force. *Inde* became in French the partitive *en,* a meaning it had already acquired in late Latin. Blaise, *Manuel,* pp. 106-7, § 153, gives examples from ecclesiastical writings. Hence line 6 means, "Live among the antipodeans, or that you may (really) be one of them, go back." Lycaon is advised to live among the antipodeans, but Luxorius seems to recall that the Romans with whom Lycaon is living are his antipodeans. Therefore the poet tells him to go back to his own kind—the people who are antipodeans of the Romans.

33

Meter: Elegiac; see above, Ch. VIII, Meter 1.

Title. sarcophago: On the spelling, see above, Ch. IX, C 3.

fuerant: On the tense, see above, Ch. VI, A 5.

1. turpia tot tumulo: On the alliteration, see above, Ch. V, B 7.

1. tumulo defixit: See note on *capiti*, 12.4, above, and cf. Vergil, *Aeneid* 1.45, scopuloque infixit acuto.

2. post superos; compact use of *post*, as if a verb were understood, "after overwhelming the gods above," contrasted with *Tartara premens*; cf. 1.1. For the bearing of the use of *superos* on the question of Luxorius' religion, cf. 81.6, and see above, Ch. III, E 2.

3. pro facinus: Like Trimalchio in Petronius, *Satiricon* 71.5-12, Balbus wants the accomplishments of which he is proud to appear on his tomb.

4. luxuriam: emendation by Riese of *luxoriam* in A. See above, Chs. III, A 3, and IX, C 3, on the exchange of *o* and *u* in the manuscript.

4. moecha: an emendation by *a* of *mecum*. This presents two difficulties—*moecha* is rarely used as an adjective, and "adulterer" or "adulteress" is boldly applied to a tomb. *Foeda* would fit better or, for a Luxorian contrast, a word like *clara* or even *pura* might be used—the deeds are foul, but the marble of the tomb is bright and pure.

34

Meter: Elegiac; see above, Ch. VIII, Meter 1.

Title. Item unde supra: Burmann (*Anthologia*, II, 597) and Riese (*Anthologia*, I, 263) think that these words refer to a previous poem, like 26 or 27. Baehrens (*PLM*, IV, 402) is just as sure that the words refer to the previous poem. These interpretations are possible, but the title may allude not to the sarcophagus of 33 but to the odd uses of different sarcophagi in Poems 33 and 34.

1. crevit: poetic cliché for "has appeared." Cf. *crescere*, 45.6. *TLL*, IV, 1176, line 32, gives *nasci* and *oriri* as synonyms of *crescere*.

2. purior: See above, Ch. VI, A 7.

2. nympha: Cf. 212R.6, Ac stupet ardentes frigida nympha lacus.

2. loco: Cf. 18.8, and see above, Ch. VI, B 4.

3. metallis: In Statius *metallum* refers to marble, or the quarry, or metal: cf. *Silvae* 1.3.47 ff.; 2.2.35; 4.3.97 ff. In this poem *metallis* most probably means "metals." Cf. 210R.1-2, Hic ubi conspicuis radiant nunc signa metallis/ Et nitido clarum marmore fulget opus. The Carthaginians used metal as well as marble for their statuary, as attested by the museums of Carthage and Tunis; see *MCAAT*, XV, 129, No. 106; 130, Nos. 114-15; 131, No. 116; and Pls. 65, 66, and 70.

4. crispatum gradum: The water runs over a curving slope or steps and falls into the coffin. Boissier describes a fountain at Tipasa near Cherchel, where the water descended from basin to basin (*L'Afrique romaine*, p. 139; see also above, Ch. 1, B 4).

7. sarcophagus: See above, Ch. IX, C 3.

7. tristis: Luxorius has used many contrasting words in this poem: *sepulcri* (line 5) and *vivis corporibus* (line 6); *tristis* (line 7) and *laetos* (line 8); *funera*

(line 7) and *vivis* (line 6); *falsa* (line 10) and *vera* (line 10). In this ecphrasis he achieves a pleasant paradox: the article intended for the dead provides water for the living.

9. signatum: Cf. Ovid, *Metamorphoses* 2.326, signant quoque carmine saxum.

10. palmiferis post praelia: On the alliteration, see above, Ch. V, B 7.

10. praelia: an emendation by Baehrens of *praemia* in A. The same change was made in 254R.1 by Riese. See below, note on *praelia, 37.5.*

10. turba: refers to the crowd of attendants and grooms.

15. potus potusque: Mariotti, *Parola del Passato,* II, (1947), 347, suggests *potus fotusque* as a borrowing from medical literature. He cites Pliny, *Natural History* 25.18.40, and 26.90.153, potu fotuque; Macrobius *Saturnalia* 7.6.3, aut potu . . . aut fotu; and Serenus Sammonicus, *Res Reconditae* 314 (*PLM,* III, 121), et potu et fotu. In 64L.11 Luxorius used *fotus.* "fomentation," but here, in spite of *salubres,* there is no evidence that the water was used for medicinal rubdowns or warm applications and poultices. Cf. W. S. Gilbert, *Utopia Limited,* Act I, where King Paramount says that his "medical adviser exhibits rum punch . . . as a draught, not as a fomentation."

16. proprius: See above, Ch. VI, A 6.

35

Meter: Elegiac; see above, Ch. VIII, Meter 1.

2. quod: Either there is an asyndeton here or *quod* is used to sum up *divitias, epulas,* and *munera.*

3. Becca: This is the only occurrence of the name *Becca* listed in *TLL,* II, 1797, where it is compared with *Becco* and *Beccus,* Celtic names. *Beccus* is found in *CIL,* XII, 2514. In Suetonius, *Vitellius* 18, *Beccus,* "rooster's beak," is given as the nickname of Antonius Primus, the slayer of Vitellius.

3. maritos: For this theme, see especially Juvenal, 2.57-60, 117-26.

6. debueras: For the tense, cf. 14.4 and 50.2, and see above, Ch. VI, A 5.

6. si bona membra dares: Becca is like Virro in Juvenal, 9.35-37, but he is generous with his wealth, even lavishing exceptional favors upon one of his debauchers. Therefore Luxorius concludes that there is something wrong with him, that he must be suffering from a foul disease, if he hands out money freely to those who should be paying him for his services—another paradox.

36

Meter: Anapaestic; see above, Ch. VIII, Meter 7.

Title. prostare faciebat: On the use of *facere* and the infinitive, see Ch. VI, A 4, also Kuehner-Stegmann, I, 694.

For the possible inspiration of this poem, see Juvenal, 9.70-90; cf. also, for different twists, 127R, *De lenone uxoris suae,* and Martial, 1.84; 6.39; 10.102; and 11.71, Et fieri quod iam non facit ipse sinit. The modern variation on the theme—more literary, more extended, and more elevated—is Eugene O'Neill's *Strange Interlude.* Cf. also D. H. Lawrence's *Lady Chatterley's Lover.*

This short poem offers more difficulties in its meter and its meaning, than any other poem of Luxorius. In spite of the many suggested and actual emendations, it is difficult to extract a satisfactory interpretation, especially of the last two lines.

2. non pater: in apposition with the subject of *audis,* "although you are not a father."

2. audis: *Audire* may be used as a copulative verb equaling *vocor;* see Kuehner-Stegmann, I, 15, § 6c. Therefore, *patrium nomen . . . audis* means, "You are called by the name of father," which equals, "You are called a father." Cf. Horace, *Epistles* 1.7.37-38, rexque paterque/ Audisti . . . , and *Satires* 2.6.20, seu Iane libentius audis.

2. carus: emended to *rarus* by Klapp (p. xi), which may at first glance seems to be an improvement. However, it destroys the bold contrast of *carus* with *adulter,* which is part of Luxorius' style. In his first edition Riese interchanged *carus* and *castae,* emending to *castus* and *carae.* He reversed himself in his 1894 edition and suggested *pravus* for *castus.* But this is a simplification; *carus,* "beloved," highlights the chasteness and devotion of the wife, who still loves her husband in spite of the indignities he forces her to undergo. She is guiltless because she is acting under duress. Or, if *carus* means "affectionate" here, it forms another paradox—the husband still loves her in spite of what he forces her to do.

2. adulter: *Damnas* clearly shows that the husband is the *adulter* but he is not reported in the poem to be the paramour of another woman, the general meaning of *adulter.* Neither is he an unnatural lover, like Pasiphae's bull, which is called *adulter* by Ovid, *Ars Amatoria* 1.304, and *Metamorphoses* 9.740, nor does the husband qualify as an *adulter* in the scriptural sense of an unchaste person or as a party to a marriage which the theologians disapproved (*OED,* I, 130, *s.v. adultery*). However, a remote resemblance to Luxorius' use of the word appears in Seneca, *Dialogues* 2, *De Constantia Sapientis* 7.4, Si quis cum uxore sua tamquam cum aliena concumbat, adulter erit, quamvis illa adultera non sit. Surely *carus adulter* is one of Luxorius' boldest and wryest paradoxes. Whenever the husband gives his wife to another, the lover is now acting as the husband in fact, and the legal husband, who is not a real husband because of his inability to procreate, becomes the *adulter pro tempore,* when he makes love to his own wife.

Baehrens rewrites Luxorius by changing *carus* to *pactus* and *damnas* to *aravit*—thereby taking away any subtlety the lines may have had.

3. coiugis: See above, Ch. VIII, A 7.

4. spurcos: See above, Ch. VIII, A 7.

5. inscia: *inscius* in A. Klapp emended to *inscia. Inscios* is also possible grammatically, but *inscia* is best for the meter.

5. quo sint semine creti: Cf. 198R.13, quo sim de semine cretus.

6. forsan: For the scansion, see above, Ch. VIII, A 7, and entry for this word in Ch. VIII, B I. Note the alliteration in this line carried over to *foeda* in the next.

7. Proconi: Apparently the only occurrence of this name; it may be derived from *proco* and *procus,* like *Proculus.*

Through line 7 the meaning of this poem is quite clear, no matter which readings are adopted for lines 1-7:

Lines 1-2. Although impotent, Proconius, you are nevertheless called a father.

Lines 3-5. You force your wife to bear children by somebody else. There are so many of these men that nobody involved knows who the real father is.

Lines 6-7. Your wish to have sons in this way might perhaps be tolerable, if—.

This leads to the crux of the problem. Under what circumstances presumably revealed in lines 8-9 would the *foeda vota* have been *ferenda*?

One might expect Luxorius to say that Proconius' shameful method of attaining his desire would have been bearable if the boy when grown up acknowledged or treated Proconius as if the latter were his father. With some effort and strain and with emendations of *ipsa* to *ipsum* or *ipse* and *matrem* to *patrem,* this interpretation can be extracted from the last two lines of the poem. *Scire* would have to be taken in the sense of "know how" (see Kuehner-Stegmann, *Grammatik,* I, 669, § 124d, on *scire* and the complementary infinitive), and *dicere* would here mean "call, name," as in Horace, *Odes* 1.2.50. The translation would then be, "If ever your son when grown up could know how to call you yourself his father."

Burmann (*Anthologia,* II, 198) thought that line 8 could be made to read *Si tu vel ipse filius umquam,* but this makes the conclusion in the next line unintelligible. Riese keeps lines 8-9 as they are in A, with the correction of *situs* to *si tuus,* which was made by Mueller. Four important versions of these two lines are:

(1) Scire vel ipsa tuus umquam
     Posset adultus dicere matrem.

                                        Riese (*Anthologia,* I, 265)

(2) Scire vel ipsum si tuus umquam
     Posset adultus dicere patrem.

                                        Baehrens (*PLM,* IV, 403)

(3) Scire vel ipse si tuus umquam
     Posset adultus dicere patrem.

                                        Mueller (*NJbb,* XCV, 784)

(4) Scire vel ipsam si tuus umquam
     Posset adultus dicere matrem.

                                        Klapp (*Quaestiones,* p. xi)

No. (1) is manifestly impossible because *ipsa* cannot modify anything in the two lines; Riese properly obelizes lines 8-9 in this version.

No. (2) seems to mean, "If at any rate the boy when grown up could say that the father himself knew." It does not show how Proconius' shame would be bearable. However, see above, end of note to line 7.

No. (3) is practically the same as (2). Mueller's change of *ipsa* to *ipse* merely shifts the emphasis to *adultus.* Moreover, the final short open vowel in *ipse* is not good metrically.

No. (4) is explained by Klapp in great detail. His interpretation is that the disgraceful longing of Proconius would have some excuse if the son could finally say that at any rate the mother knew—. But what? Klapp's answer is: If she knew from what seed the children had sprung (*quo semine creti,* line 5). He reasons that, if not even the mother knows, it will appear to the son that she had been let out (*"permissam"*) not to one but to all comers. Klapp says that this must undoubtedly be considered much more disgraceful than the mother's enforced infidelity with just one man, the boy's real father.

In this interpretation, the element of surprise is lacking. We have been told in line 5 by the word *inscia,* which is Klapp's own emendation, that the mother herself does not know. Actually, *inscios* would be better for the effect, but it is poor metrically. However, I have accepted Klapp's text in spite of its weaknesses because it is more plausible than the other suggestions. The analysis of the poem is then completed as follows:

Lines 8-9. You adopted this shameful way of being a father, Proconius. However, you are not the boy's father, and what is more, the boy can never say who is his real father because even his mother cannot tell. This makes your detestable desire intolerable.

37

Meter: Lesser Asclepiad; see above, Ch. VIII, Meter 4.

Title. in pretio ludente: The legal phrase is *in aliquid ludere.* Cf. *Digesta* 11.5.2 *Praefatio,* Senatus consultum vetuit in pecuniam ludere. See above, note on *in antra,* 7.4, on Luxorius' use of prepositions.

1. ludis ad aleam: The name of the game or the instrument with which it is played should be in the accusative or ablative without a preposition, as *aleam* or *aleā ludere*; see Kuehner-Stegmann, I, 277. For pictures of gaming tables, see *Inventaire,* III (1925), Pl. 176, and A. Maiuri, *Roman Painting* (Lausanne, 1953), p. 145.

1. Ultor: This name occurs on an inscription found in Proconsularis, *CIL,* VIII, Supp. 4, 25508.

2. tabula: Mueller, *De Re Metrica,* p. 182, emends to *tabulam.* However, if *das* is here considered a synonym of *ponis,* the ablative with *in* is correct; see Kuehner-Stegmann, I, 589, § 114a.

2. virginem: Playing dice for a woman is a scene in Erskine Caldwell's novel *Journeyman* (New York, 1938), pp. 137-50.

3. spondens: Ultor is apparently wagering the use of the girl, not actual possession of her as property.

4. das aliis: Cf. 16.8, exercens aliis.

5-6. These two lines have been subjected to many emendations, suggestions, and interpretations. The reading of A (with the obvious corrections of *grada* and *prodeest*) is:

> An tabulae melius praemia grata sunt
> Aut prodest vitium tale quod imperas.

Tabulae is a definite metrical fault and *imperas* seems meaningless. Some emended versions are:

(1)   An tali melius praemia grata sunt?
      Aut prodest vitium tale, quod impetras?
                              Mueller (*De Re Metrica*, p. 182)

Riese follows this version exactly.

(2)   An tablae melius proelia grata sunt,
      An prodest vitium tale quod impetras.
                              Schubert (*De Luxorio*, pp. 34-35)

(3)   An tali melius praemia grata sunt
      Aut forte est vitium tale quod imperat?
                              Klapp (*Quaestiones*, p. xi)

(4)   Hau tablae melius praemia grata sunt.
      At prodest vitium tale quod impetras!
                              Baehrens (*PLM*, IV, 403)

(5)   An tablae melius praelia grata sunt?
      Aut prodest vitium tale quod impetras?
                              (My text)

Mueller's change of *tabulae* to *tali* ("of the die," "dice playing") is clever but not needed since *tablae*, the syncopated form of *tabulae*, fits both the meter and the meaning and is closer to the manuscript reading. Luxorius uses syncopated forms, e.g., *saeclum*, 66.1; *saeclo*, 81.5; *periclum*, 87.7. *Tablista* is found in 47.T. *Proelia* or *praelia* is better than *praemia* because Ultor does not have to seek the rewards or winnings of dice playing, since he can always hire the girl out. Apparently, the poet is asking Ultor whether the excitement of playing is more pleasing to him than having the girl for himself. The use of *proelia* or *praelia* for the battles of the gaming table is parallelled in 47.6 and 193R.9, and in Juvenal, 1.90-93. *Praelia* (not *proelia*) is used in my text instead of *praemia* in accordance with the same change made in 34.13.

In version (3) Klapp would have it that line 6 is addressed to the other player and not to Ultor. He believes that it means that there is some fault in the girl or the player which impels him to stake the girl. This is not clear and there is no justification for the sudden change of address. It also weakens an epigram that is none too strong. In (4) Baehrens rewrites and simplifies, but he seems to be making Luxorius say what he did not say. Luxorius is asking whether the gambler is happier with the game than with the girl; Baehrens flatly says that Ultor is not happy with gambling but with his vice. I have followed Schubert in line 8 and Mueller and Riese in line 9.

5.   melius grata: See above, Ch. VI, A 7.

8.   cupere: For the scansion, see above, note on *forsan*, 36.6.

This poem is another example of the cryptic and somewhat deep type of paradox appealing to Luxorius. Ultor has a girl who means nothing to him *qua* girl. The poet may be implying that Ultor is impotent or that he looks upon the girl only as a source of revenue. He offers her to others on peculiar terms: they must play dice for the privilege of making love to her. Ultor could just as well exact a fee but he loves the roll of the dice. This is the paradox—an ancient version of "Heads, I win; tails, you lose." In either event

Ultor gets what he wants. If he wins, he still has the girl, although he will not enjoy the *blanditias et coitus* the other winners would receive. If he loses, he really loses nothing. He does not want the girl carnally and since the winner has played only for the privilege of a night with the girl, she is still the property of Ultor—and he can "sell" her again.

38

Meter: Elegiac; see above, Ch. VIII, Meter 1.

Title. quo: The antecedent may be either *Aegyptii* or *nomen* to carry out the play on names in lines 1-2.

1. Icarus et Phaethon: On their fall, see Ovid, *Metamorphoses* 2.311-29; 8.195-235.

1. Veneto nolente: The charioteer must be a member of the Greens; the Blues hate him and do not relish hearing him called by complimentary names. In Poem 42 Luxorius praises a Green charioteer. See above, Ch. I, B 14.

2. Agilis: This is capitalized here a nickname, like our "Speedy."

2. pigro ... pede ... premas: On the alliteration, see above, Ch. V, B 7.

4. insolitis ... plagis: Note the rhyme here and in line 5, below; see note on *totis ... horis*, 25.2.

5-6. Hysteron proteron; cf. 87.6-7.

6. Icare: a sudden shift to the vocative, a trick of style often found in Lucan also, e.g. *Pharsalia* 1.21, 30, 41, *et al*. See above, Ch. V, B 4. Cf. Vergil, *Aeneid* 6.31.

7. ergo: On the final *o*, see above, Ch. VIII, B 3.

7-8. The inevitable Luxorian paradox and contrast: You bear names that speedy fliers once bore but they perished; may you fall as they did so that they perish once again in your name.

8. per ... prius: Cf. the alliteration with that in line 2, above.

39

Meter: Dactylic Hexameter; see above, Ch. VIII, Meter 2.

Title. ubi: Riese queries whether this should be *qui*. However, *ubi* may refer to the scene in the painting; cf. 88.T.

1. pium facinus: oxymoron, "pious impiety." See above, Ch. V, B 1, and note on *omen*, line 3, below. Cf. also Shakespeare, *Much Ado about Nothing*, Act IV, scene 1: Thou pure impiety, and impious purity; and "the crime of piety" of Antigone, "the sinless sinner," Sophocles, *Antigone* 74.

3. c(a)edis: must be read as *cēdis* to make the line a *versus recurrens*, amphisbaena, or palindrome. (See above, Ch. V, n. 8.) Klapp, *Quaestiones*, p. xii, first noticed that the line is a palindrome. Mueller, *De Re Metrica*, p. 183, had categorically declared "pro illo aperte falso *si* restituendum sine mora *sed*." In the 1869 edition of the *Anthologia Latina*, Riese had suggested *si accipit* for *si decet* but did not change his text. Noticing that the line read the same backward and forward, Klapp tersely and almost apologetically remarks about Riese and Mueller, "utrumque aperte iudicium fefellit." *Caveat Corrector*! See above, Preface, on the scholars' use of *sine dubio* and the like.

3. omen: What was *facinus* has becomes *omen,* for Romulus is now honored, whereas Remus is forgotten. Hence *huius nomine* (line 2) may refer to the act of slaying Remus or may mean "because of the city's name". See Livy, 1.7.3, condita urbs conditoris nomine appellata.

40

Meter: Lesser Sapphic; see above, Ch. VIII, Meter 5.

Title. ad prandium clamabat. *Clamare* is used here instead of the classical *invitare* or *vocare.* Cf. Martial, 1.49.29-30. Vocabitur venator et veniet tibi/ Conviva clamatus prope, and 12.26.11, Nec venit ablatis clamatus verna lacernis. See also the late Latin *Testamentum Porcelli,* clamavit ad se suos parentes, which Haupt, *Opuscula,* II, 180, citing Luxorius, calls a plebeian use. The text of the *Testamentum Porcelli* is also found in F. Buecheler and W. Heraeus, *Petronii Saturae et Liber Priapeorum* (6th ed., Berlin, 1922), and in H. T. Peck and R. L. Arrowsmith, *Roman Life in Latin Prose and Verse* (New York, 1894), pp. 172-73. *TLL,* III, 1253, line 50, equates *clamavit* with *invitavit.*

xenia: All of Martial's Book 13 is devoted to *xenia,* gifts given to guests, and Book 14 describes *apophoreta,* likewise gifts or favors taken away by guests. Evidently the custom has taken on new proportions in Luxorius' day; the guests now bring gifts just as do visitors today when invited to dinner or for a week end. The "switch" that makes the paradox in Luxorius' poem is that the guest begs not to be invited—unlike the guests in Martial's poems, who were always seeking invitations. The guest in Luxorius' poem is being impoverished and has nothing left to eat at home.

1. nimis: See above, Ch. VI, A 7.

2. Blumarit: apparently a Germanic name meaning "flowery"; Schoenfeld, *Wörterbuch,* pp. 51-52, relates it to Gothic *bloma.*

4-6. volebam, pasceres, peteres, detur, pascas: On the sequence in this mélange of presents and imperfects, see above, Ch. VI, A 5.

6. detur: On the scansion, see above, entry for this word, Ch. VIII, B 2.

41

Meter: Dactylic Hexameter; see above, Ch. VIII, Meter 2.

1. Pascasium: *Pascasius* and *Pascasia* are names frequently found in African inscriptions: the index of *CIL,* V.I, 105, lists *Pascasius* about ten times, *Pascasi,* thirteen times, and *Pascasia,* five times. A number of African bishops were named *Pascasius;* see list in Victor of Vita, *Notitia Provinciarum et Civitatum Africa,* ed. by M. Petschenig, *CSEL* (Vienna, 1881), VII, 117-34 (*PL.* LVII, 270-6). The name may be related to *paschalis,* "Passover, Easter"; it was also written *Paschasius,* as in Ambrose, *Epistulae* 11.5 (*PL,* XVI, 987A). From *paschalis* are derived the names Pask, Pascoe, Pascowe, Pascal, and Paskell, also Pasquale. (See Pl. III, A.)

1. populi: Cf. *populos,* 20.2, and see above, Ch. VI, B 5.

3. papulis: an emendation by Doehner of *populis* in A. Meyer's emendation to *plagis* may seem better on the surface because *papulae* are not normally caused by falls. However, *papulis* is closer to the manuscript reading and Luxorius cannot be expected to be medically exact.

3. amica ruinis: a bold phrase, "accident-prone."

5-6. cadit ... et cadit: a reminiscence of Juvenal, 6.483-84, et caedit ... et caedit. Line 6 is adapted from Juvenal, 10.60, Caedit et inmeritis franguntur crura caballis.

8. potius: See above, Ch. VI, A 7.

8. gryphum: *TLL*, VI, 2, 2341, lines 30-33, 55-57, in giving occurrences of *gryphum*, calls this one *obscurius in carmine irrisorio*. However, glosses by Donatus and Servius on Vergil, *Bucolics* 8.27, iungentur iam grypes equis, call the griffin an enemy of the horse. See also *RE*, VII, 1923, 1927. Hence, the implication by Luxorius may well be that, like a griffin seeking to kill a horse, the charioteer seems to be trying to destroy his horses by his poor driving.

Schubert, *De Luxorio*, p. 36, emends *gryphum* to *grillum*, as a "*bestiola*" that falls and rises again. This is tempting, but Luxorius is not usually that direct.

For representations of griffins in ancient art, see *Inventaire*, Fasciculus 1, No. 301, and Fasciculus 2, Nos. 909-13; Reinach *Répertoire de peintures*, pp. 347-48; *Répertoire de la statuaire*, V.2, 579.

8. proprium: See above, Ch. VI, A 6.

42

Meters: Elegiac; see above, Ch. VIII, Meter 1.

Title. laude aurigae: On the honors paid to charioteers, see above, Ch. I, n. 72.

Prasini: Cf. Poem 38.1, and see above, Ch. I, B 14, on factions.

1. Iectofian: a name otherwise unknown.

3. suetus: nominative with vocative *Iectofian*, line 1; see above, note on *Fauste*, 1.3-4, and Ch. VI, A 12.

5. Tantalides ... humero eburno: Pelops was killed by his father Tantalus, cut into small pieces, and served as a dish to the gods and goddesses, all of whom spurned the repast, except hungry Demeter, who ate the shoulder. Later the gods restored Pelops to life and replaced the missing shoulder with one of ivory. Poseidon gave him winged steeds with which he outraced Oenomaos, son of Ares and king of Pisa in Elis. As a reward Pelops won Hippodamia, daughter of Oenomaos. See Ovid, *Metamorphoses* 6. 404-11; Grimal, *Dictionnaire de la Mythologie, s.v. Hippodamia, Oenomaos*, and *Pelops;* cf. Hyginus, *Fabulae* 83, umero non perpetuo eburneum eius loco Ceres aptavit. Uranius, a charioteer of Constantinople, was called Pelops because of his victories (*Anthologia Palatina* 15.48.4).

43

Meter: Elegiac; see above, Ch. VIII, Meter 1.

1. foedas puellas: For a poem in a similar vein, cf. Martial, 3.76, especially line 2, Nec formosa tibi sed moritura placet.

1. Myrro: The name is spelled *Myro* elsewhere; see Juvenal, 8.102; Martial, 4.39.2; *CIL*, VIII, Supp. 4, 22759, 24023; XIV. 2, 4126; *et al. Myro* is found on a mosaic; see *Inventaire*, II, Fasciculus 2, 511; and *MCAAT*, VII, 28, No. 137.

2. viderit: For the subjunctive, cf. *vicerit,* 47.10.

3. est: On the use of the indicative in an indirect question, see above, Ch. VI, A 3.

3. fatere: This is the reading of A, which was corrected to *fateri* by Riese. Although the exclamatory infinitive adds vigor, I have kept *fatere,* "you confess," since the form fits grammatically and makes good sense.

3. Myrro: a shift to the vocative; see above, Ch. V, B 4.

4. non placeat Pontica, sed Garamas: These two names are placed in opposition to denote a contrast between either beautiful and ugly, or white and black. The use of *Pontica* seems strained and recondite. Medea is associated with Pontus, as in Cicero, *De Imperio Pompei* 9.22, ex eodem Ponto Medea, but she was more noted for magic than for her beauty. It is not clear why Luxorius should have chosen the inhabitants of Pontus as the symbols of beauty or whiteness. *Garamas* may represent a Negro. According to modern scholarship, the Garamantes, an African tribe, were not Negroes, but to the ancients anthropology was a rudimentary branch of learning; see above, Ch. I, n. 11, and Courtois, *Les Vandales,* p. 102. Luxorius may therefore have considered the Garamantes Negroes; at any rate, they were probably swarthy. Contrasting a Carthaginian girl with a foreign maiden of darker hue, Petschenig, *ZöstG,* XXVIII, 490, suggests *Poenica* for *Pontica* ("Ich zweifle nicht das er [Luxorius] Poenica schrieb"). Luxorius did not draw the color line in the case of athletes; see Poems 7 and 67. That there was some bias against Garamantians and Negroes on the part of an African poet or two is attested by 183R,1-2, Faex Garamantarum nostrum processit ad axem/ Et piceo gaudet corpore verna niger, and by 189R.5-6, on Memnon's aid to Troy, Iam tunc monstratur, maneat qui Pergama casus,/ Cum nigrum Priamus suscipit auxilium.

5. quaeris: See note on *est,* line 3.

6. dare: *sensu obsceno;* see note on *das,* 31.5.

44

Meter: Elegiac; see above, Ch. VIII, Meter 1.

This is another of the poems about performing animals, a genre familiar to us from Martial, especially in his *Liber de Spectaculis*; cf. also his 14.202. Monkeys were pets in Rome in early times; see Plautus, *Miles Gloriosus* 162 and 179. Jennison, *Animals for Show and Pleasure,* pp. 127-29, lists a number of allusions to domesticated monkeys, apes, and baboons in Greek and Latin authors, including Aelian and Pliny; reference is also made to Pompeian paintings. Keller, *Die antike Tierwelt,* I, 2, 5, has an illustration of a long-tailed monkey on a Roman tombstone. Monkeys were popular in Africa, and performed in the market place.

Luxorius' poem has other implications, an allegorical overtone to the effect that animals know the deference due to their masters, who in turn know how to calm the nature of wild beasts. (See introductory note on Poem 19, also Poems 5 and 74.) The theme is set forth in Martial, 1.104.21-22, Haec clementia non paratur arte,/ Sed norunt cui serviant leones, and in 195R.8-9, Vis humana potest rabiem mutare ferinam;/ Ecce hominem parvum belua magna timet.

Finally, this particular poem may have some historical significance. Line 1 indicates that peace had returned after a long period of war, and line 3 sounds like the annunciation of a new reign. Schubert, *De Luxorio*, pp. 16-17, discusses the possible occasions on which Carthage could have been said to be freed from war and on which she had a new ruler in Luxorius' lifetime. (See above, Ch. III, D 2.) There are three possibilities:

(1.) In 523, after the death of Thrasamund, his widow, Amalafrida, conspired with her Gothic troops against Hilderic, the new king. When the revolt was crushed, Hilderic's kingdom could be said to be *felix*. (See note on Poem 59.)

(2.) In 534, when Belisarius defeated Gelimer, the rule of Justinian's general could also be called *felix*.

(3.) In 530, when Gelimer deprived Hilderic of his kingdom, the same adjective could have been used.

Schubert rejects (3) because Gelimer imprisoned Oageis, whom Luxorius praises in Poems 59 and 83. However, there is not enough evidence to fix the event referred to in this poem. If it is any of the three, (1) is the most likely choice, especially because of the leniency of the mild and gentle Hilderic, who was tolerant toward the Romans and the different religious groups.

Title. simiis: For the possible bearing of the use of the plural in the title and of the singular (*simia*, line 2) in the same poem on the authorship of the title, see above, Ch. VII, 2-4, 6, and note on *stabulo*, 26. T.

dorso: For the case, see note on *capiti*, 12.4.

1. Tyriis: Cf. 3.8.

1. mira: Cf. 74.6; 79.5; 81.5.

2. sedeat canem: See above, note on *corde sedent*, 17.2, and cf. 26.4 and 27.4.

3. quanto magna: The reading of A is *quanto*. Meyer emended this to *quantum*, which Riese and Baehrens accepted. However, the chance is unnecessary. Although *multum, tantum,* and *quantum* instead of the ablative of measure of difference with a comparative are found in all periods of Latin, in late Latin the ablative is used even with a positive: see Kuehner-Stegman, I, 402-3, 81, Remarks 19-21. Klapp, *Quaestiones*, p. vii, thinks that *quantum* (*quanto*) replaces *quam* in this passage.

For the thought of lines 3-4, cf. Martial, *De Spectaculis* 10.5-6, Quos decet esse hominum tali sub principe mores,/ Qui iubet ingenium mitius esse feris.

45

Meter: Elegiac; see above Ch. VIII, Meter 1.

1. lambere: At the end of the hibernating period the female bear gives birth to her cubs, usually two in number. "They are born in a much less developed condition than the young of the dog and cat tribes, for the bear cubs are at first almost naked, as well as blind, they are also extremely small, weighing only about a pound at birth. In few other animals, except marsupials, are the young so tiny compared with the adult" (Ray Palmer, "The Bear Tribe," in *Wild Life the World Over* [New York, 1947], p. 158). This has

given rise to the belief that the mother bear licks her young into shape; cf. 690R.3 (Petronius, Fragment 26, in Buecheler, *Petronius,* p. 119, and Sage, *Petronius,* p. 140), Sic format lingua fetum cum protulit ursa; Pliny, *Natural History* 8.54.126, hanc lambendo paulatim figurant; also Aelian, *De Natura Animalium* 2.19.

1. prolis: Note the synonyms used by Luxorius: *genus, subolem, pignus.* He does not often pay such attention to a choice of words; see above, Ch. VI, B 4, and note to 34.7.

2. ferox placido: See above, Ch. V, B 1, on Luxorius' use of contrasting words.

6. sculpendo: On the short final *o,* see above, Ch. VIII, B 3.

6. facit crescere: See Ch. VI, A 4, on *facere* and the infinitive. So Vergil is supposed to have written the *Georgics* by working on a small number of verses a day, non absurde carmen se more ursae parere dicens et lambendo demum effingere (Suetonius, *Vita Vergilii* 22). Aulus Gellius, *Noctes Atticae* 17.10.2-5, tells the story in greater details, Namque ut illa bestia fetum ederet ineffigiatum informemque conformaret et fingeret, etc.

6. crescere: Cf. *crevit,* 34.1.

8. lingua magistra: This may be a reminiscence of Vergil, *Aeneid* 8.442, arte magistra. Luxorius is saying that two organs of the mother's body shape the cub: first her womb, and then her tongue.

46

Meter: Phalaecean; see above, Ch. VIII, Meter 3.

Title. Eugeti: It is impossible to identify this Eugetus. Meerman (in Burmann, *Anthologia,* II, 602, note on Book VI, *Epigram* 45) thinks he is the Oageis of Poems 59 and 83. Schubert, *De Luxorio,* pp. 13-14, and Riese, *Anthologia,* I, xxvii, argue to the contrary; Courtois, *Les Vandales,* p. 339, reasons equivocally. He doubts that Oageis (or Hoageis) is the same as Eugetus on the basis of philology, but on the other hand he thinks that Poem 83 may confirm the hypothesis that the two men, Oageis and Eugetus, are the same.

This poem, another ecphrasis (see above, note on Poem 18), is a division of that genre called the *locus amoenus* or pleasance, which forms the principal motif of all descriptions of nature from the days of the Roman Empire to the sixteenth century. It includes the poetical description of gardens as well as of ideal groves and forests. For a fuller treatment, see Curtius, *European Literature,* pp. 295-300. In the present poem Luxorius follows the tradition of Martial and especially of Statius, who wrote about beautiful estates. Cf. also 18L and 83L; Asmenius, *De Laude Horti* (Poem 635R); and the *Amnis ibat* poem of Tiberian.

1. hortus: nominative, although it is being addressed; see above, note on *Fauste,* 1.3.

1. Napaeae: The dell nymphs; cf. Vergil, *Georgics* 4.535; Statius, *Thebais* 4.255.

2. quo: See note to 3.5, above.

2. virente choro: For the scansion, see above, entry for *choro,* Ch. VIII, B 1.

5. teretes: This is an unusual word to apply to the torch of Cupid. It is

possible that Luxorius thought of the flames as weapons and transferred the epithet so often given to smooth and well rubbed weapons to the fires used as the weapons. Cf. the following concatenation in 253R.9-10, flammantes sagittas and teretes catenas, also the coupling of arrows and flames in Seneca, *Hippolytus* 275 ff.

5. flammas: Cf. *facibus,* 61.2. Many statues and reliefs of Cupid and his torch have been found in North Africa; see *MCAAT,* VII, 75-76, No. 890, 78, and No. 906; XV, 63, No. 1082, 66, No. 1112, 69, and No. 1146; XX, 54, No. 1332. See also Reinach, *Répertoire de la statuaire,* II.2, 413, Nos. 2-3, and *Répertoire de peintures,* p. 68.

5. liber: For the scansion, see above, Ch. VIII, A 3.

                                                                    ni
7. quo sese Aonides: The reading in A is *quos elacodes* (with *-is* corrected to *-es*). In the margin Saumaise wrote *Heliconiades,* which does not fit the Phalaecean meter at all. Mueller, *De Re Metrica,* p. 180, changes the line to *Quo ferunt se Heliconides puellae.* Baehrens, is his usual manner, goes far afield, writing *Quo se Acidaliae,* thereby bringing the Graces on the scene. Riese's text has *Quo se Laconides.* This must be rejected on two grounds. In the first place, Riese does not make the second foot a dactyl (see above, Ch. VIII, A 3, for method of scanning Phalaeceans). Luxorius uses a dactyl without exception in that foot; it is strange that an editor who again and again calls Luxorius a careless poet should saddle him with an unnecessary and unwarranted flaw. Evidently some editors considered Luxorius so negligent that they did not hesitate to make unmetrical emendations as if they were appropriate to Luxorius. In the second place, Spartan girls are introduced after only lesser and greater divinities have been mentioned. Would the Vandal nobles have been complimented by the intrusion of girls from a poor part of the world into their gardens? Riese cites in his *apparatus criticus* Petschenig's comparison with Vergil, *Aeneid* 1.498, Qualis in Eurotae ripis aut per iuga Cynthi/ Exercet Diana choros. Even if the term "Spartan maidens" can be applied to Diana's followers, she and her nymphs have already been mentioned in line 3. Riese also refers to Plato, *Laws* 7.806A, a passage on the training of Laconian girls in music. It is not at all certain that Luxorius had ever read Plato or that he knew that, in the late Roman Empire, Sparta was one of the few places where formal and regular education in the dance was given (Marrou, *Histoire de l'éducation,* p. 193).

Riese's comment on Mueller's change to *Heliconides* is, "Musarum locus hic nullus." Baehrens seconds this, "Sed Musis hic locum esse recte negavit Riesius." Of course, they cannot mean that Helicon is not a place for the Muses; see Hesiod, *Theogony* 1-2; Lucretius, 3.1037, Heliconiadum comites; Ovid, *Metamorphoses* 5.254, Virgineumque Helicona petit; Persius, *Prologue* 4; *et al.* They must mean that the garden is not a spot for the Muses. But the Muses frequented the springs and mountaintops; they would be just as much at home in a garden as Cupid and Venus. Mueller's emendation is acceptable if one does not object to the transposition of the words; otherwise, Burmann's version is satisfactory. It is the one I use. *Que sese Aonides* is metrically correct and, of course, the Aonides are the Muses; see Vergil, *Georgics* 3.11, Aonio rediens deducam vertice Musas, and Juvenal, 7.59, fontibus Aonidum.

8. minus: This either modifies *amoena* or it may be used as a noun; cf. Lucan, *Pharsalia* 1.1, Bella per Emathios plus quam civilia campos.

8. amoena frondis: Meyer, *Anthologia,* I, 130, note on Poem 343, calls *frondis* a nominative. Klapp, *Quaestiones,* p. xii, refused to believe this and emended to *aroma.* However, *frondis* is clearly a nominative in Serenus Sammonicus, *Res Reconditae* 185, Tum Delphica frondis addatur, and in 567, Prodest praeterea cum Baccho Punica frondis. *Frondis* can be considered a nominative in this line of Luxorius.

9. amoma: The manuscript repeats *amoena* from the preceding line. Burmann did not like this inept repetition but did nothing about it; Baehrens emended to *amoma,* which Riese accepted. *Amomum* or *amomon* is an aromatic plant from which the Romans prepared a costly balsam used as a hair lotion. Cf. Martial, 5.64.3, Pinguescat nimio madidus mihi crinis amomo, and 8.77.3, where he advises a young man to let his locks glisten *Assyrio amomo.* See also Vergil, *Bucolics* 3.89; Statius, *Silvae* 2.4.34; Lucan, 10.168; and Persius, 3.104.

12. dulcis: For the scansion, see above, entry for this word, Ch. VIII, B 1.

12. avium canor: Cf. 635R.19 f., aves canorae, and Tiberian, *Amnis ibat* 15, ales plus canora.

12. resultat: The manuscript has *resultans,* which is kept by Baehrens, who indicates a lacuna. Riese emends to *resultat* and also indicates a missing line, although there is no lacuna with his reading. The garden is addressed in line 1 and then described in a series of subordinate clauses; the last two lines sum up the entire poem in a complete sentence. For poems of similar structure, cf. Martial, 5.24, consisting of fifteen lines without a main verb, in which *Hermes* is the first word of every line, and 389R. in which lines 36-58 begin with *Sol.*

14. hoc uno . . . loco: Cf. 18.8 and 27.4; see above, Ch. VI, B 4.

14. famulans: See above, Ch. VI, B 4.

14. subaptat: Souter, listing only this occurrence, translates by "adapt(?)." This word is not found in classical Latin; see above, Ch. VI, B 1, and note on *praemedicante,* 83.4.

47

Meter: Elegiac; see above, Ch. VIII, Meter 1.

Title. tablista: Neither *tablista* nor *tabulista* is found in classical Latin. Forcellini lists only *tablistis,* 196R.7, which he relates to the late Latin verb *tablisso.* On the syncopation, see note on *tablae,* 37.5. For poems on dice playing, see Poems 82R, 192R-194R, and, for a most complicated game, see *Anthologia Palatina,* 9.482. See also *DarSag,* III, 1403 ff., for descriptions of dice games.

1. Vatanans: The only occurrence of this name: Meerman (in Burmann, *Anthologia,* II, 603) thinks it should be *Vatanas,* which he calls a Gothic-Vandal name like *Rhodanas.*

2. puncta: like our points at dice. Cf. 82R.15, Vulnere plus crescunt punctis,

quam bella sagittis, and Suetonius, *Nero* 30.3, Quadringenis in punctum sestertiis aleam lusit.

4. ore fremit: Cf. Vergil, *Aeneid* 1.559 and 9.341.

6. proelia: Cf. *praelia* in 34.13 and 37.5, and 254R.21, all emendations of *praemia.* In 254R.1, the word is written *prelia,* with the mark under the *e* to denote the diphthong *ae.* However, a scribe clearly wrote *proelia* in 193R.9 and in this line. I have observed the scribal lack of uniformity in respect to this word; see above, Ch. IX, C 3, on the variation of spelling in A.

7. tabulam ... pyrgum: On the asyndeton, see above, Ch. V, B 2.

8. Harpyacis: apparently the only occurrence of this word, which is not listed in Forcellini or *TLL; Harpyacis aera* is actually an emendation of *arpia cisera.*

10. vicerit: Cf. *viderit,* 43.2.

12. vincens ... superatus: a typical Luxorian contrast; see above, Ch. V, B 1.

12. quam superatus erat: a compact expression, with ellipsis of a temporal conjunction.

13. non iam: Baehrens emends to *iam non,* for which there is no necessity, since the *h* of *huic,* the next word, makes position and avoids hiatus (see above, entry for *quis,* Ch. VIII, B 1).

13. ludum sapientum: This game was played with tablets and dice. For a description of such games, see *RE,* XIII.2, 1900-2029, *s.v. Lusoria Tabula. MCAAT,* XIX, 35, Nos. 5-6, describes tablets found in the Amphitheater of Carthage; see also *Inventaire,* III (1925), Pl. 176. There are three lines of letters or signs arranged in two columns. If words are used, they form a maxim. The game resembled forms of backgammon; it required reflection and calculation. Three examples found in Africa follow:

INVIDA	PUNCTA		VENARI	LAVARI		PATRUS	ET FILI
IUBENT	FELICE		LUDERE	RIDERE		SERVUS	PLENUS
LUDERE	DOCTUM		OCCEST	VIVERE		EXIVIT	ARATOR
			[hoc]				

The left-hand one (*CIL,* VIII.1, 7998) was found in Philippeville (ancient Rusicade); the center one (*CIL,* Supp. 2, 17938) is part of the pavement of the Timgad Forum (see Boissier, *l'Afrique Romaine,* p. 194); the right-hand one (*CIL,* VIII.2, 8407) was found in Ain-Kebria, Mauretania Sitifensis.

There are thirty-six letters, with each half line consisting of a word or word group of six letters. Some such scheme is followed in the dactylic hexameters of the *Carmina Duodecim Sapientum,* 495R-505R. The rare use of *felice* in the left-hand inscription as an adverb or in place of *felicem* is most probably due to the need for a six-letter word; see *TLL,* VI.1, 455.

The translations of the three examples given above are, from left to right: "The unfriendly points [dice] bid the skillful player to play with luck"; "Hunting, bathing, playing, laughing—this is living"; "The old ploughman, the slave of the father and son, has died."

The last line of Luxorius' poem is missing. He might have given advice to his irrational player, who took victory and defeat in the same objectionable

way, giving vent to anger and supercharged emotion. Good counsel is contained in some of the lines of the *Carmina* mentioned in the previous paragraph. See also *Anthologia Palatina* 9.767, where the players are advised not
to blame the dice—neither to be elated when winning nor put out when losing.
However, Luxorius' last line would more probably present a contrast. Luxorius
might have said, since the demented Vatanans was playing the game, that the
Game of the Wise Men was now the Game of the Unwise, or that Vatanans
should be playing with the Furies. Accordingly, a final line could be *Sed
potius furiae nomina talus habet* or *Qui possit potius ludere cum furiis.*

48

Meter: Elegiac; see above, Ch. VIII, Meter 1.

Title. venatore: For other representations of hunters, see notes to 18.13
and 67.T.

in manibus oculos habente: a remarkably primitive style of painting. The
eye has been used as a pictorial symbol from the days of the Egyptians to
the present. Its purpose has been apotropaic and anthropomorphic: to ward
off evil, to bring good luck, to guide ships or to provide vision to the dead,
to denote watchfulness, intelligence, and omniscience (as in this poem), and to
serve as a key symbol of eroticism, as in the surrealist paintings of Frederick
Kiesler, Man Ray, and Salvador Dali.

Eyes were depicted on Egyptian coffins and ships, on Greek vases of the
late Ionic period known as eye-cups, and on Greek and Roman ships. Eyes are
still painted on small boats in different parts of the world, especially in the
Mediterranean; I have seen them on Portuguese fishing vessels and on small
craft in Yugoslavian harbors. (See Pl. IV, B.)

References to the eye as a symbol are found in Aeschylus, *Suppliants* 716,
and Philostratus, *Imagines* 1.19.3. In modern literature Aubrey Menen, *The
Ramayana* (New York, 1954), p. 170, so describes an Indian boat, "She was
black, with two painted eyes in her prow, a lateen sail, and a high red tiller."
Isak Dinesen, in the story "Peter and Rosa" contained in *Winter's Tales* (New
York, 1942), pp. 274-75, has written a chilling and frightening account of
the effect of a pair of blue stones used as eyes in the carved figurehead of a
ship.

The purpose of the eye in the painting described by Luxorius is almost like
that of a figure of speech. Just as we say of a wide-awake person that he
has eyes in the back of his head, or of a ball that finds its mark that it has eyes
on it, so the painter put eyes on the fingers of the hunter's hands as a testimonial
to his accuracy.

For a discussion and illustrations of the symbolism of the eye, see H. T.
Bailey and E. Pool, *Symbolism for Artists* (Worchester, Mass., 1925), p. 100;
A. M. Blackman, "The Stela of Nobipusen Wosret, British Museum 101,
"Journal of Egyptian Archaeology, XXI (1935), 1-9; D. von Bothmer, "Greek
Vases from the Hearst Collection," Metropolitan Museum of Art Bulletin
(March, 1957), p. 172; C. Connolly, "Surrealism," *Art News Annual,* II (1951),
Part 2, 131-70, and Pls., pp. 158-59; A. Furtwaengler and K. Reichhold,

Griechische Vasenmalerei (Munich, 1904), Series 1, pp. 218-19, 227, 269; J. Hornell, "Survival of the Use of Oculi in Modern Boats," *Journal of the Royal Anthropological Institute of Great Britain and Ireland,* LIII (1923), 289-321; G. Picard, *Le Monde de Carthage,* p. 181 and Pl. 42; C. A. Robinson, Jr., *The Spring of Civilization* (New York, 1954), Pl. 67; and C. Torr, *Ancient Ships* (Cambridge, 1895), p. 69.

1. docta manus: Cf. use of same words in 173R.3, 174R.3, 176R.10, and see above, Ch. IV, 6.

1. ursis: Pliny erroneously says that the bear was not native to Africa, *Natural History* 8.54.131, cum in Africa ursum non gigni constet.

4. visum: Cf. "the sights of a gun."

49

Meter: Elegiac; see above, Ch. VIII, Meter 1.

1. manibus locavit: See note on *capiti,* 12.4.

2. manet: Riese suggests *nitet*; Schubert, *De Luxorio,* p. 36, feels that *manet* cannot be tolerated and thinks that *micat* is better. *Nitet* or *micat* will naturally brighten the picture, but it is not necessary to rewrite Luxorius to add sparkle to his style.

4. signatum: a vivid expression, "as if it had the victim's name on it," like our "The bullet has his number on it."

6. visus: accusative plural.

6. proprios: See above, Ch. VI, A 6.

50

Meter: Phalaecean; see above, Ch. VIII, Meter 3.

1. praecedis: a play upon words in the repetition of this verb. The manuscript reading of the first verb is *precedis*; Meyer and Baehrens prefer *procedis*. Riese explains the paronomasia, "Ire pergis, nec tamen ceteros superas." For the scansion, see above, Ch. VIII, A 3.

1. Vico: apparently the only occurrence of this name.

2. debueras: Cf. 35.6, and see above, Ch. VI, A 5.

2. tenere partem: Cf. 31.7, and see note on *partem* as used there. Shakespeare uses "parts" in a similar way, as when Falstaff boasts, "Page's wife . . . examined my parts with most judicious oeilliades" (*The Merry Wives of Windsor,* Act I, scene 3), and "setting the attraction of my good parts aside, I have no other charms" (Act II, scene 2).

The exact meaning of Luxorius' poem is obscure. Just how the corruptor prevents the charioteer from winning is not made clear, nor is the remedy explained. There may be an obscene connotation in the apparent punning and word play contained or rather concealed in *tenere* and *teneris,* and a double-entendre in the use of the word *retro,* line 5.

3. teneris: Cf. *teneris,* 40.7.

5. ponendus: For the scansion, see Ch. VIII, A 3.

51

Meter: Elegiac; see above, Ch. VIII, Meter 1.

Title. paranympho: not used in classical Latin; see Souter, *Glossary,* p. 286; Blaise, *Dictionnaire,* p. 593; and Augustine, *De Civitate Dei* 14.18 (*PL,* XLI, 426). *Paranymphus,* of course, is from the Greek word for the friend of the groom who rode with him and the bride after the ceremony from her home to that of the husband. There was no real equivalent in the Roman ceremony; the *auspex* or witness (see below, *auspice,* line 5) did not accompany the married pair.

delatore: Titus drove the tribe of *delatores* out of Rome; see Suetonius, *Titus* 8.5. Martial, *De Spectaculis* 4 and 4b, rejoiced at their banishment. Centuries later in Carthage, Luxorius reveals in this poem that a different type of informer appeared. What and to whom is the *delator* supposed to report? He may expose family secrets or, having seen the wealth of the groom and his parents on display, he may give information to a treasury official for tax purposes; see Courtois, *Les Vandales,* pp. 258-59, on tax collections by the Vandal kings. For the theme of this poem, see especially Juvenal, 3.113.

1. Hermes: an aptly chosen name, since the god Hermes also flitted about and was the patron of thieves. E. Guhl and W. Koner, *The Life of the Greeks and Romans,* tr. from the 3rd German ed. by F. Hueffer (new ed., London, 1889), p. 193, refer to a Greek vase on which Hermes is depicted at the head of a wedding procession.

2. pronubus: The feminine *pronuba* is classical Latin for the woman who took care of the marriage arrangements for the bride; the masculine is very late Latin; Souter, *Glossary,* p. 327, dates it from the time of Tertullian. See note on *paranymphus,* above, and Blaise, *Dictionnaire,* p. 673.

5. famulatur: See above, Ch. VI, B 4.

6. potius: See above, Ch. VI, A 7.

7. te: See above, Ch. V, B 4; 24.7-8; 38.6; and 43.3.

7. non sua sortitur: Actually, the bridegroom does not pray for his own prosperity but for that of the informer: another Luxorian paradox.

7. auspice: the technical and classical word (from *auspex nuptiarum*) for the person who witnessed the signing of the marriage contract and took care of other formalities. Originally he was the taker of the auspices. See Cicero, *De Divinatione* 1.16.28; Suetonius, *Divus Claudius,* 26.2; and Juvenal, 10.336.

52

Meter: Elegiac; see above, Ch. VIII, Meter 1.

Title. litigiosa: Cf. Juvenal, 6.242-45, for a portrait of a litigious woman.

1. Gorgoneos vultus: At first the Gorgons were considered only as monsters, but later Medusa was deemed to be a beautiful woman. See Grimal, *Dictionnaire,* p. 168, *s.v. Gorgone*; and Reinach, *Répertoire de peintures,* p. 204, No. 8, for ancient pictures of Medusa. Luxorius combines both conceptions; see line 6. This poem embodies another Luxorian antithesis: Catucia is beautiful in looks, foul in temper. See also *RE, VII,* 1636, for allusions to the beauty of the Gorgons.

1. Catucia: The only occurrence of this name listed in *TLL, Onomasticon,* II, 273. Related names are *Catulatus, Catullius,* and *Catulus.* The masculine

form of *Catucia* is found in the name *Q. Catucius Autolycus, CIL,* VI.2, 14601.

2. dum . . . foret: On use of *dum* as an adversative, see above, Ch. VI, A 1.

3. rixando: On the short *o,* see above, Ch. VIII, B 3.

4. stultius: See above, Ch. VI, A 7.

6. horrebat: The reading in A is *herebat,* which Baehrens interprets as *haerebat.* This is also good.

7. tandem haec: no hiatus or elision; cf. *iam huic,* 47.13; and see above, entry for *quis,* 4.2, Ch. VIII, B 1.

7. ferre: For this particular use of the infinitive, as if to express result, cf. *inesse,* 6.1, and see above, Ch. VI, A 4. Klapp, *Quaestiones,* p. viii, calls it a rather unusual Greek construction. Similar examples are found in Lucan; for a list, see Haskins, *Lucani Pharsalia,* p. cv.

53

Meter: Elegiac; see above, Ch. VIII, Meter 1.

1-2. conpedibus . . . carceris: On the alliteration and the *c* sound, see above, Ch. V, B 7.

7-8. On *sententiae,* see above, Ch. V, B 5.

8. poenis . . . arma: another paradox.

54

Meter: Elegiac; see above, Ch. VIII, Meter 1.

Title. concuba: late Latin for *concubina*; see Isidore, *Origines* 10.229 (*PL,* LXXXII, 391B-C), Pellex apud Graecos proprie dicitur, a Latinis concuba.

Charitem: The writer of the title used the Latinized form of *Charis,* the Greek word for a Grace. In Greek, *Charites,* the plural, is generally found, like *Gratiae* in Latin. *Charita* is the more proper Latin accusative singular; see Pliny, *Natural History* 35.36.79. Luxorius refers to the lawyer's mistress as *Veneris famula* (line 4), which can mean a Grace, since the Graces were among the attendants of Venus. However, Luxorius does not say directly that the lawyer called his girl friend a Grace, as the title specifically asserts he did. For the bearing of the use of the name in the title and its omission in the poem itself on the authorship of the title, see above, Ch. VII, A 3.

This is another poem on the vices and failings of a professional; see note to 8.T.

1. facundia: the first *a* is properly long here; cf. *făcundior,* 9.5.

1. nervo: *membrum virile,* as in Horace, *Epodes* 12.19; Juvenal, 9.34 and 10.205.

2. impleret . . . negotii: a bold figure, to be taken in an obscene sense to carry out the idea of *nervo.* On the spelling of *impleret,* see above, Ch. IX, C 4.

2. negotii: For the scansion, see above, entries for this word, Ch. VIII, B 1 and 2. See also above, Ch. VIII, A 1 f.

3-4. These two lines are a contrast to lines 1-2. The lawyer is weak in his profession, but he should be strong in making love, for like Priapus he possesses the proper implement. Nevertheless, even in the court of love he is not so good, for he has to plead with his Grace (*famula Veneris*), who should be easy to win over because of her association with Venus. Klapp, *Quaestiones,*

p. xii, thinks that the meaning is that Luxorius is twitting the lawyer because he thinks about his cases *in concubitu.* The two interpretations can be combined: if the lawyer's eloquence were equal to his manly power, he would be a great lawyer, but he has to think of his cases even at night—when he is making love, he is still the inept lawyer and performer, in spite of his equipment.

55

Meter: Elegiac; see above, Ch. VIII, Meter 1.

Title. ministrum: Technically, the *ministri* were subordinate officials in the palace of the Vandal kings; see Courtois, *Les Vandales,* pp. 252-53.

1. nocteque: unnecessarily emended by Riese to *noctuque*; see above, entry for this word, Ch. VIII, B 1.

1. Eutychus: a transliteration of *Bonifatius*; see Mueller, *De Re Metrica,* p. 441. The Greek Εὐτυχής means "a fortunate or prosperous man." The name *Eutychus,* also spelled *Eutichus, Eutychos,* and *Eutyches,* is found not only in African inscriptions, as in *CIL,* VIII.1, 502, 7646, but also in literature and history. According to Suetonius, *Divus Augustus* 96.2, Octavian met an ass-driver named Eutychus before the battle of Actium. Caligula, as related by Suetonius, *Caligula* 55.2, gave the charioteer Eutychus 2,000,000 sesterces. *Eutychius martyr* are the opening words of poem 307 in F. Buecheler, *Carmina Epigraphica,* Fasciculus 1 (Leipzig, 1886), p. 149. The title of *Epigram* 339, Burmann, *Anthologia,* II, 249, Book IV, begins with *Eutycheti Aurigae.* Eutychus is a character in Plautus' *Mercator,* and a man named Eutychos appears in Martial, 6.68.4. On the change of *Bonifatius* into *Eutychus* as a possible indication of Luxorius' knowledge of Greek, see above, Ch. V, A 6-8. Courtois, *Les Vandales,* p. 255, n. 12, does not think that Boni-fatius or Boniface, the official of Gelimer, is to be identified with the Eutychus of Luxorius' poem. However, the chances are that he is the one meant.

During the war with Belisarius, Gelimer entrusted his treasure to Boniface; see Procopius, *Bellum Vandalicum,* 2.4.33-41, and Courtois, p. 270. Although originally loyal to Gelimer, Boniface eventually came to terms with Belisarius and kept a great part of Gelimer's wealth for himself. His rapacity was of the kind attributed to the king's official by Luxorius; see Victor Tunnunensis, *Chronica* (*PL,* LXVIII, 954c), Geilimer . . . multorumque substantias per Boni-facium tollit, and Corippus, *Johannis* 3.269-70. Schubert uses Luxorius' poem to fix an important date: see above, Ch. II, p. 28.

4. "Regis habenda," nimis: Riese interprets this as "Clamat magna voce, omnia putanda esse regis" (Everything here belongs to the king).

4. nimis: See above, Ch. VI, A 7.

5. gravius: For the scansion, see above, entry for this word, Ch. VIII, B 1.

5. implet: a play upon words—*implere* has two meanings, "to fulfil a duty of office" and "to accomplish, perpetrate." On *-in* or *-im,* see above, Ch. IX, C 4; cf. *impleret,* 54.2. For parallels to this line, see Vergil, *Bucolics* 3.16, Quid domini facient, audent cum talia fures? and Ovid, *Heroides* 8.11-12, Quid gravius capta Lacedaemone serva tulissem,/ Si raperet Graias barbara turba nurus?

6. dominus: an official title of the Vandal kings; there is no documentary evidence that it was applied to them before Huneric (477-84), but it is not impossible that Genseric also used the title; see Courtois, *les Vandales,* pp. 243-45 and note to 83.T, below. Dracontius used the title often in reference to Thrasamund; e.g., *Satisfactio* 107 (*PL,* LX, 914A), regi dominoque; 110 (*PL,* LX, 914A), rex dominusque; 309 (*PL,* LX, 932A), regnanti domino.

56

Meter: Elegiac; see above, Ch. VIII, Meter 1.
1. famulis: See above, Ch. VI, B 4.
4. manet: According to Riese, I, 273, "Quamvis v. 3 abire iussus."
5. ergo: For the scansion, see above, Ch. VIII, B 3.
7. nemo: See *ergo,* above.
8. fulmina dei: For the bearing of these words on Luxorius' alleged Christianity, see above, Ch. III, E 2-3, 6.

57

Meter: Elegiac; see above, Ch. VIII, Meter 1.
Title. concubas: See note on *concubam,* 54.T. Riese keeps *et,* the last word of the title in A, but I have dropped it, for there is nothing in the poem that requires it, and the point is made sharper without any further explanations.
Compare with this poem and the next, Martial, 3.43; 4.78; and 6.70, which are also about old men who do not act their age.
1. proprios: See above, Ch. VI, A 6.
1. canos: Cf. *Priapea* 76.1-2 (Buecheler, *Petronius,* p. 167, or Burmann, II, 551, Book VI, *Epigram* 78), Quod sim iam senior, meumque canis/ Cum barba caput albicet capillis.
2. phoenicis: Riese spelled this with a small initial letter in his 1869 edition, but wrote *Phoenicis* in the 1894 edition. The ostensible reason is given in his *apparatus criticus,* p. 273: "Ziehen cf. Ilias 9,607." Ziehen apparently thought that Luxorius used Phoenix, the aged tutor of Achilles, as the criterion of old age. This is not acceptable, for the clichés referring to old age are Priam, Hecuba, Nestor, the crow, the raven, the stag, the elephant, and the phoenix, but not the Homeric Phoenix. See Pliny, *Natural History* 6.19.22 and 10.2.4-5; Martial, 6.70.12-13; 7.96.7; 9.29.1; 10.38.14; *et al.;* Juvenal, 10.246-47; Ausonius, *Griphus* 11-17, *Carmina* 7.5.1-8, and 18.24.8-10; and, of course, Lactantius, *De Ave Phoenice* 32. In the *Anthologia Palatina* it is the same story. Myrinus (11.67) speaks of somebody as old as a crow and as Hecuba, grandmother of Sisyphus and sister of Deucalion, an array like that of 15 L. Bassus of Smyrna (11.72) uses Nestor and a stag; Lucilius (11.389) evokes a stag and a crow. See also 58L.1-2.
2. grandior a senio: Klapp, *Quaestiones,* p. viii, thinks that the use of the genitive *phoenicis* is scarcely believable and that the ablative should have been used. In his 1869 edition Riese suggested this, but omitted the idea in the 1894 edition. Klapp probably wanted the phrase to mean "older than the phoenix in age." Luxorius, however, does not express the thought in that way; he uses a trope, "older than the old age of the phoenix." After a com-

parative, *a* with the ablative (instead of the ablative of comparison) is occasionally found in classical authors, more often in late Latin; see Kuehner-Stegmann, I, 496. Cf. Ovid, *Heroides* 18.69, A Veneris facie non est prior ulla tuaque; Juvenal, 10.246-47, Rex Pylius, magno si quicquam credis Homero,/ Exemplum vitae fuit a cornice secundae. Roensch, "Zur lateinischen Anthologie," *RhM* (neue Folge) XXXI (1876), 477-79, calls this construction a Hebraism; Woelfflin, "Der Genetivus Comparationis und die präpositionalem Umschreibungen," *ALL*, VII (1892), 124-26, equates the phrase with *grandior quam phoenix confectus.* See also W. A. Baehrens, "Vermischtes," *Eranos*, XIII (1913), 20-21.

4. te facis esse: See above, Ch. VI, A 4, on *facere* and the infinitive.

5-6. Another Luxorian antithesis. The old man wants his youth again and thinks that he will hide his old age if he has a number of girls at his service. Instead this *luxus* (cf. 37.8) only points up his age; the would-be youth turns out to be a boring old man (*gravis senior*) through the very means he selected as his Fountain of Youth.

6. sis . . . ut: For the inversion, cf. 32.6.

58

Meter: Elegiac; see above, Ch. VIII, Meter 1.

Title. mori: present instead of future infinitive, as in Plautus and later writers; cf. *rumpere,* line 5, below, and *existimabant eum . . . casurum et mori,* Acts, 28.6.

diceret: See above, Ch. VII, B 2.

1. Priami: See note on *phoenicis,* 57.2.

2. elephans: See above, Ch. IX, C 3.

3. dum: See above, Ch. VI, A 1.

5. Lachesim: used here, as often by the poets, for all three Fates; see note on *mors invida,* 59.1.

5. rumpere: The use of the present instead of the future infinitive with *credis* here is analogous to the construction with *spero* and *confido*; cf. Caesar, *Bellum Civile* 3.8.3, reliquos terreri sperans, and see Kuehner-Stegmann, I, 689-90, Remark 1.

7. veniet mors ultima: a poetic and epigraphic commonplace. Cf. Burmann, *Anthologia,* I, 597, Book III, *Epigram* 150, 1, Mors non una venit, sed, quae rapit, ultima mors est, and Petronius, *Satiricon* 89.63-64 (*Halosis Troiae*), Obtruncat et continuat in mortem ultimam/ Somnos.

8-9. See above, Ch. V, B 5, on the use of *sententiae.* For the thought, cf. Martial, 6.70.15, Non est vivere, sed valere, vita est. See also Juvenal, 10.188-272, on the ills of old age, especially 190-91, Sed quam continuis et quantis longa senectus/Plena malis! Luxorius is telling the old man that a life prolonged through suffering and disease is really death-in-life and should be cut short, that he is not really living but making his life last too long.

See Plato, *Republic* 3.14 (406 B-C), and notes on this passage by Paul Shorey in the Loeb Classical Library translation of the *Republic,* I (London and Cambridge, Mass., 1946), 274-75. It is amazing to see how many ideas and turns of phrase employed by Luxorius occur in the works of other writers, usually greater, both earlier ones whom Luxorius probably never read, or later ones who may never have heard of Luxorius.

9. potius: See above, Ch. VI, A 7.

59

Meter: Dactylic Hexameter; see above, Ch. VIII, Meter 2.

Title. Oageis: See Poems 46 and 83. He is apparently the Euagees (Εὐαγεής) mentioned by Procopius, *Bellum Vandalicum* 1.9.2, 14. Schoenfeld, *Wörterbuch, s.v. Euagees*, p. 81, and *Oageis*, p. 173, calls it a Gothic name with the same root as *Geiseric* or *Gaiseric*, the Gothic *-gais*, "spear." Euagees was a kinsman of King Hilderic and brother of the general Oamer or Hoamer, whom Procopius calls the Achilles of the Vandals. Upon seizing power in 530, Gelimer imprisoned Hilderic, Oamer, and Euagees. Oamer was blinded and soon died, but Hilderic and Euagees languished in prison until the troops of Belisarius invaded Africa. Acting upon the orders of Gelimer, his brother Ammatas put Hilderic and Euagees to death in 533 (Procopius, *Bellum Vandalicum* 1.17.11-12; see also Courtois, *Les Vandales*, pp. 398-99, for other references to Oamer and Euagees). Victor Tunnunensis, *Chronica (PL*, LXVIII, 954B), confirms this in part, Oamerdigum multosque nobilium Gelimer perimit. Procopius does not refer to Euagees as a general and it is difficult to determine what was the glorious victory in line 18 of Luxorius' poem.

The Vandals were defeated by the Moors in a signal disaster when Thrasamund was king, and again in the reign of Hilderic, his successor. After this defeat the Vandals turned against the Goths, took Amalafrida, widow of Thrasamund, prisoner, and put her followers to death on the pretext that they had conspired against Hilderic and the Vandals; see Procopius, *Bellum Vandalicum* 1.8.14-1.9.5; Courtois, *Les Vandales*, p. 401; Schmidt, *Geschichte*, p. 118; see also above, notes on Poem 44. Schubert, *De Luxorio*, pp. 12-13, thinks the victory over the Goths is the one Luxorius had in mind and sets the date as shortly after the beginning of Hilderic's accession in 523. He also believes that "naturally" Euagees was with his brother at this battle, but there is no evidence to that effect in the writings of the chroniclers of that period; Courtois, p. 399, on the basis of this poem, thinks that Euagees was a general against the Moors, but he presents no other testimony.

infantula: a late Latin word, used by Apuleius, *Metamorphoses* 10.28, and by later authors.

1. mors invida: a variation of this expression occurs frequently in sepulchral inscriptions. *Lachesis, Persephone, Parcae, sors,* and *fata* replace *mors; invidere* is sometimes used in place of the adjective. See F. Buecheler, *Carmina Latina Epigraphica* (Leipzig, 1897), Vol. II, Poem 1375.1, Quamvis, nate, tuos mors invida ruperit annos; and Poems 974.1; 1011.1; 1122.7; 1149.1; 1206.1; 1279.5; 1301.3; 1311.3; 1388.2; and 1409.8. See also Martial, 9.76.6, Invidit de tribus una soror, 10.53.2, Invida quem Lachesis, and *Anthologia Palatina* 7.13.4, where the poet speaks of envious Hades.

3. Damira: This is the only occurrence of the name listed in *TLL* and

Forcellini. Schoenfeld, *Wörterbuch,* p. 70, calls it probably Germanic or Visigothic.

5. offuscant: a late and ecclesiastical word; Souter, *Glossary,* p. 276, translates it as "obscure, blacken, depreciate."

5. iucundum tristia: On the juxtaposition of contrasting words, see above, Ch. V, B 1.

6. nemo: On the short *o,* see above, Ch. VIII, B 3.

6. rosam albentem . . . carpit: On the use of *sententiae,* see above, Ch. V, B 5. Cf. Ovid, *Ars Amatoria* 3.182, albentesve rosas.

6. fuerit: Cf. *viderit,* 43.2, and *vicerit,* 47.10. On the tense, see above, Ch. VI, A 5.

8. nimis: See above, Ch. VI, A 7.

8. verecundo: For the scansion, see above, entry for this word, Ch. VIII, B 2.

8. garrula: Cf. Martial, 5.34.8, Et nomen blaeso garriat ora meum.

9. Cf. this line with Buecheler (cited above in note to line 1), Poem 1165.7-8, Forma et sensu mirabilis et super annos/ Docta decens dulcis grataque blanditiis.

9. superaverat: For the use of *superare* in this sense, cf. 73.9, vincit membra.

10. dulce loquebatur: a reminiscence of Horace, *Odes* 1.22.24, dulce loquentem.

11. mellea murmur: effective alliteration and sound pattern.

12. avium . . . cantus: Cf. 46.12; one of the few similes in Luxorius. See above, Ch. V, B 3.

13. stellantis regia caeli: from Vergil, *Aeneid* 7.210.

14. iustis: For deductions from this word and other parts of lines 13-14 by Schubert and others that Luxorius was a Christian, see above, Ch. III, E 2-4, 6.

14. inter . . . esse: tmesis.

18. Victoria: Since the poem is an epitaph to be inscribed on a tomb, the likelihood is that a statue of a weeping Victory was placed above the poem. Ziehen (cited by Riese, p. 274) thinks it may have been an angel. This is not substantiated by the poem. All that the line may mean is that, figuratively, Victory herself was saddened by the news—Oageis took no joy from his victory when he learned the sad news.

60

Meter: Elegiac, see above, Ch. VIII, Meter 1.

This poem is another indication of the luxurious manner of living enjoyed by the Romans in Africa and by the Vandals who took their place. A private amphitheater was erected on land that could have been used for agriculture, but Luxorius argues that it really does not matter. In his paradoxical way, he reasons that so many wild beasts will be removed from their haunts for use in the arena that the land from which they have been cleared will be used for cultivation. Cf. 178R, *De balneis cuiusdam pauperis,* which tells about thermae built by a poor man: Nam nova in angusto erexit balnea campo. See above, Ch. I, B 5, note to Poem 64, and Courtois, *Les Vandales,* p. 221.

2. cernit: Luxorius uses synonyms for this: *spectat,* line 3, and *videt,* line 4. Cf. similar use of synonyms in Poems 45 and 76.

3. arando: On the short *o,* see above, Ch. VIII, B 3. Here the gerund replaces the present participle; see above, Ch. VI, A 10.

4. gaudia mixta: "different forms of entertainment."

6. metuunt: Cf. 64.2, metuenda feris.

61

Meter: Elegiac; see above, Ch. VIII, Meter 1.

1. salutifero: an odd term to apply to Cupid's fire, which inflames passion. For an opposite idea, see Ovid, *Amores* 1.2.46, Fervida vicino flamma vapore nocet.

1. omnia flammans: Cf. 46.5, Cupido flammas, and see note on it, above. Cf. also Ovid, *Amores* 1.2.43, Tunc quoque non paucos, si te bene novimus, ures; *Metamorphoses* 1.461-62, Tu face nescio quos esto contentus amores/ Inritare tua.

2. propriis arte: See above, Ch. VI, A 6, B 4. Ziehen, *Neuen Studien,* p. 6, thinks that *arte* should be *utre* and lists statues of "Eros mit dem Schlauch" to prove his point. But *arte* is a favorite word of Luxorius and is certainly in place here; cf. 49.2. I have accepted Meyer's emendation of *probrias* in A to *propriis* instead of Riese's *proprias. Propriis* strengthens the paradox: instead of using his characteristic equipment (*facibus propriis*), Cupid is made by art to offer the opposite—water. For a similar conceit, see *Anthologia Palatina* 9.826, attributed to Plato, on a statue of Cupid and a satyr, in which the latter is pouring water instead of wine.

2. ministrat aquas: Cf. 64.8.

62

Meter: Elegiac; see above, Ch. VIII, Meter 1.

Title. Neptuno: Neptune is also the god of some fresh waters, of *stagna* as well as *maria;* see Catullus, 31.3, uterque Neptunus. Riese, *Anthologia,* I, 275, quotes Ziehen to the effect that the ocean or some river god is here wrongly considered as Neptune. However, it is difficult to see why Luxorius, with his knowledge of mythology, would have been unable to distinguish between a statue of the ocean or a river god and one of Neptune. Moreover, the poet has made his antithesis quite clear. Neptune is represented as pouring out (*fundente* in the title) water instead of waving his trident; he is better off in this fresh water than in the salty sea. Modern statues of Neptune are abundant in European cities, e.g., the Trevi Fountain in Rome, the Fountain of Neptune in the Plaza de Canovas del Castello, Madrid, etc., etc.

marmoreo alveo: An emendation by Baehrens of *marmoreo calido* in A.

1. quam melior: Klapp, *Quaestiones,* p. vii, thinks that *quanto* or *quantum* should have been used here. However, *quam* is occasionally found with a comparative; see Vergil, *Georgics* 3.306, quam magis. It is true that *quam* and the comparative should be correlative to *tanto* or *tam magis* expressed or understood; Luxorius' use of *quam* is analogous to only half of the con-

struction. See Kuehner-Stegmann, II, 485, Remark 27, for examples of the complete construction, and see above, notes on *quantum,* 24.4, and *quanto,* 44.3.

2. post pelagus: Cf. the use of *post* in 1.1 and 33.2.

2. dantur: A possible play on words; Neptune is given the water which he then gives to others. There is some ambiguity here, if *tibi* is considered a dative of the agent.

63

Meter: Elegiac; see above, Ch. VIII, Meter 1.

1. quis hunc: Riese and Baehrens change the order of these two words as found in A to *hunc quis,* but this is unnecessary; see above, entry for *quis,* 4.2, Ch. VIII, B 1.

1. credat: For the scansion, see above, entry for this word, Ch. VIII, B 1.

1. Syrtibus: See description in Lucan, *Pharsalia* 9.302 ff. The Syrtes, two great gulfs off the eastern half of the northern coast of Africa, are sea swamps, neither entirely wet nor dry. A fresh river flowing through them would be doubly impossible, just as the birth of a spring from a dry mountain is doubly unexpected—another Luxorian paradox.

2. viscere: a cliché, "the bowels of the earth." Cf. Vergil, *Aeneid* 3.575, Interdum scopulos avulsaque montis. Burmann, *Anthologia,* I, 474, cites a great many examples in different authors.

64

Meter: Elegiac; see above, Ch. VIII, Meter 1.

Title. Cirnensibus: an emendation of *Cernensibus* in A, made by Meerman, who conjectures (in Burmann, *Anthologia,* II, 610, n.) that the designated place is Cirna, a mountain in Zeugitana or Proconsularis. It is not possible to identify the site of the spa referred to in this poem. Numerous hot springs exist in Tunisia today; the thermal establishment at Hammam Lif, ten miles from Tunis, still active, is the Aquae Persianae of the Romans. Ruins of Roman baths are found at Korbous, the ancient Aquae Carpitanae, opposite to Carthage across the gulf; its waters are still used for cures. These spas had been established by the Romans before the Vandals came; the watering place described in the poem was apparently built by the Vandals. Other poems in the *Anthologia Latina* reveal the intense delight taken in hot springs and thermae of North Africa, some of them privately owned. Vandal rulers, notably Thrasamund and Hilderic, and members of the royal family erected thermal establishments; see above, note on Poem 60, and Poems 110R, 119R-124R, 210R-214R; and especially *CIL,* VIII, Supp. 4, 25362, referring to the baths built by Gebamundus or Gibamundus, a nephew of Gelimer. The text of this is also in Courtois, *Les Vandales,* p. 382. See also *Anthologia Palatina* 9. 630-32, on hot baths.

1-2. ardua ... culmina: an interesting arrangement of nouns and adjectives with hyperbaton of *splendentia.*

2. metuenda feris: Cf. 60.6, metuunt ... ferae.

3. quo: Riese emends to *cum.* Baehrens follows Klapp's change to *quae* but *quo* (for *ubi*) can be kept; see above, note to 3.5.

4. sederat ... viam: See above, note on *sedent*, 17.2.

7. ignitus tepet: an emendation by Froehner of *ignota stupet*; Baehrens prefers *ignotus*.

7. ad praetoria: Cf. Juvenal, 10.161, cliens sedet ad praetoria regis, 68 L. 12, ad Manes; and see notes on *quo*, 3.5, and *ad antra*, 7.4.

8. plenior: See above, Ch. VI, A 7.

8. ministrat aquas: Cf. 61.2.

9-10, 13-14. These lines, as first noted by Heynse, are interpolated from Claudian, 26(49), *Aponus* 19-22, whether by a scribe or by Luxorius himself cannot be determined.

65

Meter: Dactylic Hexameter: see above, Ch. VIII, Meter 2.

Title. philosophorum: Here the scribe of A used *ph* at the beginning and *f* inside the word, illustrating his inconsistency. See above, Ch. IX, C 3.

The list of the Seven Wise Men first appears in Plato, *Protagoras* 343A. With the exception of the substitution of Periander of Corinth for Myson of Chen, Luxorius' Seven are the same as Plato's. However, the canon was not fixed: Diogenes Laertius, 1.40-42, lists twenty-three philosophers from whom different writers made their selections of seven. Nor were the different sayings fixed in their authorship or content. Stobaeus (5th century A.D.) compiled a list of the various sayings, 128 in all. For the lives and the sayings of the Seven Sages, see Diogenes Laertius, 1.21-122; Bohren, *De Septem Sapientibus;* H. Diels, *Die Fragmente der Vorsokratiker* (7th ed., Berlin, 1954), I, 63-66; W. A. Mullach, *Fragmenta Philosophorum Graecorum* (Paris, 1860), I, 203-36.

Luxorius' Seven Wise Men belong to the standard list—the one met most often. It is also found in Sidonius Apollinaris, *Carmina* 2.156-63; 15.42-50; 23.101-10; Ausonius, *Ludus Septem Sapientum*; in Poem 882R; Hyginus, *Fabulae* 221; Antipater in the *Anthologia Palatina* 7.81; and Stobaeus.

Plutarch, in *Septem Sapientum Convivium* (*Moralia* 146-64), substitutes Anacharsis for Periander. Augustine, *De Civitate Dei* 8.2 (*PL*, XLI, 225-26), refers to the Wise Men, but he names only Thales. Courcelle, *Les lettres grecques,* pp. 179-81, 240-41, thinks that Sidonius, Ausonius, Augustine, and Luxorius used a common source, some handbook of philosophy. His choice is a work by a certain Celsus or Celsinus. Courcelle and W. Brandes, *Beiträge zu Ausonius* (Wolfenbüttel, 1895), p. 30, characterize the variations upon the theme of the Seven Wise Men as school declamations and poetical exercises in the form of a game.

The sayings attributed to the Seven Wise Men by Luxorius are also standard with the exception of the declaration he puts into the mouth of Thales. Among the many sayings ascribed to the latter, one appears more prominently than all the others: Ἐγγύα, πάρα δ'ἄτη, which was inscribed on the temple of Apollo at Delphi. (See Wilkins, *The Delphic Maxims,* pp. 1-3, 11-18.) The Roman poets took this advice to mean "Shun suretyship," e.g., Sidonius Apollinaris, 15.44, Thales Mileto genitus vadimonia damnat.

Nowhere in the lists of the maxims of the Seven Wise Men is there any saying remotely resembling line 8 of this poem. However, the question of the responsibility of men or the gods for the faults of men was often treated in Greek and Latin literature. A distich from one of Solon's poems touches upon the theme, but his lines deal with a specific situation and are not in the form of a gnomic saying. In his poem to the Athenians on the tyranny of Pisistratus (Diogenes Laertius, 1.52; Bergk, *PLG,* [4th ed., Leipzig, 1882], II, 40, Fragment 11 [19]) Solon comments that if they are suffering bitterly on account of their own wickedness, they must not blame the gods. In Homer, *Odyssey* 1.33, Zeus declares that mortals say that all evil comes from the gods. A distant resemblance to Luxorius' line may be seen in Xenophanes, Fragments 11 and 12 in Diels, *Die Fragmente* (cited above in this note), I, 132. Xenophanes accuses Homer and Hesiod of attributing to the gods everything that passes for disgrace and reproach among men. Luxorius, however, expresses an opposite idea: the faults of men do not come from the gods. See also Euripides, *Hippolytus* 1433-34; Plato, *Republic* 2.19(380) and 3.5(391E); Diogenes Laertius, 10.124; and Lucretius, *De Rerum Natura* 5.195-200 and 1185-1240.

Finally, Ate (Delusion, Error) thrust from Olympus by Zeus, lived only among men (Homer, *Iliad* 19. 127-31); see also Ovid, *Metamorphoses* 12.59.

The thought expressed by Luxorius may have been developed from such sources or may have been found by him in a book like the one attributed to Celsus or Celsinus mentioned above in note on Poem 79.1-2; see also Augustine, *Confessions,* 1.16.

Inde, the first word of line 9, which follows the saying of Thales, implies that Bias' maxim is the consequence of Thales' words, as if part of a discussion. This does not appear in the imaginary conversation of the Seven Wise Men in Plutarch's *Convivium,* mentioned above.

distichi: an adjectival form used as a noun. The nominative plural form of the noun is *disticha. TLL* does not list this use of *distichi* as a noun.

1. Solon: For the scansion, see above, entry for this name, Ch. VIII, B 4. See Herodotus, 1.32, for the story of the occasion when Solon gave this advice to Croesus. See also V. H. Collins, *A Book of English Proverbs* (London, 1959), p. 43, No. 104, on "Look to (*or* Mark) the end" (*Respice finem*), and p. 60, No. 171, for a discussion of the Solon and Croesus story, and for variations on "Call no man happy until he is dead (*or* dies)." Collins quotes Erasmus, *Vitae finem specta* ("Look at the end of life"). See also Sophocles, *Oedipus Rex* 1528-30; Aristotle, *Nicomachean Ethics* 1.10; Aeschylus, *Agamemnon* 928-30; *Libation Bearers* 1018-20; Euripides, *Trojan Women* 509-10; *et al.*

2. prolixae ... vitae: See above, note on *totis ... horis,* 25.2.

2. dixit te cernere: For the use of *dixit* like a verb of ordering, advising, etc., see above, Ch. VI, A 4, and Kuehner-Stegmann, I, 682-83.

3. Chilon: Spartan ephor, 556-55 B.C.; see Diogenes Laertius, 1.68; and Pausanias, 3.16.4.

3. Lacedaemona: Cf. *Laida,* 88.1; *Colchidarum,* 17R (title between lines 24 and 25); and *Calydona,* 199R.68. Burmann, I, 645, n., gives as examples

of a nominative singuar formed from the Greek accusative ending *-a, Briseïda, Chalcida, Gorgona, Amazona,* etc. Mueller, *De Re Metrica,* pp. 492-93, points out that this process had been going on in Latin and gives as examples *placenta, cratera,* and *chlamyda,* also *cassida* alongside of *cassis.* Likewise, a neuter nominative singular in *-a* was often considered feminine, e.g., *diploma, schema, syrma,* and *dogma* (*CIL,* VIII. 1, 1027, n.). Petronius illustrates both trends with *stigmam* and *stateram, Satiricon* 45.9, and 67.8.

4. ut . . . possis: in apposition with *hoc,* where the infinitive construction might be expected. Cf. *cernere,* line 2, and see Kuehner-Stegmann, II, 221.

5. Pittacus: *ca.* 650-570 B.C., a democratic lawgiver, contemporary of Solon.

6. exquirere: Cf. *cernere,* line 2.

7. Thales: statesman, scientist, philosopher, sixth century B.C. For the scansion, see above, entry for this name, Ch. VIII, B 4.

8. caelitus: late Latin for *divinitus.*

9. Bias: *fl. ca.* 550 B.C., a powerful speaker and a statesman of Priene in Asia Minor. For the scansion, see above, entry for this name, Ch. VIII, B 4.

10. malos divina: On the use of contrasting words, see above, Ch. V, B. 1.

11. Periander: tyrant of Corinth, 625-585 B.C.; see Herodotus, 1.20-23; 3.48-53; 5.92; and Pausanias, 5.17. At his court was held the feast of the Seven Wise Men described by Plutarch.

11. fama Corintho est: Klapp, *Quaestiones,* p. vii, thinks that *fama* is used here in a unusual way to mean "famous name." If *fama* had its usual meaning of "fame, renown, report," the construction of *Corintho* would be awkward, for it would have to be taken with *urbe,* from which it is widely separated, "in the city of Corinth, to which there is fame," or *Corintho* would have to be considered in apposition with *cui,* "to which, Corinth, there is fame." Klapp's suggestion makes the construction normal, as with *nomen;* cf. 565R.1, Vergilio mihi nomen est. See notes on *Pasiphaae,* 79.T, and *Marina,* 82.T.

12. meditando: On the short *o,* see above, Ch. VIII, B 3.

13. Cleobolus: lived about 580 B.C. He and his daughter, Cleobuline or Cleobule, were famous for their riddles. For the scansion of his name, see above, entry for this name, Ch. VIII, B 4.

13. proprium: See above, Ch. VI, A 6.

13. Lindia: Lindos is on the island of Rhodes.

14. quod mensura optima librat: The thought of this line is similar to that of *ne quid nimis,* line 6. In addition to Μηδὲν ἄγαν, "Nothing too much," the Greeks had other maxims that expressed the golden mean. See Hesiod, *Works and Days* 40, "How much more the half is better than the whole," and 694, "Observe due measure, for proportion is best in all things." To Cleobolus was attributed a variation of the latter saying: ἄριστον μέτρον. This was translated into Latin as *optimus modus;* see Ausonius, *Ludus Septem Sapientum* 6. Luxorius' phrase, *mensura optima,* is merely a variant, probably his own, of *optimus modus.* See Wilkins, *Delphic Maxims,* Ch. 3.

66

Meter: Elegiac; see above, Ch. VIII, Meter 1.

Title. Ianuario: Mariotti, *Phil, C* (1956), 325-26, points out that the subject of the poem is Janus, not January. See above, Ch. VII, 2, on the authorship of the titles. However, there may not be a discrepancy. Ovid, *Fasti* 2.1, refers to January as Janus: Ianus habet finem. See also *Fasti* 2.48-49.

For other poems on the days, months, and seasons, see Burmann, *Anthologia*, II, 358-77, Book V, *Epigrams* 71-88; Riese, *Anthologia*, Poems 116, 117, 394, 395, 488, 639, 640, 665, 689, 736, 864, 868. Nos. 639 and 640 are Ausonius, *Eclogues* 9 and 16; Ausonius wrote on the same topic in *Eclogues* 8, 10-15, 17, and 18. See also Dracontius, *De Mensibus* (*PLM*, V, 235-36) and *Anthologia Palatina* 9.384 and 9.580 on the Roman months.

Line 2 of Luxorius' poem is missing in A; the scribe copied line 3 twice. A possible way to fill the lacuna may be inferred from the lines on Janus in other authors. See, for example, Ausonius, 7.9.1 (639R.1), Primus Romanas ordiris, Iane, Kalendas, and 7.10.1-2, Iane nove, primo qui das tua nomina mensi,/ Iane bifrons spectas tempora bina simul; 665R.1-2, Primus, Iane, tibi sacrator nomine mensis,/ Undique cui semper cuncta videre licet; and above all, Martial, 8.8.1-2, to which Luxorius' first line bears some resemblance in the use of forms of *annus* and *saec(u)lum*, "Principium des, Iane, licet velocibus annis/ Et renoves voltu saecula longa tuo." Some line like *principium faciens, omnia tu renovas* might be inserted to complete the thought; the use of trisyllables at the end of each member is not infrequent in Luxorius; see 20.2; 22.4; 43.4; 49.4; 57.2; *et al.* On Janus, see Horace, *Satires* 2.6.20-24; Ovid, *Fasti* 1.90 ff.; Martial, 10.28; Macrobius, *Saturnalia* 1.7.20 and 1.9.4; Dio Cassius, *Roman History* 1, Fragments 6-7.

1. saeclis: Many suggestions have been made for the correction of various words in this poem. The manuscript reading is *seclis sol Iane secundus.* Baehrens prefers *saeclis, o Iane.* Riese thinks *saecli* may be possible. Klapp, *Quaestiones,* p. xiii, changes *et* to *es* and *secundus* to *sequendus.* Maehly, *ZöstG,* XXII (1871), 578, suggests *caeli.* I have followed A, which is kept in Riese's text. The thought is "As the sun is to the day, Janus is to the centuries—a second sun." Cf. 395R.3, Annorum saecli caput.

3. tu: The manuscript shows four different forms of this pronoun in two lines. Luxorius apparently emphasized it designedly, perhaps to show the dual nature of Janus. Riese changes *tu* to *est,* but Baehrens retains it, as does my text. Klapp sees no meaning in *tu* and rewrites the line, turning it into *It rota tua circum sine fine laboris.* The expression *Tu rota certa tui* may be another example of Luxorius' cryptic and compressed style, his own peculiar way of saying that Janus revolves in a fixed orbit like a wheel and he is his own wheel turning by himself. For a similar idea, see Macrobius, *Saturnalia* 1.9.11, dum in orbem volvitur et ex se initium faciens, in se refertur.

4. itque reditque: Cf. Ovid, *Fasti* 1.126-27, It redit officio Iuppiter ipse meo/ Inde vocor Ianus.

4. venit: Here, as in *venient,* line 6, *venire* may stand for *evenire;* see Löfstedt, *Coniectanea,* pp. 100-1.

6. venient: The future with *necdum* is most troublesome here. We should expect Luxorius to say in conclusion that Janus sees what has been and what

will be or, if *necdum* is used, what has not yet come. However, an emendation to *vēnerint* or *vēnērunt* is metrically impossible. Buecheler emends to *demum venient,* and Baehrens rewrites to *quaeve olim venient,* which simplifies the thought but takes great liberties. Klapp, *Quaestiones,* p. xiii, argues that the future is impossible, for who ever heard of future things that will not yet come? He therefore changes the line to *Quaeve dein venient quaeve fuere vides,* another simplification. The original reading of A does not imply that the future will not come, as Klapp infers. Luxorius combines two ideas in an extremely compressed way: Janus sees what will happen later but has not yet happened. Cf. Macrobius, *Saturnalia* 1.7.20, qui et praeterita nosset et futura prospiceret, and 1.9.4, et praeterita sciverit et futura providebit.

6. quaeve: *-ve* equals *vel,* consequently *et,* here. See above, Ch. VI, A 8; also Kuehner-Stegmann, *Grammatik,* II, 111, § 169.8, and Schmalz, *Lateinische Grammatik,* p. 677, par. 249.

67

Meter: Dactylic Hexameter: see above, Ch. VIII, Meter 2.

Title: venatore: The popularity of *venatores,* professional hunters in the arena, rivaled that of ancient charioteers (see above, Ch. I, n. 72) or of modern boxers, baseball stars, or bullfighters, so that even Roman emperors condescended, or, according to one's point of view, elevated themselves on occasion to become hunters in the arena. Jennison, *Animals for Show and Pleasure,* pp. 87-90, refers to the hunting activities of Commodus, Caracalla, and Elagabalus; he also cites many ancient authors on *venationes,* which originated with the baiting of animals for amusement or as part of a religious rite and developed into tremendous spectacles. During the final years of Vandal rule, *venationes* and animal turns seem to have been popular sports in Carthage; see Poems 44, 48, 49, and 68. Mosaics of trained animals and hunts in the amphitheater are described and illustrated in *Inventaire* and *MCAAT*; see especially *Inventaire,* I, Fasciculus 2 (1922), Pls. 1072, 1247, 1399; II (1914), Pls. 64, 71, 72, 463, 511a, 607; *MCAAT,* VII, 7, No. 353; and Reinach, *Répertoire de peintures,* pp. 287, 297-305.

1. causa favoris: Cf. Martial, 10.53.2, on the hunter Scorpus: Plausus, Roma, tui deliciaeque breves.

2. fortior: See above, Ch. IV, A 7. Cf. 384R.1 on the hunter Juvenal, Excipit ingentem Iuvenalis fortior aprum.

2. Olympie: On this form of the vocative, see above, note on *Marcie,* 28.1,8. The name *Olympius* is found in *CIL,* VI.1, 406, 751, VI.2, 8464; *Olympianus, Olympias, Olympius,* and *Olympus* are listed in the index of *CIL,* VIII.1, 1030. See H. Wuilleumier, "Etude historique sur l'emploi et la signification des signa," *MPAI,* XIII (1933), 580-81, on the significance of the name.

3. signas: Cf. *signatum,* 34.9.

4. On the long asyndeta and the sound effects in this line and the next, see above, Ch. V, B 2, 7.

4. collo, cervice: There may be some physiological distinction between *col-*

lum and *cervix,* but not enough to justify the use of both words to list different parts of the athlete's body. Sometimes the two words are coupled for emphasis, as in Cicero, *In Verrem* II.5.42.108, cum istius avaritiae poenam collo et cervicibus suis sustinerent.

4. nigro . . . colore: See above, notes to Poem 7, on Negroes as athletes in the Roman world, and note to 43.4 on color prejudice. Cf. also Shakespeare, *Merchant of Venice,* Act II, scene 1, "Mislike me not for my complexion," and Song of Solomon, 1.5, "I am black, but comely."

7. For the original MS reading of this line see Reise, *Anthologia,* I. 278. I have followed Baehrens' correction, which Riese also adopted. Baehrens, *PLM,* IV, 415, and Riese, *Anthologia,* I, 278, list the major emendations made by other scholars. To these must be added a new one, *Asiae* for *atrum,* made by Mariotti, "Congetture all'Anthologia Latina," *Parola del Passato,* II (1947), 347. Mariotti cites Vergil, *Georgics* 2.116-17, sola India nigrum/ fert hebenum, but the emphasis in Luxorius' poem is on blackness, for which he uses several synonyms.

7. atrum: The idea of darkness of complexion is stressed by this word, *nigrae,* line 9, *tetras,* line 10, *obscuros,* line 11, and *nigredo,* line 12. For a similar variety in choice of words, cf. Poems 45, 60, and 76.

8. parvo depressa: Riese obelizes but retains *magno* of A, which I have replaced by *parvo.* The murex is small, only a few inches in size, so that *magnus* is an inappropriate adjective to apply to it—unless the poet was thinking of its commercial importance. *Parvo murice* is more in Luxorius' style: the paradox is that a tiny mollusk contains rich, glowing, purple dye, although it is so small and insignificant. Haupt, *Opuscula,* III, 538, prefers *nigro* to *magno.* Klapp, *Quaestiones,* p. xiii, makes the same change and avers that *depressa* should undoubtedly be read *deprensa.* Schubert, *De Luxorio,* p. 37, likewise thinks that *depressa* is undoubtedly wrong and would replace it with *deprensa* on the analogy of *deprendier,* 4L.5. Riese prefers *caeco* to *magno,* after having suggested *madido* in his 1869 edition. Klapp also believes that *picea facie* is better than *pretiosum* in line 7; apparently, objections are taken to *magno* because the commentators want Luxorius to carry out the idea of blackness in every comparison in lines 7-12. However, he had already used *nigro* in line 6 and in this poem he was careful in choosing different words. Moreover, in line 8, Luxorius may have been thinking of *purpura* as something dark rather than of the murex. Finally, *depressa* may remain, for the poet's image may denote that the fluid furnishing the dye is deep in the murex.

On the change from *magno* to *parvo,* see A. E. Housman, *D. Iunii Iuvenalis Saturae* (Cambridge, 1931), p. 100, n. to 10.351, and "Remarks on the *Ciris,*" *CR,* XVII (July, 1903), 309 (remarks on *Ciris* 441).

The dull red fluid from which the Tyrian purple was made was obtained by squeezing out the fleshy parts of the murex. The banded murex (*trunculus*), the commonest of the Mediterranean species, was used. This murex has brown shells with bands of purple; its length is about three inches. The straight-spine murex (*brandaris*), whose shells are brown and whose length is two to three inches, was also used. See J. E. Rogers, *The Shell Book* (Boston, 1908), pp. 32-

33, W. F. Webb, *Handbook for Shell Collectors,* (4th ed., Rochester, N.Y., 1936), pp. 28, 33-34, 56, 61, 73-76, and Julian Huxley, *From an Antique Land* (London, 1954), pp. 73-76.

11. elephans: See above, Ch. X, 3.

11. ad artus: Klapp, *Quaestiones,* p. viii, compares this construction with the Greek accusative of specification. Cf. Cicero, *In Catilinam* I.5.12, ad severitatem lenius et ad communem salutem utilius. See also Kuehner-Stegmann, I, 523, § 97, on development of *ad* and the accusative as instrumentals in late Latin.

12. placessit: late Latin synonym of *placeo;* this is the only occurrence listed by Souter. Cf. use of intensive, inceptive, desiderative verbs in Petronius; see Sage, *Petronius,* p. xxxii, D. 1.

13. pulcrescis: also late Latin.

14. foedior . . . pulcher: On the use of contrasting words, see above, Ch. V, B 1.

14. quantum used as correlative with *tanto,* line 13. See above, note on *quam melior,* 62.1.

14. pulcher: This is *pulcer* in A; the scribe preferred the spelling without *h* for all forms of this word. His preference is respected by editors except in this form of the adjective.

In this poem Luxorius has displayed a variety of poetic and rhetorical pyrotechnics: asyndeta, antitheses, alliteration, building up of effects through color words, synonyms, and a lengthy development of comparisons and similes. See note to 59.12.

68

Meter: Dactylic Hexameter; see above, Ch. VIII, Meter 2.

Title. in: "concerning," but it may be omitted in translation; see above, Ch. VII, A 7.

1. nimis: For the scansion, see above, entry for this word, Ch. VIII, B 1; on the use, see above, Ch. VI, A 7.

2. gratus, fortissimus: On the use of the nominative with the vocative, see above, note on *Fauste,* 1.3, and Ch. VI, B 12. On the asyndeton, cf. 67.4-5, and see above, Ch. V, B 2.

3. advixeris: a correction by Klapp, *Quaestiones,* p. xiii, of *adunxeris* in A. *Advivo* is found mainly in late writers and in epitaphs; see Statius, *Thebais* 12.424, and *CIL,* VI.3, 17297, adbixit mecum. On the use of the subjunctive with *dum* and on the sequence, see above, Ch. VI, A 1, 5.

5. propria: See above, Ch. VI, A 6.

5. populis: See above, Ch. VI, B 5.

6. praestabas: On the late Latin use of *praestare,* "help," see Souter, *Glossary,* p. 319; *Löfstedt, Coniectanea,* pp. 33-36; and Blaise, *Dictionnaire,* p. 655.

9. mortis livore: a variation on the theme of *mors invida,* 59.1; see note to 59.1.

10. triumpho: Here the scribe of A used *ph* instead of his usual *f,* as in *anfeatrali* on the same line; see above, Ch. IX, C 3.

10-11. Cf. Shakespeare, *Henry IV*, Part 1, Act V, scene 4:

> Ill-weav'd ambition, how much art thou shrunk!
> When that this body did contain a spirit,
> A kingdom for it was too small a bound;
> But now two paces of the vilest earth
> Is room enough; this earth, that bears thee dead,
> Bears not alive so stout a gentleman.

12. ad Manes: Cf. *ad praetoria*, 64.7. *Ad* in this line may be equivalent to *apud*; see Kuehner-Stegmann, I, 520.

69

Meter: Phalaecean; see above, Ch. VIII, Meter 3.
Title. Chimaera: For a description of the Chimera, see 98R:

> Ore leo tergoque caper postremaque serpens
> Bellua tergemino mittit ab ore faces.

> Having the mouth of a lion, the back of a
> goat, and the tail of a serpent, the beast
> discharges fire from its triform mouth.

Illustrations of ancient statues of Chimeras are found in Reinach, *Répertoire de la statuaire*, II.2, 695, and III, 205.

1. aeris ... metallo: See note on *metallis*, 34.3.
1. fulgiduli: a rare word, correction by Burmann of *fulgidi*, which does not fit the meter. See above, Ch. VIII, n. 44.
3. melior: Luxorius is again struck by a paradoxical situation: the living Chimera spouts fire; her statue is made with the help of fire, which improves the Chimera since she is no longer harmful. Cf. use of *melior, 62.1.*

70

Meter: Lesser Asclepiad; see above, Ch. VIII, Meter 4.
Title. De statua Veneris: This is the title of Poem 34R:

> In gremio Veneris quoddam genus herba virescit.
> Sensit dura silex quo foco exaestuet ignis.

> On the bosom of Venus a certain type of plant
> is growing. The hard stone has realized in what
> brazier the fire is glowing.

1. candidulo: *Candenti*, the reading of A, kept but obelized by Riese, was corrected to *candidulo* by *a*, and is retained in my text. *Candidulo* is metrically correct; cf. *fulgiduli*, 69.1. Baehrens emends to *tereti.*
3. propriis: See above, Ch. VI, A 6.
4. in statuam: Riese questions whether this should be *in statua ... sua.* However, *in* and the accusative are found with verbs that signify being at rest; see above, notes on *quo*, 3.5, *in antra*, 7.4; Ch. VI, A 9; and Kuehner-Stegmann,

I, 593-94, § 114b. The idea implied in *viveret* may be that Venus is sending life into the statue; cf. 80.4, fluxit in hanc ... Venus.

5. mendax locus: Luxorius uses *locus* indefinitely; see above, Ch. VI, B 4, and cf. 18.16; 34.2, 46.14; and 83.7. Here it may refer to the statue, the soil, or the entire situation.

5. qui violas feret: *Qui* is used as if *locus* is understood but *si* is also possible. The manuscript reading is *qui viole forent,* which Saumaise changed to *qui violas ferat.* Riese's text has *qui violas feret,* but he indicates that *quo violae florent* is possible. But the word is *flōrent* and Riese, who often calls attention to metrical faults in Luxorius, would gratuitously inflict another flaw upon him. *Feret* parallels *servabit* and is bolder than *florent*—hence more like Luxorius. Cf. Shakespeare, *Hamlet,* Act V, scene 1:

> And from her fair and unpolluted flesh
> May violets spring!

6. famulas: See above, Ch. VI, B 4.

71

Meter: Anapaestic; see above, Ch. VIII, Meter 7.

Title. caecum: For a treatment of this theme in modern literature, see Roger Heppenstall, *The Blaze of Noon* (New York and Toronto, 1940), a novel about a blind masseur, especially pp. 30-36, 121, 137-38.

1. viduae frontis: a bold expression, "with his forehead deprived of eyes."

6. ille: For the scansion, see above, entry for this word; Ch. VIII, B 1.

6. nolit: On the subjunctive with *quod* in an indirect statement, see above, Ch. VI, A 3.

8. cui: On the short *i,* see above, entry for this word, Ch. VIII, B 2.

72

Meter: Lesser Sapphic; see above, Ch. VIII, Meter 5.

Title. nocte: Riese inconsistently allows *nocte* to remain, although elsewhere he emended to *noctu,* even in a title, where there are no metrical considerations; see above, notes on 32.T, and 55.1.

This poem is another in the series on the shortcomings of professionals (see note to 8.T); specifically, it is one in the long line of literary jokes and barbs against philosophers, especially those who are supposed to practice virtue, but who, not following their own preachments, become voluptuaries.

1. hispidus: The beard is associated with philosophers; see Horace, *Satires* 1.3.133-34, and 2.3.35, sapientem pascere barbam; Persius, 4.1; Juvenal, 2.11, and 14.12; and Martial, 14.81.1.

4. tantum: Cf. 21.3. If taken with *modestum,* cf. Horace, *Satires* 2.3.313, tantum dissimilem.

5. die: For amatory activities during the daytime, see Ovid, *Amores* 1.5, especially line 26, Proveniant medii sic mihi saepe dies!

5. patrare: to be taken *sensu obsceno,* commonly used in this way, especially

in late Latin. See Burmann, *Anthologia* I, 607, Book III, *Epigram* 160.3, Non oculos: etenim sunt lusci oculi atque patrantes; Persius, 1.18, patranti fractus ocello; and Quintilian's explanation of this word in *Institutio Oratoria* 8.3.44, mala consuetudine in obscenum intellectum sermo detortus est. He declares that *patrare bella,* which was good usage in Sallust (*Jugurtha* 75.2), was laughed at in his day.

6. lateasque: *Ut* is omitted and its force is supplied from the previous *ne;* see Kuehner-Stegmann, II, 27-28, § 154.6, and 211, c.

7. lumbo: used here as in Juvenal, 9.59, and Persius, 1.20 and 4.35.

9. incubus: The classical form is *incubo,* a word applied to spirits that watched over treasures; see Petronius, *Satiricon* 38.8. Later the word became *incubus* and changed its meaning. In this line *incubus* is first used in poetry. It first occurs in prose in the writings of Jerome (d. 420) and Augustine (d. 430). For its meaning, see Jerome, *Vita Sancti Pauli Primi Eremitae* 8 (*PL,* XXIII, 23B), Mortalis ego sum, et unus ex accolis eremi, quos vario delusa errore Gentilitas Faunos, Satyrosque, et Incubos vocans incolit. Jerome also uses *incubones* in *Commentarium in Isaiam Prophetam* 5.13.21 (*PL,* XXIV, 163B), Pilosi saltabunt ibi, vel incubones, vel satyros vel silvestres quosdam homines, quos nonnulli fatuos ficarios vocant, aut daemonum genera intelligunt. Augustine, *De Civitate Dei* 15.23 (*PL,* XLI, 468), says on the same topic, . . . audisse confirmant Silvanos et Faunos, quos vulgo incubos vocant, improbos saepe exstitisse mulieribus et earum appetisse ac peregisse concubitum . . . Isidore of Seville, *Origines* (or *Etymologia*) 8.11.104 (*PL,* LXXX, 326) and 11.3.22 (*PL,* LXXXII, 422A), amplifies the definition of *incubus* along these lines. Mainly because of the interpretation of Jerome, the Graeco-Roman concept of fauns and satyrs as woodland creatures, as uninhibited children of nature, developed into the medieval image of satanic demons haunting women in their sleep, tempting them, inducing them to enter into unholy compacts, and ravishing them. From such unions witches and other demons were born; female counterparts of *incubi* called *succubae* were invented. Finally, in the demonology of the Middle Ages, distinctions among the woodland divinities were blotted out and all were classed as *incubi.* See R. Bernheimer, *Wild Men in the Middle Ages* (Cambridge, Mass., 1952), pp. 93-101, and M. Summers, *The History of Witchcraft,* (2nd ed., New York, 1956), pp. 89-103, 105-9.

10. Cato: On the quantity of the *o,* see above, entry for this name, Ch. VIII, B 4. Cato was the standard of strict morality; see Martial, 10.19.21; 11.2.1; 11.39.15; *et al.;* Juvenal, 2.40; and Petronius, *Satiricon* 132.15.1, Quid me constructa spectatis fronte, Catones?

73

Meter: Elegiac; see above, Ch. VIII, Meter 1.

A genre piece, this poem has a classical tradition that carried over to later times; see Sells, *Animal Poetry,* Chs. 2-6. As models, Luxorius had the famous *Passer* poem, Catullus, 3; Martial's poem on Issa, a pet lap dog, 1.109, his epitaph for a dog, 11.69, and the couplet on *catella,* 14.198; and Statius, *Silvae* 2.4, an elegy on a parrot.

3. famulans: See above, Ch. VI, B 4.

5. nec monstrosum aliquid: She is a miniature dog like our toy terriers or Chihuahuas, tiny but perfectly proportioned and not stunted.

7-8. mollior, saevior: See above, Ch. VI, A 7.

8. catis: The *a* must be short for the line to scan properly. The alternate spelling of the word is *cattus*, as in 89.1 and in 181R.3, Cattus in obscuro cepit pro sorice picam; in both instances a long *a* is demanded by the meter. The scribes often wrote *catus* instead of *cattus*; Ellis, "Some New Latin Fragments," *JP*, VIII (1879), 122, reports this line with *catus*; see also *TLL*, III, 620-21, *s.v. catus*; and Riese, *Anthologia*, I, 154-55. Other occurrences of the word in poetry are not reported; from the evidence of 89.1 and 181R.3 it seems that the *a* is long whether followed by one *t* or two *t*'s in the manuscripts. Luxorius changed its quantity in this line out of metrical necessity. Baehrens solves the problem by emending to *catus*, "shrewd," which is clever, except that the context seems to call for a word meaning "cats" in contrast with *muribus*.

Cattus or *catus* came into Latin late and is first found in Palladius (*fl. ca.* A.D. 350), *Opus Agriculturae* 4.9.4, Contra talpas prodest cattos frequenter habere. The feminine, *catta*, is also found in late Latin writers; see Souter, *Glossary*, p. 43, *s.v. catta. Stercus cattae* and *stercus catti* appear in the prescriptions of Sextus Placitus (5th century), *Liber Medicinae* 18.1.4 (*CML*, IV, 277). *Cattae* is found in Martial, 13.69, but there the reference is most probably to birds. On the question whether this is the same word as *catta*, "a cat," see Ernout and Meillet, *Dictionnaire*, I, 188; Friedlaender, *Martial, II*, 282; and Jennison, *Animals for Show and Pleasure*, p. 129.

Just as the word for horse in the Romance languages comes from *caballus* and not from *equus*, so *cattus*, not *felis*, gives to those languages the word for cat. See Ernout and Meillet (as cited in the preceding paragraph) on these derivatives. *Cattus* is believed to be of North African origin. *Aeluros*, a transliteration of αἴλουρος, was also used by Latin writers; see Juvenal, 15.7, and Aulus Gellius, *Noctes Atticae* 20.8.6. On cats in the Roman world, see *CIL*, VI.2, 14223, and VIII, Supp. 1, 14823; Jennison, *Animals for Show and Pleasure*, pp. 19, 20, 129; and Keller, *Die Antike Tierwelt*, I, 76-78.

9. vincit: Cf. 59.9, modicos superaverat annos.

9. nimis: See above, Ch. VI, A 7.

9. parvola: The manuscript has *forcia turba*, which Riese emended to *fortia torvo*. However, *fortia* does not seem to belong, unless we take *membra fortia* to mean "strong dogs," i.e., the small dog overcomes the large ones by her barking. *Parvola* appears better: the tiny dog has a savage bark that far exceeds her weak body—a Luxorian contrast. Cf. the loud voice in the small body, Poem 10.

10. ab arte: Cf. 49.2, and see above, Ch. VI, B 4.

74

Meter: Iambic Trimeter (Senarius) Acatalectic; see above, Ch. VIII, Meter 6.

Title. pardis: The *pardus* is the hunting leopard or cheetah, whose spots are small and solid instead of in circles or rosettes like the leopard's. The cheetah is smaller than the leopard, reaching about seven feet in length. It is not a true cat, for it belongs to a separate genus. The leopard is too fierce and untrustworthy to be used for hunting, whereas the cheetah can easily be trained and can be kept as a pet. In A. Conan Doyle's Sherlock Holmes story, "The Speckled Band," Dr. Grimesby Roylott kept a baboon and a cheetah, which were allowed to roam freely on his grounds at Stoke Moran. Cheetahs have been timed at seventy miles an hour. See A. R. Dugmore, "Cats of the Wild," in *Wild Life the World Over* (New York, 1947), p. 49, and R. Hegner, *Parade of the Animal Kingdom* (New York, 1943), pp. 610, 613.

On the various meanings of *pardus, panthera, varia,* and *leopardus,* together with a list of references in Greek and Latin authors, see Jennison, *Animals for Show and Pleasure,* pp. 183-87; cf. also 762R.50, Panther caurit amans, pardus hiando felit.

Martial has a number of poems on the tameness of wild animals, some of which, however, occasionally reverted to type: see *De Spectaculis* 10, 17, 18, 21, 30, and 1.14; 1.22; 1.48; 1.51; 1.60; and 1.104.

2. lynces: For the conquest of India by Bacchus, see Ovid, *Metamorphoses* 4.20-21, 605-6, and 15.413, Victa racemifero lyncas dedit India Baccho; Vergil, *Georgics* 3.264; and Propertius, 3.17.8.

3. duxit ille bestias: Bacchus is generally depicted as being drawn by tigers or panthers; see *Inventaire,* II, *Plates,* Fasciculus 2 (1914), 67, 139; III, *Plates* (1925), 455; *MCAAT,* III, 70, and Pl. 7; and R. V. Schoder, *Masterpieces of Greek Art* (Greenwich, Conn., 1960), Pl. 75.

5. domarent: On the use of the subjunctive, see above, Ch. VI, A 1.

6. mira: See note to 44.1.

8-10. quaerere, ferre: in apposition with *forma*; see above, Ch. VI, A 4.

10. baiulo: "portatory"; used as a noun in classical Latin but as an adjective and noun in late Latin. See Souter, *Glossary,* p. 27, and *TLL,* II, 1687, s.v. *baiulus.* See Cyprian, *Epistola I ad Donatum* (PL, IV, 198), per arundines baiulus repunt, and Ambrose, *in Epistolam I ad Thessalonicenses* 4.16 (PL, XVII, 475C), rapiemur una cum illis baiulis nubibus . . .

13. morsum . . . audeant: The reading of A is *morsu repertis et cibis non audeant,* which Burmann keeps in his text but in a note (*Anthologia,* II, 617) he suggests *morsu repertos ut cibos non adpetant.* Baehrens follows Burmann completely. Klapp, *Quaestiones,* p. xiv, changes only one word in A, *morsu* to *morsum,* which Riese accepts. The latter also followed Burmann's suggested change of *et* to *ut. Audeant* is a strong word in keeping with the spirit of the poem and with Luxorius' boldness of language. The use of the direct object with *audere* is normal in the poets, historians, and especially in late Latin; see Kuehner-Stegmann, I, 264.

75

Meter: Lesser Asclepiad: see above, Ch. VIII, Meter 4.

Title. in: Cf. *de* in 76.T; see above, Ch. VII, A 7.

psaltriam: On forms of entertainment in Carthage, see above, Ch. I, B 17.

For sculptures of musicians in North Africa, see *MCAAT,* VIII, Part 1, 115, No. 4; 130, No. 5; XVIII, 40-44, Nos, 2-6; XIX, 9, No. 1, and Pl. 3.

1. Gattula: *TLL,* VI, 1701, equates this name with *Gantula,* a bird like a hazel hen or a grouse. *Ganta* is a goose, perhaps more fitting in Luxorius' mind to this dancer. Her name might have been *Gaetula;* cf. Gaetula in pace, *Inventaire,* II, 336, No. 1055.

3. potius . . . probo psaltriam: On *potius,* see Ch. VI, A 7; on the alliteration, see above, Ch. V, B 7.

5. dum displiceas . . . iocos. *Dum* may be used here instead of *cum;* see Ch. VI, A 1. "Although you displease the people, you will put up with any jokes at your expense." Another possibility is, "You are crazy enough to put up with their jokes while you do not please the people."

5. quosque: a rare use of the plural; "each and every."

5. feras iocos: Cf. *ferre iocos,* 22R.2.

6. populos: See above, Ch. VI, B 5.

6. mulceant: For the mood, See above, Ch. VI, A 3 in his 1869 edition, Riese put a question mark after *deserat,* line 6, but not after *mulceant.* In 1875 Klapp, *Quaestiones,* p. xiv, had the opinion that? belongs after *mulceant,* giving no reason except, 'Si quid video." In 1882 Baehrens used Klapp's punctuation, as did Riese in 1894. I have also followed Klapp because the sense is clearer and the syntax more explicable if lines 6-8 are broken into two sentences. Maehly, 'Literarische Anzeigen," *ZöstG,* XXII (1871), 579, feels that something is missing after line 6 and supplies "omnes esse tui quam cupidissimos." *Quod* would them introduce a causal clause, but if it introduces an indirect statement, as in my translation, nothing need be supplied. Luxorius is generally terse in the closing lines of his epigrams; the reader must infer the idea suggested by Maehly's addition. Gattula thinks she is winning over the people by her playing, but, Luxorius assures her, the auditors will give up their delight in hearing music, if they have to watch her ugly gestures and grimaces.

8. pro te: Riese equates this with *apud te* or *te visa.* However, it may mean "instead of you," a concise way of saying, "instead of listening to you," or *pro* may mean "on account of." Cf. 19.8, and see above, Ch. VI, A 9.

76

Meter: Elegiac; see above, Ch. VIII, Meter 1.

Another Luxorian contrast, in the same vein as its companion piece, Poem 75. The poet is willing to pay Gattula that he may not receive her favors. This has a modern flavor, like "How much will you take to stop singing?" Cf. Poem 40.

Title. de: See note on *in,* 75.T.

1. quid: This is the reading of A and seems properly used here, but Riese emends to *qui* and Mueller to *cui.*

1. pretium: Luxorius uses synonyms in this poem: *praemia,* line 3, *munera,* line 3, and *dona,* line 8. Cf. Poems 45, 60, and 67 for a similar variety of language. See above, Ch. VI, B 4, and note on *prolis,* 45.1.

2. te oderis: On the hiatus, see above, Ch. VIII, A 1a.

3. tantis: used for *tot,* a late and medieval Latin usage; see Beeson, *Primer,* p. 13, § 1a; Browne, *British Latin,* p. xxii; Strecker, *Introduction to Medieval Latin,* pp. 21 and 55.

77

Meter: Elegiac; see above, Ch VIII, Meter 1.

Title. satis: See above, Ch. VI, A 7.

Cf. Martial, 2.50, and 3.87, on the theme of reversal of parts of the body; Luxorius has kept it somewhat cleaner.

2. superior: See above, entry for this word, Ch. VIII, B 1.

3. Follonia: See M. Lambertz, "Zur Ausbreitung des Supernomen oder Signum in romischen Reiche," *Glotta,* IV (1913), 101-2, on this name: see *CIL,* VIII.1, 7364, and Index, p. 999, for listing of the name *Fullonus* derived from *fullo,* "a fuller."

4. horridius: See above, Ch. VI, A 7.

78

Meter: Elegiac; see above, Ch. VIII, Meter 1.

1. pulcrior: See above, Ch. VI, A 7.

4. Pallas . . . Cypris: For a similar comparison, see Martial, 1.102, and Paul the Silentiary, *Anthologia Palatina* 5.272.5, and 5.293.10-12.

7. est animo: apparently used like *cordi est.*

7. mulier conparis: The point is that although opposed to sexual pleasure, the lady has a fancy for marriage—a paradox. She should therefore marry a man who is equally opposed to love so that they can be chaste together. If an obscene meaning is implied, *conparis* may refer to another woman; cf. Martial, 6.64.5, et possit sponsam te sponsa vocare.

79

Meter: Elegiac; see above, Ch. VIII, Meter 1.

Title. Pasiphaae: spelled in A with a double *s* in this poem and in 148R.12, 176R.14, 199R.92, and 253R.182, and with an *f* instead of *ph;* see above, Ch. XI, C 3. The name is written *Pasifae* in a painting of Pasiphae leaning on a white bull. This painting was found in a villa on the road to Ardea and is now in the Vatican Museum; see D. Raoul-Rochette, *Peintures antiques inédites* (Paris, 1836), pp. 396-99 and Pl. 2.

The first *a* of *Pasiphae* is long both in Greek and in Latin. The double *s* in the forms of this name found in A may be due to scribal errors or an anxiety on the part of some poets of the *Anthologia Latina* to leave no doubt about the original long quantity of this *a.* It is possible that in their time the first *a* of *Pasiphae* was pronounced short (see above, Ch. II, n. 32), and that the poets added an *s* to make the syllable long by position.

In the texts of Burmann, Meyer, and Riese (1869 ed.,), the forms of *Pasiphae* have one *s,* but in Baehrens' text and the 1894 edition of Riese, the double *s* appears. All the citations *s. v. Pasiphae* in Forcellini, *Onomasticon* II, show only the spelling with one *s.*

The case of *Pasiphaae* may be genitive or dative; see notes on *Corintho,* 65.11, and *Marina,* 82.T.

1-2. disciplinarum ... Aristoteles: This manner of distinguishing man from all other animals is cited by ancient and medieval grammarians and rhetoricians as an example of a perfect definition. See, for example, Sergius, *Explanationes in Artem Donatum, Liber* I, *De Nomine* (Keil, *GL* IV, 489, 22-24; see also *Pompei Commentum Artis Donati* [Keil, V, 137, 36]): Habemus in Aristote-licis et in Stoicis praeceptis et fere omnium hanc esse perfectam definitionem, quae separat a ceteris communibus rem et suam proprietatem ostendit, ut puta, homo est animal rationale, mortale, risus capax. Martianus Capella, who lived about a century before Luxorius, develops this definition at length or alludes to it several times in *Liber de Nuptiis Mercurii et Philologiae,* ed. by A. Dick (Leipzig, 1925) 4.100G.348, p. 160; 4.101G.349, p. 161; 5.156G.479, p. 238; 5.103G.354, p. 163; and 5.123G.398, p. 192. The definition recurs in the work of Clemens Scotus, a contemporary of Alcuin (end of eighth century): Diffinitio est brevis oratio unam quamque rem propria significatione con-cludens, ut homo animal est mortale, rationale, risus capax (Keil, *De Gram-maticis Quibusdam,* p. 14, lines 13-15). Cf. Seneca, *Epistulae Morales* 41.8, Rationale enim animal est homo.

As in the case of his poem on the Seven Wise Men (see above, note to 65), Luxorius may have picked up this definition in a grammatical work circulating in his time. Aristotle refers to man's desire and ability to learn in *Metaphysics* 1.1-3 (980a22-b22), but he implies that some other animals are also capable of learning. The observation that man is the only living creature that laughs occurs twice in Aristotle, *On the Parts of Animals* 3.10(673a), but not as a definition. Why then did Luxorius combine two of man's qualities in a state-ment attributed to Aristotle?

The clue lies in the quotation from Sergius above. He does not say that the definition cited by him as a perfect definition is by Aristotle himself but he uses it as an illustration of the type of definition found in the teachings of the Stoics, Aristotle, and almost all other philosopers. Luxorius, however, credited it to Aristotle directly. According to the *OCD,* the date of Sergius is unknown, but he may be the learned Sergius mentioned by Coronatus (see Appendix III, A, below). He is often confused with Servius in the manu-scripts; the latter lived before the time of Luxorius. Hence, Luxorius may have seen this definition in the works of Sergius or Servius, or of Pompeius (cited in this note, above), who lived in the fifth century A.D.

Rabelais' adaptation of Aristotle's original thought, which is found in the last line of his address to his readers (*Aux Lecteurs*) at the beginning of *Gargantua,* "Pour ce que rire est le propre de l'homme," has become a familiar saying in its own right. The opening sentence of William Hazlitt's essay, "On Wit and Humor," in *Lectures on the British Comic Writers* is "Man is the only animal that laughs and weeps." Nietzsche, *The Will to Power,* 1.91, is of the opinion that man is the only animal that laughs because he alone suffers so deeply that he has had to invent laughter.

3. cum: A omits this word, which is supplied by *a.* Baehrens prefers *si.*

Klapp, *Quaestiones,* p. xiv, changes *cum* to *sic,* arguing that, if Burdo is a man, the truth has not been turned about, for, according to Aristotle, men both laugh and reason. Klapp's idea is that the poet is facetiously doubting whether Burdo is a man. Baehrens changes *vel* in line 4 to *nec,* thereby playing horse or mule with Luxorius' little joke and making a joke of his own to the effect that Burdo, if a man, is only half a man, for he laughs but cannot reason. *Vel* here means "and"; see above, Ch. VI, A 8.

Luxorius is of course playing upon the word *burdo.* A mule cannot laugh and reason as a man does. Therefore the definition is not true when (*cum*), or since (*cum*), or if (*si*) a man is a mule, or a mule is a man, as in this case. Burdo as a man follows the definition but, since his name means "mule," *burdo* then upsets the definition—creating a paradox.

5. Cf. the idea in 44.1.

6. Pasiphae: The poet is struck by the odd combination of names: Burdo, a "mule" that can laugh and reason, and Pasiphae, who was mated with a bull. See Ovid, *Metamorphoses,* 8.132-36, and 9.736.40. Hence, a double *monstrum* has appeared in "our time." Cf. Martial's reference to the return of Pasiphae, *De Spectaculis* 5.1-2, Iunctam Pasiphaen Dictaeo credite tauro:/ Vidimus, accepit fabula prisca fidem. Nero actually had the myth reenacted in the arena (Suetonius, *Nero* 12).

80

Meter: Elegiac; see above, Ch. VIII, Meter 1.

Title. rosae centumfoliae: *Centumfolius* is a new adjective; *TLL,* III, 820, lists only this occurrence and gives *centifolia, centifolium, centu(m)folia,* and *centifolia* as glosses. It cannot be determined whether Luxorius coined the word, since the title may not be his (see above, Ch. VII, 2). Pliny, *Natural History* 21.10. 17-18, uses *centifoliam.* In line 3 of this poem *centum* is separated from *foliis*; writing *centumfoliae* as one word in the title may be analogous to *centifoliae* or a scribal error.

The flower is still cultivated; it is known today as *Rosa Centifolia,* the cabbage rose, or the Rose of Provence. One variety is the moss rose. It has a long history: Herodotus, 8.138, mentions the garden of Midas, son of Gordius, in Macedonia, where roses grew by themselves, each with sixty petals, and Theophrastus, *Historia Plantarum* 6.6.4, speaks of roses bearing a hundred petals. This variety was brought to France via Morocco and Spain, reached Germany and Austria by other routes, and was extensively cultivated in the Netherlands. It appears in the paintings of Flemish masters, among them Jan de Heem and Van Huysum. See R. C. Allen, *Roses for Everybody* (New York, 1948), p. 42, and *American Rose Annual, 1949* (Harrisburg, Pa., 1949), p. 33.

There is a record of its growth in this country in 1633. It is pink, grows to a height of three to six feet, is hardy, needs little care, and is used a great deal in old-fashioned gardens. Herodotus noted that it surpassed other flowers in fragrance; this is still true. See L. H. Bailey, *The Standard Cyclopedia of Horticulture* (New York, 1941) III, 2989.

This is one of Luxorius' better poems and has been included in anthologies (see above, Ch. IX, D 5). It is part of a long tradition of flower poems, especially on roses, from ancient times down to the lovely flower poems of Waller and Herrick. Cf. Martial, 6.80, and 7.89; also 84R-87R; 646R, attributed to Ausonius; 866R; and the charming poem by Dracontius, *De Origine Rosarum* (*PLM*, V, 237).

1. proprio: See above, Ch. VI, A 6.

2. radiis . . . suis: On the rhyme, see note on *totis . . . horis*, 25.2.

3. rosa Cypridis: On the rose as a flower of Venus, see 646R.18, Sideris et floris nam domina una Venus.

4. fluxit . . . sanguine: Cf. 70.3-4, infudit . . . statuam.

5. sidus: See above, entry for this word, Ch. VIII, B 1.

81

Meter: Dactylic Hexameter; see above, Ch. VIII, Meter 2.

Title. statua: Strabo, *Geography* 13.32, refers to a monument of Achilles at Sigeum, and, 13.29, to the sacred precinct of Hector at Ophrynium, but there is no mention in ancient authorities of opposing statues of Hector and Achilles in Troy. It is possible that Luxorius is describing a painting or a mosaic.

sudat: On the sweating of statues, see Cicero, *De Divinatione* 1.43.98, and 2.27.58.

1. Ilion in medium: See notes on *quo*, 3.5, *in antris*, 7.4, and *in medium*, 18.7.

2. Phrygius: For the scansion, see above, entry for this word, Ch. VIII, B 1.

2. vel: On use as *et*, see above, Ch. VI, A 8.

4. falsum . . . formidat: On the alliteration, see above, Ch. V, B 7.

4. fictus: For the scansion, see above, entry for this word, Ch. VIII, B 1.

5. mirum: See note to 44.1.

6. credo . . . reddunt: For the mood, see above, Ch. VIII, A 3.

6. superi animas: For the hiatus, see above, Ch. VIII, A 2. For the meaning of *superi*, cf. 13.8 and 33.2; also see above, Ch. III, E 2, 6, on the relation of this word to the question of Luxorius' religion.

7. barathri: Cf. Dracontius, *Romulea* 134, Rhadamanthus habet commune barathri. Usually the second *a* is short, as in Lucretius, 3.966 and 6.606; Catullus, 68.108,117; and Vergil, *Aeneid* 3.241, but when the word comes at the end of the hexameter line, the second *a* is long, as in this line, in the quotation from Dracontius, Vergil, *Aeneid* 8.245, and Valerius Flaccus, *Argonautica* 2.86.

8. si horum: a harsh elision.

8. extat: The reading of A is *certus stat*, emended by Baehrens to *certe stat* and by Riese, to *certe exstat*. I have omitted the *s* on the basis of *extat*, 80.3, and *extitit*, 87.7; see also note on *extructa*, 18.9.

9. viva . . . mortem: On Luxorius' juxtaposition of contrasting words, see above, Ch. V, B 1.

82

Meter: Elegiac; see above, Ch. VIII, Meter 1.

Title. Marina vocabulo: *Vocabulum* may govern the genitive, as in Tacitus, *Annales* 11.17, libertatis vocabulum; see Kuehner-Stegmann, I, 419, a. However, the name may also agree with another noun, as in Tacitus, *Annales* 12.66, artifex vocabulo Locusta, or with *vocabulum* itself, as in Tacitus, *Annales* 13.12, cui vocabulum Acte fuit. *Marina* may therefore be considered an ablative in apposition with *muliere* or even with *vocabulo;* see notes on *Corintho,* 65.11, and *Pasiphaae,* 82.T.

A variation on the theme of this poem is found in Martial, 4.22, but Luxorius is probably classicizing on Martial, 11.21.10, Hanc in piscina dicor futuisse marina. Medical opinion consulted on the feasibility of this feat differed, one *medicus eruditissimus* with a classical background quipping, "It is only littorally possible."

3. potius: See above, Ch. VI, A 7; for the inversion, *potius sed,* see note on *quam magis,* 1.8.

4. mare: The ablative singular in *-e* is sometimes found; see Ovid, *Tristia* 5.2.20, and Kuehner, I, 329, § 71B.1.

4. foret: On the imperfect subjunctive after the present, *est,* see above, Ch. VI, A 5. The use of *quod* may be causal, or *quod* may here introduce an indirect statement after *memor est;* see Ch. VI, A 3.

83

Meter: Elegiac; see above, Ch. VIII, Meter 1.

Title. horto: On the genre of poems describing gardens, see note to Poem 18.

domni: The short form of *dominus* occurs in manuscripts from the fourth century on; sometimes both *dominus* and *domnus* are found in the same manuscript; note the use of *domino* for metrical reasons in line 2. Cf. *Julia Domna,* the name of the wife of Septimius Severus; and see *TLL,* V.1, 1907. In Ennodius the short form is used with a name, the long form, solo, as in this poem.

In North Africa the title *dominus* was applied to the Vandal Kings; cf. 55.6, and see Courtois, *Les Vandales,* pp. 243-45. However, as elsewhere in the Roman world, it could be merely a title of respect; see Sidonius, *Epistulae* 4.12.2 (*PL,* LVIII, 58, 518A), Constantem . . . pro foribus vidi a dominis Simplicio et Apollinari redeuntem.

Oageis: See above, note to 59.T, and Ch. III, D 2.

This poem is a document on ancient medicine, but it is also a eulogy (*laudatio*) of a great man's estate for its superhuman qualities manifested in the healing powers of the garden's herbs. For an ancient herbal profusely illustrated with modern pictures, see *Pseudo-Musae de Herba Vettonica Liber, CML,* IV, 1-11, and *Pseudo-Apulei Platonici Herbarius, CML,* IV, 13-225.

1. parietibus: For the scansion, see above, entry for this word, Ch. VIII, B 1.

2. aptior: See above, Ch. VI, A 7.

4. praemedicante: The verbs *medico* and *medicor* and the participle *praemedicatus* are found in earlier Latin. Luxorius is using here a form not found elsewhere; Souter, *Glossary,* p. 316, lists *praemedicor,* "cure beforehand," citing only this occurrence. However, *praemedicor* may be the same as *medicor* in meaning, for late Latin writers formed new compounds that retained the meaning of the simple verb. Cf. *resordet,* 25.3; *subaptat,* 46.14; *adcognosco Cappadocem,* Petronius, *Satiricon,* 69.2; and see above, Ch. VI, B 1.

5. nil . . . tenet: Baehrens emends *nil* to *hinc*. Riese keeps the reading of A and explains (p. 285) that *tenet* here means *retinet, non permittit*. The emendation and the explanation do not take into account the meaning of *parandum*, "to be bought, procured." The line means "All the science of medicine does not mention a single drug that has to be brought from outside into this garden—everything is here."

7-8. caeli locus . . . numina regnant: Luxorius implies that there is some kind of heavenly place because death can be overcome by the use of the right herbs, which were put into this garden for men to use after they had learned their nature and application. This may only be his poetic way of extolling the power of the herbs; his idea of *caeli locus* may not be evidence of a belief in Christianity. Cf. 81.6, and see above, Ch. III, E 2, 6, on *numina* and its application to Luxorius' supposed Christianity.

7. est: On the indicative in an indirect statement, see above, Ch. VI, A 3.

8. cum datur: On the mood, see above, Ch. VI, A 1.

84

Meter: Elegiac; see above, Ch. VIII, Meter 1.

Title. pica: The magpie was a favorite talking bird among the Romans; see Jennison, *Animals for Show and Pleasure,* pp. 117-21, on talking birds kept as pets by the Romans, and for literary allusions to these pets. See also Martial, 7.87.6, and 14.76; Petronius, *Satiricon* 28.9; Statius, *Silvae* 2.4.19; and Pliny, *Natural History* 10.59.118-19, on the magpie's ability to imitate the human voice.

1. cuncta ante: See above, entry for *cunctaque,* Ch. VIII, B 1.

4. Picus: Some involved and perhaps belabored pun may be contained in the use of this word; cf. *gryphum,* 41.8, and *Burdo,* 79.3,6. *Picus* is a woodpecker or griffin, but it is also the name of an ancient king of Latium who had the gift of prophecy and was attended by a green woodpecker. Some myths have it that he too was changed into a woodpecker; see Vergil, *Aeneid* 7.189-91, and Ovid, *Metamorphoses* 14.312-96. Although Luxorius is generally correct in his knowledge of mythology, he is mistaken here, as far as I know, if he is thinking of Picus as a magpie, or he may be confusing the metamorphosis of Picus with that of the daughters of Pierus, who were turned into magpies after their unsuccessful contest with the Muses; see Ovid, *Metamorphoses* 5.293-345, 662-78.

85

Meter: Elegiac; see above, Ch. VIII, Meter 1.

Title. disco: Originally, the *discus* was a thing for throwing and could be applied to any natural object convenient for throwing, especially a stone; E. M. Gardiner, *Athletics of the Ancient World* (Oxford, 1930), p. 26. Later, *discus* was the name of any circular piece of metal, stone, or clay used for a variety of purposes—trays, coasters, dishes, and plates. They were mostly only a few inches in diameter. Specimens made of metal or terra cotta can be seen in the museums of Carthage and Tunis. Some of them are unadorned or have simple geometric designs; others bear decorative figures in relief of animals, human beings, or gods. Many others tell a story, like the disk described by Luxorius. For illustrations and descriptions of disks found in North Africa, see *MCAAT*, VII, 7, No. 65, disk with concentric circles; 144, No. 112, disk with two gods; 144, No. 113, circus scenes; VIII, 115, No. 4, flute player; 130, No. 5, warrior; 214, No. 5, copper disk used as a support for an oenochoe; XX, 157, No. 67, four sphinxes; 160, No. 107, three hearts, rings, and bands; 160, No. 108, globule, rays, and ring, etc.

spinam tollit de planta: The subject, drawing a thorn from a shoeless foot, is famous in ancient art. See M. Bieber, *Sculpture of the Hellenistic Age* (New York, 1955), Figures 550 and 635; Reinach, *Répertoire de le statuaire,* III, 21, No. 3, for Pan and a satyr, V. 1, 257, No. 5, for Cupid and a satyr; G. Rodenwaldt, *Die Kunst der Antike* (Berlin, 1927), p. 470, a single grotesque figure; and Ziehen, *Festschrift,* pp. 50-57. As far as I know, there is no ancient work of art which depicts a scene such as the one Luxorius describes. The one which comes closest is a group from a fountain showing Pan drawing a thorn from the foot of a satyr. The latter is in wild pain, as in Luxorius' poem; Pan, just like the country girl, is all attention and solicitude. This group, now in the Vatican Museum, exhibits capital humor—but there is no Cupid on the scene. For a description, see Helbig, *Fuehrer,* I, 336 (74).

1. nimis: See above, Ch. VI, A 7.

2. vulneris alta: Cf. Ovid, *Remedium Amoris* 369, altissima venti; Seneca, *Oedipus* 390, alta caeli; and Valerius Flaccus, *Argonautica* 1.160, Aegaei . . . alta profundi. The singular, *altum,* is more frequently found, either in its meaning of "the sea," or with the genitive of words expressing place—literal or figurative. For the usual manner of expressing Luxorius' idea, see Vergil, *Aeneid* 10.857, alto vulnere.

3-4. illum . . . flere. The reading of A is *illum pandorii soletur . . . pariete teste gemere.* Burmann corrects this to *illam pandurii solatur . . . inridens parili teste carere (Anthologia,* II, 620-21, Book VI, *Epigram* 80). He explains in a long note that the *planta Satyricum* is the orchid, that *virum* is the girl's lover, and that Cupid is consoling her because her friend's testes are not like the shape of the plant she is plucking. Wildly fanciful: the thorn itself would not resemble a flower or a bulb, orchids do not have thorns—although Burmann explains how this plant would! *Illum,* not *illam,* must be read in line 3. The satyr needs consoling because, deep in his foot, he has a thorn that has to be worked out slowly and painfully. The girl needs no consoling; she is not the one who is suffering. The satyr has limped up to her and cried out for help. He is an uninhibited child of nature; he might be grimacing, perhaps writhing and weeping as the girl begins to operate. Cupid, a bystander, cheers him by playing pretty tunes, but cannot help smiling and laughing with contempt at the sight of a man groaning and weeping over the extraction of a thorn. Both Baehrens and Riese accept Burmann's suggested reading of line 4: *Inridens parili teste carere virum.* If we do not agree with Burmann that *virum* refers to the husband or friend of the girl, then it must mean the satyr. But it is inconceivable to think of a satyr, of all male beings, as lacking part of his virility; the line must be further emended to something like *inridens tali flere virum*, which describes the situation adequately.

3. panduri: The pandora, pandura, or pandurina is a lutelike instrument with two or three strings plucked with the fingers. It originated in Assyria or Persia and eventually came to Rome via Asia Minor and Greece. It was modified in Rome to a four-stringed instrument. One version was pear-shaped with inward curves; the Romans used an oval shape without inward curves. See *Encyclopédie de la Musique*, Part 1, *Antiquité-Moyen Age* (Paris, 1924), p. 446 and Pls. 45-46; *EB*, 11th ed., XX, 675-76, 14th ed., XVII, 181; and *RE*, XVIII. 3, 559. The pandora was played in North Africa and from there made its way into Spain. Modern parallel instruments, counterparts, or descendants, modified in respect to the number of strings and the use of a plectrum or quill instead of the fingers, are the colascione of Italy, the san-hsien or sientze of China, the samisen of Japan, also the bandore, mandore, banjo, and mandolin, which are etymologically related to *pandura* and *pandurium*; see *OED*, VII, 418, *s.v. pandora*². For ancient references to the pandora, see Julius Pollux, *Onomasticon* 4.60, and Athenaeus, 4.183. For a painting of Cupid as a musician, see Reinach, *Répertoire de peintures*, p. 87; the *Guide du Musée Alaoui*, p. 57, lists a pandora player. See also *The New Oxford History of Music* (London, 1957), I, 244-45, on the name *pandore* and on Assyrian representations in art.

5. nil falsum: The lifelike nature of statues and paintings is a commonplace of ancient poetry; see Martial, 1.109.18-23; 3.35.41; 6.13; Philostratus, *Imagines* 1.28; also 150R, 173R, 174R, 274R, 894R.2, sub marmore viva fuit, with which cf. 70L; *Anthologia Palatina* 6.175; 9.713-43, 793; 16.97; and especially 16.245 by Leontius Scholasticus on a satyr in pain who is being pitied by Dionysus. See also Theocritus, *Idylls* 15.80-86.

5. credas: Cf. 90.6.

6. The Luxorian paradox: the copies are more lifelike than life itself.

86

Meter: Phalaecean; see above, Ch. VIII, Meter 3.

Title. colocasia: an Egyptian plant frequently mentioned by ancient writers, e.g., Vergil, *Bucolics* 4.20, and Martial, 8.33.13. Pliny, *Natural History* 21.51. 87, describes its very broad leaves, which were plaited into goblets and trays. He says of it, "In Aegypto nobilissima est colocasia, quam cyamon aliqui vocant." Columella, *De Re Rustica* 8.15.4, says it was grown in ponds where waterfowl were being reared—quae inopacant avium receptacula. Theophrastus, *Historia Plantarum* 1.17 and 1.6.9-11, calls it the *uingon*.

In modern nomenclature colocasia is called *Colocasia Antiquorum* and also *Arum Aegyptium*. It is the same as taro and is cultivated in the tropics and southern Europe; see *The Royal Horticultural Society Dictionary of Gardening*, ed. by F. J. Chittenden (Oxford, 1951), II, 528. From it are made poi and taro. It is also identified with the elephant's ear, has enormous leaves, and is grown chiefly out of doors, although a dwarf species is potted; see L. H. Bailey, *The Standard Cyclopedia of Horticulture* (New York, 1941) I, 830.

Luxorius may be referring to some such diminutive species. Colocasia is one of the *Araceae*; varieties of it are still grown in Tunis according to A. Cuénod, G. Pottier-Alapetite, and A. Lalbe, *Flore analytique et synoptique de la Tunisie* (Tunis, 1954), p. 184. F. Thonner, *The Flowering Plants of Africa* (London, 1915), p. 116, reports that colocasia is cultivated and sometimes naturalized in tropical and northern Africa, that its tubers and leaves are eaten, used in medicine, or serve as ornaments. The ancients confused the colocasia with the Egyptian bean; see A. L. P. P. de Candolle, *Origine de plantes cultivées* (Paris, 1883), pp. 58-60. The Egyptian bean, also called the sacred bean or the Egyptian lotus, is *Nelumbium Speciosum* or *Nelumbo Nucifera* or *Speciosa* (*Nelumbo* is a Cingalese word); see Chittenden (cited at the beginning of this paragraph), III, 1359.

populante: In earlier Latin *populor* or *populo* means "to destroy" and *populatio* means "destruction." Forcellini gives only the earlier meanings of *populor* and *populo* but under *populatio* he cites Sedulius, *Carmen Paschale* 4.275 (*PL*, XIX, 627), flebat populatio praesens. Souter alludes to the same passage. However, the verb in the meaning of "inhabit" does not appear until much later (Sedulius is late fifth century). Du Cange gives *populi coetus* as a meaning of *populatio* and refers to the use of *populare* in medieval documents as a word coupled with *habitare*. Luxorius' use of *populante*, "living in, growing," may either be unique for his period or may be taken as evidence that this title was written by somebody living after the time of Luxorius; see above, Ch. VII, B 4.

2. ampliores: an emendation by Burmann of *eorum*, obelized by Riese, who grants that *ampliores* may be correct. The latter is metrically correct, the use of the comparative is in accordance with Luxorius' style, and the sense is perfect in the light of the description of the colocasia above. *Eorum* is manifestly impossible, metrically and syntactically.

5. famulans: See above, Ch. VI, B 4.

5. opaca: Riese emends to *opella*, but from the description of the plant above, especially Columella's specific mention of the shade provided by the plants (*inopacant*), it seems best to retain *opaca*.

6. solet quam: inverted word order; cf. *quam magis*, 1.8.

6. quam horto: no elision and *h* does not make position here; see above, entry for these words, and for *quis*, 4.2, Ch. VIII, B 1.

The entire line is an example of Luxorius' antithetical style: the plant is better off in a house than in a garden.

87

Meter: Dactylic Hexameter; see above, Ch. VIII, Meter 2.

Title. podium: A balcony, balustrade, or platform was set above the wall running about the amphitheater or arena. Here sat important personages—see Juvenal, 2.147, omnibus ad podium spectantibus. Nero watched the games while reclining on a couch placed on the podium (Suetonius, *Nero* 12.2).

saliebat: *Salire* is not used without a prefix or preposition in the ordinary sense of jumping; Klapp therefore suggests *transiliebat* (*Quaestiones*, p. vii).

However, *volavit*, line 11, also has no preposition. Klapp thinks that the meaning is different, that the young man leaped *over* the podium but flew *to* the top of the *fastiga*. This may be a fine distinction, but *podium* and *fastigia* refer to the same thing here—whether the athlete jumped or flew, he went *over* the podium. The omission of a preposition with *saliebat* may be a scribal error or loose usage either by Luxorius, if he wrote the title, or by somebody else who wrote it. At any rate, it is startling.

1. amphitheatralem podium: On the gender of *podium* here, see above, Ch. VI, A 11.

The podium varied from 4'6" to 11'6" in the different arenas; the podium of the Colosseum was almost 11 feet high; see Jennison, *Animals for Show and Pleasure,* pp. 156-57, for statistics. Incidentally, a few modern high jumpers have cleared a height of seven feet. *Anthologia Palatina* 16.53 tells about a young man named Ladas, who either jumped or flew over the Stadium of Constantinople.

3. potius: See above, Ch. VI, A 7. On the inverted word order, *potius sed,* see note on *quam magis,* 1.8.

3. gessit: an emendation by Riese of *geret,* which α changed to *gerat.* Baehrens emends to *vera,* following Mueller; Klapp prefers *certa;* here I prefer to keep a form of the verb called for by the manuscript.

4. posui: "wagered" or "set up as a prize"; cf. Vergil, *Bucolics* 3.36, pocula ponam, *Aeneid* 5.292, praemia ponit; Phaedrus, *Fabulae* 2.15.9, posito praemio; Martial, *De Spectaculis* 29.5, posita palma.

4. Dorica vina: Although Theognis, *Elegies* 879-84, pays tribute to the wine from grapes grown below Mt. Taygetus, and Alcman, Fragment 117, *PLG, Pars* III, *Poetae Melici,* ed. by J. Rubenbauer, (4th ed., Leipzig, 1914), p. 70, is quoted by Athenaeus in praise of Laconian wine, Doric wines were nevertheless not particularly notable. The great wines of Greece and the islands came from Chios, Cos, and Lesbos; see Strabo, 10.1.6, Athenaeus, 1.31 e-f, and *DarSag,* V, 914 ff. Hence, *Dorica* here means "Greek" by metonymy, as in Vergil, *Aeneid* 2.27.

6-7. It is possible that these lines are reversed in thought, for the athlete would first have to do the feat described in line 7 to receive the reward promised. Cf. 38.5-6.

7. gravior levis: On the juxtaposition of contrasting words, see above, Ch. V, B 1. The idea is that the leaper, though weighed down by the wager, is still light and nimble enough when he leaps. It is somewhat like the modern expression "That horse carries all my cash," or "All I have rides on that nag."

8. mirabor: Both Riese and Baehrens change this reading of A to *mirabar,* possibly to keep the tense in harmony with that of *obstipui,* line 10. But *non iam* should look to the future: Luxorius was amazed at the young man's feat, but he will nevermore be surprised by the story of Daedalus. Cf. *notabo,* 41.2.

8. Daedale: a sudden invocation, like *Icare,* 38.6; see above, Ch. V, B 4.

9. natura errante: "contrary to the laws of nature."

11. fastigia summa volavit: See note on *saliebat* in the title of this poem.

88

Meter: Elegiac; see above, Ch. VIII, Meter 1.

Title. De Diogene... Cupido mingit: This poem is obviously a satirical piece on a philosopher who has denied the power of love and now finds himself mocked by a beautiful woman. Like Poem 72 it is a stricture against transgressing philosophers (see note to 8.T). Cupid is not named in the poem itself—to what extent can the title be trusted? See above, Ch. VII, A 3.

No statue, painting, or mosaic remotely resembling the scene depicted by Luxorius is listed in the *Répertoires* of Reinach or in the catalogues of the North African museums. However, this does not prove that some such picture may not have been in existence when Luxorius was alive. Mueller, *"Sammelsurien", NJbb,* XCV, 785-86, thinks that the title was added by a scribe. However, *mingit* in the title is picked up again by *mingitur* in line 6. It is hardly likely that Lais, or Laida, as Luxorius calls her, was micturating on Diogenes, for she was occupied with plucking his beard. A third figure must have been present, who might just as well have been Cupid, for he appears as a bystander or participant in other art groups; cf. Poem 85.

Moreover, Diogenes himself was not above playing such filthy tricks as the one he is being subjected to in the poem. Diogenes Laertius, 6.46, reports that at a feast the philosopher played a dog's trick and drenched certain people who threw bones at him. In 6.69 it is said of Diogenes that he did everything in public—the works of Demeter and Aphrodite alike. The tables were turned on him when he received a thorough drenching where he stood (6.41). It may well be that the artist was familiar with these stories about Diogenes and painted the scene accordingly.

menetrix: Nonius derives this word from *maneo* by folk etymology; Nonius Marcellus, ed. by L. Mueller (Leipzig, 1888), II, 4-5 (423-24, Mercer), or by W. M. Lindsay (Leipzig, 1903), III, 684. See also P. Thielmann, "Miscellen," *ALL,* III, (1884), 539-40. *Meretrix* is the earlier word and is used in line 1 of this poem. If *menetrix* in the title is not a scribal error, then it is reasonable to presume that the title is the work of a later writer; see above, Ch. VII, B 4.

barbam: See note on *hispidus,* 72.1.

evellit: Cf. Horace, *Satires* 1.3.133-34, vellunt tibi barbam/ Lascivi pueri.

1. Laida: See note on *Lacedaemona,* 65.3. *Tirentia Lais* is a name on an inscription found in Carthage (*CIL,* VIII, Supp. 1, 12831).

2. amica Venus: "the girl friend."

3. castae semitae vitae: Cf. Juvenal, 10.363-64, semita certa/ Tranquillae per virtutem patet unica vitae, and *Anthologia Palatina* 16.334.3-4, by Antiphilus of Byzantium on Diogenes:

Μοῦνος ἐπεὶ βιοτᾶς αὐτάρκεα δόξαν ἔδειξας

Θνητοῖς, καὶ ζωῆς δίμον ἐλαφροτάτην.

Since you [Diogenes] alone showed to mortals the rule
of self-sufficiency and the easiest path of life.

4. turpiter esse: For this use of the infinitive with *revocat,* cf. Propertius, 1.16.11-12, Nec tamen illa suae revocatur parcere famae/ Turpior et saecli

vivere luxuria. See Kuehner-Stegmann, II, 683, § 125-6c. For the use of the adverb *turpiter* with *esse*, cf. *suaviter sit, suavius esse, suaviter fuit*, Petronius, *Satiricon* 59.1; 61.2, 4; 65.11; and *sit tibi suaviter*, CIL, VI. 4.2, 35979.

6. nimis: See above, Ch. VI, A 7.

6. arte sophus: an emendation by Klapp, *Quaestiones*, p. xv, of *artis opus* in A, so made because it is Diogenes and not the picture that is being drenched. Klapp points to the use of *arte* by Luxorius in 61.2. Cf. also 34.12; 49.2; 173R.4. Baehrens emends to *inter opus;* Riese's text has *archisophus*, from *archisofus* credited to Froehner. *TLL* lists *archipirata, archipontifex, archisacerdos,* and similar words, but *archisophus* is not found in Latin or Greek authors.

89

Meter: Elegiac; see above, Ch. VIII, Meter 1.

Title. catto: See note on *catis,* 73.8.

maiorem: "very large" or "rather large"; see above, Ch. VI, A 7. With this poem, cf. 181R.

1. vorasset: For the use of the pluperfect subjunctive with *dum,* cf. *devorasset* in the title, and see above, Ch. VI, A, 1, 5.

1. membra: "body"; cf. 10.5; 14.4; 24.6.

2. crudior: See above, Ch. VI, A 7.

4. vitam moriens: For the juxtaposition of antithetical words, see above, Ch. V, B 1. This is another example of the Luxorian paradox; the thought remotely resembles a distorted version of Juvenal, 8.84, Et propter vitam vivendi perdere causas.

90

Meter: Elegiac; see above, Ch. VIII, Meter 1.

Title. See above, Ch. IV, 2-3, on the authorship of this poem.

in: "concerning"; see above, Ch. VII, A 7.

Anclas: In Procopius, *Bellum Vandalicum* 2.7.13-14, Aklae is the name of a suburb of Carthage; cf. 215R.

salutatorium: a late Latin word for a reception room or a visitors' room; see Souter, *Glossary*, p. 362, *s.v. salutatorium* for citations, and Cassiodorus, *Historia Ecclesiastica* 9.30 (*PL, LXIX*, 1146B), et inveniens eum in salutatorio, supplicabat ut eius vincula resolveret.

domini regis: See note to 55.6, on the use of *dominus* as a title by the Vandal kings. *Domini* is not written out in the manuscripts: it could therefore be *domni,* as in 83.T. See note to 83.T.

1. Hildirici regis: See above, Ch. I, A 21.

1. mirabile factu: On the building activities of the Vandals, see above, Ch. I, A 20, and note on Poem 60.

2. arte ... pretio: On the asyndeton, see above, Ch. V, B 2.

5-6. These two lines are found in BV but not in A. This has led to a belief that they are a separate epigram. Baehrens thinks that something is missing between lines 4 and 5. However, lines 5-6 do seem to continue the description of the preceding lines; see Burmann, *Anthologia,* I, 476-77, note on Book III, *Epigram* 27, for a discussion of this poem; Baehrens, *PLM,* IV, 331; and Riese, *Anthologia,* I, 176, for variant readings and proposed emendations.

5. nube: either "cloud," to carry out the figure of *dies,* line 4, or "blemish, dark spot, flaw," as applied to crystal by Pliny, *Natural History* 37.10.28, infestantur plurimis vitiis, scabro ferumine, maculosa nube. Petschenig, *ZöstG,* XXVIII (1877), 486, thinks the word means that snow has fallen without clouds and suggests *solo nix iacta.*

6. steterint: For the mood with *dum,* see above, Ch. VI, A 1; cf. *viderit,* 43.2, and *vicerit,* 47.10.

6. credas: Cf. 63.1, Quis non credat; 85.5, Nil falsum credas; and Claudian, 26(49), *Aponus* 49, facta manu credas.

91

Meter: Dactylic Hexameter.

Title. Fridi: For the meaning of this name, see note to 18 T.

viro clarissimo et spectabili: On titles of honor, see above, Ch. III, C 1-10.

dictum centone: *Centone* is here used with *dictum* as an ablative of means, "an epithalamium spoken by (in the form of) a cento." *Cento* in apposition with *epithalamium* would seem to be the normal construction, "an epithalamium composed as a cento," or "a cento written as an epithalamium," on the analogy of *poema facere, componere,* or *scribere.* Cf. Claudian, I, *Panegyricus dictus Probino,* etc.; 30; *Epithalamium dictum Palladio,* etc.

Cento is derived from κέντρων, "a patched cloth." A cento is a patchwork of verses put together from the works of other poets to form a new poem. Aristophanes used it for comic effects in *Peace* 1090-94, *Frogs* 1264 ff., 1285 ff., and 1309 ff. See *OCD,* pp. 179-80, *s.v. cento,* for the history of this genre in Greek and Roman literature; also Mueller, *De Re Metrica,* pp. 585-88; Migne, *PL,* II, 63, n. 79; and Isidore, *Origines* 1.38.25 (*PL,* LXXXII, 120C-121A).

The *Anthologia Latina* contains a group of centos, Poems 7R-18R, of which the one by Luxorius is the last. No. 17R, *Medea,* a tragedy in 461 lines by Hosidius Meta, a contemporary of Tertullian, is mentioned by the latter in *De Praescriptionibus Hereticorum* 39 (*PL,* II, 64A-65A). The composition of such works marks a perversity of taste, a breakdown of creative power, but it does attest the popularity of Vergil (see above, Ch. I, C 7). Even Christian writers used his lines for the making of centos to write Biblical history; see the long cento by Valeria Faltonia Proba (fourth century) in *PL,* XIX, 805-18.

The best-known Latin cento is *Cento Nuptialis* by Ausonius (fourth century, a work of 131 lines, done at the request of Emperor Valentinian. In his dedicatory letter to Paulus, Ausonius declares that it is annoying to degrade Vergil's majestic poems with such trifling.

Ausonius sets down the rules of cento writing. Two half lines can be joined together to form one line, or a line and a half can be joined with a half line. To put two whole lines of the original side by side is weak and to use three whole lines in succession is frivolous. The original lines can be cut at any caesura. Finally, the unrelated lines must fit so that a relationship is established; all must harmonize at the end and the various pieces must show "no light between."

In a nuptial cento, the innocent lines of Vergil are put to what would be considered today an indecent use. Ausonius follows line 131 with a message of extenuation and exculpation. He refers to his work as *lasciva . . . pagina* and explains in prose that marriage calls for Fescennine songs and freedom of speech, saying that he himself blushes at making Vergil so immodest. However, he cites in self-defense a long list of authors who were sometimes coarse in their writing and quotes from Martial, 1.4.8, Lasciva est nobis pagina, vita proba. It is in this spirit that the lewdness of many ancient satirical pieces must be taken; see above, Ch. V, C 2.

The cento is a monument to the ingenuity of the "stitcher," who certainly had to know Vergil thoroughly to find the parts suitable for agglutination. It would be a waste of labor to analyze in detail whether Luxorius followed the rules laid down by Ausonius. Commenting on *Hippodamia* (11R), one of these centos, Burmann, *Anthologia,* I, 115, note on Book I, *Epigram* 170, remarks that these poems will scarcely please a delicate palate accustomed to the dishes of a better age. He also characterizes the task of discovering what lines of Vergil were used by Luxorius as a thankless one, "labore fatis ingrato" (II, 624, note on Book VI, *Epigram* 84). I agree; nevertheless, I have checked the lines independently. My conclusion is that Luxorius was not a true expert. He used as many as four Vergilian lines in succession. Now and then he substituted for a word of Vergil's text because he could not fit in Vergil's exact words. Occasionally, the parts stitched together do not harmonize and light does show between.

The references below are to the *Aeneid,* unless designated by *G* for *Georgics.* More than half of the lines come from Books, 1, 4, and 6, which may indicate the popularity of these books in Luxorius' time.

Where a line of the cento is formed from more than one Vergilian segment, the first citation denotes the beginning of the line, and the Latin word thereafter indicates the beginning of a different segment. A change by Luxorius of a word used by Vergil is denoted by a hyphen placed between Vergil's word and Luxorius' word, e.g., *Vergil-Luxorius.*

1. 4.607; *lustras-lustrat.*
2. 8.591.
3. 8.717.
4. 8.608.
5. 1.492.
6. 1.679 or 11.479; *pacem,* 4.99.
7. 7.74; *Capitolia,* 8.653.
8. 1.338; *vides-videns.*
9. 1.500; *et,* 1.734.
10. 4.141 or 5.553; *pariter,* 10.756; *ad,* 1.734; *litora-limina.*
11. 7.170.

12. 7.175; *atque* inserted; *ordine*, 1.395 or 1.703.
13. 7.176.
14. 5.830 or 8.105; *magna*, 1.497.
15. 4.166; *faciemque*, 5.619; *reponit-reponunt*.
16. 4.167.
17. 4.168; *mediisque*, 1.638.
18. 1.725.
19. 1.726; *ubi*, 9.618.
20. 9.503.
21. 9.504; *mollitque*, 1.57.
22. 5.451; *cithara*, 1.740.
23. 6.646.
24. 6.647.
25. 1.707.
26. 1.708.
27. 1.335; *tum-tunc; aligerum*, 1.663.
28. 1.664.
29. 6.788; *illam*, 11.374; *illum-illam*.
30. 11.375; *qui-quae; insignis*, 9.583; *viridique*, 5.295.
31. 7.53.
32. 12.225.
33. 12.226; *erat-inest, et*, 2.773.
34. 6.129; *thalamos*, 10.649.
35. 4.12 and 6.848; *nova*, 6.104.
36. G.1.56 or G.3.103,250; *quantum*, 4.150; *tantum-quantum*.
37. 1.589; *cui*, 10.137; *crinis-colla;* or 8.660; *tum-cui*.
38. 8.661; *crines*, 4. 138.
39. 4.139.
40. 10.134; *qualis Nereia*, 9.102.
41. 9.103.
42. 11.586; *cara-cura*.
43. 9.287.
44. 4.525; *noctem*, 1.683.
45. 1.73 or 4.126.
46. 4.127; *monumentum*, 5.538 or 5.572.
47. 11.741.
48. 1.688; *paribusque*, 4.102.
49. 4.103; *Phrygio-Fridus*.
50. 11.355; *quin-cui*.
51. 11.356; *des-dat; iungit-firmes*.
52. 1.689.
53. 1.690; *sic*, 9.319.
54. 4.115; *si*, 4.382; *pia-mea;* or 9.446, *carmina-numina*.
55. 1.687.
56. 5.429.
57. 2.620; *solitam*, 8.389; *datur*, 5.844.

58. 4.122; *et,* 4.125; without *et,* 7.548.
59. 6.105.
60. 7.434; *sentiat-sentiet; atque,* 3.611.
61. 8.251; *ille-illa.*
62. 4.414.
63. 4.55.
64. 12.70; *ramum,* 6.406.
65. 10.788; *flagranti,* 9.72; *implet-infert;* cf. 10.788.
66. 9.434.
67. 6.637; *geminam,* 1.274, with omission of *partu.*
68. 6.786.

APPENDIX I. COLLATION OF
THE DIFFERENT EDITIONS

This Edition	Riese	Baehrens	Meyer	Burmann (Bk. VI, Except as Otherwise Noted)
1	287	441	299	1
2	288	442	300	2
3	289	443	301	3
4	290	444	302	4
5	291	445	303	5
6	292	446	304	6
7	293	447	305	7
8	294	448	306	8
9	295	449	307	9
10	296	450	944	III, 164
11	297	451	308	10
12	298	452	309	11
13	299	453	310	12
14	300	454	311	13
15	301	455	312	14
16	302	456	313	15
17	303	457	314	16
18	304	458	315	17
19	305	459	316	18
20	306	460	317	19
21	307	461	318	20
22	308	462	319	21
23	309	463	320	22
24	310	464	321	23
25	311	465	322	24
26	312	466	323	25
27	313	467	324	26
28	314	468	325	27
29	315	469	326	28

This Edition	Riese	Baehrens	Meyer	Burmann (Bk. VI, Except as Otherwise Noted)
30	316	470	327	29
31	317	471	328	30
32	318	472	329	31
33	319	473	330	32
34	320	474	331	33*
35	321	475	332	34
36	322	476	333	35
37	323	477	334	36
38	324	478	335	37
39	325	479	336	38
40	326	480	337	39
41	327	481	338	40
42	328	482	339	41
43	329	483	340	42
44	330	484	341	43
45	331	485	342	44
46	332	486	343	45
47	333	487	344	46
48	334	488	345	47
49	335	489	346	48
50	336	490	347	49
51	337	491	348	50
52	338	492	349	51
53	339	493	350	52
54	340	494	351	53
55	341	495	352	54
56	342	496	353	55
57	343	497	354	56
58	344	498	355	57
59	345	499	356	58
60	346	500	916	III, 14
61	347	501	587	I, 29
62	348	502	571	I, 16
63	349	503	176	III, 25
64	350	504	357	III, 32 VI, 59
65	351	505	358	60
66	352	506	359	61
67	353	507	360	62
68	354	508	361	63
69	355	509	362	64

* Misnumbered XXXI in Burmann.

This Edition	Riese	Baehrens	Meyer	Burmann (Bk. VI, Except as Otherwise Noted)
70	356	510	363	65
71	357	511	364	66
72	358	512	365	67
73	359	513	366	68
74	360	514	367	69
75	361	515	368	70
76	362	516	369	71
77	363	517	370	72
78	364	518	371	73
79	365	519	372	74
80	366	520	373	75
81	367	521	374	76
82	368	522	375	77
83	369	523	376	78
84	370	524	377	79
85	371	525	378	80
86	372	526	379	81
87	373	527	380	82
88	374	528	381	83
89	375	529	1094	V, 163
90	203	382	383	III, 27
91	18	208	382	84
III, A	p. xxvi, Note 1 (contains only part)			
III, B	37	260	296	II, 579
IV	80	267	297	II, 579
V, A	pp. xxvii-xxviii	547		
V, B				
V, C	p. xxviii (first item only)	547 (first item only)		
V, D	p. xxvii (first item only)	547 (first item only)		
V, E				

APPENDIX II. VARIATIONS
FROM RIESE'S TEXT

Variations from Riese's text are listed below; capitalization changes are disregarded. Reasons for the changes are given in the Commentary in the notes on the specific words as required. See introductory remarks, Index Nominum et Verborum, below.

4.11 vitio *to* vitia
6.8 sic *to* sit
15.5 elefans *to* elephans
17.4 fialas *to* phialas
18.9 exstructa *to* extructa
22.5 vacuo, oge *to* vanum, inguen
25.6 lagunam *to* lagonam
32.T noctu *to* nocte
34.7 sarcofagus *to* sarcophagus
36.4 spurios *to* spurcos
36.8 ipsa *to* ipsam
37.5 tali *to* tablae; praemia *to* praelia
43.3 fateri *to* fatere
43.6 sed *to* se; solet *to* potest
44.3 quantum *to* quanto
46.7 se Laconides *to* sese Aonides
55.1 noctu *to* nocte
57.T et *omitted*

58.2 elefans *to* elephans
61.2 proprias *to* propriis
63.1 hunc quis *to* quis hunc
64.3 cum *to* quo
67.8 magno *to* parvo
67.11 elefans *to* elephans
70.1 candenti *to* candidulo
73.9 fortia *to* parvola
76.1 qui *to* quid
79.T Passiphaae *to* Pasiphaae
79.6 Passiphae *to* Pasiphae
81.8 exstat *to* extat
85.3 illam *to* illum
85.4 parili teste carere *to* tali vulnere flere
86.2 eorum *to* ampliores
86.5 opella *to* opaca
87.8 mirabar *to* mirabor
88.6 archisophus *to* arte sophus

APPENDIX III. TESTIMONIA

Here are the only *testimonia* mentioning Luxorius.

A. Letter of Coronatus, text in H. Keil, *De Grammaticis Quibusdam Latinis Infimae Aetatis Commentatio,* p. 4. Keil put the following version together from two manuscripts, Codex Monacensis 14252 (EM 252)[1] and Codex Lavantinus (St. Paul, Lavanthal in Carinthia, Austria), ninth century.

Domino eruditissimorum (domino eruditissimo peritissimorum *Lav.*) atque inlustri fratri Luxorio Coronatus. Cum considerarem temporis nostri lectores, vidi quam plurimos ad fontes vel flumina venisse librorum bibentes avide et sitim propriae cupiditatis explesse, sed multorum animalium more pedibus pocula conculcasse, quibus prius fuerant dilectati, et fluenta splendidissima ab imis vadis commota pravorum facta imitare porcorum, sed tu amicior carissime quae mihi (*f.* [*fortasse*] praebe mihi) magis ac magis luxorium (*f.* Luxori) peritiam tuam et ardorem tui excellentiorem ingenii. in tuo gremio sofistarum novi cuncta versari, quae (*l.* [*lege*] quia) videlicet meam consuetudinem ex longitudine studiorum fallere nequivisset, quod tu proba diligas ac defendas et que utilia (*l.* quae inutilia) et inepta cognoscas te saepius damnare cognovi. et licet parvus labor ceteris videtur, tua peritia praesumptum me omnibus reddit, et novi q̅m̅ dum de (*f.* quo modo) solertium ingenia iudicamus, nos ab omnibus iudicandos. Quis doctus aut inperitus cum in suis manibus hoc volumen adsumpserit, quae ac solertum cana (*f.* queat sollertum inventa) respuere, quae lectitat? et non statim clamans erumpat me falsarium et temerarium, qui audiat (l. audeat) aliquid post veterum librorum doctrina (*l.* doctrinam) [aliquid] minuere vel superaddere. itaque in hac regula artium breviata conantem post peritissimum Sergium, qui cognitus est omnibus peritissimis artilator existire (*l.* existere), quaeso pertractes et, si oportet publicis minumentis (monumentis uti *Lav.*), tractando eas, ne forsitan mea temeritas rennuatur et plus tuae scientiae postlatae (praelatae *Lav.*) quam meae ignorantiae a ceteris scribatur (ascribatur *Lav.*)

To Luxorius, most learned teacher and my illustrious brother:
When I considered the readers of our time, I saw how very many had come to the fountains or, rather, rivers of literature drinking greedily and had satisfied the thirst of their eagerness, but I also saw that in the manner of many

---

[1] Emmeramensis, Regensburg; the manuscript is now in Munich.

animals they had trampled with their feet upon the cups from which they had previously derived pleasure, and having disturbed the very glistening streams from their very depths, they were imitating the actions of disgraceful swine, but you, my dearest friend Luxorius, are displaying to me your knowledge and the remarkable brilliance of your keen mind more and more. I know that in your heart there dwells all the knowledge of scholars because I could not possibly have failed to notice on account of my long dedication to learning that you cherish and defend all that is good, and I know that you often condemn what you know to be useless and insipid.

Although it seems of little consequence to others, your learning causes me to appear bold before all, and I know that as we judge the abilities of intelligent persons, so must we be judged by all. What person, whether learned or ignorant, upon taking this volume into his hands and reading it, could look down upon the writings of skillful writers found in it? Which of these persons would not immediately cry out that I am deceitful and rash for daring to take away or add anything after the scholarly work of the old writers? And so, I beg of you that you look over my efforts in this digest of the arts made after the most learned Sergius, who is known to be the inspirer of learning to all the greatest scholars. If it is necessary to use the public records, do go and look at them, lest perhaps others should put more blame upon your preeminent knowledge than upon my ignorance.

B.　　Poem 37R. (For the translation of this poem, see above, Ch. III, B 1.)

De titulo Luxorii cum versibus

Priscos, Luxori, certum est te vincere vates;
Carmen namque tuum duplex Victoria gestat.

APPENDIX IV. SERPENTINE POEM

Serpentine poem, the last of a group, 38R-80R, attributed to Luxorius by Meyer and Baehrens.

Epitaphion

Nil mihi mors faciet: pro me monumenta relinquo.
Tu modo vive, liber: nil mihi mors faciet.

Death will do nothing to me: I am leaving behind
a monument for myself. But you, my book, live on:
death will do nothing to me.

APPENDIX V. LISORIUS

Following are references to the grammarian Lisorius and all lines at present attributed to Lisorius.

A. Robinson Ellis, "Some New Latin Fragments," *JP,* VIII (1879), 122-24. This article is a discussion of a twelfth-century Latin glossary (Sir Thomas Phillipps Ms., Cheltenham 4626, now Brussels, Bibliothèque Royale, II.1049).[1]

Admirabilis per d non per duo m m scribi debet. Unde lisorius in ortographia dicit quod d ante omnes consonantes mutari potest praeter m et q ut adquiro admitto admodum quemadmodum. Adbrevio quoque dicendum, non abbrevio.[2]

Candaces olim vocabantur regine ethiopum, unde lisorius:

> Candacis ethiopum ditant eraria parvos.[3]

Obrizum dicitur aurum optimum rubrum vel ut alii dicunt rude. hoc obrizum i vel haec obriza e. Lisorius:

> prompserat obrizum dum licida sterteret aurum.

Reditus i pensio unde lisorius:

> annuus ut reditus quo pascar vestiar ungar.

Supina . . . frondui tum . . . florui tum. Lisorius:

> nec fronditura pinus nec floritura ficus.

Ysopus est herba pectori mundativa unde lisorius:

> pectus ysopo mundatur cerebrumque sinapi.

Peritus a verbo pereo ris corripit penultimam peritus i doctus ab eo quod est perior periris producit quod utrumque ostendit. lisorius uno brevi versiculo dicens:

> non peritum tendis si vis audire peritum.[4]

B. Charles Thurot, "Notices et extraits de divers manuscrits latins pour servir à l'histoire des doctrines grammaticales du moyen âge," *NE,* XII.2 (1868), 435. This is a report on grammar in Europe from Charlemagne to the Renaissance, in which Thurot cites the following by Guillermus, a learned

[1] Information in letters from L. M. J. Delaissé (November 6, 1956), H. G. Fletcher (August 9, 1956), and A. N. L. Munby (August 11, 1956). See above, Preface, for the identification of the correspondents mentioned here, and below, n. 5.

[2] Cf. E, below.

[3] For emendation of lines in this section, see Baehrens, *PLM,* IV, No. 547, and Riese, *Anthologia,* I, xxvii-xxviii.

[4] Cf. first quotation from Luxorius, C, below.

grammarian (in Ms. S.V. 17, thirteenth century, Abbey of St. Victor, now Paris, latin 14744):[5]

Tertia declinatio corripit specular solum. Contra Lisorius:

> Ipsa specular habens confert cristillina secum.[6]

C. Charles Thurot (as cited in B, above), n. 6, quotes from Aimeric, De Arte Lectoria, Ms. Paris 11277, fourteenth century:

Peritum, cum a deponenti est perior, periris, unde experior compositum, producitur, cum a neutro pereo, peris, correptum: quod pulchre Lisorius (liso *Cod.*) in uno versu sic ostendit:

> Non peritum si vis, tendis audire peritum.

Lisorius (liso *Cod.*):

> Veste decora me decora, decoraberis ipse.

Lisorius in poemate:

> Non tribules damnans externos sive tribules.

Lisorius:

> Si corvos amicis, delirus nonne videris?

Lisorius:

> Estibus hic algens Garamantide nudus Arabas.

Lisorius:

> Ab (*sic*) ambitibus pernitar ut unda remanet.

Item:

> Ipse releget nos ad prata virentia pastum.

Lisorio in Cornicio (*sic*):

> Dirutus heu strupis Helene fit Pergamus omnis.

Lisorius in Cornu:

> Expeditque vafer minuens sibi probra noverce.

Risor, risoris, ristrix. Lisorius in Cornicio:

> Puelle ristricis osorem me profiteor.

liso in versu quodam sic ait:

> Coniux est generum nomen commune duorum.

liso:

> Stulte, ministerio semper dederis iniquo.

Ministerium, cum est IIII sillabarum, hoc est secretum, cum V, est officium.

D. Charles Thurot, "Mois de septembre, séance de vendredi 2," *CRAI*, n.s. VI (1870), 248, citing again from Aimeric in Ms. St. Gatien de Tours 416, now Bibliothèque Municipale Tours 843, twelfth century(?).

Lisorius in Cornicio:

> Candacis Ethiope ditant aeraria parvos.

Lisorius:

> nec fastus Arsacis horret.

[5] Identification of the French manuscripts in B-E in letters from Mlle J. Vielliard (March 4 and 11, 1957).

[6] Cf. Possidonius, Hic specular renitens fert et crystallina mira (Baehrens, *PLM*, IV, No. 547).

Idem:

> Rasacis eloquium compti non extimet unus.

Lisorius:

> Conspicue, mathesi, reserasti plurima ludens.

Lisorius:

> Herba pascibili locus is vestitur et omnium est oculo gratus.

E. Paul Meyer, "Notice sur les Corrogationes Promethei d'Alexandre Neckam," *NE,* XXXV (1896), 665, on Ms. Bibliothèque Municipale Evreux 72, thirteenth century:

D in compositione mutatur in c, sequente c, ut in hoc exemplum quod positum est accio. Sequente vero q, remanet d, ut adquiro. Lisorius in Orthographia sua metrica: D subiens cunctas, m q tamen esse recusat.

quasi diceret: D [in] compositione ante omnes consonantes mutari potest in sequentem, preterquam in m et q, ut admitto, admiror, adquiro.

BIBLIOGRAPHY

1. Texts and Editions

Baehrens, Emil. Poetae Latini Minores, 5 vols. Leipzig, 1879-83, 1910-23, 1930.

Burmann, Peter. Anthologia Veterum Latinorum Epigrammatum et Poematum sive Catalecta Poetarum Latinorum in VI Libros Digesta. 2 vols. Amsterdam, 1759, 1773.

Heinemann, Otto von. Die Handschriften der Herzoglicher Bibliothek zu Wolfenbüttel. 9 vols. Wolfenbüttel, 1884-1913.

Lowe, E. A. Codices Latini Antiquiores. 7 vols. Oxford, 1950-56.

Meyer, Heinrich. Anthologia Veterum Latinorum Epigrammatum et Poematum. 2 vols. Leipzig, 1835.

Meyer, Paul. "Notice sur les Corrogationes Promethei d'Alexandre Neckam," Notices et Extraits de la Bibliothèque Nationale, XXXV (1896), 665.

Omont, H. Anthologie de poètes dite de Saumaise. Paris, 1903.

Riese, Alexander. Anthologia Latina sive Poesis Latinae Supplementum. 2 vols. Fasciculus I, Libri Salmasiani Aliorumque Carmina. Leipzig, 1869. Fasciculus II, Reliquorum Librorum Carmina. Leipzig, 1870. 2nd ed., revised. Fasciculus I, Leipzig, 1894. Fasciculus II, Leipzig, 1906.

Thurot, Charles. "Mois de septembre, séance de vendredi 2," Comptes rendus de l'Académie des inscriptions et belles-lettres, n.s., VI (1870), 248.

———— "Notices et extraits de divers manuscrits latins pour servir à l'histoire des doctrines grammaticales du moyen âge," Notices et extraits des manuscrits de la Bibliothèque Impériale et autres Bibliothèques, XXII.2 (1868), 435.

Zangemeister, K., and W. Wattenbach. Exempla codicum latinorum litteris maiusculis scriptorum. Heidelberg, 1876.

2. Other Sources

Albertini, Eugène. L'Afrique romaine. 5th ed., ed. by Louis Leschi. Algiers, 1955.

Allen, J. H., and J. B. Greenough. Allen and Greenough's New Latin Grammar. Rev. ed., ed. by B. L. D.'Ooge, J. B. Greenough, A. A. Howard, and G. L. Kittredge. Boston, 1916.

Allen, P. S. The Romanesque Lyric. With renderings into English verse by H. M. Jones. Chapel Hill, N.C., 1928.

Audollent, A. Carthage romaine. Paris, 1901.

Aymard, A., and J. Auboyer. Rome et son empire. Vol. II of Histoire générale des civilisations, ed. by M. Crouzet. Paris, 1954.

Baehrens, Emil. "Kritische Satura," *Neue Jahrbücher für das klassischer Altertum,* CVII (1873), 60-66.

———— "Zur lateinischen Anthologie," *Rheinisches Museum für Philologie,* XXXI (1876), 254-62, 602-13.

Baehrens, W. A. "Vermischtes," *Eranos,* XIII (1913), 18-29.

Bailly, Auguste. Byzance. Paris, 1939.

Bardenhewer, O. Geschichte der altkirchlichen Literatur. 5 vols. Freiburg, 1914-32.

Bechtel, E. A. Sanctae Silviae Peregrinatio. Preprint from Vol. IV, the University of Chicago Studies in Classical Philology. Chicago and Leipzig, 1902.

Beeson, C. H. A Primer of Medieval Latin. Chicago, 1925.

Birt, T. Das antike Buchwesen. Berlin, 1882. Reprinted 1959.

Blaise, Albert. Dictionnaire latin-français des auteurs chrétiens, Ed. by H. Chirat. Strasbourg, 1954.

———— Manuel du latin chrétien. Strasbourg, 1955.

Blatt, Franz. Précis de syntaxe latine. Vol. VIII of the Collection, Les Langues du Monde, published under the direction of Henri Hierche. Lyon and Paris, 1952.

Bohren, F. E. De Septem Sapientibus. Bonn, 1867.

Boissier, Gaston. La fin du paganisme. 7th ed. 2 vols. Paris, 1922.

———— L'Afrique romaine. 9th ed. Paris, 1901.

———— Review of A. Riese, Anthologia Latina, *Revue critique d'histoire et de littérature,* 4th part, 1st semester (1869), 198-201.

Bouchier, E. S. Life and Letters in Roman Africa. Oxford, 1913.

Brittain, F. The Medieval Latin and Romance Lyric to A.D. 1300. 2nd. ed. Cambridge, 1951.

Browne, R. A., British Latin Selections A.D. 500-1400. Oxford, 1954.

Buecheler, F. "Coniectanea," *Rheinisches Museum für Philologie,* XXXV (1880), 405-7.

———— Petronii Saturae et Liber Priapeorum. 6th ed., ed. by W. Heraeus. Berlin, 1922.

Cagnat, R. Carthage, Timgad, Tébessa. Paris, 1927.

Cambridge Ancient History, ed. by J. B. Bury. 12 vols. and 5 vols. of plates. Cambridge, 1923-39.

Cambridge Medieval History, planned by J. B. Bury. 8 vols. Cambridge, 1913-36.

Carthage autrefois: Carthage aujourd'hui, par deux Pères Blancs. 10th ed. Tunis, 1957.

Carton, L. B. C. Pour visiter Carthage. Tunis, 1924.

Christ, W. Metrik der Griechen und Römer. 2nd ed. Leipzig, 1879.

Conrads, F. W. In Anthologiae Latinae Librum IV, Exercitationes Criticae et Exegeticae. Bonn, 1853.

Corpus Inscriptionum Latinarum, ed. by authority of Academia litterarum regiae Borussiae. 16 vols. in 38; 16 supplements in 15. Berlin, 1862—.

Corpus Medicorum Latinorum, ed. by E. Howald and H. E. Sigerist. 5 vols. Leipzig, 1915-28.

Courcelle, P. Histoire littéraire des grandes invasions germaniques. Paris, 1948.

────── Les lettres grecques en occident de Macrobe à Cassiodore. New. ed. Paris, 1948.

Courtois, Christian. Les Vandales et l'Afrique. Paris, 1955.

────── Victor de Vita et son oeuvre. Algiers, 1954.

Curtius, E. R. European Literature and the Middle Ages, tr. by W. R. Trask of Europäische Literatur und lateinisches Mittelalter (Bern, 1948). (Bollingen Series XXXVI.) New York, 1953.

Daremberg, C., and E. Saglio. Dictionnaire des antiquités grecques et romaines. 5 vols. in 9. Paris, 1873-1917. Index by J. Normand. Paris, 1919.

Dill, S. Roman Society in the Last Century of the Western Empire. 2nd ed. London, 1905.

Du Cange, C. du Fresne. Glossarium Mediae et Infimae Latinitatis, ed. by L. Favre. Supp. by D. P. Carpenter and G. A. L. Henschel. 10 vols. New ed. Paris, 1937.

Duebner, F. "Poetae anonymi oratiuncula recitationi praemissa," *Rheinisches Museum für Philologie,* III (1835), 470-83.

Dunlop, John. Selections from the Latin Anthology. Edinburgh, 1838.

Dwyer, W. F. The Vocabulary of Hegesippus (Vol. XXVII of Patristic Studies, Catholic University of America). Washington, 1931.

Ebert, Adolf. Allgemeine Geschichte der Literatur des Mittelalters in Abendlands. 3 vols. Vol. I, 2nd. ed., Leipzig, 1889; Vol. II, 1880; Vol. III, 1887.

Ehwald, R. "Curae Exegeticae," *Philologus,* XLVI (1888), 632-39.

────── "Miscellen," *Philologus,* XLVII, neue Folge 1 (1889), 764-65.

Ellis, Robinson. A Commentary on Catullus. 2nd ed. Oxford, 1889.

────── "Some New Latin Fragments," *Journal of Philology,* VIII (1879), 122-24.

Ernout, A., and P. Meillet. Dictionnaire étymologique de la langue latine. 3rd ed., 2 vols. Paris, 1951.

────── , and F. Thomas. Syntaxe latine. 2nd. ed. Paris, 1953.

Fischer, G. Latin Grammar. 2 vols. New York, 1876.

Fletcher-Allen, E. A Wayfarer in North Africa: Tunisia and Algeria. London, 1931.

Forcellini, E. Lexicon Totius Latinitatis, ed. by J. Furlanetto, F. Corradini, and J. Perin. 4th ed., 6 vols, of which Vols. V and VI are the Onomasticon, ed. by J. Perin. Padua, 1940.

Friedlaender, Ludwig. Petronii Cena Trimalchionis. Leipzig, 1891.

────── "Die Circusparteien zu Rom in der Kaiserzeit," *Neue Jahrbücher für das klassischer Altertum,* LXXIII (1856), 745-50.

────── M. Valerii Martialis Epigrammaton Libri. 2 vols. Leipzig, 1886.

Gaselee, Stephen. The Transition from the Late Latin to the Medieval Love Poems. Cambridge, 1931.

Getty, Sister Marie Madeleine. The Life of the North Africans as Revealed in the Sermons of St. Augustine (Vol. XXVIII of Patristic Studies, Catholic University of America). Washington, 1931.

Gildersleeve, B. L., and Gonzalez Lodge. Gildersleeve's Latin Grammar. 3rd ed. Boston, 1894.

Goossens, R. "Note sur les factions du cirque à Rome," *Byzantion,* XIV (1939), 205-9.

Graham, Alexander. Roman Africa. London, 1902.

Grimal, Pierre. Dictionnaire de la mythologie grecque et romaine. Paris, 1951.

Gsell, S. Histoire ancienne de l'Afrique du Nord. 8 vols. Paris, 1914-28.

Hadas, Moses. A History of Greek Literature. New York, 1950.

Haight, E. H. Aspects of Symbolism in the Latin Anthology and in Classical and Renaissance Art. New York, 1952.

Hall, F. W. A Companion to Classical Texts. Oxford, 1913.

Hardie, W. R. Res Metrica. Oxford, 1920.

Harvey, Paul. The Oxford Companion to Classical Literature. 4th. ed. Oxford, 1951.

Haskins, C. E. M. Annaei Lucani Pharsalia. London, 1887.

Haupt, M. Opuscula. 3 vols. in 2. Leipzig, 1875-76.

Haywood, R. M. Roman Africa. Part 1 of Vol. IV, An Economic Survey of Ancient Rome, ed. by Tenney Frank. Baltimore, 1938.

Helbig. W. Führer durch die offentlichen Sammlungen Klassischer Altertumer in Rom. Vol. I, 3rd ed., ed. by W. Amelung, E. Reisch, and F. Weege. Leipzig, 1912.

Inventaire des mosaïques de la Gaule et de l'Afrique. Institut de France, Paris —Académie des Inscriptions et de Belles-lettres. 3 vols. of text, 3 vols. of plates. Paris, 1909-25.

Irwin, J. F. Liber I, Dracontii de Laudibus Dei. Philadelphia, 1942.

Jennison, George. Animals for Show and Pleasure in Ancient Rome. Manchester, 1937.

Julien, Charles-André. Histoire de l'Afrique du Nord. 2nd ed., ed. by C. Courtois. Paris, 1951.

Juret, A-C. Principes de métrique grecque et latine. 2nd ed. Paris, 1938.

Keenan, Sister Mary Emily. The Life and Times of St. Augustine as Revealed in His Letters (Vol. XLV of Patristic Studies, Catholic University of America). Washington, 1935.

Keil, H. De Grammaticis Quibusdam Latinis Infimae Aetatis Commentatio. Erlangen, 1868.

——— Grammatici Latini. 7 vols. Leipzig, 1857-60.

Keller, O. Die antike Tierwelt. 2 vols. Leipzig, 1909-13.

Kenyon, F. G. Books and Readers in Ancient Rome and Greece. Oxford, 1932.

Klapp, H. "Quaestiones de Anthologiae Latinae Carminibus Nonnullis," Jahresbericht, Höhere Bürgerschule mit Gymnasialeclassen zu Wandsbeck. Wandsbeck, 1875.

Koster, W. J. W. Traité de métrique grecque suivi d'un précis de métrique latine. 2nd ed. Leiden, 1953.

Kuehner, R. Ausführliche Grammatik der lateinischen Sprache. 2 vols. in 3. Vol. I, 2nd ed., ed. by F. Holzweissig. Hanover, 1912. Vol. II, Part 1, 2nd. ed., ed. by C. Stegmann. Hanover, 1912. Vol. II, Part 2, 2nd ed., ed. by C. Stegmann. Hanover, 1914.

Kuehner, R., and C. Stegmann. Ausführliche Grammatik der lateinischen

Sprache. 3rd ed., 2 vols., supervised by A. Thierfelder. Leverkusen, 1955. This is a new edition of only Vol. II of Kuehner, above. Vol. I (1955) corresponds to Vol. II, Part 1 (1912), and Vol. II (1955) corresponds to Vol. II, Part 2 (1914).

Kuhnmuench, O. J. Early Christian Poets from the 4th to the 6th Century. Chicago, 1929.

Labriolle, P. de. Histoire de la littérature latine chrétienne, rev. by G. Bardy. 3rd ed., 2 vols. Paris, 1947.

Lane, G. M. A Latin Grammar. Rev. ed. New York, 1903.

Lapeyre, G. G., and A. Pellegrin. Carthage latine et chrétienne. Paris, 1950.

Lavedan, P., and S. Besques. Histoire de l'art. 2 vols. Paris, 1949.

Leclercq, H. L'Afrique chrétienne. 2 vols. Paris, 1904.

Lewis, C. T., and C. Short. Harper's Latin Dictionary. New York, 1907. Reprinted 1955.

Lindsay, Jack. Song of a Falling World. London, 1948.

Lindsay, W. M. The Latin Language. Oxford, 1894.

———— A Short Historical Latin Grammar. 2nd ed. Oxford, 1915.

Loewe, G. "Beiträge zu Placidus," Rheinisches Museum für Philologie, XXXI (1876), 55-75.

Löfstedt, E. Coniectanea: Untersuchungen auf dem Gebiete der antiken und mittelalterlichen Latinität. Upsala and Stockholm, 1950.

———— Philologischer Kommentar zur Peregrinatio Aetheriae. Upsala and Leipzig, 1911.

Maas, Paul. Griechische Metrik. 2nd ed. Leipzig and Berlin, 1929.

Maehly, J. "Literarische Anzeigen," a review of Riese's Anthologia Latina, Zeitschrift für die Oesterreichischer Gymnasien, XXII (1871), 550-90.

Manitius, Max. Geschichte der lateinischen Literatur des Mittelalters. 3 vols. Munich, 1911-31.

Mariotti, Scaevola. "Adnotatiunculae ad Epigrammata Bobiensa et Anthologiam Latinam," Philologus, C (1956), 323-26.

———— "Congetture all'Anthologia Latina," Parola del Passato, II (1947), 346-48.

Marrou, H. I. Histoire de l'éducation dans l'antiquité. Paris, 1948.

Martroye, F. Genséric, la conquête vandale et la destruction de l'empire d'occident. Paris, 1907.

———— L'Occident à l'époque byzantine: Goths et Vandales. Paris, 1907.

Mayor, J. E. B. Thirteen Satires of Juvenal with a Commentary. 2nd ed., 2 vols. London, 1880-81.

Merlin, A. Report on excavations in Carthage, especially on mosaics. In "Séance du premier octobre," Comptes rendus de l'Académie des inscriptions et belles-lettres (1920), pp. 337-38.

Merlin, A., and L. Poinssot. Guide du Musée Alaoui (Musée du Bardo). Fasciculus 1, Musée antique, reedited by P. Quondam. Tunis, 1957.

Merrill, E. T. Catullus. Boston, 1893.

Migne, J. P. Patrologiae Cursus Completus; Series Latina. 221 vols. Paris, 1844-64.

Mohrmann, Christine. "Le latin commun et le latin des chrétiens," *Vigiliae Christianae*, I, No. 1 (January, 1947), 1-12.

———— "Les éléments vulgaires du latin des chrétiens," *Vigiliae Christianae*, II, No. 2 (April, 1948), 89-101, and II, No. 3 (July, 1948), 163-84.

———— "Les origines de la latinité chrétienne à Rome," *Vigiliae Christianae*, III, No. 2 (April, 1949), 67-106, and III, No. 3 (July, 1949), 163-83.

———— "Les emprunts grecs dans la latinité chrétienne," *Vigiliae Christianae*, IV, No. 4 (October, 1950), 193-211.

———— Latin vulgaire, latin des chrétiens. Paris, 1952.

Mommsen, T. The Provinces of the Roman Empire from Caesar to Diocletian, tr. by W. P. Dickson of Die Provinzen von Caesar bis Diocletian, Vol. V of Römische Geschichte. 2 vols. Rev. by F. Haverfield from the 5th German ed. (1904). London, 1909.

Monceaux, P. Les Africans, étude sur la littérature latine d'Afrique: les Païens. Paris, 1894.

———— Histoire littéraire de l'Afrique depuis les origines jusqu'à l'invasion arabe. 7 vols. Paris, 1894.

Mueller, Lucian. De Re Metrica Poetarum Latinorum praeter Plautum et Terentium. 2nd ed. St. Petersburg and Leipzig, 1894.

———— "Sammelsurien," *Neue Jahrbücher für das klassischer Altertum*, XCIII (1866, Part 1), 555; XCV (1867, Part 1), 783-86, 801-2.

———— "Zur lateinischen Anthologie," *Rheinisches Museum für Philologie*, XVIII (1863), 432-40.

———— "Zu Meyer's Anthologie," *Rheinisches Museum für Philologie*, XX (1876), 633-37.

Musées et collections archéologiques de l'Algérie et de la Tunisie. 26 fasciculi in 22 vols. Paris, 1893-1928.

Nelson, H. L. W. Petronius en Zijn "Vulgair" Latijn. Alphen, The Netherlands, 1947.

Ohl, Raymond T. "Some Remarks on the Latin Anthology," *Classical Weekly*, XLII (February 21, 1949), 147-53.

———— The Enigmas of Symphosius. Philadelphia, 1928.

O'Sullivan, J. F. The Writings of Salvian, the Presbyter. New York, 1947.

Oxford Classical Dictionary, ed. by M. Cary, J. P. Denniston, J. W. Duff, A. D. Nock, W. D. Ross, and H. H. Scullard. Oxford, 1944.

Pauly, A. F. von, G. Wissowa, and W. Kroll. Real-Encyclopädie der Altertumswissenschaft. First series, Vols. I-XXIII. I; second series, Vols. I.A.1-VIII and 8 supplements. Stuttgart, 1894—.

Peiper, R. "Ebrius Debrius," *Neue Jahrbücher für das klassischer Altertum*, CVII (1873), 340.

———— "Zur Anthologie des Luxorius," *Rheinisches Museum für Philologie*, XXXI (1876), 183-200.

Pétré, H. Ethérie, Journal de voyage. Paris, 1948.

Petschenig, M. "Beitrage zu Kritik lateinischer Schriftsteller—2. Zur Anthologie der Liber Salmasianus," *Zeitschrift für die oesterreichischer Gymnasien*, XXVIII (1877), 480-92.

Picard, Colette. Carthage. Paris, 1951.

Picard, Gilbert. Le Monde du Carthage. Paris, 1956.

Platnauer, M. Latin Elegiac Verse. Cambridge, 1951.

Postgate, J. P. Prosodia Latina. Cambridge, 1923.

Raby, F. J. E. A History of Christian-Latin Poetry from the Beginnings to the Close of the Middle Ages. 2nd ed. Oxford, 1953.

———— A History of Secular Latin Poetry in the Middle Ages. 2nd ed., 2 vols. Oxford, 1957.

Reinach, Salomon. Répertoire de peintures grecques et romaines. Paris, 1922.

———— Répertoire de reliefs grecs et romains. 3 vols. Paris, Vol. I, 1909, Vols. II, III, 1912.

———— Répertoire de la statuaire grecque et romaine. 6 vols. in 8. Paris, 1913-30.

Riese, Alexander. "Jahresbericht über die Literatur aus den Jahren 1878 und 1879 zur Anthologia Latina," *Jahresbericht über die Fortschritte der classischen Altherthumswissenschaft,* XIV (1880), 258-66.

———— "Zur lateinischen Anthologie," *Neue Jahrbücher für das klassischer Altertum,* XCVII (1868), 698-710, CIX (1880, Part 1), 259-63.

Roberts, C. H. "The Codex," *Proceedings of the British Academy,* XL (1954), 169-204.

Roensch, H. "Zur lateinischen Anthologie," *Rheinisches Museum für Philologie,* n. F. XXXI (1876), 477-79.

Sage, Evan T. Petronius: The Satiricon. New York, 1929.

Saint Margaret, Sister Mary. Dracontii Satisfactio. Philadelphia, 1936.

Sandys, J. E. Latin Epigraphy. 2nd ed., rev. by S. G. Campbell. Cambridge, 1927.

Sanford, E. M. "Classical Latin Authors in the Libri Manuales," *Transactions of the American Philological Association,* LV (1924), 190-248.

Schanz, M., C. Hosius, and G. Krueger. Geschichte der römischen Litteratur bis zum Gesetzgebungswerk des Kaisers Justinian. Vol. IV.2 of Schanz-Hosius, Römische Litteratur-Geschichte, and VIII.4.2 of Handbuch der Altertumswissenschaft. Munich, 1920.

Schenkl, K. "Zur lateinischen Anthologie," *Wiener Studien, Zeitschrift für classischen Philologie,* I (1879), 59-74.

———— "Handschriftliches zur lateinischen Anthologie," *Wiener Studien,* II (1880), 296-300.

Schmalz, Joseph Hermann. Lateinische Grammatik. 5th ed., ed. by M. Leumann and J. B. Hoffman. Vol. II.2 of Handbuch der Altertumswissenschaft. Munich, 1928.

Schmidt, Ludwig. Geschichte der Wandalen. 2nd ed. Munich, 1942.

Schoenfeld, Moritz. Wörterbuch der altgermanischen Personen- und Völkernamen. Heidelberg, 1911.

Schubart, W. Das Buch bei den Griechen und Römern. Berlin, 1907.

Schubert, Otto. Quaestionum de Anthologia Codicis Salmasiani, Pars I, de Luxorio. Weimar, 1875.

Schulze, Wilhelm. Zur Geschichte lateinischen Eigennamen. Berlin, 1904.

Sedgwick, W. B. The Cena Trimalchionis of Petronius. 2nd ed. Oxford, 1950.

Sells, A. L. Animal Poetry in French and English Literature and the Greek Tradition. Bloomington, Indiana, 1955.

Sladen, Douglas. Carthage and Tunis. 2 vols. London, 1906.

Snell, Bruno. Griechische Metrik. Göttingen, 1955.

Snowden, Frank. M., Jr. "The Negro in Classical Italy," *American Journal of Philology,* LXVIII (1947), 266-92.

Souter, Alexander. A Glossary of Later Latin to 600 A.D. Oxford, 1949.

Strecker, Karl. Introduction to Medieval Latin, tr. by Robert B. Palmer, with revisions, of Einführung in das Mittellatein. Berlin, 1957.

Teuffel, W. S. Geschichte der römischer Literatur. 1st ed., Leipzig, 1872. 5th ed., ed. by L. Schwabe, Leipzig, 1890.

Thesaurus Linguae Latinae. 26 vols. in 27, ed. by the Academies of Berlin, Göttingen, Leipzig, Munich, and Vienna. 1900—.

Thieling, W. Der Hellenismus in Kleinafrika. Leipzig, 1910.

Thielmann, P. "Miscellen," *Archiv für lateinische Lexikographie und Grammatik,* III (1884), 539-40.

Thomson, George. Greek Lyric Metre. Cambridge, 1929.

Traube, L. Review of Paul Meyer's "Notice sur les Corrogationes d'Alexandre Neckam," *Berliner philologische Wochenschrift,* XVIII (1898), 1068-70.

——— "Zur lateinischen Anthologie," *Philologus,* LIV (1895), 124-35.

Vollmer, F. "Rezensionen und Anzeigen," *Berliner philologische Wochenschrift,* XXVII (1907), 809-12.

Waddell, Helen. Mediaeval Latin Lyrics. 5th ed. London, 1948.

Warmington, B. H. The North African Provinces from Diocletian to the Vandal Conquest. Cambridge, 1954.

——— Carthage. London, 1960.

Weyman, C. Beiträge zur Geschichte der christlich-lateinischen Poesie. Munich, 1926.

Wilkins, E. G. The Delphic Maxims in Literature. Chicago, 1929.

Woelfflin, E. "Der Genetivus Comparationis und die präpositionalen Umschreibungen," *Archiv für lateinische Lexikographie und Grammatik,* VII (1892), 115-31.

——— "Die Lokalsätze in Lateinischen," *Archiv für lateinische Lexikographie und Grammatik,* IX (1896), 447-52.

Ziehen, Julius. "Archäologische Bemerkungen zur lateinischen Anthologie," Festschrift für Otto Benndorf, pp. 49-58. Vienna, 1898.

——— Archäologische-textkritische Bemerkungen zur Salmasianusanthologie," *Philologus,* LIX, n. F. XIII (1900), 305-11.

——— "Geschichtlich-textcritische Studien zur Salmasianusanthologie," *Philologus,* LXIII, n. F. XVII (1904), 362-77.

——— Neue Studien zur lateinischen Anthologie. Frankfurt a/M. and Berlin, 1909.

——— "Textkritisches zur lateinischen Dichtern," *Rheinisches Museum für Philologie,* LXII, n. F. LIII (1898), 273.

INDEX NOMINUM ET VERBORUM

Where a reading in my text differs from one in Riese's text, the former is indicated by (MR), the latter, by (R). T after a number refers to the title of the poem in which the word occurs. Words in the superscriptions are grouped with those in the titles. The words in the cento, 91L, are not included here. The words of 64.9-10, 13-14, are indicated by (C); see above, Ch. VIII, n. 1.

A

a 30.T; 57.2; 91.T.
ab 5.T; 7.1; 38.6; 49.2; 73.10; 74.2; 76.7; 77.1.
abeo: abis 17.1.
ac 5.6; 18.12; 23.3; 25.4; 40.1; 51.2; 74.4.
accendo: accendens *m.* 18.15.
acceptorarius: acceptorarium 14.T.
accipio: accipe 76.4.
accuso: accusas 57.1.
acer: acri *abl. n.* 65.7.
acerbus: acerbo *abl. n.* 68.12.
Achilles 7.5; 81.2: Achillem 81.T, 4.
actus (*noun*): actu 4.7: actus *acc.* 72.9.
ad 1.T; 2.T; 3.T, 1; 17.T; 19.T; 30.5; 32.T, 6; 33.4; 34.1; 37.1; 40.T; 51.T; 64.7; 67.11; 68.3, 12; 73.T, 3.
admiror: admiranda est 18.13: admirande 67.5.
adsiduo (*adv.*) 26.3.
adsuesco: adsuetae *gen.* 89.3.
adsum: adesse 60.2.
adtendo: adtendat 4.3.
adulter 36.2.
adulterium 22.6; 82.2.
adultus 36.9.
advivo: advixeris *perf. subj.* 68.3.
advocatus: advocatum 9.T.
Aegyptius: Aegyptii *gen. m.* 38.T: Aegyptio (*adj.*) *abl. m.* 7.T; 67.T.
aeneus: aenea *abl.* 69.T.
Aeolus 7.4.
aequor: aequore 38.5.
aequoreus: aequoreae *nom. pl.* 19.3.
aes: aeris 69.1: aera *acc. pl.* 47.8.
aetas 1.9: aetatem 59.7: aetate 20.7; 58.3.
aeternus: aeterno *abl. n.* 58.6.
aether: aethera 38.3.

aetherius: aetherios 87.9: aetherias 18.5.
Africa 41.8.
ager 60.5: agris *abl.* 80.5.
agilis 38.2 (R); 68.2: Agilis 38.2 (MR).
agito: agitas 22.1.
agmen 74.9: agmine 3.3.
agnosco 43.5: agnovi 9.9.
ago: agis 9,6: agit 54.4; 55.6; 57.6; 88.5: egit 53.5: agas 20.10: agat 34.16.
agrestis 60.3.
aio: ait 65.4.
albeo: albentem *f.* 59.6.
Alcides 67.4.
alea: aleam 37.1.
aleator: aleatore 37.T.
ales: alites *nom.* 30.6: alitibus *abl.* 19.1.
alienus: alienas 55.T.
aliquis 55.3; 76.7: aliquid *acc.* 13.7; 30.4; 73.5.
aliter 27.T; 43.2; 49.T; 56.T.
alius: aliam 47.10: aliud *acc.* 41.2: alii *nom.* 20.8: aliis *dat. m.* 16.8; 37.4; 68.6: alios 88.5.
almus 80.5.
alter 67.14: altera *nom. f.* 90.4: alterius *m.* 10.4; 20.5.
altus: altis *abl. m.* 83.1: alta (*noun*) *acc.* 85.2.
alveus: alveo *abl.* 62.T.
amabilis: *nom. f.* 73.1.
amator 71.2; 76.5.
ambitus (*noun*): ambitus *gen.* 2.8: ambitu 29.5; 40.2.
amica (*noun*) 26.4; 88.2: amicas 43.5.
amicus (*noun*) 56.3: amice 1.1: amicis *dat. pl.* 51.5: amicos 40.T.
amicus (*adj.*): amica *acc.* 41.3.
amitto: amittens *masc.* 71.2.
amnis: *gen.* 5.4: amnes *acc.* 63.1.

Blumarit: *voc.* 40.2.
bonum (*noun*): bona *nom.* 40.4: *acc.* 35.T: bonis *abl.* 1.18.
bonus: bona *nom. f.* 59.6: bona *acc.* 35.6: bonis *abl. m.* 2.2: melior *f.* 62.1; 69.3: optima *nom. f.* 65.14.
brachium: brachia *acc.* 41.4.
brevis: *nom. f.* 73.1: brevibus *abl. n.* 4.5: brevior *fem.* 24.3: brevissima *abl.* 73.T.
Burdo 79T,3: burdo 79.6.
bustum: busta *acc.* 23.1.

C

caballus: caballo *abl.* 21.7: caballis *dat.* 41.6.
cado: cadis 38.6: cadit 41.5 (*bis*), 6: cecidit 38.3: cecidisse 18.20: cadente 41.T.
caecus 71.2: caecum *acc. m.* 71.T.
caedes: c(a)edis 39.3: caedem 53.5.
caedo: ceciderunt 53.T.
caelitus 65.8.
caelum: caeli 17.4; 59.13; 83.7.
calculus 47.13.
calidus: calidas 64.8: calidis *abl. f.* 64.T.
calor 64.12: caloribus *abl.* 70.3.
calx: calcibus *abl.* 53.5.
candeo: candenti (R) *abl. n.* 70.1.
candidulus: candidulo (MR) *abl. n.* 70.1.
canis: canem 44.2: canum 44.T; 74.9: canibus *abl.* 74.T.
cano: canunt 30.7; canam *fut. or subj.* 64.5.
canor 46.12.
canto: cantaret 30.T.
cantus 59.12: cantu 13.6.
canus: canos 57.1.
capax: capacem *m.* 79.1.
capesso: capessunt 74.10.
capillus: capillo *abl.* 12.1.
capio: capit 6.3; 21.3; 35.4; 68.10; 90.3: capiebant 5.T; 38.T: capiant 10.5: capi 72.6.
caprea: capreas 21.1.
caput: capitis 72.2: capiti 12.4: *acc.* 41.3: capite 70.T.
carcer: carceris 53.2.
careo: carere 85.4 (R).
carmen: carminis 1.25: carmine 4.8; 30.2; 64.5: carminum 8.1: carmina *acc.* 13.5.
Carthago 68.14: Carthaginis 68.10.
carus 36.2: cara *nom. f.* 2.6.
cassus, *see* incassum.
castigo: castigas 20.4.
castitas: castitati 78.T.
castus: casta *nom. f.* 18.2: castae *gen.* 36.3; 88.3.
casus: casu 59.18.
catena: catenas 53.7.

caterva: catervas 23.2: catervis *dat.* 59.14.
Cato 72.10.
cattus 89.1: catto *abl.* 89.T.
Catucia 52.1.
catula: catulae *gen.* 73.1: catula *abl.* 73.T.
catus: catis *dat.* 73.8.
caupo: cauponis 17.T.
causa *voc.* 67.1: causam 1.25; 53.2: causis *dat.* 54.3: causas 9.6.
causidicus: causidici *gen.* 54.1: causidico *abl.* 54.T.
cautes: cautes (C) *nom. pl.* 64.13.
cautus: cauta *nom. f.* 85.1.
cavatus: cavato *abl. m.* 63.T.
cedo: cessit 74.1.
celo: celas 35.5: celare 57.3.
celsus: celsas 18.1.
cento: centone 91.T.
centum 80.3.
centumfolius: centumfoliae *gen.* 80.T.
Ceres: Cereris 15.9; 25.3.
cerno: cernit 60.2: cernebat 52.5: cernere 65.2; 71.7.
certe 81.8.
certus: certa *nom. f.* 66.3: certis *abl. n.* 85.2.
cervix: cervice 67.4.
cervus: cervos 21.1.
Chaos 15.3.
Charis: Charitem 54.T.
Chilon 65.3.
Chimaera 69.3: *abl.* 69.T.
chirurgus: chirurge 16.11; 23.6.
chorus: choro 46.2.
cibus 73.7: cibos 5.T, 2: cibis *abl.* 74.13.
cicada: cicadis *dat.* 10.1.
cinaedus: cinaedum 35.T.
cingo: cingunt 18.9; 34.3: cinguntur 18.3: cinctus 3.3.
circum (*prep.*) 34.12.
circus 20.1; 34.16: circi *gen.* 26.T; 34.T, 1; 38.T: circo *dat.* 41.8.
Cirnensis: Cirnensibus *abl.* 64.T.
cito (*adv.*) citius: 4.8.
civis: civem 65.13.
clamo: clamat 47.4; 55.4; 65.13: clamabat 40.T.
clamor 10.6: clamore 10.1.
clamosus: clamosum *acc. m.* 10.T.
clareo: clares 72.3.
clarus: clara *nom. n.* 34.3: clarissimi *gen. m.* 1.T: clarissimo *abl. m.* 91.T.
claudo: claudit 34.7: clauditur 59.3: claudere *imperative* 3.9: clausa *nom. f.* 4.8; 18.11; 27.4: clausas 5.1; 22.3.
Cleobolus 65.13.
clunis: clune 22.1.
cocta(C), *see* coquo.

vendo: vendere *inf.* 35.6; 37.8.
venenum: venena *acc.* 11.7.
Venetus: Veneto *abl.* 38.1.
venio: venit *pres.* 66.4: veniet 58.7: venient 66.6: veneris *fut. perf.* 3.3: venire 23.18.
venter: ventris 5.8.
Venus 46.4; 80.4; 88.2: Veneris 6.8; 54.4; 61.1; 70.T; 82.4.
ver: veris 4.4.
verbum: verba *nom.* 29.5: verba *acc.* 30.3: verbis *abl.* 1.22; 8.4; 47.5.
verecundus: verecundo *abl. m.* 59.8.
vereor: verendi (*gerundive*) *gen. n.* 72.2.
verna (*noun*) 5.1.
verno: vernant (C) 64.9; 67.9.
vernus: verna *nom. n.* 59.12.
vernum: verni 46.9.
vero (adv.) 1.T (R); 18.5.
versus (*noun*): versus *nom. pl.* 1.T (R): versus *acc.* 1.6: versibus *abl.* 2.6.
vertex: vertice 5.7.
verto: vertit 86.5: versum est 79.3.
verum (*noun*) 79.3.
verus 81.3: vera *nom. f.* 52.6: verum *m.* 27.1: veram 70.2: verum *acc. n.* 67.3: vera *acc.* 20.8; 34.10; 47.6.
vestis: vestem 23.16.
veto: vetat 56.3: vetant 10.2.
vetulus: vetulam 15.T.
vetus: veteres *acc. m.* 1.1.
via: viam 64.4.
vicinus: vicina *abl. f.* 60.T: vicinum 28.T.
Vico: *voc.* 50.1.
victor 42.5: victores *acc.* 20.2; 34.14.
Victoria 59.18.
video 9.9; vides 66.6: videt 51.6; 59.14; 60.4; 81.T: videas 28.8: viderit *subj.* 43.2: videre *inf.* 16.12, 14; 78.6: videnti *abl. f.* 87.10: videtur 23.11: visa *nom. f.* 73.6.
viduus: viduae *gen.* 71.1: viduam 23.T.
vigeo: viget 79.4: vigeat 86.6.
vigilia: vigilias 32.3.
vigilo: vigilabat 32.T.
villa: villa *abl.* 60.T.
vincio: vincti erant 53.T.
vinclum: vincla *nom.* 53.6 (*bis*); 74.5.
vinco: vincit 73.9: vincebat 7.T: vicerunt 49.5: vincas 37.7: vicerit *subj.* 47.10: vincere *inf.* 5.8; 50.4; 68.6; 83.8: vincens *m.* 47.12: vincentem *m.* 50.T: victus 20.10; 38.6; 87.6: victum *m.* 20.T, 1: vincendi (*gerund*) 26.3.
vinum: vina *acc.* 87.4.
viola: violae *nom.* 67.9; 70.T: violas 70.5.

vir: viri *gen.* 1.T; 9.1: viro *dat.* 15.14: virum 16.13; 22.2; 31.2; 57.4; 85.4; 88.4: viro *abl.* 91.T: viris *dat.* 1.16; 72.4.
vireo: viret (C) 64.14: virens *f.* 86.3: virente *abl. m.* 46.2.
virgo: *voc.* 15.1: virginem 15.T; 37.2, 7: virgine 24.3.
viridarium: viridario *abl.* 18.T.
virtus 88.3: virtutis 18.13, 15: virtute 20.7.
vis: vim 55.4: vi *abl.* 55.T: vires *acc.* 56.7: viribus *abl.* 67.14.
viscus: viscere 2.5; 63.2: viscera *acc.* 36.3; 54.2; 89.3.
visus (*noun*): visum 20.3; 48.4: visus *acc.* 49.6.
vita 33.3; 59.4: vitae *gen.* 65.2; 88.3: vitam 58.9: 89.4.
vitalis: vitales *nom. f.* 83.3.
vitium 37.6: vitio (R) *dat.* 4.10: *abl.* 40.7: vitia *nom.* 4.10 (MR).
vivo: vivis 28.8: vivet 68.13: vivas 32.6: viveret 70.4: vivere 32.4; 58.1.
vivus 23.8: viva *abl.* 81.9: viva *nom. n.* 85.6: vivis *dat. n.* 34.6: vivos 27.2.
vocabulum: vocabulo *abl.* 82.T.
voco: vocat 15.1: vocabat 54.T: vocabo 25.5: vocet 41.8: vocaris 38.1: vocari 8.8; 21.4; 40.8: vocatus 5.3: vocate (*voc.*) 23.7.
volatus: volatum 19.T: volatu 19.7.
volo (volare): volavit 87.11.
volo (velle): vis 9.11; 16.13; 28.6: volebam 40.4: velis 42.4: velit 51.3.
volucer: volucres *nom. f.* 19.3.
voluptas 1.25; 18.11; 31.4; 44.1; 78.7: voluptatis 67.1.
vomo: vomit 34.10: vomebat 69.2.
voro: vorasset 89.1.
vos: *acc.* 64.5: *voc.* 34.11; *see* tu.
votum: vota *nom.* 36.7: *acc.* 51.1, 7.
vox 10.3: vocem 73.3: voce 65.10; 85.4: voces *acc.* 84.T, 1.
vulnus: vulneris 85.2: vulnere 85.4 (MR): vulnera *acc.* 18.21.
vultus: vultum 27.1: vultu 59.8: vultus *acc.* 15.5; 52.1.

X

xenium: xenia *acc.* 40.T.

Z

zelor: zeleris 28.1.
zelus: zelo *abl. m.* 22.1.
Zenobius: Zenobi *voc.* 30.2.
Zephyrus: Zephyri *gen.* 7.4.

GENERAL INDEX

Only some of the annotated words in the Latin text appear below, Consult the Index Nominum et Verborum and check in the Commentary for possible notes on words not listed here.

Villas, 13-15, Plates II, A, IV, A
Vincentinus, 26
Virgil, *see* Vergil
Virgin, aged, *see under* Aged persons
Viridarium, 14, Plate II, A; Poem *18,* 122, 123, (Title), 189
Visigoths, 7-9
Vocative, *see under* Cases
Vollmer, F., 107 n. 34
Voltaire, François Marie Arouet de, 9 n. 29
Voss, Isaac, 100, 102; *see also* Codex Vossianus
Vowels, changes of quantity of, 33 n. 32, 73, 75, 77, 78 nn. 38-41, 83, 85-95, Poem 79 (Title), 239; *see also* Quantity
Vulgate, 47 n. 54, 59

Waddell, Helen, 35
Warmington, B. H., 40
Weber, S. H., 108
Weddings, Poem *51,* 140-43, (ll. 1, 7), 217; *see also* Epithalamium; Marriage
Wells, Poem *63,* 148, 149, (l. 1), 225
Weyman, C., 46 n. 49
Whitman, Walt, Poem *3* (Title), 178
Wine, excessive use of, Poem *25,* 126, 127, (l. 2), 196; Greek, Poem *87* (l. 4), 248; *see also* Love; Reversal of parts

Witchcraft, Poem *13* (Title), 186; *see also* Charms; Magic; *Magus*
Withycombe, E. G., Poem *18* (Title), 189
Woelfflin, E., Poem *57* (l. 2), 221
Wolfenbüttel, Library in, 100
Woman, beautiful and chaste, Poem *78,* 156, 157, (ll. 4, 7), 239; drunken, Poem *77,* 156, 157; dwarf, Poem *24,* 126, 127, (l. 8), 194; married, Poem *15,* 120, 121, Poem *23,* 124-27, Poem *36,* 133-34; quarrelsome, Poem *52,* 142, 143, (Title), 217; ugly musician, Poems *75, 76,* 156, 157; *see also* Marina, Pasiphae
Woodpecker, Poem *84* (l. 4), 244
Wuilleumier, H., Poem *67* (l. 2), 230

Xenia, Poem *40,* 134, 135, (Title), 207
Xenophanes, 54, Poem *65* (Title), 227
Xenophon, Poem *18* (l. 20), 192

Yeats-Brown, Francis, Poem *18* (l. 20), 191-92

Zeugitana, 4, Poem *64* (Title), 225
Zeus, Poem *65* (Title), 227
Ziehen, Julius, cited, Poem *18* (Title), 190, Poem *57* (l. 2), 220, Poem *59* (l. 18), 223, Poem *62* (Title), 224

HIC LOCUS EST METAE: LIBER EXPLICIT, ATQUE VALETE.

(Colophon of a manuscript of Persius: Bodleianus 8879.)